T0100418

New Paradigms in Computer Aided Verification

New Paradigms in Computer Aided Verification

Edited by Tyler Keating

www.statesacademicpress.com

States Academic Press,
109 South 5th Street,
Brooklyn, NY 11249, USA

Visit us on the World Wide Web at:
www.statesacademicpress.com

ISBN: 978-1-63989-690-5

Trademark Notice: Registered trademark of products or corporate names are used only for explanation and identification without intent to infringe.

Cataloging-in-publication Data

New paradigms in computer aided verification / edited by Tyler Keating.
    p. cm.
Includes bibliographical references and index.
ISBN 978-1-63989-690-5
1. Computer software--Verification. 2. Electronic digital computers--Evaluation.
3. Computer programs--Verification. I. Keating, Tyler.
QA76.76.V47 N49 2023
005.14--dc23

Contents

Permissions

List of Contributors

Index

Preface

Computer aided verification process (CAV) comprises mathematically based strict approaches for the verification, specification and development of hardware and software systems. The goal of CAD is to make such systems more robust, correct and dependable. Mathematical theories, design phase and specification formalism are used to categorize verification methods. Methods for verification during the design phase comprise testing, specification and implementation. Markov chains, process algebras and timed automata are the processes done in specification formalism. Static analysis, model checking and theorem proving are part of the verification process in mathematical theories. SPIN, NuSMV, UPPAAL, CBMC, TLA+, dafny, and PRISM are some of the tools that can be utilized in CAV. This book elucidates the concepts and innovative models and prospective developments with respect to computer science and information technology. It will also provide interesting topics for research which interested readers can take up.

After months of intensive research and writing, this book is the end result of all who devoted their time and efforts in the initiation and progress of this book. It will surely be a source of reference in enhancing the required knowledge of the new developments in the area. During the course of developing this book, certain measures such as accuracy, authenticity and research focused analytical studies were given preference in order to produce a comprehensive book in the area of study.

This book would not have been possible without the efforts of the authors and the publisher. I extend my sincere thanks to them. Secondly, I express my gratitude to my family and well-wishers. And most importantly, I thank my students for constantly expressing their willingness and curiosity in enhancing their knowledge in the field, which encourages me to take up further research projects for the advancement of the area.

Editor

Quantified Invariants via Syntax-Guided Synthesis

Grigory Fedyukovich[1]([✉])[iD], Sumanth Prabhu[2],
Kumar Madhukar[2], and Aarti Gupta[1]

[1] Princeton University, Princeton, USA
{grigoryf,aartig}@cs.princeton.edu
[2] TCS Research, Pune, India
{sumanth.prabhu,kumar.madhukar}@tcs.com

Abstract. Programs with arrays are ubiquitous. Automated reasoning about arrays necessitates discovering properties about ranges of elements at certain program points. Such properties are formally specified by universally quantified formulas, which are difficult to find, and difficult to prove inductive. In this paper, we propose an algorithm based on an enumerative search that discovers quantified invariants in stages. First, by exploiting the program syntax, it identifies ranges of elements accessed in each loop. Second, it identifies potentially useful facts about individual elements and generalizes them to hypotheses about entire ranges. Finally, by applying recent advances of SMT solving, the algorithm filters out wrong hypotheses. The combination of properties is often enough to prove that the program meets a safety specification. The algorithm has been implemented in a solver for Constrained Horn Clauses, FREQ-HORN, and extended to deal with multiple (possibly nested) loops. We show that FREQHORN advances state-of-the-art on a wide range of public array-handling programs.

1 Introduction

Formally verifying programs against safety specifications is difficult. This problem worsens in the presence of data structures like lists, arrays, and maps, which are ubiquitous in real-world applications. For instance, proving an array-handling program safe often requires discovering an inductive invariant that is universally quantified over ranges of array elements. Such invariants help to prove the unreachability of error states independently of the size of the array. However, the majority of invariant synthesis approaches are limited to quantifier-free numerical invariants. The approach presented in this paper advances the knowledge by an effective technique to discover quantified invariants over arrays and linear integer arithmetic.

Syntax-guided techniques [3] have recently been applied to synthesize quantifier-free numerical invariants [15–17,34] in the approach called FREQ-HORN. In a nutshell, FREQHORN collects various statistics from the syntactical patterns occurring in the program's source code and uses them to construct a set of formal grammars that specify a search space for invariants. It is often sufficient to perform an *enumerative search* over the formulas produced from these grammars and identify a set of suitable inductive invariants among them using an off-the-shelf solver for Satisfiability Modulo Theories (SMT). The presence of arrays complicates this reasoning in a few respects: it is hard to find suitable candidates and difficult to prove them inductive.

In this paper, we present a novel technique that extends the approach of enumerative search in general, and its instantiation in FREQHORN in particular, to reason about quantifiers. It discovers invariants over arrays in multiple stages. First, by exploiting the program syntax, it identifies ranges of elements accessed in each loop. Second, it identifies potentially useful facts about individual elements and generalizes them to hypotheses about entire ranges. The SMT-based validation of candidates, which are quantified formulas, is often inexpensive as they are constructed using the same syntactic patterns that appear in the source code. Furthermore, for supporting certain corner cases, our approach allows specifying additional rules that help in generalizing learned properties. The combination of properties proven inductive by an SMT solver is often enough to prove that the program meets a safety specification.

We show that FREQHORN advances state-of-the-art on a selection of array-handling programs from SVCOMP[1] and literature. For instance, it can prove completely automatically that an array is monotone after applying a sorting algorithm. Furthermore, FREQHORN is able to discover quantifier-free invariants over integer variables in the program, use them as inductive relatives while checking inductiveness of quantified candidates over arrays; and vice versa.

While a detailed discussion of the related work comes later in the paper (Sect. 6), it is noteworthy that being syntax-guided crucially helps us overcome several limitations of other techniques to verify array-handling programs [2,9, 11,35]. Most of them avoid inferring quantified invariants explicitly and thus do not produce checkable proofs. As a result, tools are fragile and in practice often output false positives (see Sect. 5 for concrete results). By comparison, our approach never produces false positives, and its results can be validated by existing SMT solvers.

The core contributions made through this work are:

- a novel syntax-guided approach to generate universally quantified invariants for programs manipulating arrays;
- an algorithm and its fully automated implementation; and
- a thorough experimental evaluation comparing our technique with state-of-the-art in verification of array-handling programs.

The rest of the paper is structured as follows. In Sect. 2, we give background and notation and illustrate our approach on an example. Our main contributions are then presented in Sect. 3 (main algorithm) and Sect. 4 (important design choices). In Sect. 5, we show the evaluation and comparison with state-of-the-art. Finally, the related work and conclusion complete the paper in Sects. 6 and 7, respectively.

---

[1] Software Verification Competition.

2 Background

The Satisfiability Modulo Theories (SMT) task is to decide whether there is an assignment m of values to variables in a first-order logic formula φ that makes it true. We write $\varphi \implies \psi$, if every satisfying assignment to φ is also a satisfying assignment to some formula ψ. By *Expr* we denote the space of all possible quantifier-free formulas in our background theory and by *Vars* a range of possible variables.

2.1 Programs as Constrained Horn Clauses

To guarantee expected behaviors, programs require proofs, such as inductive invariants, ranking functions, or recurrence sets. It is becoming increasingly popular to consider a verification task as a *proof synthesis* task which is formulated as a system of SMT formulas involving unknown predicates, also known as *constrained Horn clauses* (CHC). The synthesis goal is to discover a suitable interpretation of all unknown predicates that make all CHCs true. CHCs offer the advantages of flexibility and modularity in designing verifiers for various systems and languages. CHCs can be constructed in a way that captures the operational semantics of a language in question, and an off-the-shelf CHC solver can be used for solving the resulting formulas.

Definition 1. *A* linear constrained Horn clause *(CHC) over a set of uninterpreted relation symbols $\mathcal{R}$ is a formula in first-order logic that has the form of one of three implications (called respectively a* fact, *an* inductive clause, *and a* query*):*

$$\varphi(\vec{x_1}) \implies inv_1(\vec{x_1})$$
$$inv_1(\vec{x_1}) \wedge \varphi(\vec{x_1}, \vec{x_2}) \implies inv_2(\vec{x_2})$$
$$inv_1(\vec{x_1}) \wedge \varphi(\vec{x_1}) \implies \bot$$

where $inv_1, inv_2 \in \mathcal{R}$ are uninterpreted symbols, $\vec{x_1}, \vec{x_2}$ are vectors of variables, and φ, called a body, *is a fully interpreted formula (i.e., φ does not have applications of inv_1 or inv_2).*

For a CHC C, by $src(C)$ we denote an application of $inv \in \mathcal{R}$ in the premise of C (if C is a fact, we write $src(C) \overset{\text{def}}{=} \top$). Similarly, by $dst(C)$ we denote an application of $inv \in \mathcal{R}$ in the conclusion of C (if C is a query, we write $dst(C) \overset{\text{def}}{=} \bot$). We define functions rel and $args$, such that for each $inv(\vec{x})$, $rel(inv(\vec{x})) \overset{\text{def}}{=} inv$ and $args(inv(\vec{x})) \overset{\text{def}}{=} \vec{x}$. For a CHC C, by $body(C)$ we denote the body (i.e., φ) of C.

Example 1. Figure 1 gives a program in the C programming language that handles two integer arrays, A and B, both of an unknown size N. The A array has unknown content, and the program first identifies a value m which is smaller or

```
int N = nondetInt();
int *A = nondetArray(N);
int m = 0;
for (int i = N - 1; i ≥ 0; i--) { if (m > A[i]) m = A[i]; }
int *B = malloc(N*sizeof(int));
for (int i = 0; i < N; i++) { B[N - i - 1] = A[i] - m; }
int s = 0;
for (int i = 0; i < N; i++) { s = s + B[i]; }
assert(s ≥ 0);
```

Fig. 1. Example program: source code in C.

(A) $i'=N'-1 \wedge m'=0 \implies inv_1(A',i',m',N')$

(B) $inv_1(A,i,m,N) \wedge i \geq 0 \wedge m'=ite(m>A[i],A[i],m) \wedge i'=i-1 \implies inv_1(A,i',m',N)$

(C) $inv_1(A,i,m,N) \wedge i<0 \wedge i'=0 \implies inv_2(A,B,i',m,N)$

(D) $inv_2(A,B,i,m,N) \wedge i<N \wedge B'=store(B,N-i-1,A[i]-m]) \wedge i'=i+1 \implies inv_2(A,B',i',m,N)$

(E) $inv_2(A,B,i,m,N) \wedge i \geq N \wedge i'=0 \wedge s'=0 \implies inv_3(A,B,i',m,s',N)$

(F) $inv_3(A,B,i,m,s,N) \wedge i<N \wedge s'=s+B[i] \wedge i'=i+1 \implies inv_3(A,B,i',m,s',N)$

(G) $inv_3(A,B,i,m,s,N) \wedge i \geq N \wedge s<0 \implies \bot$

Fig. 2. Example program: CHC encoding.

equal to all elements of A (it might be either a minimal element among the content of A or 0). Then, the program populates B by values of A with m subtracted. Interestingly, the order of elements A and B is not preserved, e.g., A[0] − m gets written to B[N − 1], and so on. Finally, the program computes the sum s of all elements in B and requires us to prove that s is never negative.

Figure 2 gives a CHC encoding of the program. The system has three uninterpreted predicates, inv_1, inv_2, and inv_3 corresponding to invariants at heads of the three loops. The primed variables correspond to modified variables. Rules **B**, **D**, and **F** encode the loop bodies, and the remaining rules encode the fragments of code before, after, or between the loops. In particular, rule **G** ensures that after the third loop has terminated, a program state with a negative value of s is unreachable. Before we describe how our technique solves this CHC system (see Sect. 2.2), we briefly introduce the notion of satisfiability of CHCs.

Definition 2. *Given a set of uninterpreted relation symbols $\mathcal{R}$ and a set S of CHCs over $\mathcal{R}$, we say that S is satisfiable if there exists an interpretation that assigns to each n-ary symbol $inv \in \mathcal{R}$ a relation over n-tuples and makes all implications in S valid.*

In the paper, we assume that a relation assigned by an interpretation is represented by a formula ψ over at most n free variables.

We call a CHC C inductive when $rel(src(C)) = rel(dst(C)) = inv$ for some inv. While accessing an array in a loop, we assume the existence of an integer counter variable. More formally:

Definition 3. *Let C be an inductive CHC, $\vec{x} = args(src(C))$, and $\vec{x}' = args(dst(C))$. We say that C is* array-handling *if there exist numbers c and a, such that (1) $1 \leq c \leq |\vec{x}|$ and $1 \leq a \leq |\vec{x}|$; (2) $\vec{x}[c]$ (and consequently, its "primed copy" $\vec{x}'[c]$) has type integer, (3) either of these implications holds:*

$$body(C) \implies \vec{x}[c] < \vec{x}'[c] \tag{1}$$

$$body(C) \implies \vec{x}[c] > \vec{x}'[c] \tag{2}$$

(4) $\vec{x}[a]$ (and consequently $\vec{x}'[a]$) has type array, and (5) there is an access function *f that identifies a relationship between an access to $\vec{x}[a]$ in $body(C)$ and $\vec{x}[c]$.*

2.2 Illustrating Example

The CHC system in Fig. 2 has a solution, indicating that the program meets its specification. In particular:

$$\boldsymbol{inv}_1 \mapsto \forall j \, . \, i < j < N \implies m \leq A[j]$$
$$\boldsymbol{inv}_2 \mapsto \forall j \, . \, 0 \leq j < N \implies m \leq A[j] \, \wedge$$
$$\forall j \, . \, 0 \leq j < i \implies B[N - j - 1] = A[j] - m$$
$$\boldsymbol{inv}_3 \mapsto \forall j \, . \, 0 \leq j < N \implies m \leq A[j] \, \wedge$$
$$\forall j \, . \, 0 \leq j < N \implies B[N - j - 1] = A[j] - m$$
$$\wedge \, s \geq 0$$

The interpretation of $\boldsymbol{inv}_1$ means that as the first loop progresses (i.e, all elements $A[N - 1], A[N - 2], \ldots, A[i + 1]$ are sequentially considered), the value of m is always smaller than all the considered elements. Thus, we refer to the interpretation of $\boldsymbol{inv}_1$ as a *progress lemma*. When the first loop has terminated, clearly, this property holds for all elements from $A[0]$ to $A[N - 1]$. Because A leaks through the second loop without any changes, the interpretation of $\boldsymbol{inv}_1$ gets finalized (thus, it becomes a *finalized lemma*) and added to an interpretation of $\boldsymbol{inv}_2$.

Additionally, the interpretation of $\boldsymbol{inv}_2$ gets a relational fact about pairs of elements $A[0]$ and $B[N - 1]$, $A[1]$ and $B[N - 2]$, $\ldots$, $A[i - 1]$ and $B[N - i - 2]$, which again appears as a progress lemma and then gets finalized in an interpretation of $\boldsymbol{inv}_3$. With these two quantified invariants about all elements of A, and relation about pairs of elements of A and B, it is possible to derive the remaining lemma in the interpretation of $\boldsymbol{inv}_3$, namely, $s \geq 0$; which concludes the proof.

3 Invariants via Enumerative Search

In this work, we aim at discovering a solution for a CHC system S over a set of uninterpreted symbols $\mathcal{R}$ enumeratively, i.e., by guessing a candidate formula for each $\boldsymbol{inv} \in \mathcal{R}$, substituting it for all CHCs $C \in S$ and checking their validity.

3.1 Quantifier-Free Invariants

We build on top of an algorithm, called FREQHORN, recently proposed in [17]. Its key insight is an automatic construction of a set of formal grammars $G(inv)$ for each $inv \in \mathcal{R}$ based on either source code, program behaviors, or both. Importantly, these grammars are *conjunction-free*: they cannot be used to produce a conjunction of clauses and can give rise to only a finite number of formulas, potentially related to invariants (otherwise, the approach does not guarantee strong convergence). Since invariants are often represented by a conjunction of lemmas, FREQHORN attempts to sample (i.e., recursively apply production rules) each lemma from a grammar in separation, until a combination of them is sufficient for the inductiveness and safety, or a search space is exhausted. FREQ-HORN relies on an SMT solver to filter out unsuccessfully sampled lemmas.

The construction of formal grammars is biased by the syntax of CHC encoding. First, FREQHORN collects a set of *Seeds* by converting the body of each CHC to a Conjunctive Normal Form, extracting, and normalizing each conjunct. Then, the set of seeds could be optionally replenished by a set of *behavioral seeds* and *bounded proofs*. They are constructed respectively from the concrete values of variables obtained from actual program runs, and Craig interpolants from unsatisfiable finite unrollings of the CHC systems. Finally, the production rules are created in a way to enable producing seeds and also their *mutants* (i.e., syntactically similar formulas to seeds). In general, no specific restriction on a grammar-construction method is imposed; so in practice, the grammars are allowed to be more (or less) general to enable a broader (or more focused) search space for invariants.

3.2 Quantified Candidates from Quantifier-Free Grammars

The main obstacle for applying the enumerative search to generate array invariants is that the grammars do not allow quantifiers. Because grammars are constructed automatically from syntactic patterns which appear in the original programs, in the presence of arrays, we can expect expressions involving only particular elements of arrays (such as ones accessed via a loop counter). However, since each loop repeats certain operations over a *range* of array elements, we have to *generalize* the extracted expressions about individual elements to expressions about entire ranges.

Let a set of variables associated with a relation symbol inv be $Vars(inv) \stackrel{\text{def}}{=} IntVars(inv) \cup ArrVars(inv)$, where $IntVars(inv)$ and $ArrVars(inv)$ are disjoint and contain integer variables and array variables, respectively. A candidate quantified invariant over arrays consists of three parts:

- a set of quantified integer variables $QVars(inv)$, which are introduced by our algorithm and do not appear in $Vars(inv)$;
- a *range* formula over $QVars(inv) \cup IntVars(inv)$; and
- a quantifier-free *cell property* over $QVars(inv) \cup Vars(inv)$.

Algorithm 1. PREPARE$(S, \mathcal{R})$

Input: CHCs S over $\mathcal{R}$
Output: Formal grammars $G(\boldsymbol{inv})$, quantified variables $QVars(\boldsymbol{inv})$ and
$progressRange(\boldsymbol{inv})$ for each $\boldsymbol{inv} \in \mathcal{R}$

1 **for each** $\boldsymbol{inv} \in \mathcal{R}$ **do**
2      $Seeds \leftarrow$ SYNTSEEDS$(\boldsymbol{inv}) \cup$ BEHAVSEEDS$(\boldsymbol{inv})$;
3      $cnt \leftarrow$ GETCOUNTERS$(S, \boldsymbol{inv}, ArrVars(\boldsymbol{inv}))$;
4   **if** $\varnothing \neq cnt$ **then**
5          $QVars(\boldsymbol{inv}) \leftarrow$ COPY(cnt);
6          $progressRange(\boldsymbol{inv}) \leftarrow$ GETRANGE(cnt);
7      $G(\boldsymbol{inv}) \leftarrow$ REPLACE(GETGRAMMAR$(Seeds), cnt, QVars(\boldsymbol{inv}))$;

Algorithm 2. SOLVEARRAYCHCS$(S, \mathcal{R})$

Input: CHCs S over $\mathcal{R}$
Output: $res \in \{\text{SAT}, \text{UNKNOWN}\}$, $Lemmas : \mathcal{R} \to 2^{Expr}$

1 $\langle G, QVars, progressRange \rangle \leftarrow$ PREPARE$(S, \mathcal{R})$;
2 **for each** $\boldsymbol{inv} \in \mathcal{R}$ **do** $Lemmas(\boldsymbol{inv}) \leftarrow \varnothing$;
3 **while** $\exists C \in S . \left(\bigwedge\limits_{\ell \in Lemmas(rel(src(C)))} \ell(args(src(C))) \wedge body(C) \implies \bot \right)$ **do**
4   **if** $\forall \boldsymbol{inv} \in \mathcal{R} .$ ALLBLOCKED$(G(\boldsymbol{inv}))$ **then return** $\langle \text{UNKNOWN}, \varnothing \rangle$;
5      $\boldsymbol{inv} \leftarrow$ PICKLOOP$(\mathcal{R})$;
6   **if** $QVars(\boldsymbol{inv}) = \varnothing$ **then** $Cand(\boldsymbol{inv}) \leftarrow$ SAMPLE$(G(\boldsymbol{inv}))$;
7   **else** $Cand(\boldsymbol{inv}) \leftarrow \forall QVars(\boldsymbol{inv}) .$
         $QVars(\boldsymbol{inv}) \in progressRange(\boldsymbol{inv}) \implies$ SAMPLE$(G(\boldsymbol{inv}))$;
8      $ExtCand \leftarrow$ EXTEND$(S, \{\boldsymbol{inv}\}, Cand, Lemmas)$;
9   **if** $\forall \boldsymbol{inv}' \in \mathcal{R} . ExtCand(\boldsymbol{inv}') = \top$ **then** $G(\boldsymbol{inv}) \leftarrow$ BLOCK$(G, Cand, \boldsymbol{inv})$;
10   **else**
11   **for each** $\boldsymbol{inv}' \in \mathcal{R}$ **do**
12              $Lemmas(\boldsymbol{inv}') \leftarrow Lemmas(\boldsymbol{inv}') \cup \{ExtCand(\boldsymbol{inv}')\}$;
13              $G(\boldsymbol{inv}') \leftarrow$ BLOCK$(G, ExtCand, \boldsymbol{inv}')$;
14 **return** $\langle \text{SAT}, Lemmas \rangle$;

A naive idea for getting a range formula and a cell property is to sample them separately, and then to bind them together using some $QVars(\boldsymbol{inv})$. But it would result in a large search space. Algorithm 1 gives a more tailored procedure on the matter. The central role in this process is taken by an analysis of the loop counters which are used to access array elements (line 3). This analysis is performed once for each loop before the main verification process, and thus its results are reused in all iterations of the verification process.

Our algorithm identifies $QVars(\boldsymbol{inv})$ by creating a fresh variable for each counter, including counters of nested loops (line 5). It then generates range formulas based on the results of the analysis (line 6) such that: (1) the range formula itself is an inductive invariant for $\boldsymbol{inv}$, and (2) the range formula is expressed over the initial values of counters of $\boldsymbol{inv}$ and the counters themselves. Finally, only a cell property is going to be produced from the grammar $G(\boldsymbol{inv})$,

---

Algorithm 3. WEAKEN(S', $\mathcal{R}'$, $Cand$, $Lemmas$)

Input: CHCs S' over $\mathcal{R}'$, candidates $Cand(\boldsymbol{inv})$; learned $Lemmas(\boldsymbol{inv})$ for
　　　　each $\boldsymbol{inv} \in \mathcal{R}'$
Output: weakened $Cand$

1　$toRecheck \leftarrow \bot$;
2　**for all** $C \in S'$ **do**
3　　　**if** $\bigwedge\limits_{\ell \in Lemmas(rel(src(C)))} \ell(args(src(C))) \wedge Cand(rel(src(C)))(args(src(C))) \wedge$
　　　　$body(C) \implies\!\!\!\!\!/\ \ Cand(rel(dst(C)))(args(dst(C)))$ **then**
4　　　　　**if** IsFINALIZEDARRAYCAND($Cand$, $rel(dst(C))$) **then**
5　　　　　　　$Cand(rel(dst(C)))) \leftarrow$ GETREGRESSCAND($Cand$, $rel(dst(C))$);
6　　　　　**else**
7　　　　　　　$Cand(rel(dst(C))) \leftarrow \top$;
8　　　　　$toRecheck \leftarrow \top$;
9　　　　　**break**;
10　**if** $toRecheck$ **then return** WEAKEN(S', $\mathcal{R}'$, $Cand$, $Lemmas$);
11　**else return** $Cand$;

Algorithm 4. EXTEND(S, $\mathcal{R}$, $Cand$, $Lemmas$), cf [17].

Input: CHCs S over $\mathcal{R}$; $\mathcal{R}' \subseteq \mathcal{R}$, candidates $Cand(\boldsymbol{inv})$; learned $Lemmas(\boldsymbol{inv})$
　　　　for each $\boldsymbol{inv} \in \mathcal{R}'$
Output: extended $Cand$

1　$Cand \leftarrow$ WEAKEN(S', $\mathcal{R}'$, $Cand$, $Lemmas$);
2　**for all** $C \in S$ **s.t.** $rel(src(C)) \in \mathcal{R}'$ **do**
3　　　$Cand(rel(dst(C))) \leftarrow$ PROPAGATE(C, $Cand$);
4　　　$Cand \leftarrow$ EXTEND(S, $\mathcal{R}' \cup \{rel(dst(C))\}$, $Cand$, $Lemmas$);
5　**return** $Cand$;

---

constructed from the seeds (recall Sect. 3.1), in which all counters are replaced by the corresponding variables from $QVars(\boldsymbol{inv})$ (line 7). Thus, the only part of the candidate formula where the counter can appear is the range formula.

Once grammars, $QVars$, and ranges are detected, our approach proceeds to sample candidates and to check them with an SMT solver. The general flow of this algorithm is illustrated in Algorithm 2. For each $\boldsymbol{inv} \in \mathcal{R}$, it initiates a set $Lemmas(\boldsymbol{inv})$ (line 2). Then it iteratively guesses lemmas until a combination of them is inductive and safe, or a search space is exhausted (lines 3–4).

Compared to the baseline approach from [17], our new algorithm fixes a shape for the candidates for arrays. At the same time, it permits to sample quantifier-free candidates (line 6): they could be either formulas over counters or any other variables in the loop, or even formulas over isolated array elements (if, e.g., accessed by a constant). Then (line 8), Algorithm 2 propagates candidates through all available implications in CHCs using quantifier elimination and identifies lemmas among the candidates. This step is similar to the baseline approach from [17], but for completeness of presentation, we provide the pseudocode in Algorithms 3 and 4. The only differences are (1) in the implementation of the candidate propagation for array candidates and (2) in the weakening of failed candidates (both in Algorithm 3, to be discussed in Sects. 4.3 and 4.4, respectively).

Both successful and unsuccessful candidates are "blocked" from their grammars to avoid re-sampling them in the next iterations. This fact together with the property of grammars being conjunction-free gives the main hint for proving the following theorem.

Theorem 1. *Algorithm 2 always makes a finite number of iterations, and if it returns with* SAT *then the CHC system is satisfiable.*

Next section discusses a particular instantiation of important subroutines that make our invariant synthesizer effective in practice.

4 Design Choices

Our main contribution is a completely automated algorithm for finding quantified invariants for array-handling loops. In this section, we first show how by exploiting the program syntax we can identify ranges of elements accessed in each loop (Sect. 4.1). Second, we present an intuitive justification to why our candidates can often be proved as lemmas by an off-the-shelf SMT solver (Sect. 4.2). Finally, we extend our algorithm to handle more complicated cases of multiple loops (Sects. 4.3–4.4), and benchmarks of the tiling [9] technique, which are adapted from the industrial code of battery controllers (Sect. 4.5).

4.1 Discovery of Progress Lemmas

We start with the simplest scenario of a single loop handling just one array. Let S be a system of CHCs over a set of uninterpreted relation symbols $\mathcal{R}$. Let $inv \in \mathcal{R}$ correspond to a loop, in which arrays are accessed using some counter variable i (counters are automatically identified by posing and solving queries of forms (1) and (2)).

Recall that we do not necessarily require the array elements to be accessed directly by i, and we allow an access function f to identify relationships between i and an index of the accessed element. However, we assume that the counter is unique in the loop because it is the case in most of the practical applications. In principle, our algorithm can be extended to loops handling several independent counters (although it is rare in practice), with the help of additionally discovered lemmas that describe relationships among counters. We leave a discussion about this to future work.

Definition 4. *A* range *of inv and a counter i is a formula over IntVars(inv) and a free variable v having form $L < v \wedge v < U$, such that either of formulas $L < i$ or $i < U$ is a lemma for inv. A* progress lemma *is either a formula $L < v \wedge v < i$ (if $L < i$ is a lemma), or a formula $i < v \wedge v < U$ (if $i < U$ is a lemma).*

Both ranges and progress ranges can be identified statically. Let C_1 and C_2 be two CHCs, such that $\boldsymbol{inv} = rel(dst(C_1)) = rel(src(C_2)) = rel(dst(C_2))$ and $\boldsymbol{inv} \neq rel(src(C_1))$. It is common in practice that $body(C_1)$ identifies a symbolic bound b on the initial value of i: it could be either a lower bound (if i increments in $body(C_2)$) or an upper bound (if i decrements). In this case, a progress range of $\boldsymbol{inv}$ is simply computed as a lemma for $\boldsymbol{inv}$ over i and b. A range of $\boldsymbol{inv}$ can often be constructed as a conjunction of the progress range with the negation of the termination condition of $body(C_2)$.[2]

Example 2. For the CHC-encoding of the program is shown in Fig. 2, the ranges of $\boldsymbol{inv}_1, \boldsymbol{inv}_2$ and $\boldsymbol{inv}_3$ are all equal to $-1 < v < N$. The progress range of $\boldsymbol{inv}_1$ is $i < v < N$, and the progress ranges of $\boldsymbol{inv}_2$ and $\boldsymbol{inv}_3$ are $-1 < v < i$.

We call candidates, that use progress ranges in their left sides, *progress candidates*:

$$\forall \vec{q} \, . \, progressRange(\boldsymbol{inv})(\vec{q}) \implies cand$$

where $\vec{q} = QVars(\boldsymbol{inv})$ and *cand* is a quantifier-free formula over $QVars(\boldsymbol{inv}) \cup IntVars(\boldsymbol{inv})$. As can be seen from Algorithm 1, all sampled candidates are progress candidates. However, during the next steps of the algorithm (i.e., propagation and weakening) we will use other kind of candidates (namely, *regress* and *finalized*, see Sects. 4.3 and 4.4 respectively).

If a progress candidate is proven inductive, we call it a *progress lemma*.

4.2 SMT-Based Inductiveness Checking

We rely on recent advances of SMT solving to identify successful candidates, a conjunction of which is directly used to prove the desired safety specification. In general, solving quantified formulas for validity is a hard task, however, in certain cases, the initiation and inductiveness queries can be simplified and reduced to a sequence of (sometimes even quantifier-free) formulas over integer arithmetic. We illustrate such proving strategy, inspired by the *tiling* approach [9], on the following example.

Example 3. Recall the CHC system from Fig. 2. Consider a progress candidate $\forall j \, . \, i < j < N \implies m \leq A[j]$ for $\boldsymbol{inv}_1$. Checking its initiation (i.e., for CHC **A**) requires deciding validity of the following quantified formula:

$$i' = N' - 1 \wedge m' = 0 \implies \left(\forall j \, . \, i' < j < N' \implies m' \leq A'[j] \right) \tag{3}$$

The range formula $i' < j < N'$ simplifies to $N' - 1 < j < N'$, which is always false, making formula (3) always valid.

---

[2] Thus, we explicitly require guards of loops to have the forms of an inequality, which is the most common array access pattern.

Checking the inductiveness of the candidate (i.e., for CHC **B**) boils down to solving a more complicated formula:

$$\left(\forall j\,.\,i < j < N \implies m \leq A[j]\right)$$
$$\wedge\, i \geq 0 \wedge m' = ite(m > A[i], A[i], m) \wedge i' = i - 1 \implies$$
$$\left(\forall j\,.\,i' < j < N \implies m' \leq A[j]\right) \qquad (4)$$

Although quantifiers are present on both sides of (4), proving its validity is not hard. Indeed, the query is reducible to two implications:

$$\left(\forall j\,.\,i < j < N \implies m \leq A[j]\right) \wedge m' = ite(m > A[i], A[i], m) \implies m' \leq A[i]$$

$$\left(\forall j\,.\,i < j < N \implies m \leq A[j]\right) \wedge$$
$$m' = ite(m > A[i], A[i], m) \implies \left(\forall j\,.\,i < j < N \implies m' \leq A[j]\right)$$

The former does not require any information about $A[i+1], \ldots, A[N-1]$, so the entire quantified conjunction is ignored, and $A[i]$ could be replaced by a fresh integer variable. The latter is trickier: it requires to prove that if all elements in a range are greater or equal than m, then they are also greater or equal to $ite(m > A[i], A[i], m)$. This again is reduced to a quantifier-free formula over integer arithmetic:

$$m \leq A[j] \wedge m' = ite(m > A[i], A[i], m) \implies m' \leq A[j]$$

Thus, because formulas (3) and (4) are valid, the progress candidate is proved a progress lemma.

In general, we cannot always conduct proofs that easily. Often, the prerequisite for success is the commonality of an access function f in the candidate and the body of the CHC. Fortunately, our algorithm ensures that all access functions used in the candidates are borrowed directly from bodies of CHCs. Thus, in many cases, FREQHORN is able to check large amounts of candidates quickly.

4.3 Strategy of Lemma Propagation

In this subsection, we identify a useful strategy for propagation of quantified lemmas through adjacent CHCs in the given system, inspired by [17]. Let some $\boldsymbol{inv}_1 \in \mathcal{R}$ have the following lemma:

$$\forall \vec{q}\,.\,\rho(\vec{q}) \implies \ell$$

where $\vec{q} = QVars(\boldsymbol{inv}_1)$, formula ρ over $\vec{q} \cup IntVars(\boldsymbol{inv}_1)$ is either a range or a progress range, and ℓ is over $\vec{q} \cup Vars(\boldsymbol{inv}_1)$. Let then a CHC C be such that $rel(src(C)) = \boldsymbol{inv}_1$ and $rel(dst(C)) = \boldsymbol{inv}_2$, and its body be $\varphi(\vec{x}_1, \vec{x}_2)$.

Definition 5. Forward propagation *of lemma* $\forall \vec{q} . \rho(\vec{q}) \implies \ell$ *through* C *gives a formula of the following form:*

$$\forall \vec{q} . (\exists \vec{x}_1 . \rho(\vec{q})(\vec{x}_1) \wedge \varphi(\vec{x}_1, \vec{x}_2)) \implies (\exists \vec{x}_1 (\vec{x}_1, \vec{q}) . \ell \wedge \varphi(\vec{x}_1, \vec{x}_2))$$

Example 4. Recall the example from Fig. 2 and the following lemma for $\boldsymbol{inv}_1$:

$$\forall j . i < j < N \implies m \le A[j]$$

The body of $\mathbf{C}$ is $i < 0 \wedge i' = 0$, thus the forward propagation gives the following formula:

$$\forall j . (\exists i . i < j < N \wedge i < 0 \wedge i' = 0) \implies (\exists i . m \le A[j] \wedge i < 0 \wedge i' = 0)$$

Applying quantifier elimination to both sides of the implication, we get the following formula:

$$\forall j . 0 \le j < N \implies m \le A[j]$$

Note that this formula is not going to be immediately learned as a lemma, but instead should be checked by the solver for inductiveness. Intuitively, such a candidate represents some facts about array elements that were accessed during a loop that has terminated. If after the propagation it appeared that the candidate uses the entire range then we refer to such candidate to as a *finalized* candidate.

4.4   Weakening Strategy

Whenever a finalized candidate cannot be proven inductive, we often do not want to withdraw it completely. Instead, our algorithm runs *weakening* and proposes *regress candidates*. The main idea is to calculate a range of elements which have not been touched by the loop yet. This is an inverse of the procedure outlined in Sect. 4.1.

Definition 6. *Given* $\boldsymbol{inv} \in \mathcal{R}$*, its* $Range(\boldsymbol{inv})$ *and* $progressRange(\boldsymbol{inv})$ *formulas, we call a* regress range *a formula of the following kind:*

$$regressRange(\boldsymbol{inv}) \overset{\text{def}}{=} Range(\boldsymbol{inv}) \wedge \neg progressRange(\boldsymbol{inv})$$

We call candidates that use regress ranges in their left sides as *regress candidates*. Clearly, a regress candidate is weaker than the corresponding finalized candidate. Thus, from the failure to prove inductiveness of the finalized candidate it does not follow that the regress candidate is not inductive; and it makes sense to try proving it in the next iteration.

4.5   Learning from Sub-ranges

In complicated scenarios of loops with multiple iterators, multiple array variables or multiple access functions, the iterative process of lemma discovery, might end up in a large number of quantified formulas and get lost while checking a candidate for inductiveness (recall Sect. 4.2). To overcome current limitations in existing SMT solvers, it appeared to be useful to help the solver while generalizing learned lemmas. In particular, a property could be learned for two subranges of an array, and then combined in the following way:

```
int N = nondetInt();
int *A = nondetArray(2*N);
int val1 = 1, val2 = 3, m = nondetInt();
for (int i = 1; i ≤ N; i++) {
  if (m < val2) A[2*i-2] = val2; else A[2*i-2] = 0;
  if (m < val1) A[2*i-1] = val1; else A[2*i-1] = 0; }
for (int i = 0; i < 2*N; i++) assert(A[i]==0 || A[i] ≤ m);
```

Fig. 3. Learning from sub-ranges.

Lemma 1. *Let for some **inv** $\in \mathcal{R}$ two lemmas be of the following kind:*

$$\forall \vec{q} . \rho_1(\vec{q}) \implies \ell \qquad\qquad \forall \vec{q} . \rho_2(\vec{q}) \implies \ell \qquad\qquad (5)$$

*Then, the following is also a lemma for **inv**:*

$$\forall \vec{q} . \rho_1(\vec{q}) \vee \rho_2(\vec{q}) \implies \ell$$

Example 5. Figure 3 shows a program from the tiling benchmark suite [9]. If lemmas $\forall j . 0 < j < N \implies A[2*j-1] = 0 \vee A[2*j-1] \leq m$ and $\forall j . 0 < j < N \implies A[2*j-2] = 0 \vee A[2*j-2] \leq m$ are discovered, then formula $\forall j . 0 \leq j < 2*N-1 \implies A[j] = 0 \vee A[j] \leq m$ is also a lemma.

5 Evaluation

We have implemented our algorithm on top of the FREQHORN[3] tool. It takes a system of CHCs with arrays as input and performs an enumerative search as presented in Sect. 4. The tool uses Z3 [12] to solve SMT queries.

We have evaluated FREQHORN on 137 satisfiable CHC-translations of publicly available C programs (whose assertions are safe) taken from the SVCOMP ReachSafety Array subcategory and literature. These programs include variations of standard array copying, initializing, maximum, minimum, sorting, and tiling benchmarks. Among these 137 benchmarks, 79 have a single loop, and 58 have multiple loops, including 7 that have nested loops. These programs are encoded using the theories of Arrays, Linear (LIA) and Non-linear Integer Arithmetic (NIA). Our experiments have been performed on an Ubuntu 18.04 machine running at 2.5 GHz and having 16 GB memory, with a timeout of 100 s for every benchmark. FREQHORN solved 129 benchmarks within the timeout, of which 73 solved benchmarks had a single loop and 56 had multiple loops.

We have compared our tool with SPACER (Z3 v4.8.3) [26], that implements a recent QUIC3 [22] algorithm, BOOSTER (v0.2) [2], VIAP (v1.0) [35], and VERI-ABS (v1.3.10) [11]. The last two tools performed well in the ReachSafety Array

---

[3] The source code and benchmarks are available at https://github.com/grigoryfedyuk ovich/aeval/tree/rnd.

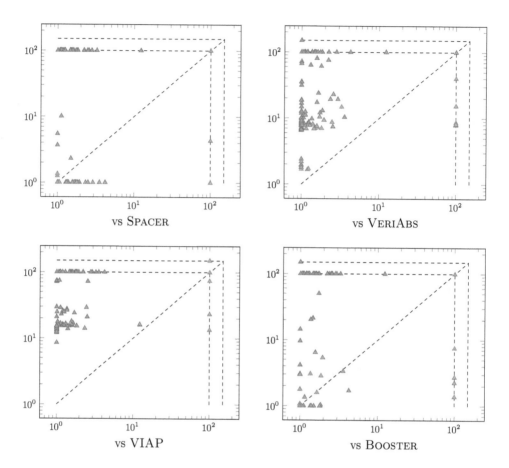

Fig. 4. FREQHORN vs competitors. Each point in a plot represents a pair of the run times (sec × sec) of FREQHORN (x-axis) and a competitor (y-axis). Timeouts are placed on the inner dashed lines; false alarms, unsupported cases, and crashes are on the outer dashed lines.

subcategory at SVCOMP 2019[4]. Figure 4 gives a comparison of FREQHORN timings against timings of these tools.[5]

Compare to 129 benchmarks solved by FREQHORN, only 81 were solved by SPACER, 108 – by VERIABS, 70 – by VIAP, and 48 – by BOOSTER.

FREQHORN solved 54 benchmarks on which SPACER diverged. Our intuition is that SPACER works poorly on programs with non-deterministic assignments and NIA operations, which our tool can handle.

FREQHORN solved 27 benchmarks on which VERIABS diverged. VERIABS failed to solve programs with nested loops and when array values were dependent on access indices. Furthermore, it decided one of the programs as unsafe, Time-wise, FREQHORN significantly outperformed VERIABS on all benchmarks.

---

[4] https://sv-comp.sosy-lab.org/2019/results/results-verified/.
[5] The time taken for every benchmark is available at: http://bit.ly/2VS5Mtf.

Importantly, the short time taken by FREQHORN includes the time for generating a checkable witness – quantified invariant – an essence that VERIABS cannot produce by design. On the other side, VERIABS solved several benchmarks after merging loops. No quantified invariant satisfying the FREQHORN's restrictions exists for these benchmarks before this program transformation.

FREQHORN solved 60 programs on which VIAP diverged. VIAP decided one program as unsafe. There were no programs on which FREQHORN took more time than VIAP. Finally, FREQHORN solved 83 programs on which BOOSTER diverged. And again, BOOSTER decided two programs as unsafe.

6   Related Work

Our algorithm for quantified invariant synthesis extends the prior work on checking satisfiability of CHCs [15–17], where solutions do not permit quantifiers. It works in a similar – enumerate-and-check – manner, but there are two crucial changes: (1) introduction of quantifiers, to formulate hypotheses over a subset of array indices, and (2) a generalization mechanism, to derive properties that may hold over the entire range of array indices.

Many existing approaches for verifying programs over arrays are extensions of well-known techniques for programs over scalar variables to quantified invariants. For example, by extending predicates with Skolem variables in predicate abstraction [30], by exploiting the MCMT [19] framework in lazy abstraction with interpolants [1] and its integration with acceleration [2], and, recently, QUIC3 [22], that extends IC3 [8, 14] to universally quantified invariants. Apart from the skeletal similarity, however, these approaches rely on orthogonal techniques.

Partitioning of arrays has also been used to infer invariants in many different ways. It refers to splitting an array into symbolic segments, and may be based on syntax [20,23,25] or semantics [10,31]. Invariants may be inferred for each segment separately and generalized for the entire array. The partitioning need not be explicit, as in [13]. However, most of these techniques (except [13,31]) are restricted to contiguous array segments, and work well when different loop iterations write to disjoint array locations or when the segments are non-overlapping. Tiling [9], a property-driven verification technique, overcomes these limitations for a class of programs by inferring array access patterns in loops. But identifying tiles of array accesses is itself a difficult problem, and the approach is currently based on heuristics developed by observing interesting patterns.

There are a number of approaches that verify array programs without inferring quantified invariants explicitly. A straightforward way is to smash all array elements into a single memory location [4], but it is quite imprecise. Every array element might also be considered a separate variable, but it is not possible with unknown array sizes. There are also techniques that abstract an array to a fixed number of elements, e.g. k-distinguished cell abstraction [32,33] and k-shrinkability [24,29]. Such abstractions usually reduce array modifying loops with unknown bounds to a known, small bound. It may even be possible to get rid of such loops altogether, by accelerating (computing transitive closures of) transition relations involving array updates in that loop [7]. Along similar lines, VIAP [35] resorts to reasoning with recurrences instead of loops. It translates the input program, including loops, to a set of first-order axioms, and checks if they derive the property. But all these techniques do not obtain quantified invariants explicitly, unlike ours. Besides, many of these transformations produce an abstraction of the original program, i.e., they do not preserve safety.

Alternatively, there are approaches that use sufficiently expressive templates to infer quantified invariants over arrays [5, 21, 27]. However, the templates need to be supplied manually. For instance, [6] uses a template space of quantified invariants and reduces the problem to quantifier-free invariant generation. Thus, universally quantified solutions for unknown predicates in a CHC system may be obtained by extending a generic CHC solver to handle quantified predicates. Learning need not be limited to user-supplied templates; one may do away with the templates entirely and learn only from examples and counterexamples [18]. Alternatively, [36] chooses a template upfront and refurbishes it with constants or coefficients appearing in the program source. Similarly, [28] proposes to infer array invariants without any user guidance or any user-defined templates or predicates. Their method is based on automatic analysis of predicates that update an array and allows one to generate first-order invariants, including those that contain alternations of quantifiers. But it does not work for nested loops. By comparison, our technique supports multiple as well as nested loops, enables candidate propagation between loops and, more importantly, generates the grammar automatically from the syntactical constructions appearing in the program's source.

7   Conclusion

We have presented a new algorithm to synthesize quantified invariants over array variables, systematically accessed in loops. Our algorithm implements an enumerative search that guesses invariants based on syntactic constructions which appear in the code and checks their initiation, inductiveness, and safety with an off-the-shelf SMT solver. Key insights behind our approach are that individual accesses to array elements performed in the loop can be generalized to hypotheses about entire ranges, and the existing SMT solvers can be used to validate these hypotheses efficiently. Our implementation on top of a CHC solver FREQHORN confirmed that such strategy is effective on a variety of practical examples. In a vast majority of cases, our tool outperformed competitors and provided checkable guarantees that prevented from reporting false positives.

Acknowledgements. This work was supported in part by NSF Grant 1525936. Any opinions, findings, and conclusions expressed herein are those of the authors and do not necessarily reflect those of the NSF.

References

1. Alberti, F., Bruttomesso, R., Ghilardi, S., Ranise, S., Sharygina, N.: Lazy abstraction with interpolants for arrays. In: Bjørner, N., Voronkov, A. (eds.) LPAR 2012. LNCS, vol. 7180, pp. 46–61. Springer, Heidelberg (2012). https://doi.org/10.1007/978-3-642-28717-6_7
2. Alberti, F., Ghilardi, S., Sharygina, N.: Booster: an acceleration-based verification framework for array programs. In: Cassez, F., Raskin, J.-F. (eds.) ATVA 2014. LNCS, vol. 8837, pp. 18–23. Springer, Cham (2014). https://doi.org/10.1007/978-3-319-11936-6_2
3. Alur, R., et al.: Syntax-guided synthesis. In: FMCAD, pp. 1–17. IEEE (2013)
4. Bertrane, J., et al.: Static analysis and verification of aerospace software by abstract interpretation. Found. Trends Program. Lang. **2**(2–3), 71–190 (2015)
5. Beyer, D., Henzinger, T.A., Majumdar, R., Rybalchenko, A.: Invariant Synthesis for combined theories. In: Cook, B., Podelski, A. (eds.) VMCAI 2007. LNCS, vol. 4349, pp. 378–394. Springer, Heidelberg (2007). https://doi.org/10.1007/978-3-540-69738-1_27
6. Bjørner, N., McMillan, K., Rybalchenko, A.: On solving universally quantified horn clauses. In: Logozzo, F., Fähndrich, M. (eds.) SAS 2013. LNCS, vol. 7935, pp. 105–125. Springer, Heidelberg (2013). https://doi.org/10.1007/978-3-642-38856-9_8
7. Bozga, M., Habermehl, P., Iosif, R., Konečný, F., Vojnar, T.: Automatic verification of integer array programs. In: Bouajjani, A., Maler, O. (eds.) CAV 2009. LNCS, vol. 5643, pp. 157–172. Springer, Heidelberg (2009). https://doi.org/10.1007/978-3-642-02658-4_15
8. Bradley, A.R.: SAT-based model checking without unrolling. In: Jhala, R., Schmidt, D. (eds.) VMCAI 2011. LNCS, vol. 6538, pp. 70–87. Springer, Heidelberg (2011). https://doi.org/10.1007/978-3-642-18275-4_7
9. Chakraborty, S., Gupta, A., Unadkat, D.: Verifying array manipulating programs by tiling. In: Ranzato, F. (ed.) SAS 2017. LNCS, vol. 10422, pp. 428–449. Springer, Cham (2017). https://doi.org/10.1007/978-3-319-66706-5_21
10. Cousot, P., Cousot, R., Logozzo, F.: A parametric segmentation functor for fully automatic and scalable array content analysis. In: POPL, pp. 105–118 (2011)
11. Darke, P., et al.: VeriAbs: verification by abstraction and test generation. In: Beyer, D., Huisman, M. (eds.) TACAS 2018, Part I. LNCS, vol. 10806, pp. 457–462. Springer, Cham (2018). https://doi.org/10.1007/978-3-319-89963-3_32
12. de Moura, L., Bjørner, N.: Z3: an efficient SMT solver. In: Ramakrishnan, C.R., Rehof, J. (eds.) TACAS 2008. LNCS, vol. 4963, pp. 337–340. Springer, Heidelberg (2008). https://doi.org/10.1007/978-3-540-78800-3_24
13. Dillig, I., Dillig, T., Aiken, A.: Fluid updates: beyond strong vs. weak updates. In: Gordon, A.D. (ed.) ESOP 2010. LNCS, vol. 6012, pp. 246–266. Springer, Heidelberg (2010). https://doi.org/10.1007/978-3-642-11957-6_14
14. Eén, N., Mishchenko, A., Brayton, R.K.: Efficient implementation of property directed reachability. In: FMCAD, pp. 125–134. IEEE (2011)
15. Fedyukovich, G., Bodík, R.: Accelerating syntax-guided invariant synthesis. In: Beyer, D., Huisman, M. (eds.) TACAS 2018, Part I. LNCS, vol. 10805, pp. 251–269. Springer, Cham (2018). https://doi.org/10.1007/978-3-319-89960-2_14
16. Fedyukovich, G., Kaufman, S., Bodík, R.: Sampling invariants from frequency distributions. In: FMCAD, pp. 100–107. IEEE (2017)
17. Fedyukovich, G., Prabhu, S., Madhukar, K., Gupta, A.: Solving constrained horn clauses using syntax and data. In: FMCAD, pp. 170–178. IEEE (2018)

18. Garg, P., Löding, C., Madhusudan, P., Neider, D.: Learning universally quanti-
    fied invariants of linear data structures. In: Sharygina, N., Veith, H. (eds.) CAV
    2013. LNCS, vol. 8044, pp. 813–829. Springer, Heidelberg (2013). https://doi.org/
    10.1007/978-3-642-39799-8_57

19. Ghilardi, S., Ranise, S.: MCMT: a model checker modulo theories. In: Giesl, J.,
    Hähnle, R. (eds.) IJCAR 2010. LNCS (LNAI), vol. 6173, pp. 22–29. Springer,
    Heidelberg (2010). https://doi.org/10.1007/978-3-642-14203-1_3

20. Gopan, D., Reps, T., Sagiv, M.: A framework for numeric analysis of array opera-
    tions. In: POPL, pp. 338–350 (2005)

21. Gulwani, S., McCloskey, B., Tiwari, A.: Lifting abstract interpreters to quantified
    logical domains. In: POPL, pp. 235–246. ACM (2008)

22. Gurfinkel, A., Shoham, S., Vizel, Y.: Quantifiers on demand. In: Lahiri, S.K., Wang,
    C. (eds.) ATVA 2018. LNCS, vol. 11138, pp. 248–266. Springer, Cham (2018).
    https://doi.org/10.1007/978-3-030-01090-4_15

23. Halbwachs, N., Péron, M.: Discovering properties about arrays in simple programs.
    In: PLDI, pp. 339–348 (2008)

24. Jana, A., Khedker, U.P., Datar, A., Venkatesh, R., Niyas, C.: Scaling bounded
    model checking by transforming programs with arrays. In: Hermenegildo, M.V.,
    Lopez-Garcia, P. (eds.) LOPSTR 2016. LNCS, vol. 10184, pp. 275–292. Springer,
    Cham (2017). https://doi.org/10.1007/978-3-319-63139-4_16

25. Jhala, R., McMillan, K.L.: Array abstractions from proofs. In: Damm, W.,
    Hermanns, H. (eds.) CAV 2007. LNCS, vol. 4590, pp. 193–206. Springer, Heidelberg
    (2007). https://doi.org/10.1007/978-3-540-73368-3_23

26. Komuravelli, A., Gurfinkel, A., Chaki, S.: SMT-based model checking for recursive
    programs. In: Biere, A., Bloem, R. (eds.) CAV 2014. LNCS, vol. 8559, pp. 17–34.
    Springer, Cham (2014). https://doi.org/10.1007/978-3-319-08867-9_2

27. Kong, S., Jung, Y., David, C., Wang, B.-Y., Yi, K.: Automatically inferring quan-
    tified loop invariants by algorithmic learning from simple templates. In: Ueda, K.
    (ed.) APLAS 2010. LNCS, vol. 6461, pp. 328–343. Springer, Heidelberg (2010).
    https://doi.org/10.1007/978-3-642-17164-2_23

28. Kovács, L., Voronkov, A.: Finding loop invariants for programs over arrays using
    a theorem prover. In: Chechik, M., Wirsing, M. (eds.) FASE 2009. LNCS, vol.
    5503, pp. 470–485. Springer, Heidelberg (2009). https://doi.org/10.1007/978-3-
    642-00593-0_33

29. Kumar, S., Sanyal, A., Venkatesh, R., Shah, P.: Property checking array programs
    using loop shrinking. In: Beyer, D., Huisman, M. (eds.) TACAS 2018, Part I.
    LNCS, vol. 10805, pp. 213–231. Springer, Cham (2018). https://doi.org/10.1007/
    978-3-319-89960-2_12

30. Lahiri, S.K., Bryant, R.E.: Constructing quantified invariants via predicate abstrac-
    tion. In: Steffen, B., Levi, G. (eds.) VMCAI 2004. LNCS, vol. 2937, pp. 267–281.
    Springer, Heidelberg (2004). https://doi.org/10.1007/978-3-540-24622-0_22

31. Liu, J., Rival, X.: Abstraction of arrays based on non contiguous partitions. In:
    D'Souza, D., Lal, A., Larsen, K.G. (eds.) VMCAI 2015. LNCS, vol. 8931, pp. 282–
    299. Springer, Heidelberg (2015). https://doi.org/10.1007/978-3-662-46081-8_16

32. Monniaux, D., Alberti, F.: A simple abstraction of arrays and maps by program
    translation. In: Blazy, S., Jensen, T. (eds.) SAS 2015. LNCS, vol. 9291, pp. 217–234.
    Springer, Heidelberg (2015). https://doi.org/10.1007/978-3-662-48288-9_13

33. Monniaux, D., Gonnord, L.: Cell morphing: from array programs to array-free horn
    clauses. In: Rival, X. (ed.) SAS 2016. LNCS, vol. 9837, pp. 361–382. Springer,
    Heidelberg (2016). https://doi.org/10.1007/978-3-662-53413-7_18

34. Prabhu, S., Madhukar, K., Venkatesh, R.: Efficiently learning safety proofs from appearance as well as behaviours. In: Podelski, A. (ed.) SAS 2018. LNCS, vol. 11002, pp. 326–343. Springer, Cham (2018). https://doi.org/10.1007/978-3-319-99725-4_20

35. Rajkhowa, P., Lin, F.: Extending VIAP to handle array programs. In: Piskac, R., Rümmer, P. (eds.) VSTTE 2018. LNCS, vol. 11294, pp. 38–49. Springer, Cham (2018). https://doi.org/10.1007/978-3-030-03592-1_3

36. Sharma, R., Aiken, A.: From invariant checking to invariant inference using randomized search. In: Biere, A., Bloem, R. (eds.) CAV 2014. LNCS, vol. 8559, pp. 88–105. Springer, Cham (2014). https://doi.org/10.1007/978-3-319-08867-9_6

Proving Unrealizability for Syntax-Guided Synthesis

Qinheping Hu[1(✉)], Jason Breck[1], John Cyphert[1], Loris D'Antoni[1], and Thomas Reps[1,2]

[1] University of Wisconsin-Madison, Madison, USA
qhu28@wisc.edu
[2] GrammaTech, Inc., Ithaca, USA

Abstract. We consider the problem of automatically establishing that a given syntax-guided-synthesis (SYGUS) problem is *unrealizable* (i.e., has no solution). Existing techniques have quite limited ability to establish unrealizability for general SYGUS instances in which the grammar describing the search space contains infinitely many programs. By encoding the synthesis problem's grammar G as a nondeterministic program P_G, we reduce the unrealizability problem to a reachability problem such that, if a standard program-analysis tool can establish that a certain assertion in P_G always holds, then the synthesis problem is unrealizable.

Our method can be used to augment existing SYGUS tools so that they can establish that a successfully synthesized program q is *optimal* with respect to some syntactic cost—e.g., q has the fewest possible if-then-else operators. Using known techniques, grammar G can be transformed to generate the set of all programs with lower costs than q—e.g., fewer conditional expressions. Our algorithm can then be applied to show that the resulting synthesis problem is unrealizable. We implemented the proposed technique in a tool called NOPE. NOPE can prove unrealizability for 59/132 variants of existing linear-integer-arithmetic SYGUS benchmarks, whereas all existing SYGUS solvers lack the ability to prove that these benchmarks are unrealizable, and time out on them.

1 Introduction

The goal of program synthesis is to find a program in some search space that meets a specification—e.g., satisfies a set of examples or a logical formula. Recently, a large family of synthesis problems has been unified into a framework called *syntax-guided synthesis* (SYGUS). A SYGUS problem is specified by a regular-tree grammar that describes the search space of programs, and a logical formula that constitutes the behavioral specification. Many synthesizers now support a specific format for SYGUS problems [1], and compete in annual synthesis competitions [2]. Thanks to these competitions, these solvers are now quite mature and are finding a wealth of applications [9].

Consider the SYGUS problem to synthesize a function f that computes the maximum of two variables x and y, denoted by $(\psi_{\mathtt{max2}}(f, x, y), G_1)$. The goal is to create e_f—an expression-tree for f—where e_f is in the language of the following regular-tree grammar G_1:

$$\text{Start} ::= \text{Plus}(\text{Start}, \text{Start}) \mid \text{IfThenElse}(\text{BExpr}, \text{Start}, \text{Start}) \mid x \mid y \mid 0 \mid 1$$
$$\text{BExpr} ::= \text{GreaterThan}(\text{Start}, \text{Start}) \mid \text{Not}(\text{BExpr}) \mid \text{And}(\text{BExpr}, \text{BExpr})$$

and $\forall x, y . \psi_{\text{max2}}(\llbracket e_f \rrbracket, x, y)$ is valid, where $\llbracket e_f \rrbracket$ denotes the meaning of e_f, and

$$\psi_{\text{max2}}(f, x, y) := f(x, y) \geq x \wedge f(x, y) \geq y \wedge (f(x, y) = x \vee f(x, y) = y).$$

SyGuS solvers can easily find a solution, such as

$$e := \text{IfThenElse}(\text{GreaterThan}(x, y), x, y).$$

Although many solvers can now find solutions efficiently to many SyGuS problems, there has been effectively no work on the much harder task of proving that a given SyGuS problem is *unrealizable*—i.e., it does not admit a solution. For example, consider the SyGuS problem $(\psi_{\text{max2}}(f, x, y), G_2)$, where G_2 is the more restricted grammar with if-then-else operators and conditions stripped out:

$$\text{Start} ::= \text{Plus}(\text{Start}, \text{Start}) \qquad \mid x \mid y \mid 0 \mid 1$$

This SyGuS problem does *not* have a solution, because no expression generated by G_2 meets the specification.[1] However, to the best of our knowledge, current SyGuS solvers cannot prove that such a SyGuS problem is unrealizable.[2]

A key property of the previous example is that the grammar is infinite. When such a SyGuS problem is realizable, any search technique that systematically explores the infinite search space of possible programs will eventually identify a solution to the synthesis problem. In contrast, proving that a problem is unrealizable requires showing that *every* program in the *infinite* search space *fails to satisfy* the specification. This problem is in general undecidable [6]. Although we cannot hope to have an algorithm for establishing unrealizability, the challenge is to find a technique that succeeds for the kinds of problems encountered in practice. Existing synthesizers can detect the absence of a solution in certain cases (e.g., because the grammar is finite, or is infinite but only generate a finite number of functionally distinct programs). However, in practice, as our

---

[1] Grammar G_2 only generates terms that are equivalent to some linear function of x and y; however, the maximum function cannot be described by a linear function.

[2] The synthesis problem presented above is one that is generated by a recent tool called QSyGuS, which extends SyGuS with quantitative syntactic objectives [10]. The advantage of using quantitative objectives in synthesis is that they can be used to produce higher-quality solutions—e.g., smaller, more readable, more efficient, etc. The synthesis problem $(\psi_{\text{max2}}(f, x, y), G_2)$ arises from a QSyGuS problem in which the goal is to produce an expression that (i) satisfies the specification $\psi_{\text{max2}}(f, x, y)$, and (ii) uses the smallest possible number of if-then-else operators. Existing SyGuS solvers can easily produce a solution that uses one if-then-else operator, but cannot prove that no better solution exists—i.e., $(\psi_{\text{max2}}(f, x, y), G_2)$ is unrealizable.

experiments show, this ability is limited—no existing solver was able to show unrealizability for any of the examples considered in this paper.

In this paper, we present a technique for proving that a possibly infinite SyGuS problem is unrealizable. Our technique builds on two ideas.

1. We observe that unrealizability can often be proven using *finitely many input examples*. In Sect. 2, we show how the example discussed above can be proven to be unrealizable using four input examples—$(0,0)$, $(0,1)$, $(1,0)$, and $(1,1)$.
2. We devise a way to encode a SyGuS problem $(\psi(f,\bar{x}),G)$ over a finite set of examples E as a *reachability problem in a recursive program* $P[G,E]$. In particular, the program that we construct has an assertion that holds if and only if the given SyGuS problem is unrealizable. Consequently, *unrealizability* can be proven by establishing that the assertion always holds. This property can often be established by a conventional program-analysis tool.

The encoding mentioned in item 2 is non-trivial for three reasons. The following list explains each issue, and sketches how they are addressed

(1) Infinitely many terms. We need to model the infinitely many terms generated by the grammar of a given synthesis problem $(\psi(f,\bar{x}),G)$.

To address this issue, we use non-determinism and recursion, and give an encoding $P[G,E]$ such that (i) each non-deterministic path p in the program $P[G,E]$ corresponds to a possible expression e_p that G can generate, and (ii) for each expression e that G can generate, there is a path p_e in $P[G,E]$. (There is an isomorphism between paths and the expression-trees of G)

(2) Nondeterminism. We need the computation performed along each path p in $P[G,E]$ to mimic the execution of expression e_p. Because the program uses non-determinism, we need to make sure that, for a given path p in the program $P[G,E]$, computational steps are carried out that mimic the evaluation of e_p for *each* of the finitely many example inputs in E.

We address this issue by threading the expression-evaluation computations associated with each example in E through the *same* non-deterministic choices.

(3) Complex Specifications. We need to handle specifications that allow for nested calls of the programs being synthesized.

For instance, consider the specification $f(f(x)) = x$. To handle this specification, we introduce a new variable y and rewrite the specification as $f(x) = y \wedge f(y) = x$. Because y is now also used as an input to f, we will thread both the computations of x and y through the non-deterministic recursive program.

Our work makes the following contributions:

- We reduce the SyGuS unrealizability problem to a reachability problem to which standard program-analysis tools can be applied (Sects. 2 and 4).
- We observe that, for many SyGuS problems, unrealizability can be proven using *finitely many input examples*, and use this idea to apply the Counter-Example-Guided Inductive Synthesis (CEGIS) algorithm to the problem of proving unrealizability (Sect. 3).

– We give an encoding of a SyGuS problem $(\psi(f, \bar{x}), G)$ over a finite set of examples E as a reachability problem in a nondeterministic recursive program $P[G, E]$, which has the following property: if a certain assertion in $P[G, E]$ always holds, then the synthesis problem is unrealizable (Sect. 4).
– We implement our technique in a tool NOPE using the ESolver synthesizer [2] as the SyGuS solver and the SeaHorn tool [8] for checking reachability. NOPE is able to establish unrealizability for 59 out of 132 variants of benchmarks taken from the SyGuS competition. In particular, NOPE solves all benchmarks with no more than 15 productions in the grammar and requiring no more than 9 input examples for proving unrealizability. Existing SyGuS solvers lack the ability to prove that these benchmarks are unrealizable, and time out on them.

Section 6 discusses related work. Some additional technical material, proofs, and full experimental results are given in [13].

2 Illustrative Example

In this section, we illustrate the main components of our framework for establishing the unrealizability of a SyGuS problem.

Consider the SyGuS problem to synthesize a function f that computes the maximum of two variables x and y, denoted by $(\psi_{\mathsf{max2}}(f, x, y), G_1)$. The goal is to create e_f—an expression-tree for f—where e_f is in the language of the following regular-tree grammar G_1:

$$\text{Start} ::= \text{Plus(Start, Start)} \mid \text{IfThenElse(BExpr, Start, Start)} \mid x \mid y \mid 0 \mid 1$$
$$\text{BExpr} ::= \text{GreaterThan(Start, Start)} \mid \text{Not(BExpr)} \mid \text{And(BExpr, BExpr)}$$

and $\forall x, y.\psi_{\mathsf{max2}}(\llbracket e_f \rrbracket, x, y)$ is valid, where $\llbracket e_f \rrbracket$ denotes the meaning of e_f, and

$$\psi_{\mathsf{max2}}(f, x, y) := f(x, y) \geq x \wedge f(x, y) \geq y \wedge (f(x, y) = x \vee f(x, y) = y).$$

SyGuS solvers can easily find a solution, such as

$$e := \text{IfThenElse(GreaterThan}(x, y), x, y).$$

Although many solvers can now find solutions efficiently to many SyGuS problems, there has been effectively no work on the much harder task of proving that a given SyGuS problem is *unrealizable*—i.e., it does not admit a solution. For example, consider the SyGuS problem $(\psi_{\mathsf{max2}}(f, x, y), G_2)$, where G_2 is the more restricted grammar with if-then-else operators and conditions stripped out:

$$\text{Start} ::= \text{Plus(Start, Start)} \mid x \mid y \mid 0 \mid 1$$

This SyGuS problem does *not* have a solution, because no expression generated by G_2 meets the specification.[3] However, to the best of our knowledge, current

---

[3] Grammar G_2 generates all linear functions of x and y, and hence generates an infinite number of functionally distinct programs; however, the maximum function cannot be described by a linear function.

SYGUS solvers cannot prove that such a SYGUS problem is unrealizable. As an example, we use the problem $(\psi_{\mathrm{max2}}(f, x, y), G_2)$ discussed in Sect. 1, and show how unrealizability can be proven using four input examples: $(0, 0)$, $(0, 1)$, $(1, 0)$, and $(1, 1)$.

```
1  int I_0;
2  void Start(int x_0,int y_0){
3    if(nd()){  // Encodes ''Start ::= Plus(Start, Start)''
4      Start(x_0, y_0);
5      int tempL_0 = I_0;
6      Start(x_0, y_0);
7      int tempR_0 = I_0;
8      I_0 = tempL_0 + tempR_0;
9    }
10   else if(nd()) I_0 = x_0;  // Encodes ''Start ::= x''
11   else if(nd()) I_0 = y_0;  // Encodes ''Start ::= y''
12   else if(nd()) I_0 = 1;    // Encodes ''Start ::= 1''
13   else          I_0 = 0;    // Encodes ''Start ::= 0''
14 }
15
16 bool spec(int x, int y, int f){
17   return (f>=x && f>=y && (f==x || f==y))
18 }
19
20 void main(){
21   int x_0 = 0; int y_0 = 1;  // Input example (0,1)
22   Start(x_0,y_0);
23   assert(!spec(x_0,y_0,I_0));
24 }
```

Fig. 1. Program $P[G_2, E_1]$ created during the course of proving the unrealizability of $(\psi_{\mathrm{max2}}(f, x, y), G_2)$ using the set of input examples $E_1 = \{(0, 1)\}$.

Our method can be seen as a variant of Counter-Example-Guided Inductive Synthesis (CEGIS), in which the goal is to create a program P in which a certain assertion always holds. Until such a program is created, each round of the algorithm returns a counter-example, from which we extract an additional input example for the original SYGUS problem. On the ith round, the current set of input examples E_i is used, together with the grammar—in this case G_2— and the specification of the desired behavior—$\psi_{\mathrm{max2}}(f, x, y)$, to create a candidate program $P[G_2, E_i]$. The program $P[G_2, E_i]$ contains an assertion, and a standard program analyzer is used to check whether the assertion always holds.

Suppose that for the SYGUS problem $(\psi_{\mathrm{max2}}(f, x, y), G_2)$ we start with just the one example input $(0, 1)$—i.e., $E_1 = \{(0, 1)\}$. Figure 1 shows the initial program $P[G_2, E_1]$ that our method creates. The function `spec` implements the predicate $\psi_{\mathrm{max2}}(f, x, y)$. (All of the programs $\{P[G_2, E_i]\}$ use the same function `spec`). The initialization statements "int x_0 = 0; int y_0 = 1;" at line (21) in procedure `main` correspond to the input example $(0, 1)$. The recursive procedure `Start` encodes the productions of grammar G_2. `Start` is non-deterministic; it contains four calls to an external function `nd()`, which returns a non-deterministically chosen Boolean value. The calls to nd() can be understood as controlling whether or not a production is selected from G_2 during a top-down, left-to-right generation of an expression-tree: lines (3)–(8) correspond to "Start ::= Plus(Start, Start)," and lines (10), (11), (12), and (13) correspond to "Start ::= x," "Start ::= y," "Start ::= 1," and "Start ::= 0," respectively. The code in the five cases in the body of Start encodes the semantics of the respective production of G_2; in particular, the statements that are executed along any execution path of $P[G_2, E_1]$ implement the *bottom-up evaluation of some expression-tree that can be generated by* G_2. For instance, consider the path that visits statements in the following order (for brevity, some statement numbers have been elided):

$$21 \quad 22 \quad (_{\text{Start}} \quad 3 \quad 4 \quad (_{\text{Start}} \quad 10 \quad)_{\text{Start}} \quad 6 \quad (_{\text{Start}} \quad 12 \quad)_{\text{Start}} \quad 8 \quad)_{\text{Start}} \quad 23, \quad (1)$$

where $(_{\text{Start}}$ and $)_{\text{Start}}$ indicate entry to, and return from, procedure Start, respectively. Path (1) corresponds to the top-down, left-to-right generation of the expression-tree Plus(x,1), interleaved with the tree's bottom-up evaluation.

Note that with path (1), when control returns to main, variable I_0 has the value 1, and thus the assertion at line (23) fails.

A sound program analyzer will discover that some such path exists in the program, and will return the sequence of non-deterministic choices required to follow one such path. Suppose that the analyzer chooses to report path (1); the sequence of choices would be t, f, t, f, f, f, t, which can be decoded to create the expression-tree Plus(x,1). At this point, we have a candidate definition for f: $f = x + 1$. This formula can be checked using an SMT solver to see whether it satisfies the behavioral specification $\psi_{\text{max2}}(f, x, y)$. In this case, the SMT solver returns "false." One counter-example that it could return is $(0, 0)$.

At this point, program $P[G_2, E_2]$ would be constructed using both of the example inputs $(0, 1)$ and $(0, 0)$. Rather than describe $P[G_2, E_2]$, we will describe the final program constructed, $P[G_2, E_4]$ (see Fig. 2).

As can be seen from the comments in the two programs, program $P[G_2, E_4]$ has the same basic structure as $P[G_2, E_1]$.

- main begins with initialization statements for the four example inputs.
- Start has five cases that correspond to the five productions of G_2.

The main difference is that because the encoding of G_2 in Start uses non-determinism, we need to make sure that along *each* path p in $P[G_2, E_4]$, each of the example inputs is used to evaluate the *same* expression-tree. We address this issue by threading the expression-evaluation computations associated with each of the example inputs through the *same* non-deterministic choices. That is, each of the five "production cases" in Start has four encodings of the production's semantics—one for each of the four expression evaluations. By this means, the statements that are executed along path p perform *four simultaneous bottom-up evaluations* of the expression-tree from G_2 that corresponds to p.

Programs $P[G_2, E_2]$ and $P[G_2, E_3]$ are similar to $P[G_2, E_4]$, but their paths carry out two and three simultaneous bottom-up evaluations, respectively. The

```
1  int I_0, I_1, I_2, I_3;
2  void Start(int x_0,int y_0,...,int x_3,int y_3){
3    if(nd()){   // Encodes ''Start ::= Plus(Start, Start)''
4      Start(x_0, y_0, x_1, y_1, x_2, y_2, x_3, y_3);
5      int tempL_0 = I_0; int tempL_1 = I_1;
6      int tempL_2 = I_2; int tempL_3 = I_3;
7      Start(x_0, y_0, x_1, y_1, x_2, y_2, x_3, y_3);
8      int tempR_0 = I_0; int tempR_1 = I_1;
9      int tempR_2 = I_2; int tempR_3 = I_3;
10     I_0 = tempL_0 + tempR_0;
11     I_1 = tempL_1 + tempR_1;
12     I_2 = tempL_2 + tempR_2;
13     I_3 = tempL_3 + tempR_3;}
14   else if(nd()) {   // Encodes ''Start ::= x''
15     I_0 = x_0; I_1 = x_1; I_2 = x_2; I_3 = x_3;}
16   else if(nd()) {   // Encodes ''Start ::= y''
17     I_0 = y_0; I_1 = y_1; I_2 = y_2; I_3 = y_3;}
18   else if(nd()) {   // Encodes ''Start ::= 1''
19     I_0 = 1;   I_1 = 1;   I_2 = 1;   I_3 = 1;}
20   else {            // Encodes ''Start ::= 0''
21     I_0 = 0;   I_1 = 0;   I_2 = 0;   I_3 = 0;}
22 }
23
24 bool spec(int x, int y, int f){
25   return (f>=x && f>=y && (f==x || f==y))
26 }
27
28 void main(){
29   int x_0 = 0; int y_0 = 1;   // Input example (0,1)
30   int x_1 = 0; int y_1 = 0;   // Input example (0,0)
31   int x_2 = 1; int y_2 = 1;   // Input example (1,1)
32   int x_3 = 1; int y_3 = 0;   // Input example (1,0)
33   Start(x_0,y_0,x_1,y_1,x_2,y_2,x_3,y_3);
34   assert(   !spec(x_0,y_0,I_0) || !spec(x_1,y_1,I_1)
35          || !spec(x_2,y_2,I_2) || !spec(x_3,y_3,I_3));
36 }
```

Fig. 2. Program $P[G_2, E_4]$ created during the course of proving the unrealizability of $(\psi_{\text{max2}}(f, x, y), G_2)$ using the set of input examples $E_4 = \{(0,0), (0,1), (1,0), (1,1)\}$.

actions taken during rounds 2 and 3 to generate a new counter-example—and hence a new example input—are similar to what was described for round 1. On round 4, however, the program analyzer will determine that the assertion on lines (34)–(35) always holds, which means that there is no path through $P[G_2, E_4]$ for which the behavioral specification holds for all of the input examples. This property means that there is no expression-tree that satisfies the specification— i.e., the SyGuS problem $(\psi_{\text{max2}}(f, x, y), G_2)$ is unrealizable.

Our implementation uses the program-analysis tool SEAHORN [8] as the assertion checker. In the case of $P[G_2, E_4]$, SEAHORN takes only 0.5 s to establish that the assertion in $P[G_2, E_4]$ always holds.

3 SyGuS, Realizability, and CEGIS

3.1 Background

Trees and Tree Grammars. A *ranked alphabet* is a tuple (Σ, rk_Σ) where Σ is a finite set of symbols and $rk_\Sigma : \Sigma \rightarrow \mathbb{N}$ associates a rank to each symbol. For every $m \geq 0$, the set of all symbols in Σ with rank m is denoted by $\Sigma^{(m)}$. In our examples, a ranked alphabet is specified by showing the set Σ and attaching the respective rank to every symbol as a superscript—e.g., $\Sigma = \{+^{(2)}, c^{(0)}\}$. (For brevity, the superscript is sometimes omitted). We use T_Σ to denote the set of all (ranked) trees over Σ—i.e., T_Σ is the smallest set such that (i) $\Sigma^{(0)} \subseteq T_\Sigma$, (ii) if $\sigma^{(k)} \in \Sigma^{(k)}$ and $t_1, \ldots, t_k \in T_\Sigma$, then $\sigma^{(k)}(t_1, \cdots, t_k) \in T_\Sigma$. In what follows, we assume a fixed ranked alphabet (Σ, rk_Σ).

In this paper, we focus on *typed* regular tree grammars, in which each non-terminal and each symbol is associated with a type. There is a finite set of types $\{\tau_1, \ldots, \tau_k\}$. Associated with each symbol $\sigma^{(i)} \in \Sigma^{(i)}$, there is a type assignment $a_{\sigma^{(i)}} = (\tau_0, \tau_1, \ldots, \tau_i)$, where τ_0 is called the *left-hand-side type* and $\tau_1, \ldots, \tau_i$ are called the *right-hand-side types*. Tree grammars are similar to word grammars, but generate trees over a ranked alphabet instead of words.

Definition 1 (Regular Tree Grammar). *A* **typed regular tree grammar** *(RTG) is a tuple $G = (N, \Sigma, S, a, \delta)$, where N is a finite set of non-terminal symbols of arity 0; Σ is a ranked alphabet; $S \in N$ is an initial non-terminal; a is a type assignment that gives types for members of $\Sigma \cup N$; and δ is a finite set of productions of the form $A_0 \rightarrow \sigma^{(i)}(A_1, \ldots, A_i)$, where for $1 \leq j \leq i$, each $A_j \in N$ is a non-terminal such that if $a(\sigma^{(i)}) = (\tau_0, \tau_1, \ldots, \tau_i)$ then $a(A_j) = \tau_j$.*

In a SyGuS problem, each variable, such as x and y in the example RTGs in Sect. 1, is treated as an arity-0 symbol—i.e., $x^{(0)}$ and $y^{(0)}$.

Given a tree $t \in T_{\Sigma \cup N}$, applying a production $r = A \rightarrow \beta$ to t produces the tree t' resulting from replacing the left-most occurrence of A in t with the right-hand side β. A tree $t \in T_\Sigma$ is generated by the grammar G—denoted by $t \in L(G)$—iff it can be obtained by applying a sequence of productions $r_1 \cdots r_n$ to the tree whose root is the initial non-terminal S.

Syntax-Guided Synthesis. A SyGuS problem is specified with respect to a background theory T—e.g., linear arithmetic—and the goal is to synthesize a function f that satisfies two constraints provided by the user. The first constraint, $\psi(f, \bar{x})$, describes a *semantic property* that f should satisfy. The second constraint limits the *search space* S of f, and is given as a set of expressions specified by an RTG G that defines a subset of all terms in T.

Definition 2 (SyGuS). *A SyGuS problem over a background theory T is a pair $sy = (\psi(f, \bar{x}), G)$ where G is a regular tree grammar that only contains terms in T—i.e., $L(G) \subseteq T$—and $\psi(f, \bar{x})$ is a Boolean formula constraining the semantic behavior of the synthesized program f.*

A SyGuS *problem is* **realizable** *if there exists a expression $e \in L(G)$ such that $\forall \bar{x}.\psi(\llbracket e \rrbracket, \bar{x})$ is true. Otherwise we say that the problem is* **unrealizable**.

Theorem 1 (Undecidability [6]). *Given a* SyGuS *problem sy, it is undecidable to check whether sy is realizable.*

Counterexample-Guided Inductive Synthesis. The Counterexample-Guided Inductive Synthesis (CEGIS) algorithm is a popular approach to solving synthesis problems. Instead of directly looking for an expression that satisfies the specification φ on *all* possible inputs, the CEGIS algorithm uses a synthesizer S that can find expressions that are correct on a *finite* set of examples E. If S finds a solution that is correct on all elements of E, CEGIS uses a verifier V to check whether the discovered solution is also correct for all possible inputs to the problem. If not, a counterexample obtained from V is added to the set of examples, and the process repeats. More formally, CEGIS starts with an empty set of examples E and repeats the following steps:

1. Call the synthesizer S to find an expression e such that $\psi^E(\llbracket e \rrbracket, \bar{x}) \stackrel{\text{def}}{=} \forall \bar{x} \in E.\psi(\llbracket e \rrbracket, \bar{x})$ holds and go to step 2; return *unrealizable* if no expression exists.
2. Call the verifier V to find a model c for the formula $\neg \psi(\llbracket e \rrbracket, \bar{x})$, and add c to the counterexample set E; return e as a valid solution if no model is found.

Because SyGuS problems are only defined over first-order decidable theories, any SMT solver can be used as the verifier V to check whether the formula $\neg \psi(\llbracket e \rrbracket, \bar{x})$ is satisfiable. On the other hand, providing a synthesizer S to find solutions such that $\forall \bar{x} \in E.\psi(\llbracket e \rrbracket, \bar{x})$ holds is a much harder problem because e is a second-order term drawn from an infinite search space. In fact, checking whether such an e exists is an undecidable problem [6].

The main contribution of our paper is a reduction of the unrealizability problem—i.e., the problem of proving that there is no expression $e \in L(G)$ such that $\forall \bar{x} \in E.\psi(\llbracket e \rrbracket, \bar{x})$ holds—to an unreachability problem (Sect. 4). This reduction allows us to use existing (un)reachability verifiers to check whether a SyGuS instance is unrealizable.

3.2 CEGIS and Unrealizability

The CEGIS algorithm is sound but incomplete for proving unrealizability. Given a SyGuS problem $sy = (\psi(f, \bar{x}), G)$ and a finite set of inputs E, we denote with $sy^E := (\psi^E(f, \bar{x}), G)$ the corresponding SyGuS problem that only requires the function f to be correct on the examples in E.

Lemma 1 (Soundness). *If sy^E is unrealizable then sy is unrealizable.*

Even when given a perfect synthesizer S—i.e., one that can solve a problem sy^E for every possible set E—there are SyGuS problems for which the CEGIS algorithm is not powerful enough to prove unrealizability.

Lemma 2 (Incompleteness). *There exists an unrealizable* SyGuS *problem sy such that for every finite set of examples E the problem sy^E is realizable.*

Despite this negative result, we will show that a CEGIS algorithm can prove unrealizability for many SyGuS instances (Sect. 5).

4 From Unrealizability to Unreachability

In this section, we show how a SyGuS problem for finitely many examples can be reduced to a reachability problem in a non-deterministic, recursive program in an imperative programming language.

4.1 Reachability Problems

A *program* P takes an initial state I as input and outputs a final state O, i.e., $[\![P]\!](I) = O$ where $[\![\cdot]\!]$ denotes the semantic function of the programming language. As illustrated in Sect. 2, we allow a program to contain calls to an external function nd(), which returns a non-deterministically chosen Boolean value. When program P contains calls to nd(), we use $\hat{P}$ to denote the program that is the same as P except that $\hat{P}$ takes an additional integer input n, and each call nd() is replaced by a call to a local function nextbit() defined as follows:

```
bool nextbit(){bool b = n%2; n=n»1; return b;}.
```

In other words, the integer parameter n of $\hat{P}[n]$ formalizes all of the non-deterministic choices made by P in calls to nd().

For the programs $P[G, E]$ used in our unrealizability algorithm, the only calls to nd() are ones that control whether or not a production is selected from grammar G during a top-down, left-to-right generation of an expression-tree. Given n, we can decode it to identify which expression-tree n represents.

Example 1. Consider again the SyGuS problem $(\psi_{\mathsf{max2}}(f, x, y), G_2)$ discussed in Sect. 2. In the discussion of the initial program $P[G_2, E_1]$ (Fig. 1), we hypothesized that the program analyzer chose to report path (1) in P, for which the sequence of non-deterministic choices is t, f, t, f, f, f, t. That sequence means that for $\hat{P}[n]$, the value of n is 1000101 (base 2) (or 69 (base 10)). The 1s, from low-order to high-order position, represent choices of production instances in a top-down, left-to-right generation of an expression-tree. (The 0s represent rejected possible choices). The rightmost 1 in n corresponds to the choice in line (3) of "Start ::= Plus(Start, Start)"; the 1 in the third-from-rightmost position corresponds to the choice in line (10) of "Start ::= x" as the left child of the Plus node; and the 1 in the leftmost position corresponds to the choice in line (12) of "Start ::= 1" as the right child. By this means, we learn that the behavioral specification $\psi_{\mathsf{max2}}(f, x, y)$ holds for the example set $E_1 = \{(0, 1)\}$ for $f \mapsto \mathtt{Plus(x,1)}$. □

Definition 3 (Reachability Problem). *Given a program $\hat{P}[n]$, containing assertion statements and a non-deterministic integer input n, we use re_P to denote the corresponding reachability problem. The reachability problem re_P is **satisfiable** if there exists a value n that, when bound to n, falsifies any of the assertions in $\hat{P}[n]$. The problem is **unsatisfiable** otherwise.*

4.2 Reduction to Reachability

The main component of our framework is an encoding enc that given a SYGUS problem $sy^E = (\psi^E(f,x), G)$ over a set of examples $E = \{c_1, \ldots, c_k\}$, outputs a program $P[G, E]$ such that sy^E is **realizable** if and only if $re_{enc(sy,E)}$ is **satisfiable**. In this section, we define all the components of $P[G, E]$, and state the correctness properties of our reduction.

Remark: In this section, we assume that in the specification $\psi(f, x)$ every occurrence of f has x as input parameter. We show how to overcome this restriction in App. A [13]. In the following, we assume that the input x has type τ_I, where τ_I could be a complex type—e.g., a tuple type.

Program Construction. Recall that the grammar G is a tuple $(N, \Sigma, S, a, \delta)$. First, for each non-terminal $A \in N$, the program $P[G, E]$ contains k global variables $\{g\_1\_A, \ldots, g\_k\_A\}$ of type $a(A)$ that are used to express the values resulting from evaluating expressions generated from non-terminal A on the k examples. Second, for each non-terminal $A \in N$, the program $P[G, E]$ contains a function

$$\texttt{void funcA}(\tau_I \texttt{ v1}, \ldots, \tau_I \texttt{ vk})\{ \ bodyA \ \}$$

We denote by $\delta(A) = \{r_1, \ldots, r_m\}$ the set of production rules of the form $A \to \beta$ in δ. The body $bodyA$ of $\texttt{funcA}$ has the following structure:

```
if(nd()) {Enδ(r1)}
else if(nd()) {Enδ(r2)}
...
else {Enδ(rm)}
```

The encoding $\text{En}_\delta(r)$ of a production $r = A_0 \to b^{(j)}(A_1, \cdots, A_j)$ is defined as follows (τ_i denotes the type of the term A_i):

```
funcA1(v1,...,vk);
τ1 child_1_1 = g_1_A1;...;τ1 child_1_k = g_k_Aj;
...
funcAj(v1,...,vk);
τj child_j_1 = g_1_A1;...;τj child_j_k = g_k_Aj;
g_1_A0 = enc¹b(child_1_1,...,child_1_k)
...
g_k_A0 = encᵏb(child_j_1,...,child_j_k)
```

Note that if $b^{(j)}$ is of arity 0—i.e., if $j = 0$—the construction yields k assignments of the form $\texttt{g\_m\_A0} = enc_b^m()$.

The function enc_b^m interprets the semantics of b on the mth input example. We take Linear Integer Arithmetic as an example to illustrate how enc_b^m works.

$$
\begin{aligned}
enc_{0(0)}^m &:= 0 & enc_{1(0)}^m &:= 1 \\
enc_{x(0)}^m &:= \texttt{vi} & enc_{\text{Equals}(2)}^m(L, R) &:= (L\text{=}R) \\
enc_{\text{Plus}(2)}^m(L, R) &:= L\text{+}R & enc_{\text{Minus}(2)}^m(L, R) &:= L\text{-}R \\
enc_{\text{IfThenElse}(3)}^m(B, L, R) &:= \texttt{if}(B) \ L \ \texttt{else} \ R
\end{aligned}
$$

We now turn to the correctness of the construction. First, we formalize the relationship between expression-trees in $L(G)$, the semantics of $P[G, E]$, and the number n. Given an expression-tree e, we assume that each node q in e is annotated with the production that has produced that node. Recall that $\delta(A) = \{r_1, \ldots, r_m\}$ is the set of productions with head A (where the subscripts are indexes in some arbitrary, but fixed order). Concretely, for every node q, we assume there is a function $pr(q) = (A, i)$, which associates q with a pair that indicates that non-terminal A produced n using the production r_i (i.e., r_i is the ith production whose left-hand-side non-terminal is A).

We now define how we can extract a number $\#(e)$ for which the program $\hat{P}[\#(e)]$ will exhibit the same semantics as that of the expression-tree e. First, for every node q in e such that $pr(q) = (A, i)$, we define the following number:

$$\#_{nd}(q) = \begin{cases} 1\underbrace{0\cdots 0}_{i-1} & \text{if } i < |\delta(A)| \\ \underbrace{0\cdots 0}_{i-1} & \text{if } i = |\delta(A)|. \end{cases}$$

The number $\#_{nd}(q)$ indicates what suffix of the value of n will cause funcA to trigger the code corresponding to production r_i. Let $q_1 \cdots q_m$ be the sequence of nodes visited during a pre-order traversal of expression-tree e. The number corresponding to e, denoted by $\#(e)$, is defined as the bit-vector $\#_{nd}(q_m) \cdots \#_{nd}(q_1)$.

Finally, we add the entry-point of the program, which calls the function funcS corresponding to the initial non-terminal S, and contains the assertion that encodes our reachability problem on all the input examples $E = \{c_1, \ldots, c_k\}$.

```
void main(){
    τI x1 = c1; ⋯ ;τI xk = ck;
    funcS(x1,..., xk);
    assert ⋁1≤i≤k ¬ψ(f,ci)[g_i_S/f(x)]; // At least one ci fails }
```

Correctness. We first need to show that the function $\#(\cdot)$ captures the correct language of expression-trees. Given a non-terminal A, a value n, and input values $i_1, \ldots, i_k$, we use $[\![\text{funcA}[n]]\!](i_1, \ldots, i_k) = (o_1, \ldots o_k)$ to denote the values of the variables $\{$g_1_A$, \ldots,$ g_k_A$\}$ at the end of the execution of funcA[n] with the initial value of $n = n$ and input values $x_1, \ldots, x_k$. Given a non-terminal A, we write $L(G, A)$ to denote the set of terms that can be derived starting with A.

Lemma 3. *Let A be a non-terminal, $e \in L(G, A)$ an expression, and $\{i_1, \ldots, i_k\}$ an input set. Then, $([\![e]\!](i_1), \ldots, [\![e]\!](i_k)) = [\![funcA[\#(e)]]\!](i_1, \ldots, i_k)$.*

Each procedure funcA[n]$(i_1, \ldots, i_k)$ that we construct has an explicit dependence on variable n, where n controls the non-deterministic choices made by the funcA and procedures called by funcA. As a consequence, when relating numbers and expression-trees, there are two additional issues to contend with:

Non-termination. Some numbers can cause funcA[n] to fail to terminate. For instance, if the case for "Start ::= Plus(Start, Start)" in program

$P[G_2, E_1]$ from Fig. 1 were moved from the first branch (lines (3)–(8)) to the final else case (line (13)), the number n = 0 = ...0000000 (base 2) would cause Start to never terminate, due to repeated selections of Plus nodes. However, note that the only assert statement in the program is placed at the end of the main procedure. Now, consider a value of n such that $re_{enc(sy,E)}$ is satisfiable. Definition 3 implies that the flow of control will reach and falsify the assertion, which implies that funcA[n] terminates.[4]

Shared suffixes of sufficient length. In Example 1, we showed how for program $P[G_2, E_1]$ (Fig. 1) the number n = 1000101 (base 2) corresponds to the top-down, left-to-right generation of Plus(x,1). That derivation consumed exactly seven bits; thus, any number that, written in base 2, shares the suffix 1000101—e.g., 11010101000101—will also generate Plus(x,1).

The issue of shared suffixes is addressed in the following lemma:

Lemma 4. *For every non-terminal A and number n such that $[\![funcA[n]]\!](i_1, \ldots, i_k) \neq \bot$ (i.e., funcA terminates when the non-deterministic choices are controlled by n), there exists a minimal n' that is a (base 2) suffix of n for which (i) there is an $e \in L(G)$ such that $\#(e) = n'$, and (ii) for every input $\{i_1, \ldots, i_k\}$, we have $[\![funcA[n]]\!](i_1, \ldots, i_k) = [\![funcA[n']]\!](i_1, \ldots, i_k)$.*

We are now ready to state the correctness property of our construction.

Theorem 2. *Given a SYGUS problem $sy^E = (\psi_E(f, x), G)$ over a finite set of examples E, the problem sy^E is **realizable** iff $re_{enc(sy,E)}$ is **satisfiable**.*

5   Implementation and Evaluation

NOPE is a tool that can return two-sided answers to unrealizability problems of the form $sy = (\psi, G)$. When it returns **unrealizable**, no expression-tree in $L(G)$ satisfies ψ; when it returns **realizable**, some $e \in L(G)$ satisfies ψ; NOPE can also time out. NOPE incorporates several existing pieces of software.

1. The (un)reachability verifier SEAHORN is applied to the reachability problems of the form $re_{enc(sy,E)}$ created during successive CEGIS rounds.
2. The SMT solver Z3 is used to check whether a generated expression-tree e satisfies ψ. If it does, NOPE returns **realizable** (along with e); if it does not, NOPE creates a new input example to add to E.

It is important to observe that SEAHORN, like most reachability verifiers, is only sound for **un**satisfiability—i.e., if SEAHORN returns **unsatisfiable**, the reachability problem is indeed unsatisfiable. Fortunately, SEAHORN's one-sided

---

[4] If the SYGUS problem deals with the synthesis of programs for a language that can express non-terminating programs, that would be an additional source of non-termination, different from that discussed in item **Non-termination**. That issue does not arise for LIA SYGUS problems. Dealing with the more general kind of non-termination is postponed for future work.

answers are in the correct direction for our application: to prove unrealizability, NOPE only requires the reachability verifier to be sound for unsatisfiability.

There is one aspect of NOPE that differs from the technique that has been presented earlier in the paper. While SEAHORN is sound for **un**reachability, it is not sound for reachability—i.e., it cannot soundly prove whether a synthesis problem is realizable. To address this problem, to check whether a given SYGUS problem sy^E is realizable on the finite set of examples E, NOPE also calls the SYGUS solver ESolver [2] to synthesize an expression-tree e that satisfies sy^E.[5]

In practice, for every intermediate problem sy^E generated by the CEGIS algorithm, NOPE runs the ESolver on sy^E and SEAHORN on $re_{enc(sy,E)}$ in *parallel*. If ESolver returns a solution e, SEAHORN is interrupted, and Z3 is used to check whether e satisfies ψ. Depending on the outcome, NOPE either returns *realizable* or obtains an additional input example to add to E. If SEAHORN returns **unsatisfiable**, NOPE returns **unrealizable**.

Modulo bugs in its constituent components, NOPE is sound for both realizability and unrealizability, but because of Lemma 2 and the incompleteness of SEAHORN, NOPE is not complete for unrealizability.

Benchmarks. We perform our evaluation on 132 variants of the 60 LIA benchmarks from the LIA SYGUS competition track [2]. We do not consider the other SYGUS benchmark track, Bit-Vectors, because the SEAHORN verifier is unsound for most bit-vector operations–e.g., bit-shifting. We used three suites of benchmarks. LIMITEDIF (resp. LIMITEDPLUS) contains 57 (resp. 30) benchmarks in which the grammar bounds the number of times an IfThenElse (resp. Plus) operator can appear in an expression-tree to be 1 less than the number required to solve the original synthesis problem. We used the tool QUASI to automatically generate the restricted grammars. LIMITEDCONST contains 45 benchmarks in which the grammar allows the program to contain only constants that are coprime to any constants that may appear in a valid solution—e.g., the solution requires using odd numbers, but the grammar only contains the constant 2. The numbers of benchmarks in the three suites differ because for certain benchmarks it did not make sense to create a limited variant—e.g., if the smallest program consistent with the specification contains no IfThenElse operators, no variant is created for the LIMITEDIF benchmark. In all our benchmarks, the grammars describing the search space contain infinitely many terms.

Our experiments were performed on an Intel Core i7 4.00 GHz CPU, with 32 GB of RAM, running Lubuntu 18.10 via VirtualBox. We used version 4.8 of Z3, commit 97f2334 of SEAHORN, and commit d37c50e of ESolver. The timeout for each individual SEAHORN/ESolver call is set at 10 min.

Experimental Questions. Our experiments were designed to answer the questions posed below.

> **EQ 1.** Can NOPE prove unrealizability for variants of real SYGUS benchmarks, and how long does it take to do so?

---

[5] We chose ESolver because on the benchmarks we considered, ESolver outperformed other SYGUS solvers (e.g., CVC4 [3]).

Finding: NOPE*can prove unrealizability for* 59/132 *benchmarks.* For the 59 benchmarks solved by NOPE, the average time taken is 15.59 s. The time taken to perform the last iteration of the algorithm—i.e., the time taken by SEAHORN to return **unsatisfiable**—accounts for 87% of the total running time.

NOPE can solve all of the LIMITEDIF benchmarks for which the grammar allows at most one IfThenElse operator. Allowing more IfThenElse operators in the grammar leads to larger programs and larger sets of examples, and consequently the resulting reachability problems are harder to solve for SEAHORN.

For a similar reason, NOPE can solve only one of the LIMITEDPLUS benchmarks. All other LIMITEDPLUS benchmarks allow 5 or more Plus statements, resulting in grammars that have at least 130 productions.

NOPE can solve all LIMITEDCONST benchmarks because these require few examples and result in small encoded programs.

EQ 2. How many examples does NOPE use to prove unrealizability and how does the number of examples affect the performance of NOPE?

Note that Z3 can produce different models for the same query, and thus different runs of NOPE can produce different sequences of examples. Hence, there is no guarantee that NOPE finds a good sequence of examples that prove unrealizability. One measure of success is whether NOPE is generally able to find a small number of examples, when it succeeds in proving unrealizability.

Finding: Nope used 1 to 9 examples to prove unrealizability for the benchmarks on which it terminated. Problems requiring large numbers of examples could not be solved because either ESolver or times out—e.g., on the problem max4, NOPE gets to the point where the CEGIS loop has generated 17 examples, at which point ESolver exceeds the timeout threshold.

Finding: The number of examples required to prove unrealizability depends mainly on the arity of the synthesized function and the complexity of the grammar. The number of examples seems to grow quadratically with the number of bounded operators allowed in the grammar. In particular, problems in which the grammar allows zero IfThenElse operators require 2–4 examples, while problems in which the grammar allows one IfThenElse operator require 7–9 examples.

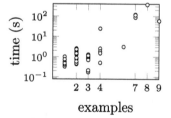

Fig. 3. Time vs examples.

Figure 3 plots the running time of NOPE against the number of examples generated by the CEGIS algorithm. *Finding: The solving time appears to grow exponentially with the number of examples required to prove unrealizability.*

6   Related Work

The SYGUS formalism was introduced as a unifying framework to express several synthesis problems [1]. Caulfield et al. [6] proved that it is undecidable to determine whether a given SYGUS problem is realizable. Despite this negative result, there are several SYGUS solvers that compete in yearly SYGUS competitions [2] and can efficiently produce solutions to SYGUS problems when a solution exists. Existing SYGUS synthesizers fall into three categories: (*i*) Enumeration solvers enumerate programs with respect to a given total order [7]. If the given problem is unrealizable, these solvers typically only terminate if the language of the grammar is finite or contains finitely many functionally distinct programs. While in principle certain enumeration solvers can prune infinite portions of the search space, none of these solvers could prove unrealizability for any of the benchmarks considered in this paper. (*ii*) Symbolic solvers reduce the synthesis problem to a constraint-solving problem [3]. These solvers cannot reason about grammars that restrict allowed terms, and resort to enumeration whenever the candidate solution produced by the constraint solver is not in the restricted search space. Hence, they also cannot prove unrealizability. (*iii*) Probabilistic synthesizers randomly search the search space, and are typically unpredictable [14], providing no guarantees in terms of unrealizability.

Synthesis as Reachability. CETI [12] introduces a technique for encoding template-based synthesis problems as reachability problems. The CETI encoding only applies to the specific setting in which (*i*) the search space is described by an imperative program with a *finite number* of holes—i.e., the values that the synthesizer has to discover—and (*ii*) the specification is given as a finite number of input-output test cases with which the target program should agree. Because the number of holes is finite, and all holes correspond to values (and not terms), the reduction to a reachability problem only involves making the holes global variables in the program (and no more elaborate transformations).

In contrast, our reduction technique handles search spaces that are described by a grammar, which in general consist of an infinite set of terms (not just values). Due to this added complexity, our encoding has to account for (i) the semantics of the productions in the grammar, and (ii) the use of non-determinism to encode the choice of grammar productions. Our encoding creates one expression-evaluation computation for each of the example inputs, and threads these computations through the program so that each expression-evaluation computation makes use of the *same* set of non-deterministic choices.

Using the input-threading, our technique can handle specifications that contain nested calls of the synthesized program (e.g., $f(f(x)) = x$). (App. A [13]).

The input-threading technique builds a *product program* that performs multiple executions of the same function as done in relational program verification [4]. Alternatively, a different encoding could use multiple function invocations on individual inputs and require the verifier to thread the same bit-stream for all input evaluations. In general, verifiers perform much better on product programs [4], which motivates our choice of encoding.

Unrealizability in Program Synthesis. For certain synthesis problems—e.g., reactive synthesis [5]—the realizability problem is decidable. The framework tackled in this paper, SYGUS, is orthogonal to such problems, and it is undecidable to check whether a given SYGUS problem is realizable [6].

Mechtaev et al. [11] propose to use a variant of SYGUS to efficiently prune irrelevant paths in a symbolic-execution engine. In their approach, for each path π in the program, a synthesis problem p_π is generated so that if p_π is unrealizable, the path π is infeasible. The synthesis problems generated by Mechtaev et al. (which are not directly expressible in SYGUS) are decidable because the search space is defined by a finite set of templates, and the synthesis problem can be encoded by an SMT formula. To the best of our knowledge, our technique is the first one that can check unrealizability of general SYGUS problems in which the search space is an *infinite set of functionally distinct terms*.

Acknowledgment. This work was supported, in part, by a gift from Rajiv and Ritu Batra; by AFRL under DARPA MUSE award FA8750-14-2-0270 and DARPA STAC award FA8750-15-C-0082; by ONR under grant N00014-17-1-2889; by NSF under grants CNS-1763871 and CCF-1704117; and by the UW-Madison OVRGE with funding from WARF.

References

1. Alur, R., et al.: Syntax-guided synthesis. In: Formal Methods in Computer-Aided Design (FMCAD), pp. 1–8. IEEE (2013)
2. Alur, R., Fisman, D., Singh, R., Solar-Lezama, A.: SyGuS-Comp 2016: results and analysis. arXiv preprint arXiv:1611.07627 (2016)
3. Barrett, C., et al.: CVC4. In: Gopalakrishnan, G., Qadeer, S. (eds.) CAV 2011. LNCS, vol. 6806, pp. 171–177. Springer, Heidelberg (2011). https://doi.org/10.1007/978-3-642-22110-1_14
4. Barthe, G., Crespo, J.M., Kunz, C.: Relational verification using product programs. In: Butler, M., Schulte, W. (eds.) FM 2011. LNCS, vol. 6664, pp. 200–214. Springer, Heidelberg (2011). https://doi.org/10.1007/978-3-642-21437-0_17
5. Bloem, R.: Reactive synthesis. In: Formal Methods in Computer-Aided Design (FMCAD), p. 3 (2015)
6. Caulfield, B., Rabe, M.N., Seshia, S.A., Tripakis, S.: What's decidable about syntax-guided synthesis? arXiv preprint arXiv:1510.08393 (2015)
7. ESolver. https://github.com/abhishekudupa/sygus-comp14
8. Gurfinkel, A., Kahsai, T., Navas, J.A.: SeaHorn: a framework for verifying C programs (competition contribution). In: Baier, C., Tinelli, C. (eds.) TACAS 2015. LNCS, vol. 9035, pp. 447–450. Springer, Heidelberg (2015). https://doi.org/10.1007/978-3-662-46681-0_41
9. Hu, Q., D'Antoni, L.: Automatic program inversion using symbolic transducers. In: Proceedings of the 38th ACM SIGPLAN Conference on Programming Language Design and Implementation (PLDI), pp. 376–389 (2017)
10. Hu, Q., D'Antoni, L.: Syntax-guided synthesis with quantitative syntactic objectives. In: Chockler, H., Weissenbacher, G. (eds.) CAV 2018. LNCS, vol. 10981, pp. 386–403. Springer, Cham (2018). https://doi.org/10.1007/978-3-319-96145-3_21
11. Mechtaev, S., Griggio, A., Cimatti, A., Roychoudhury, A.: Symbolic execution with existential second-order constraints. In: Proceedings of the 2018 26th ACM Joint Meeting on European Software Engineering Conference and Symposium on the Foundations of Software Engineering (ESEC/FSE), pp. 389–399 (2018)

12. Nguyen, T.V., Weimer, W., Kapur, D., Forrest, S.: Connecting program synthesis and reachability: automatic program repair using test-input generation. In: Legay, A., Margaria, T. (eds.) TACAS 2017. LNCS, vol. 10205, pp. 301–318. Springer, Heidelberg (2017). https://doi.org/10.1007/978-3-662-54577-5_17
13. Qinheping, H., Jason, B., John, C., Loris, D., Reps, T.: Proving unrealizability for syntax-guided synthesis. arXiv preprint arXiv:1905.05800 (2019)
14. Schkufza, E., Sharma, R., Aiken, A.: Stochastic program optimization. Commun. ACM **59**(2), 114–122 (2016)

3

Cerberus-BMC: A Principled Reference Semantics and Exploration Tool for Concurrent and Sequential C

Stella Lau[1,2]([✉]), Victor B. F. Gomes[2],
Kayvan Memarian[2], Jean Pichon-Pharabod[2],
and Peter Sewell[2]

[1] MIT, Cambridge, USA
stellal@mit.edu
[2] University of Cambridge, Cambridge, UK
{victor.gomes,kayvan.memarian,
jean.pichon-pharabod,peter.sewell}@cl.cam.ac.uk

Abstract. C remains central to our infrastructure, making verification of C code an essential and much-researched topic, but the semantics of C is remarkably complex, and important aspects of it are still unsettled, leaving programmers and verification tool builders on shaky ground. This paper describes a tool, Cerberus-BMC, that for the first time provides a principled reference semantics that simultaneously supports (1) a choice of concurrency memory model (including substantial fragments of the C11, RC11, and Linux kernel memory models), (2) a modern memory object model, and (3) a well-validated thread-local semantics for a large fragment of the language. The tool should be useful for C programmers, compiler writers, verification tool builders, and members of the C/C++ standards committees.

1 Introduction

C remains central to our infrastructure, widely used for security-critical components of hypervisors, operating systems, language runtimes, and embedded systems. This has prompted much research on the verification of C code, but the semantics of C is remarkably complex, and important aspects of it are still unsettled, leaving programmers and verification tool builders on shaky ground. Here we are concerned with three aspects:

1. The Concurrency Memory Model. The 2011 versions of the ISO C++ and C standards adopted a new concurrency model [3,12,13], formalised during the development process [11], but the model is still in flux: various fixes have been found to be necessary [9,14,26]; the model still suffers from the "thin-air problem" [10,15,35]; and Linux kernel C code uses a different model, itself recently partially formalised [7].

2. The Memory Object Model. A priori, one might imagine C follows one of two language-design extremes: a concrete byte-array model with pointers that are simply machine words, or an abstract model with pointers combining abstract block IDs and structured offsets. In fact C is neither of these: it permits casts between pointer and integer types, and manipulation of their byte representations, to support low-level systems programming, but, while at runtime a C pointer will typically just be a machine word, compiler analyses and optimisations reason about abstract notions of the provenance of pointers [27,29,31]. This is a subject of active discussion in the ISO C and C++ committees and in compiler development communities.

3. The Thread-Local Sequential Semantics. Here, there are many aspects, e.g. the loosely specified evaluation order, the semantics of integer promotions, many kinds of undefined behaviour, and so on, that are (given an expert reading) reasonably well-defined in the standard, but that are nonetheless very complex and widely misunderstood. The standard, being just a prose document, is not *executable as a test oracle*; it is not a reference semantics usable for exploration or automated testing.

Each of these is challenging in isolation, but there are also many subtle interactions between them. For example, between (1) and (3), the pre-C11 ISO standard text was in terms of sequential stepwise execution of an (informally specified) abstract machine, while the C11 concurrency model is expressed as a predicate over complete candidate executions, and the two have never been fully reconciled – e.g. in the standard's treatment of object lifetimes. Then there are fundamental issues in combining the ISO treatment of undefined behaviour with that axiomatic-concurrency-model style [10, §7]. Between (1) and (2), one has to ask about the relationships between the definition of data race and the treatment of uninitialised memory and padding. Between (2) and (3), there are many choices for what the C memory object model should be, and how it should be integrated with the standard, which are currently under debate. Between all three one has to consider the relationships between uninitialised and thin-air values and the ISO notions of unspecified values and trap representations. These are all open questions in what the C semantics and ISO standard are (or should be). We do not solve them here, but we provide a necessary starting point: a tool embodying a precise reference semantics that lets one explore examples and debate the alternatives.

We describe a tool, Cerberus-BMC, that for the first time lets one explore the allowed behaviours of C test programs that involve all three of the above. It is available via a web interface at http://cerberus.cl.cam.ac.uk/bmc.html.

For (1), Cerberus-BMC is parameterised on an axiomatic memory concurrency model: it reads in a definition of the model in a Herd-like format [6], and so can be instantiated with (substantial fragments of) either the C11 [3,9,12–14], RC11 [26], or Linux kernel [7] memory models. The model can be edited in the web interface. Then the user can load (or edit in the web interface) a small C program. The tool first applies the Cerberus compositional translation (or elaboration) into a simple Core language, as in [29,31]; this elaboration addresses (3) by making many of the thread-local subtleties of C explicit, including the loose specification of evaluation order, arithmetic conversions, implementation-defined behaviour, and many kinds of undefined behaviour. Core computation is simply over mathematical integers, with explicit memory actions to interface with the concurrency and memory object models. However, there is a mismatch between the axiomatic style of the concurrency models for C (expressed as predicates on arbitrary candidate executions) with the operational style of the previous thread-local operational semantics for Core. We address this by replacing the latter with a new translation from Core into SMT problems. This is integrated with the concurrency model, also translated into SMT, following the ideas of [5]. These are furthermore integrated with an SMT version of parts of the PNVI (provenance-not-via-integers) memory object model of [29], the basis for ongoing work within the ISO WG14 C standards committee, addressing (2). The resulting SMT problems are passed to Z3 [32]. The web interface then provides a graphical view of the allowed concurrent executions for small test programs.

The Cerberus-BMC tool should be useful for programmers, compiler writers, verification tool builders, and members of the C/C++ standards committees. We emphasise that it is intended as an executable reference semantics for small test programs, not itself as a verification tool that can be applied to larger bodies of C: we have focussed on making it transparently based on principled semantics for all three aspects, without the complexities needed for a high-performance verification tool. But it should aid the construction of such.

Caveats and Limitations. Cerberus-BMC covers many features of 1–3, but far from all. With respect to the concurrency memory model, we support substantial fragments of the C11, RC11, and Linux kernel memory models. We omit locks and the (deprecated) C11/RC11 consume accesses. We only cover compare-exchange read-modify-write operations, and the fragment of RCU restricted to `read_rcu_lock()`, `read_rcu_unlock()`, and `synchronize_rcu()` used in a linear way, without control-flow-dependent calls to RCU, and without nesting.

With respect to the memory object model, we do not currently support dynamic allocation or manipulation of byte representations (such as with `char*` pointers), and we do not address issues such as subobject provenance (an open question within WG14).

With respect to the thread semantics, our translation to SMT does not currently cover arbitrary pointer type-casting, function pointers, multi-dimensional arrays, unions, floating point, bitwise operations, and variadic functions, and only covers simple structs. In addition, we inherit the limitations of the Cerberus thread semantics as per [29].

Related Work. There is substantial prior work on tools for concurrency semantics and for C semantics, but almost none that combines the two. On the concurrency semantics side, CppMem [1,11] is a web-interface tool that computes the allowed concurrent behaviours of small tests with respect to variants (now somewhat outdated) of the C11 model, but it does not support other concurrency models or a memory object model, and it supports only a small fragment of C. Herd [6,8] is a command-line tool that computes the allowed concurrent behaviours of small tests with respect to arbitrary axiomatic concurrency models expressed in its cat language, but without a memory object model and for tests which essentially just comprise memory events, without a C semantics. MemAlloy [38] and MemSynth [16] also support reasoning about axiomatic concurrency models, but again not integrated with a C language semantics.

On the C semantics side, several projects address sequential C semantics but without concurrency. We build here on Cerberus [28,29,31], a web-interface tool that computes the allowed behaviours (interactively or exhaustively) for moderate-sized tests in a substantial fragment of sequential C, incorporating various memory object models (an early version supported Nienhuis's operational model for C11 concurrency [33], but that is no longer integrated). KCC and RV-Match [19,21,22] provide a command-line semantics tool for a substantial fragment of C, again without concurrency. Krebbers gives a Coq semantics for a somewhat smaller fragment [24].

Then there is another large body of work on model-checking tools for sequential and concurrent C. These are all optimised for model-checking performance, in contrast to the Cerberus-BMC emphasis on expressing the semantic envelope of allowed behaviour as clearly as we can (and, where possible, closely linked to the ISO standard). The former include tis-interpreter [18,36], CBMC [17,25], and ESBMC [20]. On the concurrent side, as already mentioned, we build on the approach of [5], which integrated various hardware memory concurrency models with CBMC. CDSChecker [34] supports something like the C/C++11 concurrency model, but subject to various limitations [34, §1.3]. It is implemented using a dynamically-linked shared library for the C and C++ atomic types, so implicitly adopts the C semantic choices of whichever compiler is used. RCMC [23], supports memory models that do not exhibit Load Buffering (LB), for an idealised thread-local language. Nidhugg [4] supports only hardware memory models: SC, TSO, PSO, and versions of POWER and ARM.

2   Examples

We now illustrate some of what Cerberus-BMC can do, by example.

Concurrency Models. First, for C11 concurrency, Fig. 1 shows a screenshot for a classic message-passing test, with non-atomic writes and reads of x, synchronised with release/acquire writes and reads of y. The test uses an explicit parallel composition, written {-{...|||...}-}, to avoid the noise from the extra memory actions in pthread_create. The consistent race-free UB-free execution on the right shows the synchronisation working correctly: after the i read-acquire of y=1, the l non-atomic read of x has to read x=1 (there are no consistent executions in which it does not). As usual in C/C++ candidate execution graphs, rf are reads-from edges, sb is sequenced-before (program order), mo is modification

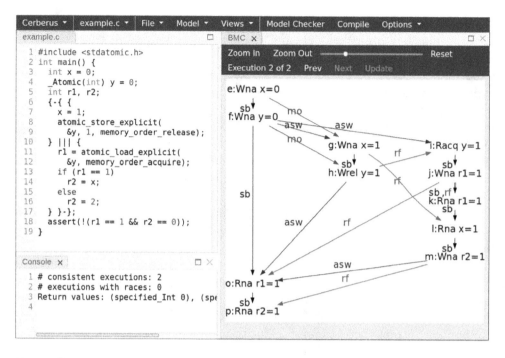

Fig. 1. Cerberus-BMC Screenshot: C11 Release/Acquire Message Passing. If the read of y is 1, then the last thread has to see the write of 1 to x.

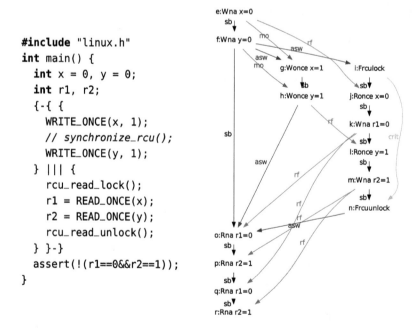

Fig. 2. Linux kernel memory model RCU lock. Without synchronize_rcu(), the reads of x and y can see 0 and 1 (as shown), even though they are enclosed in an RCU lock. With synchronization, after reading x=1, the last thread has to see y=1.

order (the coherence order between atomic writes to the same address), and asw is additional-synchronised-with, between parent and child threads and vice versa. Read and write events (R/W) are annotated na for non-atomic and rel/acq for release/acquire.

For the Linux kernel memory model, the example in Fig. 2 shows an RCU (read-copy-update) synchronisation.

Memory Object Model. The example below illustrates a case where one cannot assume that C has a concrete memory object model: pointer provenance matters.

In some C implementations, x and y will happen to be allocated adjacent (the _ _BMC_ASSUME restricts attention to those executions). Then &x+1 will have the same numeric address as &y, but the write *p=11 is undefined behaviour rather than a write to y. This was informally described in the 2004 ISO WG14 C standards committee response to

```
#include <stdint.h>
int x = 1, y = 2;
int main() {
    int *p = &x + 1;
    int *q = &y;
    __BMC_ASSUME((intptr_t)p==(intptr_t)q);
    if ((intptr_t)p==(intptr_t)q)
        *p = 11; // does this have UB?
}
```

Defect Report 260 [37], but has never been incorporated into the standard itself. Cerberus-BMC correctly reports UB found: source.c:8:5-7, UB043_indirection_invalid_value following the PNVI (provenance-not-via-integers) memory object model of [29].

ISO Subtleties. Turning to areas where the ISO standard is clear to experts but widely misunderstood, in the example on the right ISO leaves it implementation-defined whether **char** is signed or unsigned. In the former case, the ISO integer promotion and conversion semantics will make the equality test false, leading to a division by 0, which is undefined behaviour.

```
int main() {
    char c1 = 0xff;
    unsigned char c2 = 0xff;
    return 1 / (c1 == c2);
}
```

The example below shows the correct treatment of the ISO standard's loose specification of evaluation order, together with detection of the concurrency model's *unsequenced races* (ur in the diagram): there are write and read accesses to x that are unrelated by sequenced-before (sb), and not otherwise synchronised and hence unrelated by happens-before, which makes this program undefined behaviour.

```
int main() {
    int x=0;
    int w;
    w = x++ + x;
}
```

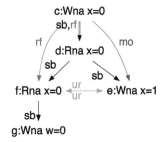

Treiber Stack. Finally, demonstrating the combination of all three aspects, we implemented a modified Treiber stack (the `push()` function is shown in Fig. 3) with relaxed accesses to struct fields. Although the Treiber stack is traditionally implemented by spinning on a compare-and-swap, as that can spin unboundedly, we instead use `__BMC_ASSUME` to restrict executions to those where the compare-and-swap succeed. Our tool correctly detects the different results from the concurrent relaxed-memory execution of threads concurrently executing the `push` and `pop` functions.

```
struct Node { int data; struct Node *next; };
struct Node * _Atomic T;
void push(struct Node *x, int v) {
    struct Node *t;
    x->data = v;
    t = atomic_load_explicit(&T, memory_order_relaxed);
    x->next = t;
    __BMC_ASSUME(atomic_compare_exchange_strong_explicit(&T, &t, x,
        memory_order_acq_rel, memory_order_relaxed));
}
```

Fig. 3. Treiber stack `push()`

```
1  proc main (): eff loaded integer :=
2    let strong x: pointer = create(Ivalignof('signed int'), 'signed int') in
3    let strong a_437: loaded integer = pure(Specified(1)) in
4    store('signed int', x, conv_loaded_int('signed int', a_437)) ;
5    kill(x) ;
6    (save ret_435: loaded integer (a_436: loaded integer:= Specified(0)) in
7      pure(a_436))
```

Fig. 4. Core program corresponding to `int main(){int x = 1}`. Core is essentially a typed, first-order lambda calculus with explicit memory actions such as **create** and **store** to interface with the concurrency and memory object models.

3   Implementation

After translating a C program into Core (see Fig. 4), Cerberus-BMC does a sequence of Core-to-Core rewrites in the style of bounded model checkers such as CBMC: it unwinds loops and inlines function calls (to a given bound), and renames symbols to generate an SSA-style program.

The explicit representation of memory operations in Core as first-order constructs allows the SMT translation to be easily separated into three components: the translation from Core to SMT, the memory object model constraints, and the concurrency model constraints.

1. Core to SMT. Each value in Core is represented as an SMT expression, with fresh SMT constants for memory actions such as `create` and `store` (e.g. lines 2 and 4), the concrete values of which are constrained by the memory object and concurrency models. The elaboration of C to Core makes thread-local undefined behaviour (as opposed to undefined behaviour from concurrency or memory layout), like signed integer overflow, explicit with a primitive `undef` construct. Undefined behaviour is then encoded in SMT as reachability of `undef` expressions, that is, satisfiability of the control-flow guards up to them.

2. Memory Object Model. As in the PNVI semantics [30], Cerberus-BMC represents pointers as pairs (π, a) of a provenance π and an integer address a. The provenance of a pointer is taken into account when doing memory accesses, pointer comparisons, and casts between integer and pointer values. Our tool models address allocation nondeterminism by constraining address values based on allocations to be appropriately aligned and non-overlapping, but not constraining the addresses otherwise.

3. Concurrency Model. Cerberus-BMC statically extracts memory actions and computes an extended pre-execution containing relations such as program order. As control flow can not be statically determined, memory actions are associated with an SMT boolean guard representing the control flow conditions upon which the memory action is executed.

Cerberus-BMC reads in a model definition in a subset of the herd `cat` language large enough to express C11, RC11, and Linux, and generates a set of quantifier-free SMT expressions corresponding to the model's constraints on relations. These constraints are based on a set of "built-in" relations defined in SMT such as `rf`. Cerberus-BMC then queries Z3 to extract all the executions, displaying the load/store values and computed relations for the user.

4   Validation

We validate correctness of the three aspects of Cerberus-BMC as follows, though, as ever, additional testing would be desirable. Performance data, demonstrating practical usability, is from a MacBook Pro 2.9 GHz Intel Core i5.

For C11 and RC11 concurrency, we check on 12 classic litmus tests. For Linux kernel concurrency, we hand-translated the 9 non-RCU tests and 4 of the RCU tests of [7] into C, and automatically translated the 40 tests of [2]. Running all the non-RCU tests takes less than 5 min; the RCU tests are slower, of the order of one hour, perhaps because of the recursive definitions involved.

For the memory object model, we take the supported subset (36 tests) of the provenance semantics test suite of [29]. These single-threaded tests each run in less than a second.

For the thread-local semantics, the Cerberus pipeline to Core has previously been validated using GCC Torture, Toyota ITC, KCC, and Csmith-generated test suites [29]. We check the mapping to BMC using 50 hand-written tests and the supported subset (400 tests) of the Toyota ITC test suite, each running in less than two minutes.

These test suites and the examples in the paper can be accessed via the CAV 2019 pop-up in the File menu of the tool.

Acknowledgments. This work was partially supported by EPSRC grant EP/K008528/1 (REMS), ERC Advanced Grant ELVER 789108, and an MIT EECS Graduate Alumni Fellowship.

References

1. CppMem: Interactive C/C++ memory model. http://svr-pes20-cppmem.cl.cam.ac.uk/cppmem/index.html
2. Litmus tests for validation LISA-language Linux-kernel memory models. https://github.com/paulmckrcu/litmus/tree/master/manual/lwn573436
3. Programming Languages — C: ISO/IEC 9899:2011 (2011). A non-final but recent version is available at http://www.open-std.org/jtc1/sc22/wg14/docs/n1539.pdf
4. Abdulla, P.A., Aronis, S., Atig, M.F., Jonsson, B., Leonardsson, C., Sagonas, K.: Stateless model checking for TSO and PSO. In: Baier, C., Tinelli, C. (eds.) TACAS 2015. LNCS, vol. 9035, pp. 353–367. Springer, Heidelberg (2015). https://doi.org/10.1007/978-3-662-46681-0_28
5. Alglave, J., Kroening, D., Tautschnig, M.: Partial orders for efficient bounded model checking of concurrent software. In: Sharygina, N., Veith, H. (eds.) CAV 2013. LNCS, vol. 8044, pp. 141–157. Springer, Heidelberg (2013). https://doi.org/10.1007/978-3-642-39799-8_9
6. Alglave, J., Maranget, L.: Herd7 (in the diy tool suite) (2015). http://diy.inria.fr/
7. Alglave, J., Maranget, L., McKenney, P.E., Parri, A., Stern, A.S.: Frightening small children and disconcerting grown-ups: concurrency in the Linux kernel. In: Proceedings of the Twenty-Third International Conference on Architectural Support for Programming Languages and Operating Systems, ASPLOS 2018, Williamsburg, VA, USA, 24–28 March 2018, pp. 405–418 (2018). https://doi.org/10.1145/3173162.3177156
8. Alglave, J., Maranget, L., Tautschnig, M.: Herding cats: modelling, simulation, testing, and data mining for weak memory. ACM TOPLAS **36**(2), 7:1–7:74 (2014)
9. Batty, M., Donaldson, A.F., Wickerson, J.: Overhauling SC atomics in C11 and OpenCl. In: Proceedings of the 43rd Annual ACM SIGPLAN-SIGACT Symposium on Principles of Programming Languages, POPL 2016, St. Petersburg, FL, USA, 20–22 January 2016, pp. 634–648 (2016). https://doi.org/10.1145/2837614.2837637
10. Batty, M., Memarian, K., Nienhuis, K., Pichon-Pharabod, J., Sewell, P.: The problem of programming language concurrency semantics. In: Vitek, J. (ed.) ESOP 2015. LNCS, vol. 9032, pp. 283–307. Springer, Heidelberg (2015). https://doi.org/10.1007/978-3-662-46669-8_12
11. Batty, M., Owens, S., Sarkar, S., Sewell, P., Weber, T.: Mathematizing C++ concurrency. In: Proceeding POPL (2011)
12. Becker, P. (ed.): Programming Languages — C++, iSO/IEC 14882:2011 (2011). A non-final but recent version is available at http://www.open-std.org/jtc1/sc22/wg21/docs/papers/2011/n3242.pdf
13. Boehm, H.J., Adve, S.V.: Foundations of the C++ concurrency memory model. In: Proceedings of PLDI, pp. 68–78. ACM, New York (2008)

14. Boehm, H.J., Giroux, O., Vafeiadis, V.: P0668R2: Revising the C++ memory model. ISO WG21 paper (2018). http://www.open-std.org/jtc1/sc22/wg21/docs/papers/2018/p0668r2.html

15. Boehm, H., Demsky, B.: Outlawing ghosts: avoiding out-of-thin-air results. In: Proceedings of the Workshop on Memory Systems Performance and Correctness, MSPC 2014, Edinburgh, United Kingdom, 13 June 2014, pp. 7:1–7:6 (2014). https://doi.org/10.1145/2618128.2618134

16. Bornholt, J., Torlak, E.: Synthesizing memory models from framework sketches and litmus tests. In: Proceedings of the 38th ACM SIGPLAN Conference on Programming Language Design and Implementation, PLDI 2017, Barcelona, Spain, 18–23 June 2017, pp. 467–481 (2017). https://doi.org/10.1145/3062341.3062353

17. Clarke, E., Kroening, D., Lerda, F.: A tool for checking ANSI-C programs. In: Jensen, K., Podelski, A. (eds.) TACAS 2004. LNCS, vol. 2988, pp. 168–176. Springer, Heidelberg (2004). https://doi.org/10.1007/978-3-540-24730-2_15

18. Cuoq, P., Runarvot, L., Cherepanov, A.: Detecting strict aliasing violations in the wild. In: Bouajjani, A., Monniaux, D. (eds.) VMCAI 2017. LNCS, vol. 10145, pp. 14–33. Springer, Cham (2017). https://doi.org/10.1007/978-3-319-52234-0_2

19. Ellison, C., Roşu, G.: An executable formal semantics of C with applications. In: Proceedings of POPL (2012)

20. Gadelha, M.Y.R., Monteiro, F.R., Morse, J., Cordeiro, L.C., Fischer, B., Nicole, D.A.: ESBMC 5.0: an industrial-strength C model checker. In: Proceedings of the 33rd ACM/IEEE International Conference on Automated Software Engineering, ASE 2018, Montpellier, France, 3–7 September 2018, pp. 888–891 (2018)

21. Guth, D., Hathhorn, C., Saxena, M., Roşu, G.: RV-Match: practical semantics-based program analysis. In: Chaudhuri, S., Farzan, A. (eds.) CAV 2016, Part I. LNCS, vol. 9779, pp. 447–453. Springer, Cham (2016). https://doi.org/10.1007/978-3-319-41528-4_24

22. Hathhorn, C., Ellison, C., Rosu, G.: Defining the undefinedness of C. In: Proceedings of the 36th ACM SIGPLAN Conference on Programming Language Design and Implementation, Portland, OR, USA, 15–17 June 2015, pp. 336–345 (2015). https://doi.org/10.1145/2737924.2737979

23. Kokologiannakis, M., Lahav, O., Sagonas, K., Vafeiadis, V.: Effective stateless model checking for C/C++ concurrency. PACMPL 2(POPL), 17:1–17:32 (2018). https://doi.org/10.1145/3158105

24. Krebbers, R.: The C standard formalized in CoQ. Ph.D. thesis, Radboud University Nijmegen, December 2015

25. Kroening, D., Tautschnig, M.: CBMC – C bounded model checker (competition contribution). In: Ábrahám, E., Havelund, K. (eds.) TACAS 2014. LNCS, vol. 8413, pp. 389–391. Springer, Heidelberg (2014). https://doi.org/10.1007/978-3-642-54862-8_26

26. Lahav, O., Vafeiadis, V., Kang, J., Hur, C., Dreyer, D.: Repairing sequential consistency in C/C++11. In: Proceedings of the 38th ACM SIGPLAN Conference on Programming Language Design and Implementation, PLDI 2017, Barcelona, Spain, 18–23 June 2017, pp. 618–632 (2017). https://doi.org/10.1145/3062341.3062352

27. Lee, J., Hur, C.K., Jung, R., Liu, Z., Regehr, J., Lopes, N.P.: Reconciling high-level optimizations and low-level code with twin memory allocation. In: Proceedings of the 2018 ACM SIGPLAN International Conference on Object Oriented Programming Systems Languages & Applications, OOPSLA 2018, part of SPLASH 2018, Boston, MA, USA, 4–9 November 2018. ACM (2018)

28. Memarian, K., Gomes, V., Sewell, P.: Cerberus (2018). http://cerberus.cl.cam.ac.uk/cerberus

29. Memarian, K., et al.: Exploring C semantics and pointer provenance. In: Proceedings of 46th ACM SIGPLAN Symposium on Principles of Programming Languages, January 2019. Proc. ACM Program. Lang. 3, POPL, Article 67
30. Memarian, K., et al.: Exploring C semantics and pointer provenance. PACMPL **3**(POPL), 67:1–67:32 (2019). https://dl.acm.org/citation.cfm?id=3290380
31. Memarian, K., et al.: Into the depths of C: elaborating the de facto standards. In: PLDI 2016: 37th Annual ACM SIGPLAN Conference on Programming Language Design and Implementation (Santa Barbara), June 2016. http://www.cl.cam.ac.uk/users/pes20/cerberus/pldi16.pdf. PLDI 2016 Distinguished Paper award
32. de Moura, L., Bjørner, N.: Z3: an efficient SMT solver. In: Ramakrishnan, C.R., Rehof, J. (eds.) TACAS 2008. LNCS, vol. 4963, pp. 337–340. Springer, Heidelberg (2008). https://doi.org/10.1007/978-3-540-78800-3_24
33. Nienhuis, K., Memarian, K., Sewell, P.: An operational semantics for C/C++11 concurrency. In: Proceedings of the ACM SIGPLAN International Conference on Object-Oriented Programming, Systems, Languages, and Applications. ACM, New York (2016). https://doi.org/10.1145/2983990.2983997
34. Norris, B., Demsky, B.: CDSchecker: checking concurrent data structures written with C/C++ atomics. In: Proceedings of OOPSLA (2013)
35. Ou, P., Demsky, B.: Towards understanding the costs of avoiding out-of-thin-air results. PACMPL **2**(OOPSLA), 136:1–136:29 (2018). https://doi.org/10.1145/3276506
36. TrustInSoft: `tis-interpreter` (2017). http://trust-in-soft.com/tis-interpreter/. Accessed 11 Nov 2017
37. WG14: Defect report 260, September 2004. http://www.open-std.org/jtc1/sc22/wg14/www/docs/dr_260.htm
38. Wickerson, J., Batty, M., Sorensen, T., Constantinides, G.A.: Automatically comparing memory consistency models. In: Proceedings of the 44th ACM SIGPLAN Symposium on Principles of Programming Languages, POPL 2017, pp. 190–204. ACM, New York (2017). https://doi.org/10.1145/3009837.3009838

4

The Marabou Framework for Verification and Analysis of Deep Neural Networks

Guy Katz[1]([✉]), Derek A. Huang[2], Duligur Ibeling[2],
Kyle Julian[2], Christopher Lazarus[2], Rachel Lim[2],
Parth Shah[2], Shantanu Thakoor[2], Haoze Wu[2],
Aleksandar Zeljić[2], David L. Dill[2],
Mykel J. Kochenderfer[2], and Clark Barrett[2]

[1] The Hebrew University of Jerusalem,
Jerusalem, Israel
guykatz@cs.huji.ac.il
[2] Stanford University, Stanford, USA
{huangda,duligur,kjulian3,clazarus,parth95,thakoor,
haozewu,zeljic,dill,mykel,clarkbarrett}@stanford.edu,
rachelim@cs.stanford.edu

Abstract. Deep neural networks are revolutionizing the way complex systems are designed. Consequently, there is a pressing need for tools and techniques for network analysis and certification. To help in addressing that need, we present *Marabou*, a framework for verifying deep neural networks. Marabou is an SMT-based tool that can answer queries about a network's properties by transforming these queries into constraint satisfaction problems. It can accommodate networks with different activation functions and topologies, and it performs high-level reasoning on the network that can curtail the search space and improve performance. It also supports parallel execution to further enhance scalability. Marabou accepts multiple input formats, including protocol buffer files generated by the popular TensorFlow framework for neural networks. We describe the system architecture and main components, evaluate the technique and discuss ongoing work.

1 Introduction

Recent years have brought about a major change in the way complex systems are being developed. Instead of spending long hours hand-crafting complex software, many engineers now opt to use *deep neural networks (DNNs)* [6,19]. DNNs are machine learning models, created by training algorithms that generalize from a finite set of examples to previously unseen inputs. Their performance can often surpass that of manually created software as demonstrated in fields such as image classification [16], speech recognition [8], and game playing [21].

Despite their overall success, the opacity of DNNs is a cause for concern, and there is an urgent need for certification procedures that can provide rigorous guarantees about network behavior. The formal methods community has taken initial steps in this direction, by developing algorithms and tools for neural network verification [5, 9, 10, 12, 18, 20, 23, 24]. A DNN verification query consists of two parts: (i) a neural network, and (ii) a property to be checked; and its result is either a formal guarantee that the network satisfies the property, or a concrete input for which the property is violated (a counter-example). A verification query can encode the fact, e.g., that a network is robust to small adversarial perturbations in its input [22].

A neural network is comprised of *neurons*, organized in layers. The network is evaluated by assigning values to the neurons in the input layer, and then using these values to iteratively compute the assignments of neurons in each succeeding layer. Finally, the values of neurons in the last layer are computed, and this is the network's output. A neuron's assignment is determined by computing a weighted sum of the assignments of neurons from the preceding layer, and then applying to the result a non-linear activation function, such as the Rectified Linear Unit (ReLU) function, $\text{ReLU}(x) = \max(0, x)$. Thus, a network can be regarded as a set of *linear constraints* (the weighted sums), and a set of *non-linear constraints* (the activation functions). In addition to a neural network, a verification query includes a property to be checked, which is given in the form of linear or non-linear constraints on the network's inputs and outputs. The verification problem thus reduces to finding an assignment of neuron values that satisfies all the constraints simultaneously, or determining that no such assignment exists.

This paper presents a new tool for DNN verification and analysis, called *Marabou*. The Marabou project builds upon our previous work on the Reluplex project [2, 7, 12, 13, 15, 17], which focused on applying SMT-based techniques to the verification of DNNs. Marabou follows the Reluplex spirit in that it applies an SMT-based, *lazy search* technique: it iteratively searches for an assignment that satisfies all given constraints, but treats the non-linear constraints lazily in the hope that many of them will prove irrelevant to the property under consideration, and will not need to be addressed at all. In addition to search, Marabou performs deduction aimed at learning new facts about the non-linear constraints in order to simplify them.

The Marabou framework is a significant improvement over its predecessor, Reluplex. Specifically, it includes the following enhancements and modifications:

- Native support for fully connected and convolutional DNNs with arbitrary piecewise-linear activation functions. This extends the Reluplex algorithm, which was originally designed to support only ReLU activation functions.
- Built-in support for a *divide-and-conquer* solving mode, in which the solver is run with an initial (small) timeout. If the timeout is reached, the solver partitions its input query into simpler sub-queries, increases the timeout value, and repeats the process on each sub-query. This mode naturally lends itself to parallel execution by running sub-queries on separate nodes; however, it can yield significant speed-ups even when used with a single node.
- A complete simplex-based linear programming core that replaces the external solver (GLPK) that was previously used in Reluplex. The new simplex

core was tailored for a smooth integration with the Marabou framework and eliminates much of the overhead in Reluplex due to the use of GLPK.
– Multiple interfaces for feeding queries into the solver. A query's neural network can be provided in a textual format or as a protocol buffer (*protobuf*) file containing a TensorFlow model; and the property can be either compiled into the solver, provided in Python, or stored in a textual format. We expect these interfaces will simplify usage of the tool for many users.
– Support for network-level reasoning and deduction. The earlier Reluplex tool performed deductions at the level of single constraints, ignoring the input network's topology. In Marabou, we retain this functionality but also include support for reasoning based on the network topology, such as symbolic bound tightening [23]. This allows for efficient curtailment of the search space.

Marabou is available online [14] under the permissive modified BSD license.

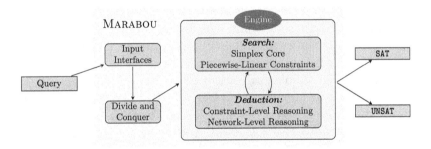

Fig. 1. The main components of Marabou.

2 Design of Marabou

Marabou regards each neuron in the network as a variable and searches for a variable assignment that simultaneously satisfies the query's linear constraints and non-linear constraints. At any given point, Marabou maintains the current variable assignment, lower and upper bounds for every variable, and the set of current constraints. In each iteration, it then changes the variable assignment in order to (1) correct a violated linear constraint, or (2) correct a violated non-linear constraint.

The Marabou verification procedure is sound and complete, i.e. the aforementioned loop eventually terminates. This can be shown via a straightforward extension of the soundness and completeness proof for Reluplex [12]. However, in order to guarantee termination, Marabou only supports activation functions that are piecewise-linear. The tool already has built-in support for the ReLU function and the Max function $\max(x_1, \ldots, x_n)$, and it is modular in the sense that additional piecewise-linear functions can be added easily.

Another important aspect of Marabou's verification strategy is deduction—specifically, the derivation of tighter lower and upper variable bounds. The motivation is that such bounds may transform piecewise-linear constraints into linear constraints, by restricting them to one of their linear segments. To achieve this, Marabou repeatedly examines linear and non-linear constraints, and also performs network-level reasoning, with the goal of discovering tighter variable bounds.

Next, we describe Marabou's main components (see also Fig. 1).

2.1 Simplex Core (*Tableau* and *BasisFactorization* Classes)

The simplex core is the part of the system responsible for making the variable assignment satisfy the linear constraints. It does so by implementing a variant of the *simplex algorithm* [3]. In each iteration, it changes the assignment of some variable x, and consequently the assignment of any variable y that is connected to x by a linear equation. Selecting x and determining its new assignment is performed using standard algorithms—specifically, the *revised simplex method* in which the various linear constraints are kept in implicit matrix form, and the steepest-edge and Harris' ratio test strategies for variable selection.

Creating an efficient simplex solver is complicated. In Reluplex, we delegated the linear constraints to an external solver, GLPK. Our motivation for implementing a new custom solver in Marabou was twofold: first, we observed in Reluplex that the repeated translation of queries into GLPK and extraction of results from GLPK was a limiting factor on performance; and second, a black box simplex solver did not afford the flexibility we needed in the context of DNN verification. For example, in a standard simplex solver, variable assignments are typically pressed against their upper or lower bounds, whereas in the context of a DNN, other assignments might be needed to satisfy the non-linear constraints. Another example is the deduction capability, which is crucial for efficiently verifying a DNN and whose effectiveness might depend on the internal state of the simplex solver.

2.2 Piecewise-Linear Constraints (*PiecewiseLinearConstraint* Class)

Throughout its execution, Marabou maintains a set of piecewise-linear constraints that represent the DNN's non-linear functions. In iterations devoted to satisfying these constraints, Marabou looks for any constraints that are not satisfied by the current assignment. If such a constraint is found, Marabou changes the assignment in a way that makes that constraint satisfied. Alternatively, in order to guarantee eventual termination, if Marabou detects that a certain constraint is repeatedly not satisfied, it may perform a *case-split* on that constraint: a process in which the piecewise-linear constraint φ is replaced by an equivalent disjunction of linear constraints $c_1 \vee \ldots \vee c_n$. Marabou considers these disjuncts one at a time and checks for satisfiability. If the problem is satisfiable when φ is replaced by some c_i, then the original problem is also satisfiable; otherwise, the original problem is unsatisfiable.

In our implementation, piecewise-linear constraints are represented by objects of classes that inherit from the *PiecewiseLinearConstraint* abstract class. Currently the two supported instances are ReLU and Max, but the design is modular in the sense that new constraint types can easily be added. *PiecewiseLinearConstraint* defines the interface methods that each supported piecewise-linear constraint needs to implement. Some of the key interface methods are:

- *satisfied()*: the constraint object needs to answer whether or not it is satisfied given the current assignment. For example, for a constraint $y = \mathrm{ReLU}(x)$ and assignment $x = y = 3$, *satisfied()* would return *true*; whereas for assignment $x = -5, y = 3$, it would return *false*.
- *getPossibleFixes()*: if the constraint is not satisfied by the current assignment, this method returns possible changes to the assignment that would correct the violation. For example, for $x = -5, y = 3$, the ReLU constraint from before might propose two possible changes to the assignment, $x \leftarrow 3$ or $y \leftarrow 0$, as either would satisfy $y = \mathrm{ReLU}(x)$.
- *getCaseSplits()*: this method asks the piecewise-linear constraint φ to return a list of linear constraints $c_1, \ldots, c_n$, such that φ is equivalent to $c_1 \vee \ldots \vee c_n$. For example, when invoked for a constraint $y = \max(x_1, x_2)$, *getCaseSplits()* would return the linear constraints $c_1 : (y = x_1 \wedge x_1 \geq x_2)$ and $c_2 : (y = x_2 \wedge x_2 \geq x_1)$. These constraints satisfy the requirement that the original constraint is equivalent to $c_1 \vee c_2$.
- *getEntailedTightenings()*: as part of Marabou's deduction of tighter variable bounds, piecewise-linear constraints are repeatedly informed of changes to the lower and upper bounds of variables they affect. Invoking *getEntailedTightenings()* queries the constraint for tighter variable bounds, based on current information. For example, suppose a constraint $y = \mathrm{ReLU}(x)$ is informed of the upper bounds $x \leq 5$ and $y \leq 7$; in this case, *getEntailedTightenings()* would return the tighter bound $y \leq 5$.

2.3 Constraint- and Network-Level Reasoning (*RowBoundTightener*, *ConstraintBoundTightener* and *SymbolicBoundTightener* Classes)

Effective deduction of tighter variable bounds is crucial for Marabou's performance. Deduction is performed at the constraint level, by repeatedly examining linear and piecewise-linear constraints to see if they imply tighter variable bounds; and also at the DNN-level, by leveraging the network's topology.

Constraint-level bound tightening is performed by querying the piecewise-linear constraints for tighter bounds using the *getEntailedTightenings()* method. Similarly, linear equations can also be used to deduce tighter bounds. For example, the equation $x = y + z$ and lower bounds $x \geq 0$, $y \geq 1$ and $z \geq 1$ together imply the tighter bound $x \geq 2$. As part of the simplex-based search, Marabou repeatedly encounters many linear equations and uses them for bound tightening.

Several recent papers have proposed verification schemes that rely on DNN-level reasoning [5,23]. Marabou supports this kind of reasoning as well, by storing the initial network topology and performing deduction steps that use this information as part of its iterative search. DNN-level reasoning is seamlessly integrated into the search procedure by (1) initializing the DNN-level reasoners with the most up-to-date information discovered during the search, such as variable bounds and the state of piecewise-linear constraints; and (2) feeding any new information that is discovered back into the search procedure. Presently Marabou implements a symbolic bound tightening procedure [23]: based on network topology, upper and lower bounds for each hidden neuron are expressed as a linear combination of the input neurons. Then, if the bounds on the input neurons are sufficiently tight (e.g., as a result of past deductions), these expressions for upper and lower bounds may imply that some of the hidden neurons' piecewise-linear activation functions are now restricted to one of their linear segments. Implementing additional DNN-level reasoning operations is work in progress.

2.4   The Engine (*Engine* and *SmtCore* Classes)

The main class of Marabou, in which the main loop resides, is called the *Engine*. The engine stores and coordinates the various solution components, including the simplex core and the piecewise-linear constraints. The main loop consists, roughly, of the following steps (the first rule that applies is used):

1. If a piecewise-linear constraint had to be fixed more than a certain number of times, perform a case split on that constraint.
2. If the problem has become unsatisfiable, e.g. because for some variable a lower bound has been deduced that is greater than its upper bound, undo a previous case split (or return UNSAT if no such case split exists).
3. If there is a violated linear constraint, perform a simplex step.
4. If there is a violated piecewise-linear constraint, attempt to fix it.
5. Return SAT (all constraints are satisfied).

The engine also triggers deduction steps, both at the neuron level and at the network level, according to various heuristics.

2.5   The Divide-and-Conquer Mode and Concurrency (*DnC.py*)

Marabou supports a *divide-and-conquer* (*D&C*) solving mode, in which the input region specified in the original query is partitioned into sub-regions. The desired property is checked on these sub-regions independently. The D&C mode naturally lends itself to parallel execution, by having each sub-query checked on a separate node. Moreover, the D&C mode can improve Marabou's overall performance even when running sequentially: the total time of solving the sub-queries is often less than the time of solving the original query, as the smaller input regions allow for more effective deduction steps.

Given a query ϕ, the solver maintains a queue Q of $\langle$query, timeout$\rangle$ pairs. Q is initialized with one element $\langle \phi, T \rangle$, where T, the initial timeout, is a configurable parameter. To solve ϕ, the solver loops through the following steps:

1. Pop a pair $\langle \phi', t' \rangle$ from Q and attempt to solve ϕ' with a timeout of t'.
2. If the problem is UNSAT and Q is empty, return UNSAT.
3. If the problem is UNSAT and Q is not empty, return to step 1.
4. If the problem is SAT, return SAT.
5. If a timeout occurred, split ϕ' into k sub-queries $\phi'_1, \ldots, \phi'_k$ by partitioning its input region. For each sub-query ϕ'_i, push $\langle \phi'_i, m \cdot t' \rangle$ into Q.

The timeout factor m and the splitting factor k are configurable parameters. Splitting the query's input region is performed heuristically.

2.6 Input Interfaces (*AcasParser* class, *maraboupy* Folder)

Marabou supports verification queries provided through the following interfaces:

- Native Marabou format: a user prepares a query using the Marabou C++ interface, compiles the query into the tool, and runs it. This format is useful for integrating Marabou into a larger framework.
- Marabou executable: a user runs a Marabou executable, and passes to it command-line parameters indicating the network and property files to be checked. Currently, network files are encoded using the *NNet* format [11], and the properties are given in a simple textual format.
- Python/TensorFlow interface: the query is passed to Marabou through Python constructs. The python interface can also handle DNNs stored as TensorFlow protobuf files.

3 Evaluation

For our evaluation we used the ACAS Xu [12], CollisionDetection [4] and TwinStream [1] families of benchmarks. Tool-wise, we considered the Reluplex tool which is the most closely related to Marabou, and also ReluVal [23] and Planet [4]. The version of Marabou used for the evaluation is available online [14].

The top left plot in Fig. 3 compares the execution times of Marabou and Reluplex on 180 ACAS Xu benchmarks with a 1 hour timeout. We used Marabou in D&C mode with 4 cores and with $T = 5$, $k = 4$, and $m = 1.5$. The remaining three plots depict an execution time comparison between Marabou D&C (configuration as above), ReluVal and Planet, using 4 cores and a 1 hour timeout. Marabou and Reluval are evaluated over 180 ACAS Xu benchmarks (top right plot), and Marabou and Planet are evaluated on those 180 benchmarks (bottom left plot) and also on 500 CollisionDetection and 81 TwinStream benchmarks (bottom right plot). Due to technical difficulties, ReluVal was not run on the CollisionDetection and TwinStream benchmarks. The results show that in a 4 cores setting Marabou generally outperforms Planet, but generally does not outperform ReluVal (though it does better on some benchmarks). These results highlight the need for additional DNN-level reasoning in Marabou, which is a key ingredient in ReluVal's verification procedure.

Figure 2 shows the average runtime of
Marabou and ReluVal on the ACAS Xu properties, as a function of the number of available cores. We see that as the number of cores
increases, Marabou (solid) is able to close
the gap, and sometimes outperform, ReluVal
(dotted). With 64 cores, Marabou outperforms ReluVal on average, and both solvers
were able to solve all ACAS Xu benchmarks
within 2 hours (except for a few segfaults by
ReluVal).

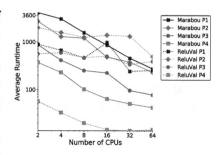

Fig. 2. A scalability comparison of
Marabou and ReluVal on ACAS
Xu.

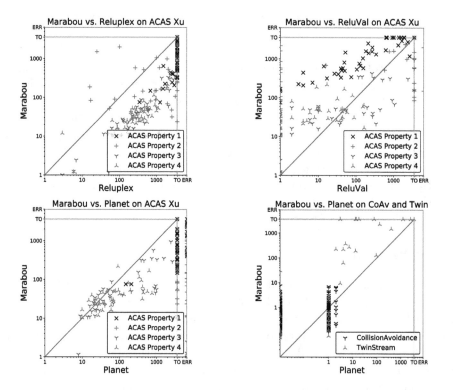

Fig. 3. A comparison of Marabou with Reluplex, ReluVal and Planet.

4　Conclusion

DNN analysis is an emerging field, and Marabou is a step towards a more mature,
stable verification platform. Moving forward, we plan to improve Marabou in several dimensions. Part of our motivation in implementing a custom simplex solver
was to obtain the needed flexibility for fusing together the solving process for linear and non-linear constraints. Currently, this flexibility has not been leveraged
much, as these pieces are solved relatively separately. We expect that by tackling

both kinds of constraints simultaneously, we will be able to improve performance significantly. Other enhancements we wish to add include: additional network-level reasoning techniques based on abstract interpretation; better heuristics for both the linear and non-linear constraint solving engines; and additional engineering improvements, specifically within the simplex engine.

Acknowledgements. We thank Elazar Cohen, Justin Gottschlich, and Lindsey Kuper for their contributions to this project. The project was partially supported by grants from the Binational Science Foundation (2017662), the Defense Advanced Research Projects Agency (FA8750-18-C-0099), the Federal Aviation Administration, Ford Motor Company, Intel Corporation, the Israel Science Foundation (683/18), the National Science Foundation (1814369, DGE-1656518), Siemens Corporation, and the Stanford CURIS program.

References

1. Bunel, R., Turkaslan, I., Torr, P., Kohli, P., Kumar, M.: Piecewise linear neural network verification: a comparative study. Technical report (2017). arXiv:1711.00455v1
2. Carlini, N., Katz, G., Barrett, C., Dill, D.: Provably minimally-distorted adversarial examples. Technical report (2017). arXiv:1709.10207
3. Chvátal, V.: Linear Programming. W. H. Freeman and Company, New York (1983)
4. Ehlers, R.: Formal verification of piece-wise linear feed-forward neural networks. In: D'Souza, D., Narayan Kumar, K. (eds.) ATVA 2017. LNCS, vol. 10482, pp. 269–286. Springer, Cham (2017). https://doi.org/10.1007/978-3-319-68167-2_19
5. Gehr, T., Mirman, M., Drachsler-Cohen, D., Tsankov, E., Chaudhuri, S., Vechev, M.: AI2: safety and robustness certification of neural networks with abstract interpretation. In: Proceedings of 39th IEEE Symposium on Security and Privacy (S&P) (2018)
6. Goodfellow, I., Bengio, Y., Courville, A.: Deep Learning. MIT Press, Cambridge (2016)
7. Gopinath, D., Katz, G., Păsăreanu, C., Barrett, C.: DeepSafe: a data-driven approach for checking adversarial robustness in neural networks. In: Proceedings of 16th International Symposium on on Automated Technology for Verification and Analysis (ATVA), pp. 3–19 (2018)
8. Hinton, G., et al.: Deep neural networks for acoustic modeling in speech recognition: the shared views of four research groups. IEEE Signal Process. Mag. **29**(6), 82–97 (2012)
9. Huang, X., Kwiatkowska, M., Wang, S., Wu, M.: Safety verification of deep neural networks. In: Proceedings of 29th International Conference on Computer Aided Verification (CAV), pp. 3–29 (2017)
10. Hull, J., Ward, D., Zakrzewski, R.: Verification and validation of neural networks for safety-critical applications. In: Proceedings of 21st American Control Conference (ACC) (2002)
11. Julian, K.: NNet Format (2018). https://github.com/sisl/NNet
12. Katz, G., Barrett, C., Dill, D.L., Julian, K., Kochenderfer, M.J.: Reluplex: an efficient SMT solver for verifying deep neural networks. In: Majumdar, R., Kunčak, V. (eds.) CAV 2017. LNCS, vol. 10426, pp. 97–117. Springer, Cham (2017). https://doi.org/10.1007/978-3-319-63387-9_5

13. Katz, G., Barrett, C., Dill, D., Julian, K., Kochenderfer, M.: Towards proving the adversarial robustness of deep neural networks. In: Proceedings of 1st Workshop on Formal Verification of Autonomous Vehicles (FVAV), pp. 19–26 (2017)
14. Katz, G., et al.: Marabou (2019). https://github.com/guykatzz/Marabou/tree/cav_artifact
15. Kazak, Y., Barrett, C., Katz, G., Schapira, M.: Verifying deep-RL-driven systems. In: Proceedings of 1st ACM SIGCOMM Workshop on Network Meets AI & ML (NetAI) (2019)
16. Krizhevsky, A., Sutskever, I., Hinton, G.: ImageNet classification with deep convolutional neural networks. In: Advances in Neural Information Processing Systems, pp. 1097–1105 (2012)
17. Kuper, L., Katz, G., Gottschlich, J., Julian, K., Barrett, C., Kochenderfer, M.: Toward scalable verification for safety-critical deep networks. Technical report (2018). arXiv:1801.05950
18. Pulina, L., Tacchella, A.: An abstraction-refinement approach to verification of artificial neural networks. In: Touili, T., Cook, B., Jackson, P. (eds.) CAV 2010. LNCS, vol. 6174, pp. 243–257. Springer, Heidelberg (2010). https://doi.org/10.1007/978-3-642-14295-6_24
19. Riesenhuber, M., Tomaso, P.: Hierarchical models of object recognition in cortex. Nat. Neurosci. **2**(11), 1019–1025 (1999)
20. Ruan, W., Huang, X., Kwiatkowska, M.: Reachability analysis of deep neural networks with provable guarantees. In: Proceedings of 27th International Joint Conference on Artificial Intelligence (IJCAI) (2018)
21. Silver, D., et al.: Mastering the game of go with deep neural networks and tree search. Nature **529**(7587), 484–489 (2016)
22. Szegedy, C., et al.: Intriguing properties of neural networks. Technical report (2013). arXiv:1312.6199
23. Wang, S., Pei, K., Whitehouse, J., Yang, J., Jana, S.: Formal security analysis of neural networks using symbolic intervals. Technical report (2018). arXiv:1804.10829
24. Xiang, W., Tran, H., Johnson, T.: Output reachable set estimation and verification for multi-layer neural networks. IEEE Trans. Neural Netw. Learn. Syst. (TNNLS) **99**, 1–7 (2018)

5

PAC Statistical Model Checking
for Markov Decision Processes
and Stochastic Games

Pranav Ashok, Jan Křetínský,
and Maximilian Weininger[(✉)]

Technical University of Munich, Munich, Germany
`maxi.weininger@tum.de`

Abstract. Statistical model checking (SMC) is a technique for analysis of probabilistic systems that may be (partially) unknown. We present an SMC algorithm for (unbounded) reachability yielding probably approximately correct (PAC) guarantees on the results. We consider both the setting (i) with no knowledge of the transition function (with the only quantity required a bound on the minimum transition probability) and (ii) with knowledge of the topology of the underlying graph. On the one hand, it is the first algorithm for stochastic games. On the other hand, it is the first practical algorithm even for Markov decision processes. Compared to previous approaches where PAC guarantees require running times longer than the age of universe even for systems with a handful of states, our algorithm often yields reasonably precise results within minutes, not requiring the knowledge of mixing time.

1 Introduction

Statistical model checking (SMC) [YS02a] is an analysis technique for probabilistic systems based on

1. simulating finitely many finitely long runs of the system,
2. statistical analysis of the obtained results,
3. yielding a confidence interval/probably approximately correct (PAC) result on the probability of satisfying a given property, i.e., there is a non-zero probability that the bounds are incorrect, but they are correct with probability that can be set arbitrarily close to 1.

One of the advantages is that it can avoid the state-space explosion problem, albeit at the cost of weaker guarantees. Even more importantly, this technique is applicable even when the model is not known (*black-box* setting) or only qualitatively known (*grey-box* setting), where the exact transition probabilities are unknown such as in many cyber-physical systems.

In the basic setting of Markov chains [Nor98] with (time- or step-)bounded properties, the technique is very efficient and has been applied to numerous domains, e.g. biological [JCL+09, PGL+13], hybrid [ZPC10, DDL+12, EGF12, Lar12] or cyber-physical [BBB+10, CZ11, DDL+13] systems and a substantial tool support is available [JLS12, BDL+12, BCLS13, BHH12]. In contrast, whenever either (i) infinite time-horizon properties, e.g. reachability, are considered or (ii) non-determinism is present in the system, providing any guarantees becomes significantly harder.

Firstly, for *infinite time-horizon properties* we need a stopping criterion such that the infinite-horizon property can be reliably evaluated based on a finite prefix of the run yielded by simulation. This can rely on the the complete knowledge of the system (*white-box* setting) [YCZ10, LP08], the topology of the system (grey box) [YCZ10, HJB+10], or a lower bound $p_{\min}$ on the minimum transition probability in the system (black box) [DHKP16, BCC+14].

Secondly, for Markov decision processes (MDP) [Put14] with (non-trivial) *non-determinism*, [HMZ+12] and [LP12] employ reinforcement learning [SB98] in the setting of bounded properties or discounted (and for the purposes of approximation thus also bounded) properties, respectively. The latter also yields PAC guarantees.

Finally, for MDP with unbounded properties, [BFHH11] deals with MDP with spurious non-determinism, where the way it is resolved does not affect the desired property. The general non-deterministic case is treated in [FT14, BCC+14], yielding PAC guarantees. However, the former requires the knowledge of mixing time, which is at least as hard to compute; the algorithm in the latter is purely theoretical since before a single value is updated in the learning process, one has to simulate longer than the age of universe even for a system as simple as a Markov chain with 12 states having at least 4 successors for some state.

Our contribution is an SMC algorithm with PAC guarantees for (i) MDP and unbounded properties, which runs for realistic benchmarks [HKP+19] and confidence intervals in orders of minutes, and (ii) is the first algorithm for stochastic games (SG). It relies on different techniques from literature.

1. The increased practical performance rests on two pillars:
   - extending early detection of bottom strongly connected components in Markov chains by [DHKP16] to end components for MDP and simple end components for SG;
   - improving the underlying PAC Q-learning technique of [SLW+06]:
     (a) learning is now model-based with better information reuse instead of model-free, but in realistic settings with the same memory requirements,
     (b) better guidance of learning due to interleaving with precise computation, which yields more precise value estimates.
     (c) splitting confidence over all relevant transitions, allowing for variable width of confidence intervals on the learnt transition probabilities.

2. The transition from algorithms for MDP to SG is possible via extending the over-approximating value iteration from MDP [BCC+14] to SG by [KKKW18].

To summarize, we give an anytime PAC SMC algorithm for (unbounded) reachability. It is the first such algorithm for SG and the first practical one for MDP.

Related Work

Most of the previous efforts in SMC have focused on the analysis of properties with *bounded* horizon [YS02a, SVA04, YKNP06, JCL+09, JLS12, BDL+12].

  SMC of *unbounded* properties was first considered in [HLMP04] and the first approach was proposed in [SVA05], but observed incorrect in [HJB+10]. Notably, in [YCZ10] two approaches are described. The first approach proposes to terminate sampled paths at every step with some probability p_{term} and re-weight the result accordingly. In order to guarantee the asymptotic convergence of this method, the second eigenvalue λ of the chain and its mixing time must be computed, which is as hard as the verification problem itself and requires the complete knowledge of the system (white box setting). The correctness of [LP08] relies on the knowledge of the second eigenvalue λ, too. The second approach of [YCZ10] requires the knowledge of the chain's topology (grey box), which is used to transform the chain so that all potentially infinite paths are eliminated. In [HJB+10], a similar transformation is performed, again requiring knowledge of the topology. In [DHKP16], only (a lower bound on) the minimum transition probability $p_{\min}$ is assumed and PAC guarantees are derived. While unbounded properties cannot be analyzed without any information on the system, knowledge of $p_{\min}$ is a relatively light assumption in many realistic scenarios [DHKP16]. For instance, bounds on the rates for reaction kinetics in chemical reaction systems are typically known; for models in the PRISM language [KNP11], the bounds can be easily inferred without constructing the respective state space. In this paper, we thus adopt this assumption.

  In the case with general *non-determinism*, one approach is to give the non-determinism a probabilistic semantics, e.g., using a uniform distribution instead, as for timed automata in [DLL+11a, DLL+11b, Lar13]. Others [LP12, HMZ+12, BCC+14] aim to quantify over all strategies and produce an ϵ-optimal strategy. In [HMZ+12], candidates for optimal strategies are generated and gradually improved, but "at any given point we cannot quantify how close to optimal the candidate scheduler is" (cited from [HMZ+12]) and the algorithm "does not in general converge to the true optimum" (cited from [LST14]). Further, [LST14, DLST15, DHS18] randomly sample compact representation of strategies, resulting in useful lower bounds if ε-schedulers are frequent. [HPS+19] gives a convergent model-free algorithm (with no bounds on the current error) and identifies that the previous [SKC+14] "has two faults, the second of which also affects approaches [...] [HAK18, HAK19]".

  Several approaches provide SMC for MDPs and unbounded properties with *PAC guarantees*. Firstly, similarly to [LP08, YCZ10], [FT14] requires (1) the mixing time T of the MDP. The algorithm then yields PAC bounds in time polynomial in T (which in turn can of course be exponential in the size of the MDP). Moreover, the algorithm requires (2) the ability to restart simulations also in non-initial states, (3) it only returns the strategy once all states have been visited (sufficiently many times), and thus (4) requires the size of the state space $|S|$. Secondly, [BCC+14], based on delayed Q-learning (DQL) [SLW+06], lifts the assumptions (2) and (3) and instead of (1) mixing time requires only (a bound on) the minimum transition probability $p_{\min}$. Our approach additionally lifts the assumption (4) and allows for running times faster than those given by T, even without the knowledge of T.

Reinforcement learning (without PAC bounds) for stochastic games has been considered already in [LN81, Lit94, BT99]. [WT16] combines the special case of almost-sure satisfaction of a specification with optimizing quantitative objectives. We use techniques of [KKKW18], which however assumes access to the transition probabilities.

2　Preliminaries

2.1　Stochastic Games

A *probability distribution* on a finite set X is a mapping $\delta : X \to [0, 1]$, such that $\sum_{x \in X} \delta(x) = 1$. The set of all probability distributions on X is denoted by $\mathcal{D}(X)$. Now we define turn-based two-player stochastic games. As opposed to the notation of e.g. [Con92], we do not have special stochastic nodes, but rather a probabilistic transition function.

Definition 1 (SG). *A stochastic game (SG) is a tuple* $G = (S, S_\square, S_\bigcirc, s_0, A, Av, \mathbb{T})$, *where* S *is a finite set of* states *partitioned[1] into the sets* $S_\square$ *and* $S_\bigcirc$ *of states of the player* Maximizer *and* Minimizer[2], *respectively* $s_0 \in S$ *is the* initial *state,* A *is a finite set of* actions, $Av : S \to 2^A$ *assigns to every state a set of* available *actions, and* $\mathbb{T} : S \times A \to \mathcal{D}(S)$ *is a* transition function *that given a state* s *and an action* $a \in Av(s)$ *yields a probability distribution over* successor *states. Note that for ease of notation we write* $\mathbb{T}(s, a, t)$ *instead of* $\mathbb{T}(s, a)(t)$.

A Markov decision process (MDP) is a special case of SG where $S_\bigcirc = \emptyset$. A Markov chain (MC) can be seen as a special case of an MDP, where for all $s \in S : |Av(s)| = 1$. We assume that SG are non-blocking, so for all states s we have $Av(s) \neq \emptyset$.

For a state s and an available action $a \in Av(s)$, we denote the set of successors by $Post(s, a) := \{t \mid \mathbb{T}(s, a, t) > 0\}$. We say a state-action pair (s, a) is an *exit* of a set of states T, written (s, a) exits T, if $\exists t \in Post(s, a) : t \notin T$, i.e., if with some probability a successor outside of T could be chosen.

We consider algorithms that have a limited information about the SG.

---

[1] I.e., $S_\square \subseteq S$, $S_\bigcirc \subseteq S$, $S_\square \cup S_\bigcirc = S$, and $S_\square \cap S_\bigcirc = \emptyset$.

[2] The names are chosen, because Maximizer maximizes the probability of reaching a given target state, and Minimizer minimizes it.

Definition 2 (Black box and grey box). *An algorithm inputs an SG as* black box *if it cannot access the whole tuple, but*

- *it knows the initial state,*
- *for a given state, an oracle returns its player and available action,*
- *given a state* s *and action* a*, it can sample a successor* t *according to* $\mathbb{T}(s, a)$,[3]
- *it knows* $p_{\min} \leq \min_{\substack{s \in S, a \in Av(s) \\ t \in Post(s,a)}} \mathbb{T}(s, a, t)$*, an under-approximation of the minimum transition probability.*

When input as grey box *it additionally knows the number* $|Post(s, a)|$ *of successors for each state* s *and action* a*.*[4]

The semantics of SG is given in the usual way by means of strategies and the induced Markov chain [BK08] and its respective probability space, as follows. An *infinite path* ρ is an infinite sequence $\rho = s_0 a_0 s_1 a_1 \cdots \in (S \times A)^\omega$, such that for every $i \in \mathbb{N}$, $a_i \in Av(s_i)$ and $s_{i+1} \in Post(s_i, a_i)$.

A *strategy* of Maximizer or Minimizer is a function $\sigma : S_\square \to \mathcal{D}(A)$ or $S_\bigcirc \to \mathcal{D}(A)$, respectively, such that $\sigma(s) \in \mathcal{D}(Av(s))$ for all s. Note that we restrict to memoryless/positional strategies, as they suffice for reachability in SGs [CH12].

A pair (σ, τ) of strategies of Maximizer and Minimizer induces a Markov chain $G^{\sigma,\tau}$ with states S, s_0 being initial, and the transition function $\mathbb{T}(s)(t) = \sum_{a \in Av(s)} \sigma(s)(a) \cdot \mathbb{T}(s, a, t)$ for states of Maximizer and analogously for states of Minimizer, with σ replaced by τ. The Markov chain induces a unique probability distribution $\mathbb{P}^{\sigma,\tau}$ over measurable sets of infinite paths [BK08, Ch. 10].

2.2 Reachability Objective

For a goal set $Goal \subseteq S$, we write $\Diamond Goal := \{s_0 a_0 s_1 a_1 \cdots \mid \exists i \in \mathbb{N} : s_i \in Goal\}$ to denote the (measurable) set of all infinite paths which eventually reach $Goal$. For each $s \in S$, we define the *value* in s as

$$V(s) := \sup_\sigma \inf_\tau \mathbb{P}_s^{\sigma,\tau}(\Diamond Goal) = \inf_\tau \sup_\sigma \mathbb{P}_s^{\sigma,\tau}(\Diamond Goal),$$

where the equality follows from [Mar75]. We are interested in $V(s_0)$, its ε-approximation and the corresponding (ε-)optimal strategies for both players.

---

[3] Up to this point, this definition conforms to black box systems in the sense of [SVA04] with sampling from the initial state, being slightly stricter than [YS02a] or [RP09], where simulations can be run from any desired state. Further, we assume that we can choose actions for the adversarial player or that she plays fairly. Otherwise the adversary could avoid playing her best strategy during the SMC, not giving SMC enough information about her possible behaviours.

[4] This requirement is slightly weaker than the knowledge of the whole topology, i.e. $Post(s, a)$ for each s and a.

Let Zero be the set of states, from which there is no finite path to any state in Goal. The value function V satisfies the following system of equations, which is referred to as the *Bellman equations*:

$$V(s) = \begin{cases} \max_{a \in Av(s)} V(s,a) & \text{if } s \in S_\square \\ \min_{a \in Av(s)} V(s,a) & \text{if } s \in S_\bigcirc \\ 1 & \text{if } s \in \text{Goal} \\ 0 & \text{if } s \in \text{Zero} \end{cases}$$

with the abbreviation $V(s,a) := \sum_{s' \in S} \mathbb{T}(s,a,s') \cdot V(s')$. Moreover, V is the *least* solution to the Bellman equations, see e.g. [CH08].

2.3 Bounded and Asynchronous Value Iteration

The well known technique of value iteration, e.g. [Put14, RF91], works by starting from an under-approximation of value function and then applying the Bellman equations. This converges towards the least fixpoint of the Bellman equations, i.e. the *value function*. Since it is difficult to give a convergence criterion, the approach of bounded value iteration (BVI, also called interval iteration) was developed for MDP [BCC+14, HM17] and SG [KKKW18]. Beside the under-approximation, it also updates an over-approximation according to the Bellman equations. The most conservative over-approximation is to use an upper bound of 1 for every state. For the under-approximation, we can set the lower bound of target states to 1; all other states have a lower bound of 0. We use the function INITIALIZE_BOUNDS in our algorithms to denote that the lower and upper bounds are set as just described; see [AKW19, Algorithm 8] for the pseudocode. Additionally, BVI ensures that the over-approximation converges to the least fixpoint by taking special care of *end components*, which are the reason for not converging to the true value from above.

Definition 3 (End component (EC)). *A non-empty set $T \subseteq S$ of states is an* end component (EC) *if there is a non-empty set $B \subseteq \bigcup_{s \in T} Av(s)$ of actions such that (i) for each $s \in T, a \in B \cap Av(s)$ we do* not *have (s,a) exits T and (ii) for each $s, s' \in T$ there is a finite path $w = s a_0 \ldots a_n s' \in (T \times B)^* \times T$, i.e. the path stays inside T and only uses actions in B.*

Intuitively, ECs correspond to bottom strongly connected components of the Markov chains induced by possible strategies, so for some pair of strategies all possible paths starting in the EC remain there. An end component T is a *maximal end component (MEC)* if there is no other end component T' such that $T \subseteq T'$. Given an SG G, the set of its MECs is denoted by $MEC(G)$.

Note that, to stay in an EC in an SG, the two players would have to cooperate, since it depends on the pair of strategies. To take into account the adversarial behaviour of the players, it is also relevant to look at a subclass of ECs, the so called *simple end components*, introduced in [KKKW18].

Definition 4 (Simple end component (SEC) [KKKW18]). *An EC T is called* simple, *if for all* $s \in T$ *it holds that* $V(s) = \text{bestExit}(T, V)$, *where*

$$\text{bestExit}(T, f) := \begin{cases} 1 & \text{if } T \cap \text{Goal} \neq \emptyset \\ \max_{\substack{s \in T \cap S_\square \\ (s,a)\, \text{exits}\, T}} f(s, a) & \text{else} \end{cases}$$

is called the best exit *(of Maximizer) from T according to the function $f : S \to \mathbb{R}$. To handle the case that there is no exit of Maximizer in T we set* $\max_\emptyset = 0$.

Intuitively, SECs are ECs where Minimizer does not want to use any of her exits, as all of them have a greater value than the best exit of Maximizer. Assigning any value between those of the best exits of Maximizer and Minimizer to all states in the EC is a solution to the Bellman equations, because both players prefer remaining and getting that value to using their exits [KKKW18, Lemma 1]. However, this is suboptimal for Maximizer, as the goal is not reached if the game remains in the EC forever. Hence we "deflate" the upper bounds of SECs, i.e. reduce them to depend on the best exit of Maximizer. T is called maximal simple end component (MSEC), if there is no SEC T' such that $T \subsetneq T'$. Note that in MDPs, treating all MSECs amounts to treating all MECs.

Algorithm 1. Bounded value iteration algorithm for SG (and MDP)

1: **procedure** BVI(SG G, target set Goal, precision $\epsilon > 0$)
2:　　INITIALIZE_BOUNDS
3:　　**repeat**
4:　　　　$X \leftarrow$ SIMULATE *until* LOOPING or state in Goal is hit
5:　　　　UPDATE(X)　　　　　　　▷ Bellman updates or their modification
6:　　　　**for** $T \in$ FIND_MSECs(X) **do**
7:　　　　　　DEFLATE(T)　　　　　▷ Decrease the upper bound of MSECs
8:　　**until** $U(s_0) - L(s_0) < \epsilon$

Algorithm 1 rephrases that of [KKKW18] and describes the general structure of all bounded value iteration algorithms that are relevant for this paper. We discuss it here since all our improvements refer to functions (in capitalized font) in it. In the next section, we design new functions, pinpointing the difference to the other papers. The pseudocode of the functions adapted from the other papers can be found, for the reader's convenience, in [AKW19, Appendix A]. Note that to improve readability, we omit the parameters G, Goal, L and U of the functions in the algorithm.

Bounded Value Iteration: For the standard bounded value iteration algorithm, Line 4 does not run a simulation, but just assigns the whole state space S to X[5]. Then it updates all values according to the Bellman equations.

---

[5] Since we mainly talk about simulation based algorithms, we included this line to make their structure clearer.

After that it finds all the problematic components, the MSECs, and "deflates" them as described in [KKKW18], i.e. it reduces their values to ensure the convergence to the least fixpoint. This suffices for the bounds to converge and the algorithm to terminate [KKKW18, Theorem 2].

Asynchronous Bounded Value Iteration: To tackle the state space explosion problem, *asynchronous* simulation/learning-based algorithms have been developed [MLG05, BCC+14, KKKW18]. The idea is not to update and deflate all states at once, since there might be too many, or since we only have limited information. Instead of considering the whole state space, a path through the SG is sampled by picking in every state one of the actions that look optimal according to the current over-/under-approximation and then sampling a successor of that action. This is repeated until either a target is found, or until the simulation is looping in an EC; the latter case occurs if the heuristic that picks the actions generates a pair of strategies under which both players only pick staying actions in an EC. After the simulation, only the bounds of the states on the path are updated and deflated. Since we pick actions which look optimal in the simulation, we almost surely find an ϵ-optimal strategy and the algorithm terminates [BCC+14, Theorem 3].

3   Algorithm

3.1   Model-Based

Given only limited information, updating cannot be done using $\mathbb{T}$, since the true probabilities are not known. The approach of [BCC+14] is to sample for a high number of steps and accumulate the observed lower and upper bounds on the true value function for each state-action pair. When the number of samples is large enough, the average of the accumulator is used as the new estimate for the state-action pair, and thus the approximations can be improved and the results back-propagated, while giving statistical guarantees that each update was correct. However, this approach has several drawbacks, the biggest of which is that the number of steps before an update can occur is infeasibly large, often larger than the age of the universe, see Table 1 in Sect. 4.

Our improvements to make the algorithm practically usable are linked to constructing a partial model of the given system. That way, we have more information available on which we can base our estimates, and we can be less conservative when giving bounds on the possible errors. The shift from model-free to model-based learning asymptotically increases the memory requirements from $\mathcal{O}(|\mathsf{S}| \cdot |\mathsf{A}|)$ (as in [SLW+06, BCC+14]) to $\mathcal{O}(|\mathsf{S}|^2 \cdot |\mathsf{A}|)$. However, for systems where each action has a small constant bound on the number of successors, which is typical for many practical systems, e.g. classical PRISM benchmarks, it is still $\mathcal{O}(|\mathsf{S}| \cdot |\mathsf{A}|)$ with a negligible constant difference.

We thus track the number of times some successor t has been observed when playing action a from state s in a variable $\#(\mathsf{s}, \mathsf{a}, \mathsf{t})$. This implicitly induces the number of times each state-action pair (s, a) has been played $\#(\mathsf{s}, \mathsf{a}) =$

$\sum_{t \in S} \#(s, a, t)$. Given these numbers we can then calculate probability estimates for every transition as described in the next subsection. They also induce the set of all states visited so far, allowing us to construct a partial model of the game. See [AKW19, Appendix A.2] for the pseudo-code of how to count the occurrences during the simulations.

3.2 Safe Updates with Confidence Intervals Using Distributed Error Probability

We use the counters to compute a lower estimate of the transition probability for some error tolerance $\delta_{\mathbb{T}}$ as follows: We view sampling t from state-action pair (s, a) as a Bernoulli sequence, with success probability $\mathbb{T}(s, a, t)$, the number of trials $\#(s, a)$ and the number of successes $\#(s, a, t)$. The tightest lower estimate we can give using the Hoeffding bound (see [AKW19, Appendix D.1]) is

$$\widehat{\mathbb{T}}(s, a, t) := \max(0, \frac{\#(s, a, t)}{\#(s, a)} - c), \tag{1}$$

where the confidence width $c := \sqrt{\frac{\ln(\delta_{\mathbb{T}})}{-2\#(s,a)}}$. Since c could be greater than 1, we limit the lower estimate to be at least 0. Now we can give modified update equations:

$$\widehat{L}(s, a) := \sum_{t:\#(s,a,t)>0} \widehat{\mathbb{T}}(s, a, t) \cdot L(t)$$

$$\widehat{U}(s, a) := \left(\sum_{t:\#(s,a,t)>0} \widehat{\mathbb{T}}(s, a, t) \cdot U(t) \right) + \left(1 - \sum_{t:\#(s,a,t)>0} \widehat{\mathbb{T}}(s, a, t) \right)$$

The idea is the same for both upper and lower bound: In contrast to the usual Bellman equation (see Sect. 2.2) we use $\widehat{\mathbb{T}}$ instead of $\mathbb{T}$. But since the sum of all the lower estimates does not add up to one, there is some remaining probability for which we need to under-/over-approximate the value it can achieve. We use

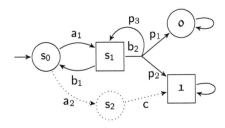

Fig. 1. A running example of an SG. The dashed part is only relevant for the later examples. For actions with only one successor, we do not depict the transition probability 1 (e.g. $\mathbb{T}(s_0, a_1, s_1)$). For state-action pair (s_1, b_2), the transition probabilities are parameterized and instantiated in the examples where they are used.

the safe approximations 0 and 1 for the lower and upper bound respectively; this is why in $\check{\mathsf{L}}$ there is no second term and in $\hat{\mathsf{U}}$ the whole remaining probability is added. Algorithm 2 shows the modified update that uses the lower estimates; the proof of its correctness is in [AKW19, Appendix D.2].

Lemma 1 (UPDATE is correct). *Given correct under- and over-approximations* L, U *of the value function* V, *and correct lower probability estimates* $\hat{\mathbb{T}}$, *the under- and over-approximations after an application of* UPDATE *are also correct.*

Algorithm 2. New update procedure using the probability estimates

---
1: **procedure** UPDATE(State set X)
2:     **for** $f \in \{\mathsf{L}, \mathsf{U}\}$ **do**   ▷ For both functions
3:        **for** $\mathsf{s} \in X \setminus$ Goal **do**   ▷ For all non-target states in the given set

4:
$$f(\mathsf{s}) = \begin{cases} \max_{\mathsf{a} \in \mathsf{Av}(\mathsf{s})} \widehat{f}(\mathsf{s}, \mathsf{a}) & \text{if } \mathsf{s} \in S_\square \\ \min_{\mathsf{a} \in \mathsf{Av}(\mathsf{s})} \widehat{f}(\mathsf{s}, \mathsf{a}) & \text{if } \mathsf{s} \in S_\bigcirc \end{cases}$$

Example 1. We illustrate how the calculation works and its huge advantage over the approach from [BCC+14] on the SG from Fig. 1. For this example, ignore the dashed part and let $\mathsf{p}_1 = \mathsf{p}_2 = 0.5$, i.e. we have no self loop, and an even chance to go to the target $\mathsf{1}$ or a sink o. Observe that hence $\mathsf{V}(\mathsf{s}_0) = \mathsf{V}(\mathsf{s}_1) = 0.5$.

Given an error tolerance of $\delta = 0.1$, the algorithm of [BCC+14] would have to sample for more than 10^9 steps before it could attempt a single update. In contrast, assume we have seen 5 samples of action b_2, where 1 of them went to $\mathsf{1}$ and 4 of them to o. Note that, in a sense, we were unlucky here, as the observed averages are very different from the actual distribution. The confidence width for $\delta_\mathbb{T} = 0.1$ and 5 samples is $\sqrt{\ln(0.1)/ - 2 \cdot 5} \approx 0.48$. So given that data, we get $\widehat{\mathbb{T}}(\mathsf{s}_1, \mathsf{b}_2, \mathsf{1}) = \max(0, 0.2 - 0.48) = 0$ and $\widehat{\mathbb{T}}(\mathsf{s}_1, \mathsf{b}_2, \mathsf{o}) = \max(0, 0.8 - 0.48) = 0.32$. Note that both probabilities are in fact lower estimates for their true counterpart.

Assume we already found out that o is a sink with value 0; how we gain this knowledge is explained in the following subsections. Then, after getting only these 5 samples, UPDATE already decreases the upper bound of $(\mathsf{s}_1, \mathsf{b}_2)$ to 0.68, as we know that at least 0.32 of $\mathbb{T}(\mathsf{s}_1, \mathsf{b}_2)$ goes to the sink.

Given 500 samples of action b_2, the confidence width of the probability estimates already has decreased below 0.05. Then, since we have this confidence width for both the upper and the lower bound, we can decrease the total precision for $(\mathsf{s}_1, \mathsf{b}_2)$ to 0.1, i.e. return an interval in the order of $[0.45; 0.55]$.   ◁

Summing up: with the model-based approach we can already start updating after very few steps and get a reasonable level of confidence with a realistic number of samples. In contrast, the state-of-the-art approach of [BCC+14] needs a very large number of samples even for this toy example.

Since for UPDATE we need an error tolerance for every transition, we need to distribute the given total error tolerance δ over all transitions in the current partial model. For all states in the explored partial model $\widehat{S}$ we know the number of available actions and can over-approximate the number of successors as $\frac{1}{p_{\min}}$. Thus the error tolerance for each transition can be set to $\delta_{\mathbb{T}} := \frac{\delta \cdot p_{\min}}{|\{a \mid s \in \widehat{S} \wedge a \in Av(s)\}|}$. This is illustrated in Example 4 in [AKW19, Appendix B].

Note that the fact that the error tolerance $\delta_{\mathbb{T}}$ for every transition is the same does *not* imply that the confidence width for every transition is the same, as the latter becomes smaller with increasing number of samples $\#(s, a)$.

3.3   Improved EC Detection

As mentioned in the description of Algorithm 1, we must detect when the simulation is stuck in a bottom EC and looping forever. However, we may also stop simulations that are looping in some EC but still have a possibility to leave it; for a discussion of different heuristics from [BCC+14, KKKW18], see [AKW19, Appendix A.3].

We choose to define LOOPING as follows: Given a candidate for a bottom EC, we continue sampling until we are $\delta_{\mathbb{T}}$-*sure* (i.e. the error probability is smaller than $\delta_{\mathbb{T}}$) that we cannot leave it. Then we can safely deflate the EC, i.e. decrease all upper bounds to zero.

To detect that something is a $\delta_{\mathbb{T}}$-*sure* EC, we do not sample for the astronomical number of steps as in [BCC+14], but rather extend the approach to detect bottom strongly connected components from [DHKP16]. If in the EC-candidate T there was some state-action pair (s, a) that actually has a probability to exit the T, that probability is at least $p_{\min}$. So after sampling (s, a) for n times, the probability to overlook such a leaving transition is $(1 - p_{\min})^n$ and it should be smaller than $\delta_{\mathbb{T}}$. Solving the inequation for the required number of samples n yields $n \geq \frac{\ln(\delta_{\mathbb{T}})}{\ln(1 - p_{\min})}$.

Algorithm 3 checks that we have seen all staying state-action pairs n times, and hence that we are $\delta_{\mathbb{T}}$-*sure* that T is an EC. Note that we restrict to staying state-action pairs, since the requirement for an EC is only that there exist staying actions, not that all actions stay. We further speed up the EC-detection, because we do not wait for n samples in every simulation, but we use the aggregated counters that are kept over all simulations.

Algorithm 3. Check whether we are $\delta_{\mathbb{T}}$-*sure* that T is an EC

1: **procedure** $\delta_{\mathbb{T}}$-*sure* EC (State set T)

2:   $requiredSamples = \frac{\ln(\delta_{\mathbb{T}})}{\ln(1 - p_{\min})}$

3:   $B \leftarrow \{(s, a) \mid s \in T \wedge \neg(s, a) \text{ exits } T\}$ ▷ Set of staying state-action pairs

4:   **return** $\bigwedge_{(s,a) \in B} \#(s, a) > requiredSamples$

We stop a simulation, if LOOPING returns true, i.e. under the following three conditions: (i) We have seen the current state before in this simulation ($s \in X$), i.e. there is a cycle. (ii) This cycle is explainable by an EC T in our current partial model. (iii) We are $\delta_{\mathbb{T}}$-*sure* that T is an EC.

Algorithm 4. Check if we are probably looping and should stop the simulation

---
1: **procedure** LOOPING(State set X, state s)
2: **if** s $\notin X$ **then**
3:   **return false**   ▷ Easy improvement to avoid overhead
4: **return** $\exists T \subseteq X.T$ is EC in partial model $\wedge$ s $\in T \wedge \delta_{\mathbb{T}}$-*sure* EC$(T)$

Example 2. For this example, we again use the SG from Fig. 1 without the dashed part, but this time with $p_1 = p_2 = p_3 = \frac{1}{3}$. Assume the path we simulated is $(s_0, a_1, s_1, b_2, s_1)$, i.e. we sampled the self-loop of action b_2. Then $\{s_1\}$ is a candidate for an EC, because given our current observation it seems possible that we will continue looping there forever. However, we do not stop the simulation here, because we are not yet $\delta_{\mathbb{T}}$-*sure* about this. Given $\delta_{\mathbb{T}} = 0.1$, the required samples for that are 6, since $\frac{\ln(0.1)}{\ln(1-\frac{1}{3})} = 5.6$. With high probability (greater than $(1 - \delta_{\mathbb{T}}) = 0.9$), within these 6 steps we will sample one of the other successors of (s_1, b_2) and thus realise that we should not stop the simulation in s_1. If, on the other hand, we are in state o or if in state s_1 the guiding heuristic only picks b_1, then we are in fact looping for more than 6 steps, and hence we stop the simulation.   ◁

3.4 Adapting to Games: Deflating MSECs

To extend the algorithm of [BCC+14] to SGs, instead of collapsing problematic ECs we deflate them as in [KKKW18], i.e. given an MSEC, we reduce the upper bound of all states in it to the upper bound of the bestExit of Maximizer. In contrast to [KKKW18], we cannot use the upper bound of the bestExit based on the true probability, but only based on our estimates. Algorithm 5 shows how to deflate an MSEC and highlights the difference, namely that we use $\widehat{U}$ instead of U.

Algorithm 5. Black box algorithm to deflate a set of states

1: **procedure** DEFLATE(State set X)
2: **for** s $\in X$ **do**
3:   U(s) = min(U(s), bestExit(X, $\widehat{U}$)

The remaining question is how to find MSECs. The approach of [KKKW18] is to find MSECs by removing the suboptimal actions of Minimizer according to the current lower bound. Since it converges to the true value function, all

MSECs are eventually found [KKKW18, Lemma 2]. Since Algorithm 6 can only access the SG as a black box, there are two differences: We can only compare our estimates of the lower bound $\widehat{L}(s, a)$ to find out which actions are suboptimal. Additionally there is the problem that we might overlook an exit from an EC, and hence deflate to some value that is too small; thus we need to check that any state set FIND_MSECs returns is a δ_T-*sure* EC. This is illustrated in Example 3. For a bigger example of how all our functions work together, see Example 5 in [AKW19, Appendix B].

Algorithm 6. Finding MSECs in the game restricted to X for black box setting

---

1: **procedure** FIND_MSECs(State set X)
2:     $suboptAct_\bigcirc \leftarrow \{(s, \{a \in Av(s) \mid \widehat{L}\,(s,a) > L(s)\} \mid s \in S_\bigcirc \cap X\}$
3:     $Av' \leftarrow Av$ without $suboptAct_\bigcirc$
4:     $G' \leftarrow G$ restricted to states X and available actions Av'
5:     **return** $\{T \in MEC(G') \mid \delta_T\text{-}sure\ EC(T)\ \}$

Example 3. For this example, we use the full SG from Fig. 1, including the dashed part, with $p_1, p_2 > 0$. Let $(s_0, a_1, s_1, b_2, s_2, b_1, s_1, a_2, s_2, c, 1)$ be the path generated by our simulation. Then in our partial view of the model, it seems as if $T = \{s_0, s_1\}$ is an MSEC, since using a_2 is suboptimal for the minimizing state s_0[6] and according to our current knowledge a_1, b_1 and b_2 all stay inside T. If we deflated T now, all states would get an upper bound of 0, which would be incorrect.

Thus in Algorithm 6 we need to require that T is an EC δ_T-*surely*. This was not satisfied in the example, as the state-action pairs have not been observed the required number of times. Thus we do not deflate T, and our upper bounds stay correct. Having seen (s_1, b_2) the required number of times, we probably know that it is exiting T and hence will not make the mistake.   ◁

3.5 Guidance and Statistical Guarantee

It is difficult to give statistical guarantees for the algorithm we have developed so far (i.e. Algorithm 1 calling the new functions from Sects. 3.2, 3.3 and 3.4). Although we can bound the error of each function, applying them repeatedly can add up the error. Algorithm 7 shows our approach to get statistical guarantees: It interleaves a guided simulation phase (Lines 7–10) with a guaranteed standard bounded value iteration (called BVI phase) that uses our new functions (Lines 11–16).

The simulation phase builds the partial model by exploring states and remembering the counters. In the first iteration of the main loop, it chooses actions randomly. In all further iterations, it is guided by the bounds that the last BVI

---

[6] For $\delta_T = 0.2$, sampling the path to target once suffices to realize that $L(s_0, a_2) > 0$.

phase computed. After $\mathcal{N}_k$ simulations (see below for a discussion of how to choose $\mathcal{N}_k$), all the gathered information is used to compute one version of the partial model with probability estimates $\widehat{\mathbb{T}}$ for a certain error tolerance δ_k. We can continue with the assumption, that these probability estimates are correct, since it is only violated with a probability smaller than our error tolerance (see below for an explanation of the choice of δ_k). So in our correct partial model, we re-initialize the lower and upper bound (Line 12), and execute a guaranteed standard BVI. If the simulation phase already gathered enough data, i.e. explored the relevant states and sampled the relevant transitions often enough, this BVI achieves a precision smaller than ε in the initial state, and the algorithm terminates. Otherwise we start another simulation phase that is guided by the improved bounds.

Algorithm 7. Full algorithm for black box setting

1: **procedure** BLACKVI(SG G, target set Goal, precision $\varepsilon > 0$, error tolerance $\delta > 0$)
2:     INITIALIZE_BOUNDS
3:     $k = 1$ $\triangleright$ guaranteed BVI counter
4:     $\widehat{S} \leftarrow \emptyset$ $\triangleright$ current partial model

5:     **repeat**
6:         $k \leftarrow 2 \cdot k$
7:         $\delta_k \leftarrow \frac{\delta}{k}$

    // Guided simulation phase
8:         **for** $\mathcal{N}_k$ times **do**
9:             $X \leftarrow$ SIMULATE
10:             $\widehat{S} \leftarrow \widehat{S} \cup X$

    // Guaranteed BVI phase
11:         $\delta_{\mathbb{T}} \leftarrow \frac{\delta_k \cdot p_{\min}}{\left|\{a \mid s \in \widehat{S} \wedge a \in Av(s)\}\right|}$ $\triangleright$ Set $\delta_{\mathbb{T}}$ as described in Section 3.2
12:         INITIALIZE_BOUNDS
13:         **for** $k \cdot \left|\widehat{S}\right|$ times **do**
14:             UPDATE($\widehat{S}$)
15:             **for** $T \in$ FIND_MSECs($\widehat{S}$) **do**
16:                 DEFLATE(T)
17:     **until** $U(s_0) - L(s_0) < \varepsilon$

Choice of δ_k: For each of the full BVI phases, we construct a partial model that is correct with probability $(1 - \delta_k)$. To ensure that the sum of these errors is not larger than the specified error tolerance δ, we use the variable k, which is initialised to 1 and doubled in every iteration of the main loop. Hence for the i-th BVI, $k = 2^i$. By setting $\delta_k = \frac{\delta}{k}$, we get that $\sum_{i=1}^{\infty} \delta_k = \sum_{i=1}^{\infty} \frac{\delta}{2^i} = \delta$, and hence the error of all BVI phases does not exceed the specified error tolerance.

When to Stop Each BVI-Phase: The BVI phase might not converge if the probability estimates are not good enough. We increase the number of iterations for each BVI depending on k, because that way we ensure that it eventually is allowed to run long enough to converge. On the other hand, since we always run for finitely many iterations, we also ensure that, if we do not have enough information yet, BVI is eventually stopped. Other stopping criteria could return arbitrarily imprecise results [HM17]. We also multiply with $|\widehat{S}|$ to improve the chances of the early BVIs to converge, as that number of iterations ensures that every value has been propagated through the whole model at least once.

Discussion of the Choice of $\mathcal{N}_k$: The number of simulations between the guaranteed BVI phases can be chosen freely; it can be a constant number every time, or any sequence of natural numbers, possibly parameterised by e.g. k, $|\widehat{S}|$, ε or any of the parameters of G. The design of particularly efficient choices or learning mechanisms that adjust them on the fly is an interesting task left for future work. We conjecture the answer depends on the given SG and "task" that the user has for the algorithm: E.g. if one just needs a quick general estimate of the behaviour of the model, a smaller choice of $\mathcal{N}_k$ is sensible; if on the other hand a definite precision ε certainly needs to be achieved, a larger choice of $\mathcal{N}_k$ is required.

Theorem 1. *For any choice of sequence for $\mathcal{N}_k$, Algorithm 7 is an anytime algorithm with the following property: When it is stopped, it returns an interval for $\mathsf{V}(\mathsf{s}_0)$ that is PAC^7 for the given error tolerance δ and some ε', with $0 \leq \varepsilon' \leq 1$.*

Theorem 1 is the foundation of the practical usability of our algorithm. Given some time frame and some $\mathcal{N}_k$, it calculates an approximation for $\mathsf{V}(\mathsf{s}_0)$ that is probably correct. Note that the precision ε' is independent of the input parameter ε, and could in the worst case be always 1. However, practically it often is good (i.e. close to 0) as seen in the results in Sect. 4. Moreover, in our modified algorithm, we can also give a convergence guarantee as in [BCC+14]. Although mostly out of theoretical interest, in [AKW19, Appendix D.4] we design such a sequence $\mathcal{N}_k$, too. Since this a-priori sequence has to work in the worst case, it depends on an infeasibly large number of simulations.

Theorem 2. *There exists a choice of $\mathcal{N}_k$, such that Algorithm 7 is PAC for any input parameters ε, δ, i.e. it terminates almost surely and returns an interval for $\mathsf{V}(\mathsf{s}_0)$ of width smaller than ε that is correct with probability at least $1 - \delta$.*

---

[7] Probably Approximately Correct, i.e. with probability greater than $1 - \delta$, the value lies in the returned interval of width ε'.

3.6   Utilizing the Additional Information of Grey Box Input

In this section, we consider the grey box setting, i.e. for every state-action pair (s, a) we additionally know the exact number of successors $|Post(s, a)|$. Then we can sample every state-action pair until we have seen all successors, and hence this information amounts to having qualitative information about the transitions, i.e. knowing where the transitions go, but not with which probability.

In that setting, we can improve the EC-detection and the estimated bounds in UPDATE. For EC-detection, note that the whole point of $\delta_{\mathbb{T}}$-*sure* EC is to check whether there are further transitions available; in grey box, we know this and need not depend on statistics. For the bounds, note that the equations for $\hat{L}$ and $\hat{U}$ both have two parts: The usual Bellman part and the remaining probability multiplied with the most conservative guess of the bound, i.e. 0 and 1. If we know all successors of a state-action pair, we do not have to be as conservative; then we can use $\min_{t \in Post(s,a)} L(t)$ respectively $\max_{t \in Post(s,a)} U(t)$. Both these improvements have huge impact, as demonstrated in Sect. 4. However, of course, they also assume more knowledge about the model.

4   Experimental Evaluation

We implemented the approach as an extension of PRISM-Games [CFK+13a]. 11 MDPs with reachability properties were selected from the Quantitative Verification Benchmark Set [HKP+19]. Further, 4 stochastic games benchmarks from [CKJ12, SS12, CFK+13b, CKPS11] were also selected. We ran the experiments on a 40 core Intel Xeon server running at 2.20 GHz per core and having 252 GB of RAM. The tool however utilised only a single core and 1 GB of memory for the model checking. Each benchmark was ran 10 times with a timeout of 30 min. We ran two versions of Algorithm 7, one with the SG as a black box, the other as a grey box (see Definition 2). We chose $\mathcal{N}_k = 10,000$ for all iterations. The tool stopped either when a precision of 10^{-8} was obtained or after 30 min. In total, 16 different model-property combinations were tried out. The results of the experiment are reported in Table 1.

In the black box setting, we obtained $\varepsilon < 0.1$ on 6 of the benchmarks. 5 benchmarks were 'hard' and the algorithm did not improve the precision below 1. For 4 of them, it did not even finish the first simulation phase. If we decrease $\mathcal{N}_k$, the BVI phase is entered, but still no progress is made.

In the grey box setting, on 14 of 16 benchmarks, it took only 6 min to achieve $\varepsilon < 0.1$. For 8 these, the exact value was found within that time. Less than 50% of the state space was explored in the case of pacman, pneuli-zuck-3, rabin-3, zeroconf and cloud_5. A precision of $\varepsilon < 0.01$ was achieved on 15/16 benchmarks over a period of 30 min.

Table 1. Achieved precision ε' given by our algorithm in both grey and black box settings after running for a period of 30 min (See the paragraph below Theorem 1 for why we use ε' and not ε). The first set of the models are MDPs and the second set are SGs. '-' indicates that the algorithm did not finish the first simulation phase and hence partial BVI was not called. m is the number of steps required by the DQL algorithm of [BCC+14] before the first update. As this number is very large, we report only $log_{10}(m)$. For comparison, note that the age of the universe is approximately 10^{26} ns; logarithm of number of steps doable in this time is thus in the order of 26.

Model	States	Explored % Grey/Black	Precision Grey	Black	$log_{10}(m)$
consensus	272	100/100	0.00945	0.171	338
csma-2-2	1,038	93/93	0.00127	0.2851	1,888
firewire	83,153	55/-	0.0057	1	129,430
ij-3	7	100/100	0	0.0017	2,675
ij-10	1,023	100/100	0	0.5407	17
pacman	498	18/47	0.00058	0.0086	1,801
philosophers-3	956	56/21	0	1	2,068
pnueli-zuck-3	2,701	25/71	0	0.0285	5,844
rabin-3	27,766	7/4	0	0.026	110,097
wlan-0	2,954	100/100	0	0.8667	9,947
zeroconf	670	29/27	0.00007	0.0586	5,998
cdmsn	1,240	100/98	0	0.8588	3,807
cloud-5	8,842	49/20	0.00031	0.0487	71,484
mdsm-1	62,245	69/-	0.09625	1	182,517
mdsm-2	62,245	72/-	0.00055	1	182,517
team-form-3	12,476	64/-	0	1	54,095

Figure 2 shows the evolution of the lower and upper bounds in both the grey- and the black box settings for 4 different models. Graphs for the other models as well as more details on the results are in [AKW19, Appendix C].

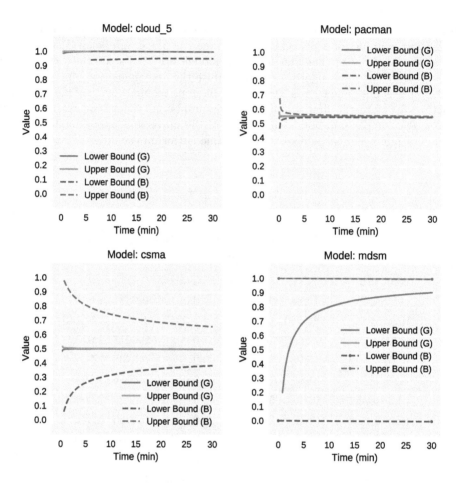

Fig. 2. Performance of our algorithm on various MDP and SG benchmarks in grey and black box settings. Solid lines denote the bounds in the grey box setting while dashed lines denote the bounds in the black box setting. The plotted bounds are obtained after each partial BVI phase, because of which they do not start at $[0, 1]$ and not at time 0. Graphs of the remaining benchmarks may be found in [AKW19, Appendix C].

5   Conclusion

We presented a PAC SMC algorithm for SG (and MDP) with the reachability objective. It is the first one for SG and the first practically applicable one. Nevertheless, there are several possible directions for further improvements. For instance, one can consider different sequences for lengths of the simulation phases, possibly also dependent on the behaviour observed so far. Further, the error tolerance could be distributed in a non-uniform way, allowing for fewer visits in rarely visited parts of end components. Since many systems are strongly connected, but at the same time feature some infrequent behaviour, this is the next bottleneck to be attacked. [KM19]

References

1. Ashok, P., Křetínský, J.: Maximilian Weininger. PAC statistical model checking for markov decision processes and stochastic games. Technical Report arXiv.org/abs/1905.04403 (2019)

2. Basu, A., Bensalem, S., Bozga, M., Caillaud, B., Delahaye, B., Legay, A.: Statistical abstraction and model-checking of large heterogeneous sys-tems. In: Hatcliff, J., Zucca, E. (eds.) FMOODS/FORTE 2010. LNCS, vol. 6117, pp. 32–46. Springer, Heidelberg (2010). https://doi.org/10. 1007/978-3-642-13464-7_4

3. Brázdil, T., et al.: Verification of markov decision processes using learning algorithms. In: Cassez, F., Raskin, J.-F. (eds.) ATVA 2014. LNCS, vol. 8837, pp. 98–114. Springer, Cham (2014). https://doi.org/10.1007/978- 3-319-11936-6_8

4. Boyer, B., Corre, K., Legay, A., Sedwards, S.: PLASMA-lab: a flexi-ble, distributable statistical model checking library. In: Joshi, K., Siegle, M., Stoelinga, M., DArgenio, P.R. (eds.) QEST 2013. LNCS, vol. 8054, pp. 160–164. Springer, Heidelberg (2013). https://doi.org/10.1007/978- 3-642-40196-1 12

5. Bulychev, P.E., et al.: UPPAAL-SMC: statistical model checking for priced timed automata. In: QAPL (2012)

6. Bogdoll, J., Ferrer Fioriti, L.M., Hartmanns, A., Hermanns, H.: Partial order methods for statistical model checking and simulation. In: Bruni, R., Dingel, J. (eds.) FMOODS/FORTE 2011. LNCS, vol. 6722, pp. 59–74. Springer, Heidelberg (2011). https://doi.org/10.1007/978-3-642-21461- 5_4

7. Bogdoll, J., Hartmanns, A., Hermanns, H.: Simulation and statistical model checking for modestly nondeterministic models. In: Schmitt, J.B.(ed.) MMB&DFT 2012. LNCS, vol. 7201, pp. 249–252. Springer, Heidel-berg (2012). https://doi.org/10.1007/978-3-642-28540-0_20

8. Baier, C., Katoen, J.-P.: Principles of Model Checking. MIT Press (2008). ISBN 978-0-262-02649-9

9. Brafman, R.I., Tennenholtz, M.: A near-optimal poly-time algorithm for learning a class of stochastic games. In: IJCAI, pp. 734–739 (1999)

10. Chen, T., Forejt, V., Kwiatkowska, M., Parker, D., Simaitis, A.: PRISM-games: a model checker for stochastic multi-player games. In: Piterman, N., Smolka, S.A. (eds.) TACAS 2013. LNCS, vol. 7795, pp. 185–191. Springer, Heidelberg (2013). https://doi.org/10.1007/978-3-642-36742- 7_13

11. Chen, T., Forejt, V., Kwiatkowska, M., Parker, D., Simaitis, A.: Auto-matic verification of competitive stochastic systems. Formal Meth. Syst. Des. **43**(1), 61–92 (2013)

12. Chatterjee, K., Henzinger, T.A.: Value iteration. In: Grumberg, O., Veith, H. (eds.) 25 Years of Model Checking. LNCS, vol. 5000, pp. 107–138. Springer, Heidelberg (2008). https://doi.org/10.1007/978-3-540-69850- 0_7

13. Chatterjee, K., Henzinger, T.A.: A survey of stochastic ω-regular games. J. Comput. Syst. Sci. **78**(2), 394–413 (2012)

14. Calinescu, R., Kikuchi, S., Johnson, K.: Compositional reverification of probabilistic safety properties for large-scale complex IT systems. In: Calinescu, R., Garlan, D. (eds.) Monterey Workshop 2012. LNCS, vol. 7539, pp. 303–329. Springer, Heidelberg (2012). https://doi.org/10.1007/ 978-3-642-34059-8_16

15. Chen, T., Kwiatkowska, M., Parker, D., Simaitis, A.: Verifying team for-mation protocols with probabilistic model checking. In: Leite, J., Torroni, P., A°gotnes, T., Boella, G., van der Torre, L. (eds.) CLIMA 2011. LNCS (LNAI), vol. 6814, pp. 190–207. Springer, Heidelberg (2011). https://doi. org/10.1007/978-3-642-22359-4 14

16. Condon, A.: The complexity of stochastic games. Inf. Comput. **96**(2), 203–224 (1992)

17. Clarke, E.M., Zuliani, P.: Statistical model checking for cyber-physical systems. In: ATVA, pp. 1–12 (2011)

18. David, A., et al.: Statistical model checking for stochastic hybrid systems. In: HSB, pp. 122–136 (2012)

19. David, A., Du, D., Guldstrand Larsen, K., Legay, A., Mikučionis, M.: Optimiz-ing control strategy using statistical model checking. In: Brat, G., Rungta, N., Venet, A. (eds.) NFM 2013. LNCS, vol. 7871, pp. 352–367. Springer, Heidelberg (2013). https://doi.org/10.1007/978-3-642-38088- 4 24

20. Daca, P., Henzinger, T.A., Křetínský, J.,Petrov,T.:Faster statisti-cal model check-ing for unbounded temporal properties. In: Chechik, M., Raskin, J.-F. (eds.) TA-CAS 2016. LNCS, vol. 9636, pp. 112–129. Springer, Heidelberg (2016). https://doi.org/10.1007/978-3-662-49674- 9 7

21. D'Argenio, P.R., Hartmanns, A., Sedwards, S.: Lightweight statistical model checking in nondeterministic continuous time. In: Margaria, T., Steffen, B. (eds.) ISoLA 2018. LNCS, vol. 11245, pp. 336–353. Springer, Cham (2018). https://doi. org/10.1007/978-3-030-03421-4 22

22. David, A., et al.: Statistical model checking for networks of priced timed autom-ata. In: Fahrenberg, U., Tripakis, S. (eds.) FORMATS 2011. LNCS, vol. 6919, pp. 80–96. Springer, Heidelberg (2011). https://doi.org/10. 1007/978-3-642-24310-3 7

23. David, A., Larsen, K.G., Legay, A., Mikučionis, M., Wang, Z.: Time for statistical model checking of real-time systems. In: Gopalakrishnan, G., Qadeer, S. (eds.) CAV 2011. LNCS, vol. 6806, pp. 349–355. Springer, Heidelberg (2011). https://doi.org/10.1007/978-3-642-22110-1 27

24. D'Argenio, P., Legay, A., Sedwards, S., Traonouez, L.-M.: Smart sampling for lightweight verification of markov decision processes. STTT **17**(4), 469–484 (2015)

25. Ellen, C., Gerwinn, S., Fr¨anzle, M.: Confidence bounds for statisti-cal model checking of probabilistic hybrid systems. In: Jurdziński, M., Ničković, D. (eds.) FORMATS 2012. LNCS, vol. 7595, pp. 123–138. Springer, Heidelberg (2012). https://doi.org/10.1007/978-3-642-33365- 1 10

26. Fu, J., Topcu, U.: Probably approximately correct MDP learning and control with temporal logic constraints. In: Robotics: Science and Sys-tems (2014)

27. Hasanbeig, M., Abate, A., Kroening, D.: Logically-correct reinforcement learn-ing. CoRR, 1801.08099 (2018)

28. Hasanbeig, M., Abate, A., Kroening, D.: Certified reinforcement learning with logic guidance. CoRR, abs/1902.00778 (2019)

29. He, R., Jennings, P., Basu, S., Ghosh, A.P., Wu, H.: A bounded statistical ap-proach for model checking of unbounded until properties. In: ASE, pp. 225–234 (2010)

30. Hartmanns, A., Klauck, M., Parker, D., Quatmann, T., Ruijters, E.: The quantitative verification benchmark set. In: TACAS 2019 (2019, to appear)

31. Hérault, T., Lassaigne, R., Magniette, F., Peyronnet, S.: Approximate probabilistic model checking. In: Steffen, B., Levi, G. (eds.) VMCAI 2004. LNCS, vol. 2937, pp. 73–84. Springer, Heidelberg (2004). https://doi.org/ 10.1007/978-3-540-24622-0_8

32. Haddad, S., Monmege, B.: Interval iteration algorithm for MDPs and IMDPs. Theor. Comput. Sci. (2017)

33. Henriques, D., Martins, J., Zuliani, P., Platzer, A., Clarke, E.M.: Statis-tical model checking for Markov decision processes. In: QEST, pp. 84–93 (2012)

34. Hahn, E.M., Perez, M., Schewe, S., Somenzi, F., Trivedi, A., Wojtczak, D.: Omega-regular objectives in model-free reinforcement learning. In: Vojnar, T., Zhang, L. (eds.) TACAS 2019. LNCS, vol. 11427, pp. 395–412. Springer, Cham (2019). https://doi.org/10.1007/978-3-030-17462- 0_27

35. Jha, S.K., Clarke, E.M., Langmead, C.J., Legay, A., Platzer, A., Zuliani, P.: A bayesian approach to model checking biological systems. In: Degano, P., Gorrieri, R. (eds.) CMSB 2009. LNCS, vol. 5688, pp. 218–234. Springer, Heidelberg (2009). https://doi.org/10.1007/978-3-642-03845- 7_15

36. Jegourel, C., Legay, A., Sedwards, S.: A platform for high performance statistical model checking – PLASMA. In: Flanagan, C., K¨onig, B. (eds.) TACAS 2012. LNCS, vol. 7214, pp. 498–503. Springer, Heidelberg (2012). https://doi.org/10.1007/978-3-642-28756-5_37

37. Kelmendi, E., Kr¨amer, J., Křetínský, J., Weininger, M.: Value iteration for simple stochastic games: stopping criterion and learning algorithm. In: Chockler, H., Weissenbacher, G. (eds.) CAV 2018. LNCS, vol. 10981, pp. 623–642. Springer, Cham (2018). https://doi.org/10.1007/978-3-319- 96145-3_36

38. Křetínský, J., Meggendorfer, T.: Of cores: a partial-exploration frame-work for Markov decision processes. Submitted 2019

39. Kwiatkowska, M., Norman, G., Parker, D.: PRISM 4.0: verification of probabilistic real-time systems. In: Gopalakrishnan, G., Qadeer, S. (eds.) CAV 2011. LNCS, vol. 6806, pp. 585–591. Springer, Heidelberg (2011). https://doi.org/10.1007/978-3-642-22110-1_47

40. Larsen, K.G.: Statistical model checking, refinement checking, optimiza-tion,. for stochastic hybrid systems. In: Jurdzi´nski, M., Niˇckovi´c, D. (eds.) FORMATS 2012. LNCS, vol. 7595, pp. 7–10. Springer, Heidelberg (2012). https://doi.org/10.1007/978-3-642-33365-1_2

41. Guldstrand Larsen, K.: Priced timed automata and statistical model checking. In: Johnsen, E.B., Petre, L. (eds.) IFM 2013. LNCS, vol. 7940, pp. 154–161. Springer, Heidelberg (2013). https://doi.org/10.1007/978- 3-642-38613-8_11

42. Littman, M.L.: Markov games as a framework for multiagent reinforcement learning. In: ICML, pp. 157–163 (1994)

43. Lakshmivarahan, S., Narendra, K.S.: Learning algorithms for two-person ze-rosum stochastic games with incomplete information. Math. Oper. Res. **6**(3), 379–386 (1981)

44. Lassaigne, R., Peyronnet, S.: Probabilistic verification and approximation. Ann. Pure Appl. Logic **152**(1–3), 122–131 (2008)

45. Lassaigne, R., Peyronnet, S.: Approximate planning and verification for large Markov decision processes. In: SAC, pp. 1314–1319, (2012)

46. Legay, A., Sedwards, S., Traonouez, L.-M.: Scalable verification of markov decision processes. In: Canal, C., Idani, A. (eds.) SEFM 2014. LNCS, vol. 8938, pp. 350–362. Springer, Cham (2015). https://doi.org/10.1007/978-3-319-15201-1_23

47. Martin, D.A.: Borel determinacy. Ann. Math. **102**(2), 363–371 (1975) Mcmahan, H.B., Likhachev, M., Gordon, G.J.: Bounded real-time dynamic programming: RTDP with monotone upper bounds and performance guarantees. In: In ICML 2005, pp. 569–576 (2005)

48. Norris, J.R.: Markov Chains. Cambridge University Press, Cambridge (1998)

49. Palaniappan, S.K., Gyori, B.M., Liu, B., Hsu, D., Thiagarajan, P.S.: Statistical model checking based calibration and analysis of bio-pathway models. In: Gupta, A., Henzinger, T.A. (eds.) CMSB 2013. LNCS, vol. 8130, pp. 120–134. Springer, Heidelberg (2013). https://doi.org/10.1007/978-3-642-40708-6_10

50. Puterman, M.L.: Markov Decision Processes: Discrete Stochastic Dynamic Programming. Wiley, Hoboken (2014)

51. Raghavan, T.E.S., Filar, J.A.: Algorithms for stochastic games – a survey. Z. Oper. Res. **35**(6), 437–472 (1991)

52. El Rabih, D., Pekergin, N.: Statistical model checking using perfect sim-ulation. In: Liu, Z., Ravn, A.P. (eds.) ATVA 2009. LNCS, vol. 5799, pp. 120–134. Springer, Heidelberg (2009). https://doi.org/10.1007/978-3-642-04761-9_11

53. Sutton, R., Barto, A.: Reinforcement Learning: An Introduction. MIT Press, Cambridge (1998)

54. Sadigh, D., Kim, E.S., Coogan, S., Sastry, S.S.S., Sanjit, A.: A learn-ing based approach to control synthesis of markov decision processes for linear temporal logic specifications. In: CDC, pp. 1091–1096 (2014)

55. Strehl, A.L., Li, L., Wiewiora, E., Langford, J., Littman, M.L.: PAC model-free reinforcement learning. In: ICML, pp. 881–888 (2006)

56. Saffre, F., Simaitis, A.: Host selection through collective decision. ACM Trans. Auton. Adapt. Syst. **7**(1), 4:1–4:16 (2012)

57. Sen, K., Viswanathan, M., Agha, G.: Statistical model checking of black-box probabilistic systems. In: Alur, R., Peled, D.A. (eds.) CAV 2004. LNCS, vol. 3114, pp. 202–215. Springer, Heidelberg (2004). https://doi. org/10.1007/978-3-540-27813-9_16

58. Sen, K., Viswanathan, M., Agha, G.: On statistical model checking of stochastic systems. In: Etessami, K., Rajamani, S.K. (eds.) CAV 2005. LNCS, vol. 3576, pp. 266–280. Springer, Heidelberg (2005). https://doi. org/10.1007/11513988_26

59. Wen, M., Topcu, U.: Probably approximately correct learning in stochas-tic games with temporal logic specifications. In: IJCAI, pp. 3630–3636 (2016)

60. Younes, H.L.S., Clarke, E.M., Zuliani, P.: Statistical verification of prob-abilistic properties with unbounded until. In: Davies, J., Silva, L., Simao, A. (eds.) SBMF 2010. LNCS, vol. 6527, pp. 144–160. Springer, Heidelberg (2011). https://doi. org/10.1007/978-3-642-19829-8_10

61. Younes, H.L.S., Kwiatkowska, M.Z., Norman, G., Parker, D.: Numerical vs. statistical probabilistic model checking. STTT **8**(3), 216–228 (2006)

62. Younes, H.L.S., Simmons, R.G.: Probabilistic verification of discrete event systems using acceptance sampling. In: Brinksma, E., Larsen, K.G.(eds.) CAV 2002. LNCS, vol. 2404, pp. 223–235. Springer, Heidelberg (2002). https://doi.org/10.1007/3-540-45657-0_17

63. Zuliani, P., Platzer, A., Clarke, E.M.: Bayesian statistical model checking with application to simulink/stateflow verification. In: HSCC, pp. 243–252 (2010)

6

Synthesizing Approximate Implementations for Unrealizable Specifications

Rayna Dimitrova[1], Bernd Finkbeiner[2], and Hazem Torfah[2(✉)]

[1] University of Leicester, Leicester, UK
[2] Saarland University, Saarbrücken, Germany
torfah@react.uni-saarland.de

Abstract. The unrealizability of a specification is often due to the assumption that the behavior of the environment is unrestricted. In this paper, we present algorithms for synthesis in bounded environments, where the environment can only generate input sequences that are ultimately periodic words (lassos) with finite representations of bounded size. We provide automata-theoretic and symbolic approaches for solving this synthesis problem, and also study the synthesis of approximative implementations from unrealizable specifications. Such implementations may violate the specification in general, but are guaranteed to satisfy the specification on at least a specified portion of the bounded-size lassos. We evaluate the algorithms on different arbiter specifications.

1 Introduction

The objective of reactive synthesis is to automatically construct an implementation of a reactive system from a high-level specification of its desired behaviour. While this idea holds a great promise, applying synthesis in practice often faces significant challenges. One of the main hurdles is that the system designer has to provide the right formal specification, which is often a difficult task [12]. In particular, since the system being synthesized is required to satisfy its requirements against all possible environments allowed by the specification, accurately capturing the designer's knowledge about the environment in which the system will execute is crucial for being able to successfully synthesize an implementation.

Traditionally, environment assumptions are included in the specification, usually given as a temporal logic formula. There are, however less explored ways of incorporating information about the environment, one of which is to consider a *bound on the size of the environment*, that is, a bound on the size of the state space of a transition system that describes the possible environment behaviours. Restricting the space of possible environments can render an unrealizable specification into a realizable one. The temporal synthesis under such bounded environments was first studied in [6], where the authors extensively study the problem, in several versions, from the complexity-theoretic point of view.

In this paper, we follow a similar avenue of providing environment assumptions. However, instead of bounding the size of the state space of the environment, we associate a bound with the sequences of values of input signals produced by the environment. The infinite input sequences produced by a finite-state environment which interacts with a finite state system are ultimately periodic, and thus, each such infinite sequence $\sigma \in \Sigma_I^\omega$, over the input alphabet Σ_I, can be represented as a *lasso*, which is a pair (u, v) of finite words $u \in \Sigma_I^*$ and $v \in \Sigma_I^+$, such that $\sigma = u \cdot v^\omega$. It is the length of such sequences that we consider a bound on. More precisely, given a bound $k \in \mathbb{N}$, we consider the language of all infinite sequences of inputs that can be represented by a lasso (u, v) with $|u \cdot v| = k$. The goal of the *synthesis of lasso precise implementations* is then to synthesize a system for which each execution resulting from a sequence of environment inputs in that language, satisfies a given linear temporal specification.

As an example, consider an arbiter serving two client processes. Each client issues a request when it wants to access a shared resource, and keeps the request signal up until it is done using the resource. The goal of the arbiter is to ensure the classical mutual exclusion property, by not granting access to the two clients simultaneously. The arbiter has to also ensure that each client request is eventually granted. This, however, is difficult since, first, a client might gain access to the resource and never lower the request signal, and second, the arbiter is not allowed to take away a grant unless the request has been set to false, or the client never sets the request to false in the future (the client has become unresponsive). The last two requirements together make the specification unrealizable, as the arbiter has no way of determining if a client has become unresponsive, or will lower the request signal in the future. If, however, the length of the lassos of the input sequences is bounded, then, after a sufficient number of steps, the arbiter can assume that if the request has not been set to false, then it will not be lowered in the future either, as the sequence of inputs must already have run at least once through it's period that will be ultimately repeated from that point on.

Formally, we can express the requirements on the arbiter in Linear Temporal Logic (LTL) as follows. There is one input variable r_i (for *request*) and one output variable g_i (for *grant*) associated with each client. The specification is then given as the conjunction $\varphi = \varphi_{mutex} \wedge \varphi_{resp} \wedge \varphi_{rel}$ where we use the LTL operators Next $\bigcirc$, Globally $\square$ and Eventually $\Diamond$ to define the requirements

$$
\begin{aligned}
\varphi_{mutex} &= \square \neg (g_1 \wedge g_2), \\
\varphi_{resp} &= \square \bigwedge\nolimits_{i=1}^{2} (r_i \rightarrow \Diamond g_i), \\
\varphi_{rel} &= \square \bigwedge\nolimits_{i=1}^{2} (g_i \wedge r_i \wedge (\Diamond \neg r_i) \rightarrow \bigcirc g_i).
\end{aligned}
$$

Due to the requirement to not revoke grants stated in φ_{rel}, the specification φ is unrealizable (that is, there exists no implementation for the arbiter process). For any bound k on the length of the input lassos, however, φ is realizable. More precisely, there exists an implementation in which once client i has not lowered the request signal for k consecutive steps, the variable g_i is set to false.

This example shows that when the system designer has knowledge about the resources available to the environment processes, taking this knowledge into account can enable us to synthesize a system that is correct under this assumption.

In this paper we formally define the synthesis problem for *lasso-precise implementations*, that is, implementations that are correct for input lassos of bounded size, and describe an automata-theoretic approach to this synthesis problem. We also consider the synthesis of *lasso-precise implementations of bounded size*, and provide a symbolic synthesis algorithm based on quantified Boolean satisfiability.

Bounding the size of the input lassos can render some unrealizable specifications realizable, but, similarly to bounding the size of the environment, comes at the price of higher computational complexity. To alleviate this problem, we further study the synthesis of *approximate implementations*, where we relax the synthesis problem further, and only require that for a given $\epsilon > 0$ the ratio of input lassos of a given size for which the specification is satisfied, to the total number of input lassos of that size is at least $1 - \epsilon$. We then propose an *approximate synthesis method* based on maximum model counting for Boolean formulas [5]. The benefits of the approximate approach are two-fold. Firstly, it can often deliver high-quality approximate solutions more efficiently than the lasso-precise synthesis method, and secondly, even when the specification is still unrealizable for a given lasso bound, we might be able to synthesize an implementation that is correct for a given fraction of the possible input lassos.

The rest of the paper is organized as follows. In Sect. 2 we discuss related work on environment assumptions in synthesis. In Sect. 3 we provide preliminaries on linear temporal properties and omega-automata. In Sect. 3 we define the synthesis problem for lasso-precise implementations, and describe an automata-theoretic synthesis algorithm. In Sect. 5 we study the synthesis of lasso-precise implementations of bounded size, and provide a reduction to quantified Boolean satisfiability. In Sect. 6 we define the approximate version of the problem, and give a synthesis procedure based on maximum model counting. Finally, in Sect. 7 we present experimental results, and conclude in Sect. 8.

2   Related Work

Providing good-quality environment specifications (typically in the form of assumptions on the allowed behaviours of the environment) is crucial for the synthesis of implementations from high-level specifications. Formal specifications, and thus also environment assumptions, are often hard to get right, and have been identified as one of the bottlenecks in formal methods and autonomy [12]. It is therefore not surprising, that there is a plethora of approaches addressing the problem of how to revise inadequate environment assumptions in the cases when these are the cause of unrealizability of the system requirements.

Most approaches in this direction build upon the idea of analyzing the cause of unrealizability of the specification and extracting assumptions that help eliminate this cause. The method proposed in [2] uses the game graph that is used to answer the realizability question in order to construct a Büchi automaton representing a minimal assumption that makes the specification realizable. The authors of [8] provide an alternative approach where the environment assumptions are gradually strengthened based on counterstrategies for the environment. The key ingredient for this approach is using a library of specification templates and user scenarios for the mining of assumptions, in order to generate good-quality assumptions. A similar approach is used in [1], where, however, assumption patterns are synthesized directly from the counterstrategy without the need for the user to provide patterns. A different line of work focuses on giving feedback to the user or specification designer about the reason for unrealizability, so that they can, if possible, revise the specification accordingly. The key challenge adressed there lies in providing easy-to-understand feedback to users, which relies on finding a minimal cause for why the requirements are not achievable and generating a natural language explanation of this cause [11].

In the above mentioned approaches, assumptions are provided or constructed in the form of a temporal logic formula or an omega-automaton. Thus, it is on the one hand often difficult for specification designers to specify the right assumptions, and on the other hand special care has to be taken by the assumption generation procedures to ensure that the constructed assumptions are simple enough for the user to understand and evaluate. The work [6] takes a different route, by making assumptions about the *size* of the environment. That is, including as an additional parameter to the synthesis problem a bound on the state space of the environment. Similarly to temporal logic assumptions, this relaxation of the synthesis problem can render unrealizable specifications into realizable ones. From the system designer point of view, however, it might be significantly easier to estimate the size of environments that are feasible in practice than to express the implications of this additional information in a temporal logic formula. In this paper we take a similar route to [6], and consider a bound on the cyclic structures in the environment's behaviour. Thus, the closest to our work is the temporal synthesis for bounded environments studied in [6]. In fact, we show that the synthesis problem for lasso-precise implementations and the synthesis problem under bounded environments can be reduced to each other. However, while the focus in [6] is on the computational complexity of the bounded synthesis problems, here we provide both automata-theoretic, as well as symbolic approaches for solving the synthesis problem for environments with bounded lassos. We further consider an *approximate version of this synthesis problem*. The benefits of using approximation are two-fold. Firstly, as shown in [6], while bounding the environment can make some specifications realizable, this comes at a high computational complexity price. In this case, approximation might be able to provide solutions of sufficient quality more efficiently. Furthermore, even after bounding the environment's input behaviours, the specification might still remain unrealizable, in which case we would like to satisfy the requirements for as many input lassos as possible. In that sense, we get closer to synthesis methods for probabilistic temporal properties in probabilistic environments [7]. However, we consider non-probabilistic environments (i.e., all possible inputs are equally likely), and provide probabilistic guarantees with desired confidence by employing maximum model counting techniques. Maximum model counting has previously been used for the synthesis of approximate non-reactive programs [5]. Here, on the other hand we are concerned with the synthesis of reactive systems from temporal specifications.

Bounding the size of the synthesized system implementation is a complementary restriction of the synthesis problem, which has attracted a lot of attention in recent years [4]. The computational complexity of the synthesis problem when both the system's and the environment's size is bounded has been studied in [6]. In this paper we provide a symbolic synthesis procedure for bounded synthesis of lasso-precise implementations based on quantified Boolean satisfiability.

3 Preliminaries

We now recall definitions and notation from formal languages and automata, and notions from reactive synthesis such as implementation and environment.

Linear-Time Properties and Lassos. A *linear-time property* φ over an alphabet Σ is a set of infinite words $\varphi \subseteq \Sigma^\omega$. Elements of φ are called *models* of φ. A *lasso* of length k over an alphabet Σ is a pair (u, v) of finite words $u \in \Sigma^*$ and $v \in \Sigma^+$ with $|u \cdot v| = k$ that induces the ultimately periodic word $u \cdot v^\omega$. We call $u \cdot v$ the *base* of the lasso or ultimately periodic word, and k the *length* of the lasso.

If a word $w \in \Sigma^*$ is a prefix of a word $\sigma \in \Sigma^* \cup \Sigma^\omega$, we write $w < \sigma$. For a language $L \subseteq \Sigma^* \cup \Sigma^\omega$, we define $Prefix(L) = \{w \in \Sigma^* \mid \exists \sigma \in L : w < \sigma\}$ is the set of all finite words that are prefixes of words in L.

Implementations. We represent implementations as *labeled transition systems*. Let I and O be finite sets of *input* and *output atomic propositions* respectively. A 2^O-labeled 2^I-transition system is a tuple $\mathcal{T} = (T, t_0, \tau, o)$, consisting of a finite set of states T, an initial state $t_0 \in T$, a transition function $\tau \colon T \times 2^I \to T$, and a labeling function $o \colon T \to 2^O$. We denote by $|\mathcal{T}|$ the size of an implementation $\mathcal{T}$, defined as $|\mathcal{T}| = |T|$. A *path* in $\mathcal{T}$ is a sequence $\pi \colon \mathbb{N} \to T \times 2^I$ of states and inputs that follows the transition function, i.e., for all $i \in \mathbb{N}$ if $\pi(i) = (t_i, e_i)$ and $\pi(i + 1) = (t_{i+1}, e_{i+1})$, then $t_{i+1} = \tau(t_i, e_i)$. We call a path *initial* if it starts with the initial state: $\pi(0) = (t_0, e)$ for some $e \in 2^I$. For an initial path π, we call the sequence $\sigma_\pi \colon i \mapsto (o(t_i) \cup e_i) \in (2^{I \cup O})^\omega$ the *trace* of π. We call the set of traces of a transition system $\mathcal{T}$ the *language of* $\mathcal{T}$, denoted $L(\mathcal{T})$.

Finite-state environments can be represented as labelled transition systems in a similar way, with the difference that the inputs are the outputs of the implementation, and the states of the environment are labelled with inputs for the implementation. More precisely, a finite-state environment is a 2^I-labeled 2^O-transition system $\mathcal{E} = (E, s_0, \rho, \iota)$. The composition of an implementation $\mathcal{T}$ and an environment $\mathcal{E}$ results in a set of traces of $\mathcal{T}$, which we denote $L_\mathcal{E}(\mathcal{T})$, where $\sigma = \sigma_0\sigma_1 \ldots \in L_\mathcal{E}(\mathcal{T})$ if and only if $\sigma \in L(\mathcal{T})$ and there exists an initial path $s_0s_1 \ldots$ in $\mathcal{E}$ such that for all $i \in \mathbb{N}$, $s_{i+1} = \rho(s_i, \sigma_{i+1} \cap O)$ and $\sigma_i \cap I = \iota(s_i)$.

Linear-Time Temporal Logic. We specify properties of reactive systems (implementations) as formulas in Linear-time Temporal Logic (LTL) [9]. We consider the usual temporal operators Next $\bigcirc$, Until $\mathcal{U}$, and the derived operators Release $\mathcal{R}$, which is the dual operator of $\mathcal{U}$, Eventually $\Diamond$ and Globally $\Box$. LTL formulas are defined over a set of atomic propositions AP. We denote the satisfaction of an LTL formula φ by an infinite sequence $\sigma \in (2^{AP})^\omega$ of valuations of the atomic propositions by $\sigma \models \varphi$ and call σ a *model* of φ. For an LTL formula φ we define the language $L(\varphi)$ of φ to be the set $\{\sigma \in (2^{AP})^\omega \mid \sigma \models \varphi\}$.

For a set of atomic propositions $AP = O \cup I$, we say that a 2^O-labeled 2^I-transition system $\mathcal{T}$ satisfies an LTL formula φ, if and only if $L(\mathcal{T}) \subseteq L(\varphi)$, i.e., every trace of $\mathcal{T}$ satisfies φ. In this case we call $\mathcal{T}$ a *model* of φ, denoted $\mathcal{T} \models \varphi$. If $\mathcal{T}$ satisfies φ for an environment $\mathcal{E}$, i.e. $L_\mathcal{E}(\mathcal{T}) \subseteq L(\varphi)$, we write $\mathcal{T} \models_\mathcal{E} \varphi$.

For $I \subseteq AP$ and $\sigma \in (2^{AP})^* \cup (2^{AP})^\omega$, we denote with $\sigma|_I$ the projection of σ on I, obtained by the sequence of valuations of the propositions from I in σ.

Automata Over Infinite Words. The automata-theoretic approach to reactive synthesis relies on the fact that an LTL specification can be translated to an automaton over infinite words, or, alternatively, that the specification can be provided directly as such an automaton. An *alternating parity automaton* over an alphabet Σ is a tuple $\mathcal{A} = (Q, q_0, \delta, \mu)$, where Q denotes a finite set of states, $Q_0 \subseteq Q$ denotes a set of initial states, δ denotes a transition function, and $\mu : Q \to C \subset \mathbb{N}$ is a coloring function. The transition function $\delta : Q \times \Sigma \to \mathbb{B}^+(Q)$ maps a state and an input letter to a positive Boolean combination of states [14].

A tree T over a set of directions D is a prefix-closed subset of D^*. The empty sequence ϵ is called the root. The children of a node $n \in T$ are the nodes $\{n \cdot d \in T \mid d \in D\}$. A Σ-labeled tree is a pair (T, l), where $l : T \to \Sigma$ is the labeling function. A *run* of $\mathcal{A} = (Q, q_0, \delta, \mu)$ on an infinite word $\sigma = \alpha_0\alpha_1 \cdots \in \Sigma^\omega$ is a Q-labeled tree (T, l) that satisfies the following constraints: (1) $l(\epsilon) = q_0$, and (2) for all $n \in T$, if $l(n) = q$, then $\{l(n') \mid n'$ is a child of $n\}$ satisfies $\delta(q, \alpha_{|n|})$.

A run tree is *accepting* if every branch either hits a *true* transition or is an infinite branch $n_0n_1n_2 \cdots \in T$, and the sequence $l(n_0)l(n_1)l(n_2) \ldots$ satisfies the *parity condition*, which requires that the highest color occurring infinitely often in the sequence $\mu(l(n_0))\mu(l(n_1))\mu(l(n_2)) \cdots \in \mathbb{N}^\omega$ is even. An infinite word σ is accepted by an automaton $\mathcal{A}$ if there exists an accepting run of $\mathcal{A}$ on σ. The set of infinite words accepted by $\mathcal{A}$ is called its *language*, denoted $L(\mathcal{A})$.

A *nondeterministic* automaton is a special alternating automaton, where for all states q and input letters α, $\delta(q, \alpha)$ is a disjunction. An alternating automaton is called *universal* if, for all states q and input letters α, $\delta(q, \alpha)$ is a conjunction. A universal and nondeterministic automaton is called *deterministic*.

A parity automaton is called a *Büchi* automaton if and only if the image of μ is contained in $\{1, 2\}$, a *co-Büchi* automaton if and only if the image of α is contained in $\{0, 1\}$. Büchi and co-Büchi automata are denoted by (Q, Q_0, δ, F), where $F \subseteq Q$ denotes the states with the higher color. A run graph of a Büchi automaton is thus accepting if, on every infinite path, there are infinitely many visits to states in F; a run graph of a co-Büchi automaton is accepting if, on every path, there are only finitely many visits to states in F.

The next theorem states the relation between LTL and alternating Büchi automata, namely that every LTL formula φ can be translated to an alternating Büchi automaton with the same language and size linear in the length of φ.

Theorem 1. [13] *For every LTL formula φ there is an alternating Büchi automaton $\mathcal{A}$ of size $O(|\varphi|)$ with $L(\mathcal{A}) = L(\varphi)$, where $|\varphi|$ is the length of φ.*

Automata Over Finite Words. We also use automata over finite words as acceptors for languages consisting of prefixes of traces. A nondeterministic finite automaton over an alphabet Σ is a tuple $\mathcal{A} = (Q, Q_0, \delta, F)$, where Q and $Q_0 \subseteq Q$ are again the states and initial states respectively, $\delta : Q \times \Sigma \to 2^Q$ is the transition function and F is the set of accepting states. A run on a word $a_1 \ldots a_n$ is a sequence of states $q_0 q_1 \ldots q_n$, where $q_0 \in Q_0$ and $q_{i+1} \in \delta(q_i, a_i)$. The run is accepting if $q_n \in F$. Deterministic finite automata are defined similarly with the difference that there is a single initial state q_0, and that the transition function is of the form $\delta : Q \times \Sigma \to Q$. As usual, we denote the set of words accepted by a nondeterministic or deterministic finite automaton $\mathcal{A}$ by $L(\mathcal{A})$.

4   Synthesis of Lasso-Precise Implementations

In this section we first define the synthesis problem for environments producing input sequences representable as lassos of length bounded by a given number. We then provide an automata-theoretic algorithm for this synthesis problem.

4.1   Lasso-Precise Implementations

We begin by formally defining the language of sequences of input values representable by lassos of a given length k. For the rest of the section, we consider linear-time properties defined over a set of atomic propositions AP. The subset $I \subseteq AP$ consists of the input atomic propositions controlled by the environment.

Definition 1 (Bounded Model Languages). *Let φ be a linear-time property over a set of atomic propositions AP, let $\Sigma = 2^{AP}$, and let $I \subseteq AP$.*

We say that an infinite word $\sigma \in \Sigma^\omega$ is an I-k-model of φ, for a bound $k \in \mathbb{N}$, if and only if there are words $u \in (2^I)^*$ and $v \in (2^I)^+$ such that $|u \cdot v| = k$ and $\sigma|_I = u \cdot v^\omega$. The language of I-k-models of the property φ is defined by the set $L_k^I(\varphi) = \{\sigma \in \Sigma^\omega \mid \sigma \text{ is a } I\text{-}k\text{-model of } \varphi\}$.

Note that a model of φ might be induced by lassos of different length and by more than one lasso of the same length, e.g., a^ω is induced by (a, a) and (ϵ, aa). The next lemma establishes that if a model of φ can be represented by a lasso of length k then it can also be represented by a lasso of any larger length.

Lemma 1. *For a linear-time property φ over $\Sigma = 2^{AP}$, subset $I \subseteq AP$ of atomic propositions, and bound $k \in \mathbb{N}$, we have $L_k^I(\varphi) \subseteq L_{k'}^I(\varphi)$ for all $k' > k$.*

Proof. Let $\sigma \in L_k^I(\varphi)$. Then, $\sigma \models \varphi$ and there exists $(u, v) \in (2^I)^* \times (2^I)^+$ such that $|u \cdot v| = k$ and $\sigma|_I = u \cdot v^\omega$. Let $v = v_1 \ldots v_k$. Since $u \cdot v_1(v_2 \ldots v_k v_1)^\omega = u \cdot (v_1 \ldots v_k)^\omega = \sigma|_I$, we have $\sigma \in L_{k+1}^I(\varphi)$. The claim follows by induction. $\square$

Using the definition of I-k-models, the language of infinite sequences of environment inputs representable by lassos of length k can be expressed as $L_k^I(\Sigma^\omega)$.

Definition 2 (k-lasso-precise Implementations). *For a linear-time property φ over $\Sigma = 2^{AP}$, subset $I \subseteq AP$ of atomic propositions, and bound $k \in \mathbb{N}$, we say that a transition system T is a k-lasso-precise implementation of φ, denoted $T \models_{k,I} \varphi$, if it holds that $L_k^I(L(T)) \subseteq \varphi$.*

That is, in a k-lasso-precise implementation T all the traces of T that belong to the language $L_k^I(\Sigma^\omega)$ are I-k-models of the specification φ.

Problem definition: Synthesis of Lasso-Precise Implementations

Given a linear-time property φ over atomic propositions AP with input atomic propositions I, and given a bound $k \in \mathbb{N}$, construct an implementation T such that $T \models_{k,I} \varphi$, or determine that such an implementation does not exist.

Another way to bound the behaviour of the environment is to consider a bound on the size of its state space. The *synthesis problem for bounded environments* asks for a given linear temporal property φ and a bound $k \in \mathbb{N}$ to synthesize a transition system T such that for every possible environment $\mathcal{E}$ of size at most k, the transition system T satisfies φ under environment $\mathcal{E}$, i.e., $T \models_\mathcal{E} \varphi$.

We now establish the relationship between the synthesis of lasso-precise implementations and synthesis under bounded environments. Intuitively, the two synthesis problems can be reduced to each other since an environment of a given size, interacting with a given implementation, can only produce ultimately periodic sequences of inputs representable by lassos of length determined by the sizes of the environment and the implementation. This intuition is formalized in the following proposition, stating the connection between the two problems.

Proposition 1. *Given a specification φ over a set of atomic propositions AP with subset $I \subseteq AP$ of atomic propositions controlled by the environment, and a bound $k \in \mathbb{N}$, for every transition system T the following statements hold:*

(1) If $T \models_\mathcal{E} \varphi$ for all environments $\mathcal{E}$ of size at most k, then $T \models_{k,I} \varphi$.
(2) If $T \models_{k \cdot |T|, I} \varphi$, then $T \models_\mathcal{E} \varphi$ for all environments $\mathcal{E}$ of size at most k.

Proof. For *(1)*, let $\mathcal{T}$ be a transition system such that $\mathcal{T} \models_{\mathcal{E}} \varphi$ for all environments $\mathcal{E}$ of size at most k. Assume, for the sake of contradiction, that $\mathcal{T} \not\models_{k,I} \varphi$. Thus, that there exists a word $\sigma \in L(\mathcal{T})$, such that $\sigma \in L_k^I(\Sigma^\omega)$ and $\sigma \not\models \varphi$.

Since $\sigma \in L_k^I(\Sigma^\omega)$, we can construct an environment $\mathcal{E}$ of size at most k that produces the sequence of inputs $\sigma|_I$. Since $\mathcal{E}$ is of size at most k, we have that $\mathcal{T} \models_{\mathcal{E}} \varphi$. Thus, since $\sigma \in L_{\mathcal{E}}(\mathcal{T})$, we have $\sigma \models \varphi$, which is a contradiction.

For *(2)*, let $\mathcal{T}$ be a transition system such that $\mathcal{T} \models_{k \cdot |\mathcal{T}|, I} \varphi$. Assume, for the sake of contradiction that there exists an environment $\mathcal{E}$ of size at most k such that $\mathcal{T} \not\models_{\mathcal{E}} \varphi$. Since $\mathcal{T} \not\models_{\mathcal{E}} \varphi$, there exists $\sigma \in L_{\mathcal{E}}(\mathcal{T})$ such that $\sigma \not\models \varphi$. As the number of states of $\mathcal{E}$ is at most k, the input sequences it generates can be represented as lassos of size $k \cdot |\mathcal{T}|$. Thus, $\sigma \in L_{k \cdot |\mathcal{T}|}^I(\Sigma^\omega)$. This is a contradiction with the choice of $\mathcal{T}$, according to which $\mathcal{T} \models_{k \cdot |\mathcal{T}|, I} \varphi$. $\qquad\square$

4.2 Automata-Theoretic Synthesis of Lasso-Precise Implementations

We now provide an automata-theoretic algorithm for the synthesis of lasso-precise implementations. The underlying idea of this approach is to first construct an automaton over finite traces that accepts all finite prefixes of traces in $L_k^I(\Sigma^\omega)$. Then, combining this automaton and an automaton representing the property φ we can construct an automaton whose language is non-empty if and only if there exists an k-lasso-precise implementation of φ.

The next theorem presents the construction of a deterministic finite automaton for the language $\mathit{Prefix}(L_k^I(\Sigma^\omega))$.

Theorem 2. *For any set AP of atomic propositions, subset $I \subseteq AP$, and bound $k \in \mathbb{N}$ there is a deterministic finite automaton $\mathcal{A}_k$ over alphabet $\Sigma = 2^{AP}$, with size $(2^{|I|} + 1)^k \cdot (k+1)^k$, such that $L(\mathcal{A}_k) = \{w \in \Sigma^* \mid \exists \sigma \in L_k^I(\Sigma^\omega). \ w < \sigma\}$.*

Idea & Construction. For given $k \in \mathbb{N}$ we first define an automaton $\widehat{\mathcal{A}}_k = (Q, q_0, \delta, F)$ over $\widehat{\Sigma} = 2^I$, such that $L(\widehat{\mathcal{A}}_k) = \{\widehat{w} \in \widehat{\Sigma}^* \mid \exists \widehat{\sigma} \in L_k^I(\widehat{\Sigma}^\omega). \ \widehat{w} < \widehat{\sigma}\}$. That, is $L(\widehat{\mathcal{A}}_k)$ is the set of all finite prefixes of infinite words over $\widehat{\Sigma}$ that can be represented by a lasso of length k. We can then define the automaton $\mathcal{A}_k$ as the automaton that for each $w \in \Sigma^*$ simulates $\widehat{\mathcal{A}}_k$ on the projection $w|_I$ of w.

We define the automaton $\widehat{\mathcal{A}}_k = (Q, q_0, \delta, F)$ such that

- $Q = (\widehat{\Sigma} \cup \{\#\})^k \times \{-, 1, \ldots, k\}^k$,
- $q_0 = (\#^k, (1, 2, \ldots, k))$,

$$
- \ \delta(q,\alpha) = \begin{cases}
(w \cdot \alpha \cdot \#^{m-1}, t) & \text{if } q = (w \cdot \#^m, t) \text{ where } 1 \leq m \leq k, \\
& \quad w \in \widehat{\Sigma}^{(k-m)}, \ t \in \{-,1,\dots,k\}^k \\[2ex]
(w, (i'_1,\dots,i'_k)) & \text{if } q = (w, (i_1,\dots,i_k)) \text{ where } w \in \widehat{\Sigma}^k, \text{ and} \\[1ex]
& i'_j = \begin{cases}
- & i_j \leq k \wedge w(i_j) \neq \alpha \text{ or } i_j = - \\[1ex]
i_j + 1 & i_j < k \wedge w(i_j) = \alpha \\[1ex]
j & i_j = k \wedge w(i_j) = \alpha
\end{cases}
\end{cases}
$$

$- \ F = Q \setminus \{(w,(-,\dots,-)) \mid w \in \widehat{\Sigma}^k\}.$

Proof. States of the form $(w \cdot \alpha \cdot \#^m, t)$ with $m \geq 1$ store the portion of the input word read so far, for input words of length smaller than k. In states of this form we have $t = (1,2,\dots,k)$, which implies that all such states are accepting. In turn, this means that $\mathcal{A}_k$ accepts all words of length smaller or equal to k. This is justified by the fact that, each word of length smaller or equal to k is a prefix of an infinite word in $L_k^I(\widehat{\Sigma}^\omega)$, obtained by repeating the prefix infinitely often. Now, let us consider words of length greater than k.

In states of the form $(u, (i_1,\dots,i_k))$, with $u \in \widehat{\Sigma}^*$, the word u stores the first k letters of the input word. Intuitively, the tuple $(i_1,\dots,i_k)$ stores the information about the loops that are still possible, given the portion of the input word that is read thus far. To see this, let us consider a word $w \in \widehat{\Sigma}^*$ such that $|w| = l > k$, and let $q_0 q_1 \dots q_l$ be the run of $\mathcal{A}_k$ on w. The state q_l is of the form $q_l = (w(1) \dots w(k), (i_1^l,\dots,i_k^l))$. It can be shown by induction on l that for each j we have $i_j^l \neq -$ if and only if w is of the form $w = w' \cdot w'' \cdot w'''$ where $w' = w(1) \dots w(j-1)$, $w'' = (w(j) \dots w(k))^k$ for some $k \geq 0$, and $w''' = (w(j) \dots w(i_j^l - 1))$. Thus, if $i_j^l \neq -$, then it is possible to have a loop starting at position j, and i_j^l is such that $(w(j) \dots w(i_j^l - 1))$ is the prefix of $w(j) \dots w(k)$ appearing after the (possibly empty) sequence of repetitions of $w(j) \dots w(k)$. This means, that if $i_j^l \neq -$, then w is a prefix of the infinite word $w' \cdot (w'')^\omega \in L_k^I(\widehat{\Sigma}^\omega)$. Therefore, if the run of $\mathcal{A}_k$ on a word w with $|w| > k$ is accepting, then there exists $\sigma \in L_k^I(\widehat{\Sigma}^\omega)$ such that $w < \sigma$.

For the other direction, suppose that for each j, we have $i_j^l = -$. Take any j, and consider the first position m in the run $q_0 q_1 \dots q_l$ where $i_j^m = -$. By the definition of δ we have that $w(m) \neq w(i_j^{m-1})$. This means that the prefix $w(1) \dots w(m)$ cannot be extended to the word $w(1) \dots w(j-1)(w(j) \dots w(k))^\omega$. Since for every $j \in \{1,\dots,k\}$ we can find such a position m, it holds that there does not exist $\sigma \in L_k^I(\widehat{\Sigma}^\omega)$ such that $w < \sigma$. This concludes the proof. $\qquad\square$

The automaton constructed in the previous theorem has size which is exponential in the length of the lassos. In the next theorem we show that this exponential blow-up is unavoidable. That is, we show that every nondeterministic finite automaton for the language $Prefix(L_k^I(\Sigma^\omega))$ is of size at least $2^{\Omega(k)}$.

Theorem 3. *For any bound $k \in \mathbb{N}$ and sets of atomic propositions AP and $\emptyset \neq I \subseteq AP$, every nondeterministic finite automaton $\mathcal{N}$ over the alphabet $\Sigma = 2^{AP}$ that recognizes $L = \{w \in \Sigma^* \mid \exists \sigma \in L_k^I(\Sigma^\omega). \ w < \sigma\}$ is of size at least $2^{\Omega(k)}$.*

Proof. Let $\mathcal{N} = (Q, Q_0, \delta, F)$ be a nondeterministic finite automaton for L. For each $w \in \Sigma^k$, we have that $w \cdot w \in L$. Therefore, for each $w \in \Sigma^k$ there exists at least one accepting run $\rho = q_0 q_1 \ldots q_f$ of $\mathcal{N}$ on $w \cdot w$. We denote with $q(\rho, m)$ the state q_m that appears at the position indexed m of a run ρ.

Let $a \in 2^I$ be a letter in 2^I, and let $\Sigma' = \Sigma \backslash \{a' \in \Sigma \mid a'|_I = a\}$. Let $L' \subseteq L$ be the language $L' = \{w \in \Sigma^k \mid \exists w' \in (\Sigma')^{k-1}, a' \in \Sigma : \ w = w' \cdot a' \text{ and } a'|_I = a\}$. That is, L' consists of the words of length k in which letters a' with $a'|_I = a$ appear in the last position and only in the last position.

Let us define the set of states

$$Q_k = \{q(\rho, k) \mid \exists w \in L' : \ \rho \text{ is an accepting run of } \mathcal{N} \text{ on } w \cdot w\}.$$

That is, Q_k consists of the states that appear at position k on some accepting run on some word $w \cdot w$, where w is from L'. We will show that $|Q_k| \geq 2^{k-1}$.

Assume that this does not hold, i.e., $|Q_k| < 2^{k-1}$. Since $|L'| \geq 2^{k-1}$, this implies that there exist $w_1, w_2 \in L'$, such that $w_1|_I \neq w_2|_I$ and there exists accepting runs ρ_1 and ρ_2 of $\mathcal{N}$ on $w_1 \cdot w_1$ and $w_2 \cdot w_2$ respectively, such that $q(\rho_1, k) = q(\rho_2, k)$. That is, there must be two words in L' with $w_1|_I \neq w_2|_I$, which have accepting runs on $w_1 \cdot w_1$ and $w_2 \cdot w_2$ visiting the same state at position k.

We now construct a run $\rho_{1,2}$ on the word $w_1 \cdot w_2$ that follows ρ_1 for the first k steps on w_1, ending in state $q(\rho_1, k)$, and from there on follows ρ_2 on w_2. It is easy to see that $\rho_{1,2}$ is a run on the word $w_1 \cdot w_2$. The run is accepting, since ρ_2 is accepting. This means that $w_1 \cdot w_2 \in L$, which we will show leads to contradiction.

To see this, recall that $w_1 = w_1' \cdot a'$ and $w_2 = w_2' \cdot a''$, and $w_1|_I \neq w_2|_I$, and $a'|_I = a''|_I = a$. Since $w_1 \cdot w_2 \in L$, we have that $w_1' \cdot a' \cdot w_2' \cdot a'' < \sigma$ for some $\sigma \in L_k^I(\Sigma^\omega)$. That is, there exists a lasso for some word σ, and $w_1' \cdot a' \cdot w_2' \cdot a''$ is a prefix of this word. Since a does not appear in $w_2'|_I$, this means that the loop in this lasso is the whole word $w_1|_I$, which is not possible, since $w_1|_I \neq w_2|_I$.

This is a contradiction, which shows that $|Q| \geq |Q_k| \geq 2^{k-1}$. Since $\mathcal{N}$ was an arbitrary nondeterministic finite automaton for L, this implies that the minimal automaton for L has at least $2^{\Omega(k)}$ states, which concludes the proof. $\square$

Using the automaton from Theorem 2, we can transform every property automaton $\mathcal{A}$ into an automaton that accepts words representable by lassos of length less than or equal to k if and only if they are in $L(\mathcal{A})$, and accepts all words that are not representable by lassos of length less than or equal to k.

Theorem 4. *Let AP be a set of atomic propositions, and let $I \subseteq AP$. For every (deterministic, nondeterministic or alternating) parity automaton $\mathcal{A}$ over $\Sigma = 2^{AP}$, and $k \in \mathbb{N}$, there is a (deterministic, nondeterministic or alternating) parity automaton $\mathcal{A}'$ of size $2^{O(k)} \cdot |\mathcal{A}|$, s.t., $L(\mathcal{A}') = (L_k^I(\Sigma^\omega) \cap L(\mathcal{A})) \cup (\Sigma^\omega \backslash L_k^I(\Sigma^\omega))$.*

Proof. The theorem is a consequence of Theorem 2 established as follows. Let $\mathcal{A} = (Q, Q_0, \delta, \mu)$ be a parity automaton, and let $\mathcal{D} = (\widehat{Q}, \widehat{q_0}, \widehat{\delta}, F)$ be the deterministic finite automaton for bound k defined as in Theorem 2. We define the parity automaton $\mathcal{A} = (Q', Q'_0, \delta', \mu')$ with the following components:

- $Q' = (Q \times \widehat{Q})$;
- $Q'_0 = \{(q_0, \widehat{q_0}) \mid q_0 \in Q_0\}$ (when $\mathcal{A}$ is deterministic Q'_0 is a singleton set);
- $\delta'((q, \widehat{q}), \alpha) = \delta(q, \alpha)_{[q'/(q', \widehat{\delta}(\widehat{q}, \alpha))]}$, where $\delta(q, \alpha)_{[q'/(q', \widehat{q}')]}$ is the Boolean expression obtained from $\delta(q, \alpha)$ by replacing every state q' by the state $(q', \widehat{q}')$;
- $\mu'((q, \widehat{q})) = \begin{cases} \mu(q) & \text{if } \widehat{q} \in F, \\ 0 & \text{if } \widehat{q} \notin F. \end{cases}$

Intuitively, the automaton $\mathcal{A}'$ is constructed as the product of $\mathcal{A}$ and $\mathcal{D}$, where runs entering a state in $\mathcal{D}$ that is not accepting in $\mathcal{D}$ are accepting in $\mathcal{A}'$. To see this, recall from the construction in Theorem 2 that once $\mathcal{D}$ enters a state in $\widehat{Q} \setminus \widehat{F}$ it remains in such a state forever. Thus, by setting the color of all states $(q, \widehat{q})$ where $\widehat{q} \notin F$ to 0, we ensure that words containing a prefix rejected by $\mathcal{D}$ have only runs in which the highest color appearing infinitely often is 0. Thus, we ensure that all words that are not representable by lassos of length less than or equal to k are accepted by $\mathcal{A}'$, while words representable by lassos of length less than or equal to k are accepted if and only if they are in $L(\mathcal{A})$. $\qquad\square$

The following theorem is a consequence of the one above, and provides us with an automata-theoretic approach to solving the lasso-precise synthesis problem.

Theorem 5 (Synthesis). *Let AP be a set of atomic propositions, and $I \subseteq AP$ be a subset of AP consisting of the atomic propositions controlled by the environment. For a specification, given as a deterministic parity automaton $\mathcal{P}$ over the alphabet $\Sigma = 2^{AP}$, and a bound $k \in \mathbb{N}$, finding an implementation $\mathcal{T}$, such that, $\mathcal{T} \models_{k,I} \mathcal{P}$ can be done in time polynomial in the size of the automaton $\mathcal{P}$ and exponential in the bound k.*

5 Bounded Synthesis of Lasso-Precise Implementations

For a specification φ given as an LTL formula, a bound n on the size of the synthesized implementation and a bound k on the lassos of input sequences, *bounded synthesis of lasso-precise implementations* searches for an implementation $\mathcal{T}$ of size n, such that $\mathcal{T} \models_{k,I} \varphi$. Using the automata constructions in the previous section we can construct a universal co-Büchi automaton for the language $L_k^I(\varphi) \cup (\Sigma^\omega \setminus L_k^I(\Sigma^\omega))$ and construct the constraint system as presented in [4]. This constraint system is exponential in both $|\varphi|$ and k. In the following we show how the problem can be encoded as a quantified Boolean formula of size polynomial in $|\varphi|$ and k.

Theorem 6. *For a specification given as an LTL formula φ, and bounds $k \in \mathbb{N}$ and $n \in \mathbb{N}$, there exists a quantified Boolean formula ϕ, such that, ϕ is satisfiable if and only if there is a transition system $\mathcal{T} = (T, t_0, \tau, o)$ of size n with $\mathcal{T} \models_{k,I} \varphi$. The size of ϕ is in $O(|\varphi| + n^2 + k^2)$. The number of variables of ϕ is equal to $n \cdot (n \cdot 2^{|I|} + |O|) + k \cdot (|I| + 1) + n \cdot k(|O| + n + 1)$.*

Construction. We encode the bounded synthesis problem in the following quantified Boolean formula:

$$\exists \{\tau_{t,i,t'} \mid t, t' \in T, i \in 2^I\}. \; \exists \{o_t \mid t \in T, o \in O\}. \tag{1}$$

$$\forall \{i_j \mid i \in I, 0 \le j < k\}. \; \forall \{l_j \mid 0 \le j < k\}. \tag{2}$$

$$\forall \{o_j \mid o \in O, 0 \le j < n \cdot k\}. \tag{3}$$

$$\forall \{t_j \mid t \in T, 0 \le j < n \cdot k\}. \tag{4}$$

$$\forall \{l'_j \mid 0 \le j < n \cdot k\}. \tag{5}$$

$$\varphi_{\det} \wedge (\varphi_{\text{lasso}} \wedge \varphi_{\in T}^{n,k} \rightarrow \llbracket \varphi \rrbracket_0^{k,n \cdot k}) \tag{6}$$

which we read as: there is a transition system (1), such that, for all input sequences representable by lassos of length k (2) the corresponding sequence of outputs of the system (3) satisfies φ. The variables introduced in lines (4) and (5) are necessary to encode the corresponding output for the chosen input lasso.

An assignment to the variables satisfies the formula in line (6), if it represents a deterministic transition system ($\varphi_{\det}$) in which lassos of length $n \cdot k$ ($\varphi_{\text{lasso} \wedge \varphi_{\in T}^{n,k}}$) satisfy the property φ ($\llbracket \varphi \rrbracket_0^{(k,n \cdot k)}$)). These constraints are defined as follows.

$\varphi_{\det}$: A transition system is deterministic if for each state t and input i there is exactly one transition $\tau_{t,i,t'}$ to some state t': $\bigwedge_{t \in T} \bigwedge_{i \in 2^I} \bigvee_{t' \in T} (\tau_{t,i,t'} \wedge \bigwedge_{t' \neq t''} \overline{\tau_{t,i,t''}})$.

$\varphi_{\in T}^{n,k}$: for a certain input lasso of size k we can match a lasso in the system of size at most $n \cdot k$. A lasso of this size in the transition system matches the input lasso if the following constraints are satisfied.

$$\bigwedge_{0 \le j < n \cdot k} \bigwedge_{t \in T} (t_j \rightarrow \bigwedge_{o \in O} (o_j \leftrightarrow o_{t_j})) \tag{7}$$

$$\wedge \; t_{00} \tag{8}$$

$$\wedge \bigwedge_{0 \le j < n \cdot k - 1} \bigwedge_{i \in 2^I} \bigwedge_{t,t' \in T} \bigwedge_{0 \le j' < k} ((\bigwedge l_{j'} \rightarrow i_{\Delta(j,k,j')}) \wedge t_j \rightarrow (\tau_{t,i,t'} \leftrightarrow t'_{j+1})) \tag{9}$$

$$\wedge \bigwedge_{i \in 2^I, t,t' \in T} \bigwedge_{0 \le j' < k} ((\bigwedge l_{j'} \rightarrow i_{\Delta(n \cdot k - 1, k, j')}) \wedge t_{n \cdot k - 1} \rightarrow (\tau_{t,i,t'} \leftrightarrow (\bigvee_{0 \le j < n \cdot k} l'_j \wedge t'_j))) \tag{10}$$

Lines (9) and (10) make sure that the chosen lasso follows the guessed transition relation τ. Line (10) handles the loop transition of the lasso, and makes sure that the loop of the lasso follows τ. Line (7) is a necessary requirement in order to match the output produced on the lasso with φ. If the output variables o_j satisfy the constraint $\llbracket \varphi \rrbracket_0^{(k,n \cdot k)}$, then the lasso satisfies φ. As the input lasso is smaller than its matching lasso in the system we need to make sure that the indices of the input variables are correct with respect to the chosen loop. This is computed using the function Δ which is given by:

$$\Delta(j, k, j') = \begin{cases} j & \text{if } j < k, \\ ((j - k) \mod (k - j')) + j' & \text{otherwise.} \end{cases}$$

φ_{lasso}: The formula encodes the additional constraint that exactly one of the loop variables can be true for a given variable valuation.

$[\![\varphi]\!]_0^{k,m}$: This constraint encodes the satisfaction of φ on lassos of size m. The encoding is similar to the encoding of bounded model checking [3], with the distinction of encoding the satisfaction relation of the atomic propositions, given below. As the inputs run with different indices than the outputs, we again, as in the lines (9) and (10), need to compute the correct indices using the function Δ.

	$h < m$	$h = m$
$[\![i]\!]_h^{k,m}$	$\bigwedge_{0 \leq j' < k} (l_{j'} \rightarrow i_{\Delta(h,k,j')})$	$\bigvee_{j=0}^{m-1} (l'_j \wedge \bigwedge_{0 \leq j' < k} (l_{j'} \rightarrow i_{\Delta(j,k,j')}))$
$[\![\neg i]\!]_h^{k,m}$	$\bigwedge_{0 \leq j' < k} (l_{j'} \rightarrow \neg i_{\Delta(h,k,j')})$	$\bigvee_{j=0}^{m-1} (l'_j \wedge \bigwedge_{0 \leq j' < k} (l_{j'} \rightarrow \neg i_{\Delta(j,k,j')}))$
$[\![o]\!]_h^{k,m}$	o_h	$\bigvee_{j=0}^{m-1} (l'_j \wedge o_j)$
$[\![\neg o]\!]_h^{k,m}$	$\neg o_h$	$\bigvee_{j=0}^{m-1} (l'_j \wedge \neg o_j)$

6 Synthesis of Approximate Implementations

In some cases, specifications remain unrealizable even when considered under bounded environments. Nevertheless, one might still be able to construct implementations that satisfy the specification in almost all input sequences of the environment. Consider for example the following simplified arbiter specification:

$$\Box(\overline{w} \rightarrow \bigcirc \overline{g}) \wedge \Box(r \rightarrow \Diamond g)$$

The specification defines an arbiter that should give grants g upon requests r, but is not allowed to provide these grants unless a signal w is true. The specification is unrealizable, because a sequence of inputs where the signal w is always false prevents the arbiter from answering any request. Bounding the environment does not help in this case as a lasso of size 1 already suffices to violate the specification (the one where w is always false). Nevertheless, one can still find reasonable implementations that satisfy the specification for a large fraction of input sequences. In particular, the fraction of input sequences where w remains false forever is less probable.

Definition 3 (ϵ-k-Approximation). *For a specification φ, a bound k, and an error rate ϵ, we say that a transition system $\mathcal{T}$ approximately satisfies φ with an error rate ϵ for lassos of length at most k, denoted by $\mathcal{T} \models_{k,I}^{\epsilon} \varphi$, if and only if, $\frac{|\{\sigma | \sigma \in L_k^I(L(\mathcal{T})), \sigma \models \varphi\}|}{|L_k^I((2^I)^\omega)|} \geq 1 - \epsilon$. We call $\mathcal{T}$ an ϵ-k-approximation of φ.*

Theorem 7. *For a specification given as a deterministic parity automaton P, a bound k and a error rate $0 \leq \epsilon \leq 1$, checking whether there is an implementation $\mathcal{T}$, such that, $\mathcal{T} \models_{k,I}^{\epsilon} P$ can be done in time polynomial in $|P|$ and exponential in k.*

Proof. For a given ϵ and k, we construct a nondeterministic parity tree automaton $\mathcal{N}$ that accepts all ϵ-k-approximations with respect to $L(P)$. For ϵ, we can compute the minimal number m of lassos from $L_k^I((2^I)^\omega)$ for which an ϵ-k-approximation has to satisfy the specification. In its initial state, the automaton $\mathcal{N}$ guesses m many lassos and accepts a transition system if it does not violate the specification on any of these lassos. The latter check is done by following the structure of the automaton constructed for P using Theorem 4. In order to check whether there is an ϵ-k-approximation for P, we solve the emptiness game of $\mathcal{N}$. The size of $\mathcal{N}$ is $(2^k)^{m+1} \cdot |P|$. $\qquad\square$

6.1   Symbolic Approach

In the following, we present a symbolic approach for finding ϵ-k-approximations based on maximum model counting. We show that we can build a constraint system and apply a maximum model counting algorithm to compute a transition system that satisfies a specification for a maximum number of input sequences.

Definition 4 (Maximum Model Counting [5]). *Let X, Y and Z be sets of propositional variables and ϕ be a formula over X, Y and Z. Let x denote an assignment to X, y an assignment to Y, and z an assignment to Z. The maximum model counting problem for ϕ over X and Y is computing a solution for $\max_x \#y.\exists z.\phi(x, y, z)$.*

For a specification φ, bounds k and n on the length of the lassos and size of the system, respectively, we can compute an ϵ-k-approximation for φ by applying a maximum model counting algorithm to the constraint system given below. It encodes transition systems of size n that have an input lasso of length k that satisfies φ.

$$\exists\{\tau_{t,i,t'} \mid t, t' \in T, i \in 2^I\}.\ \exists\{o_t \mid t \in T, o \in O\}. \tag{11}$$

$$\exists\{i_j \mid i \in I, 0 \leq j < k\}.\ \exists\{l_j \mid 0 \leq j < k\}. \tag{12}$$

$$\exists\{x_j^i \mid x \in I, 0 \leq i, j < k\} \tag{13}$$

$$\exists\{o_j \mid o \in O, 0 \leq j < n \cdot k\}. \tag{14}$$

$$\exists\{t_j \mid t \in T, 0 \leq j < n \cdot k\}. \tag{15}$$

$$\exists\{l'_j \mid 0 \leq j < n \cdot k\}. \tag{16}$$

$$\varphi_{\det} \wedge \varphi_{\text{lasso}} \wedge \varphi_{\in \mathcal{T}}^{n,k} \wedge [\![\varphi]\!]_0^{k,n \cdot k} \wedge [\![k]\!]_0 \tag{17}$$

To check the existence of a ϵ-k-approximation, we maximize over the set of assignment to variables that define the transition system (line 11) and count over variables that define input sequences of the environment given by lassos of length k. As two input lassos of the same length may induce the same infinite input sequence, we count over auxiliary variables that represent unrollings of the lassos instead of counting over the input propositions themselves (line 13).

The formulas φ_{det}, φ_{lasso}, $\varphi^{n,k}_{\in \mathcal{T}}$ and $[\![\varphi]\!]^{k,n\cdot k}_0$ are defined as in the previous section. The formula $[\![k]\!]_0$ is defined over that variables in line (13) and makes sure that input lasso that represent the same infinite sequence are not counted twice by unrolling the lasso to size $2k$.

Theorem 8. *For a specification given as an LTL formula φ, and bounds k and n, and an error rate ϵ, the propositional formula ϕ defined above is of size $O(|\varphi| + n^2 + k^2)$. The number of variables of ϕ is equal to $n \cdot (n \cdot 2^{|I|} + |O|) + k \cdot (k \cdot |I| + |I| + 1) + n \cdot k(|O| + n + 1)$.*

7 Experimental Results

We implemented the symbolic encodings for the exact and approximate synthesis methods, and evaluated our approach on a bounded version of the greedy arbiter specification given in Sect. 1, and another specification of a round-robin arbiter. The round-robin arbiter is defined by the specification:

$$\Box\Diamond w \rightarrow \Box\Diamond g_1 \wedge \Box\Diamond g_2 \wedge \Box(\neg w \rightarrow \bigcirc(\neg g_1 \wedge \neg g_2)) \wedge \Box(\neg g_1 \vee \neg g_2)$$

This specification is realizable, with transition systems of size at least 4. We used our implementation to check whether we can find approximative solutions with smaller sizes. We used the tool CAQE [10] for solving the QBF instances and the tool MaxCount [5] for solving the approximate synthesis instances.

Table 1. Experimental results for the symbolic approaches. The rate in the approximate approach is the rate of input lassos on which the specification is satisfied.

Instance					QBF				MaxCount			
Spec.	Proc.	#States	Bound	Result	#Gates	∀	∃	Time	#Max	#Count	Rate	Time
Round-Robin Arbiter	2	2	4	Unreal	15556	48	12	9.91 s	12	8	0.5	26 s
	2	3	2	Unreal	5338	40	24	2.45 s	24	4	0.88	161 s
	2	4	2	Real	13414	60	12	12.15 s	40	4	0.88	283 s
Greedy Arbiter	1	2	2	Real	1597	20	10	0.41 s	10	4	1.0	0.79 s
	1	2	3	Unreal	4749	30	10	1.95 s	10	6	0.88	3.86 s
	1	3	3	Unreal	16861	48	21	17.26 s	21	6	0.88	20.83 s
	1	4	3	Real	43692	78	36	3 min 7.44 s	36	6	1.0	2 min 43 s
	1	4	4	-	169829	104	36	TO	36	8	-	TO
	2	4	2	Real	24688	62	72	1 min. 24 s	72	6	-	TO
	2	4	3	Unreal	103433	93	72	27 min 15.2	72	12	-	TO
	3	2	2	Unreal	3985	93	72	1.39 s	38	8	0.65	4.18 s

The results are presented in Table 1. As usual in synthesis, the size of the instances grows quickly as the size bound and number of processes increase. Inspecting the encoding constraints shows that the constraint for the specification is responsible for more than 80% of the number of gates in the encoding. The results show that, using the approach we proposed, we can synthesize implementations for unrealizable specifications by bounding the environment. The results for the approximate synthesis method further demonstrate that for the unrealizable cases one can still obtain approximative implementations that satisfy the specification on a large number of input sequences.

8   Conclusion

In many cases, the unrealizability of a specification is due to the assumption that the environment has unlimited power in producing inputs to the system. In this paper, we have investigated the problem of synthesizing implementations under bounded environment behaviors. We have presented algorithms for solving the synthesis problem for bounded lassos and the synthesis of approximate implementations that satisfy the specification up to a certain rate.

We have also provided polynomial encodings of the problems into quantified Boolean formulas and maximum model counting instances. Our experiments demonstrate the principal feasibility of the approach. Our experiments also show that the instances can quickly become large. While this is a common phenomenon for synthesis, there clearly is a lot of room for optimization and experimentation with both the solvers for quantified Boolean expressions and for maximum model counting.

References

1. Alur, R., Moarref, S., Topcu, U.: Counter-strategy guided refinement of GR(1) temporal logic specifications. In: Formal Methods in Computer-Aided Design, FMCAD 2013, Portland, OR, USA, October 20–23, 2013, pp. 26–33. IEEE (2013)
2. Chatterjee, K., Henzinger, T.A., Jobstmann, B.: Environment assumptions for synthesis. In: van Breugel, F., Chechik, M. (eds.) CONCUR 2008. LNCS, vol. 5201, pp. 147–161. Springer, Heidelberg (2008). https://doi.org/10.1007/978-3-540-85361-9_14
3. Clarke, E., Biere, A., Raimi, R., Zhu, Y.: Bounded model checking using satisfiability solving. Form. Methods Syst. Des. 19(1), 7–34 (2001)
4. Finkbeiner, B., Schewe, S.: Bounded synthesis. Int. J. Software Tools Technol. Transf. 15(5–6), 519–539 (2013)
5. Fremont, D.J., Rabe, M.N., Seshia, S.A.: Maximum model counting. Technical Report UCB/EECS-2016-169, EECS Department, University of California, Berkeley, Nov 2016. This is the extended version of a paper to appear at AAAI 2017
6. Kupferman, O., Lustig, Y., Vardi, M.Y., Yannakakis, M.: Temporal synthesis for bounded systems and environments. In: Schwentick, T., Dürr, C. (eds.) 28th International Symposium on Theoretical Aspects of Computer Science, STACS 2011, March 10–12, 2011, Dortmund, Germany, vol. 9 of LIPIcs, pages 615–626. Schloss Dagstuhl - Leibniz-Zentrum fuer Informatik (2011)

7. Kwiatkowska, M., Parker, D.: Automated verification and strategy synthesis for probabilistic systems. In: Van Hung, D., Ogawa, M. (eds.) ATVA 2013. LNCS, vol. 8172, pp. 5–22. Springer, Cham (2013). https://doi.org/10.1007/978-3-319-02444-8_2

8. Li, W., Dworkin, L., Seshia, S.A.: Mining assumptions for synthesis. In: Singh, S., Jobstmann, B., Kishinevsky, M., Brandt, J. (eds.) 9th IEEE/ACM International Conference on Formal Methods and Models for Codesign, MEMOCODE 2011, Cambridge, UK, 11–13 July, 2011, pp. 43–50. IEEE (2011)

9. Pnueli, A.: The temporal logic of programs. In: Proceedings of the 18th Annual Symposium on Foundations of Computer Science, SFCS 1977, Washington, DC, USA, 1977. IEEE Computer Society (1977)

10. Rabe, M.N., Tentrup, L.: Caqe: a certifying QBF solver. In: Proceedings of the 15th Conference on Formal Methods in Computer-aided Design (FMCAD 2015), pp. 136–143, September 2015

11. Raman, V., Lignos, C., Finucane, C., Lee, K.C.T., Marcus, M.P., Kress-Gazit, H.: Sorry dave, i'm afraid I can't do that: explaining unachievable robot tasks using natural language. In: Newman, P., Fox, D., Hsu, D. (eds.), Robotics: Science and Systems IX, Technische Universität Berlin, Berlin, Germany, June 24 - June 28, 2013 (2013)

12. Rozier, K.Y.: Specification: the biggest bottleneck in formal methods and autonomy. In: Blazy, S., Chechik, M. (eds.) VSTTE 2016. LNCS, vol. 9971, pp. 8–26. Springer, Cham (2016). https://doi.org/10.1007/978-3-319-48869-1_2

13. Vardi, M.Y.: Nontraditional applications of automata theory. In: Hagiya, M., Mitchell, J.C. (eds.) TACS 1994. LNCS, vol. 789, pp. 575–597. Springer, Heidelberg (1994). https://doi.org/10.1007/3-540-57887-0_116

14. Vardi, M.Y.: Alternating automata and program verification. In: van Leeuwen, J. (ed.) Computer Science Today. LNCS, vol. 1000, pp. 471–485. Springer, Heidelberg (1995). https://doi.org/10.1007/BFb0015261

7

When Human Intuition Fails: Using Formal Methods to Find an Error in the "Proof" of a Multi-agent Protocol

Jennifer A. Davis[1], Laura R. Humphrey[2(✉)], and Derek B. Kingston[3]

[1] Collins Aerospace, Cedar Rapids, IA 52498, USA
jen.davis@collins.com
[2] Air Force Research Lab, Dayton, OH 45433, USA
laura.humphrey@us.af.mil
[3] Aurora Flight Sciences, Manassas, VA 20110, USA
kingston.derek@aurora.aero

Abstract. Designing protocols for multi-agent interaction that achieve the desired behavior is a challenging and error-prone process. The standard practice is to manually develop proofs of protocol correctness that rely on human intuition and require significant effort to develop. Even then, proofs can have mistakes that may go unnoticed after peer review, modeling and simulation, and testing. The use of formal methods can reduce the potential for such errors. In this paper, we discuss our experience applying model checking to a previously published multi-agent protocol for unmanned air vehicles. The original publication provides a compelling proof of correctness, along with extensive simulation results to support it. However, analysis through model checking found an error in one of the proof's main lemmas. In this paper, we start by providing an overview of the protocol and its original "proof" of correctness, which represents the standard practice in multi-agent protocol design. We then describe how we modeled the protocol for a three-vehicle system in a model checker, the counterexample it returned, and the insight this counterexample provided. We also discuss benefits, limitations, and lessons learned from this exercise, as well as what future efforts would be needed to fully verify the protocol for an arbitrary number of vehicles.

Keywords: Multi-agent systems · Distributed systems · Autonomy · Model checking

1 Introduction

Many robotics applications require multi-agent interaction. However, designing protocols for multi-agent interaction that achieve the desired behavior can be

---

D. B. Kingston—Supported by AFRL/RQ contract #FA8650-17-F-2220 and AFOSR award #17RQCOR417. DISTRIBUTION A. Approved for public release: distribution unlimited. Case #88ABW-2018-4275.

challenging. The design process is often manual, i.e. performed by humans, and generally involves creating mathematical models of possible agent behaviors and candidate protocols, then manually developing a proof that the candidate protocols are correct with respect to the desired behavior. However, human-generated proofs can have mistakes that may go unnoticed even after peer review, modeling and simulation, and testing of the resulting system.

Formal methods have the potential to reduce such errors. However, while the use of formal methods in multi-agent system design is increasing [2,6,8,11], it is our experience that manual approaches are still the norm. Here, we hope to motivate the use of formal methods for multi-agent system design by demonstrating their value in a case study involving a manually designed decentralized protocol for dividing surveillance of a perimeter across multiple unmanned aerial vehicles (UAVs). This protocol, called the Decentralized Perimeter Surveillance System (DPSS), was previously published in 2008 [10], has received close to 200 citations to date, and provides a compelling "proof" of correctness backed by extensive simulation results.

We start in Sect. 2 by giving an overview of DPSS, the convergence bounds that comprise part of its specification, and the original "proof" of correctness. In Sect. 3, we give an overview of the three-UAV DPSS model we developed in the Assume Guarantee REasoning Environment (AGREE) model checker [3]. In Sect. 4, we present the analysis results returned by AGREE, including a counterexample to one of the convergence bounds. Section 5 concludes with a discussion of benefits, challenges, and limitations of our modeling process and how to help overcome them, and what future work would be required to modify and fully verify DPSS for an arbitrary number of UAVs.

2 Decentralized Perimeter Surveillance System (DPSS)

UAVs can be used to perform continual, repeated surveillance of a large perimeter. In such cases, more frequent coverage of points along the perimeter can be achieved by evenly dividing surveillance of it across multiple UAVs. However, coordinating this division is challenging in practice for several reasons. First, the exact location and length of the perimeter may not be known a priori, and it may change over time, as in a growing forest fire or oil spill. Second, UAVs might go offline and come back online, e.g. for refueling or repairs. Third, inter-UAV communication is unreliable, so it is not always possible to immediately communicate local information about perimeter or UAV changes. However, such information is needed to maintain an even division of the perimeter as changes occur. DPSS provides a method to solve this problem with minimal inter-UAV communication for perimeters that are isomorphic to a line segment.

Let the perimeter start as a line segment along the x-axis with its left endpoint at $x = 0$ and its right at $x = P$. Let N be the number of UAVs in the system or on the "team," indexed from left to right as $1, \ldots, N$. Divide the perimeter into segments of length P/N, one per UAV. Then the optimal configuration of DPSS as depicted in Fig. 1 is defined as follows (see Ref. [10] for discussion of why this definition is desirable).

Definition 1. *Consider two sets of perimeter locations: (1) $\lfloor i + \frac{1}{2}(-1)^i \rfloor P/N$ and (2) $\lfloor i - \frac{1}{2}(-1)^i \rfloor P/N$, where $\lfloor \cdot \rfloor$ returns the largest integer less than or equal to its argument. The optimal configuration is realized when UAVs synchronously oscillate between these two sets of locations, each moving at constant speed V.*

Fig. 1. Optimal DPSS configuration, in which UAVs are evenly spaced along the perimeter and synchronously oscillate between segment boundaries.

The goal of DPSS is to achieve the optimal configuration in the steady state, i.e. when the perimeter and involved UAVs remain constant. The DPSS protocol itself is relatively simple. Each UAV i stores a vector $\xi_i = [P_{R_i} \quad P_{L_i} \quad N_{R_i} \quad N_{L_i}]^T$ of coordination variables that capture its beliefs (which may be incorrect) about perimeter length P_{R_i} and P_{L_i} and number of UAVs N_{R_i} and N_{L_i} to its right and left. When neighboring UAVs meet, "left" UAV i learns updated values for its "right" variables $P'_{R_i} = P_{R_{i+1}}$ and $N'_{R_i} = N_{R_{i+1}} + 1$ from "right" UAV $i + 1$, and likewise UAV $i + 1$ updates its "left" variables $P'_{L_{i+1}} = P_{L_i}$ and $N'_{L_{i+1}} = N_{L_i} + 1$. While values for these variables may still be incorrect, the two UAVs will at least have matching coordination variables and thus a consistent estimate of their shared segment boundary. The two UAVs then "escort" each other to their estimated shared segment boundary, then split apart to surveil their own segment. Note that UAVs only change direction when they reach a perimeter endpoint or when starting or stopping an escort, which means a UAV will travel outside its segment unless another UAV arrives at the segment boundary at the same time (or the end of the segment is a perimeter endpoint).

Eventually, leftmost UAV 1 will discover the actual left perimeter endpoint, accurately set $N_{L_1} = 0$ and $P_{L_1} = 0$, then turn around and update P_{L_1} continuously as it moves. A similar situation holds for rightmost UAV n. Accurate information will be passed along to other UAVs as they meet, and eventually all UAVs will have correct coordination variables and segment boundary estimates. Since UAVs also escort each other to shared segment boundaries whenever they meet, eventually the system reaches the optimal configuration, in which UAVs oscillate between their true shared segment boundaries.

An important question is how long it takes DPSS to converge to the optimal configuration. Each time the perimeter or number of UAVs changes, it is as if the system is reinitialized; UAVs no longer have correct coordination variables and so the system is no longer converged. However, if DPSS is able to re-converge relatively quickly, it will often be in its converged state.

Ref. [10] claims that DPSS converges within $5T$, where $T = P/V$ is the time it would take a single UAV to traverse the entire perimeter if there were no other UAVs in the system. It describes DPSS as two algorithms: Algorithm A, in which UAVs start with correct coordination variables, and Algorithm B, in which they do not. The proof strategy is then to argue that Algorithm A converges in $2T$ (Theorem 1) and Algorithm B achieves correct coordination variables in $3T$ (Lemma 1)[1]. At that point, Algorithm B converts to Algorithm A, so the total convergence time is $2T + 3T = 5T$ (Theorem 2)[2].

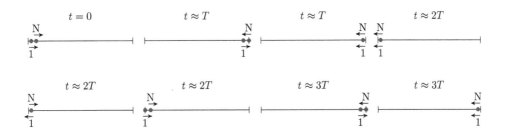

Fig. 2. Claimed worst-case coordination variable convergence for Algorithm B.

Informally, the original argument for Lemma 1 is that information takes time T to travel along the perimeter. The worst case occurs when all UAVs start near one end of the perimeter, e.g. the left endpoint, so that the rightmost UAV N reaches the right endpoint around time T. UAV N then turns around and through a fast series of meetings, correct "right" coordination variables are propagated to the other UAVs, all of which then start moving left. Due to incorrect "left" coordination variables, UAV $N - 1$ and UAV N might think their shared segment boundary is infinitesimally close to the left endpoint. The UAVs travel left until they are almost at the left perimeter endpoint around time $2T$. However, since UAV N thinks its segment boundary is near the left endpoint, it ends its escort and goes right without learning the true location of the left perimeter endpoint. Leftmost UAV 1 learns the true location of the left perimeter endpoint and this information will be passed to the other UAVs as they meet, but the information will have to travel the perimeter once again to reach the rightmost UAV N around time $3T$. This situation is depicted in Fig. 2.

Through model checking, we were able to find a counterexample to this claimed bound, which will be presented in Sect. 4. But first, we overview the model used for analysis through model checking.

3   Formal Models

We briefly overview the formal models developed in AGREE for a three-UAV version of DPSS as described by Algorithm B. Models for Algorithm A and

---

[1] We label this Lemma 1 for convenience; it is unlabeled in [10].
[2] A version of the original proof is on GitHub [1] in file dpssOriginalProof.pdf.

Algorithm B along with a more detailed description of the Algorithm B model are available on GitHub [1][3].

AGREE is an infinite-state model checker capable of analyzing systems with real-valued variables, as is the case with DPSS. AGREE uses assume/guarantee reasoning to verify properties of architectures modeled as a top-level system with multiple lower-level components, each having a formally specified assume/guarantee contract. Each contract consists of a set of assumptions on the inputs and guarantees on the outputs, where inputs and outputs can be reals, integers, or booleans. System assumptions and component assume/guarantee contracts are assumed to be true. AGREE then attempts to verify that (a) component assumptions hold given system assumptions, and (b) system guarantees hold given component guarantees. AGREE poses this verification problem as a satisfiability modulo theory (SMT) problem [4] and uses a k-induction model checking approach [7] to search for counterexamples that violate system-level guarantees given system-level assumptions and component-level assume/guarantee contracts. The language used by AGREE is an "annex" to the Architecture Analysis and Design Language (AADL) [5].

AGREE's ability to analyze systems modeled as a top-level system with multiple lower-level components provides a natural fit for DPSS. The three-UAV AGREE DPSS model consists of a single top-level system model, which we call the "System," and a component-level UAV model that is instantiated three times, which we call the "UAV(s)." The System essentially coordinates a discrete event simulation of the UAVs as they execute the DPSS protocol, where events include a UAV reaching a perimeter endpoint or two UAVs starting or stopping an escort. In the initial state, the System sets valid ranges for each UAV's initial position through assumptions that constrain the UAVs to be initialized between the perimeter endpoints and ordered by ID number from left to right. System assumptions also constrain UAV initial directions to be either left or right (though a UAV might have to immediately change this value, e.g., if it is initialized at the left endpoint headed left). These values become inputs to the UAVs. The System determines values for other UAV inputs, including whether a UAV is co-located with its right or left neighbor and the true values for the left and right perimeter endpoints. Note the true perimeter endpoints are only used by the UAVs to check whether they have reached the end of the perimeter, not to calculate boundary segment endpoints. The System also establishes data ports between UAVs, so that each UAV can receive updated coordination variable values from its left or right neighbor as inputs and use them (but only if they are co-located).

The last System output that serves as a UAV input is the position of the UAV. At initialization and after each event, the System uses the globally known constant UAV speed V and other information from each UAV to determine the amount of time δt until the next event, and then it updates the position of each

---

[3] AADL projects are in AADL_sandbox_projects. Algorithm A and B models for three UAVs are in projects DPSS-3-AlgA-for-paper and DPSS-3-AlgB-for-paper. A description of the Algorithm B model is in file modelAlgorithmB.pdf.

UAV. Determining the time of the next event requires knowing the direction and next anticipated "goal" location of each UAV, e.g. estimated perimeter endpoint or shared segment boundary. Each UAV outputs these values, which become inputs to the System. Each UAV also outputs its coordination variables P_{R_i}, P_{L_i}, N_{R_i}, and N_{L_i}, which become System inputs that are used in System guarantees that formalize Theorem 1, Lemma 1, and Theorem 2 of Sect. 2. Note that we bound integers N_{R_i} and N_{L_i} because in order to calculate estimated boundary segments, which requires dividing perimeter length by the number of UAVs, we must implement a lookup table that copies the values of N_{R_i} and N_{L_i} to real-valued versions of these variables. This is due to an interaction between AGREE and the Z3 SMT solver [4] used by AGREE. If we directly cast N_{R_i} and N_{L_i} to real values in AGREE, they are encoded in Z3 using the to_real function. Perimeter values P_{R_i} and P_{L_i} are directly declared as reals. However, Z3 views integers converted by the to_real function as constrained to have integer values, so it cannot use the specialized solver for reals that is able to analyze this model.

4 Formal Analysis Results

In this section, we discuss the analysis results provided by AGREE for Algorithm A and Algorithm B, though we focus on Algorithm B.

Algorithm A: Using AGREE configured to utilize the JKind k-induction model checker [7] and the Z3 SMT solver, we have proven Theorem 1, that Algorithm A converges within $2T$, for N = 1, 2, 3, 4, 5, and 6 UAVs. Computation time prevented us from analyzing more than six UAVs. For reference, N = 1 through N = 4 ran in under 10 min each on a laptop with two cores and 8 GB RAM. The same laptop analyzed N = 5 overnight. For N = 6, the analysis took approximately twenty days on a computer with 40 cores and 128 GB memory.

Algorithm B: We were able to prove Theorem 2, that DPSS converges within $5T$, for N = 1, 2, and 3 UAVs and with each UAV's coordination variables N_{R_i} and N_{L_i} bounded between 0 and 20. In fact, we found the convergence time to be within $(4 + \frac{1}{3}T)$. However, AGREE produced a counterexample to Lemma 1, that every UAV obtains correct coordination variables within $3T$, for N = 3. In fact, we incrementally increased this bound and found counterexamples up to $(3 + \frac{1}{2})T$ but that convergence is guaranteed in $(3 + \frac{2}{3})T$.

One of the shorter counterexamples provided by AGREE shows the UAVs obtaining correct coordination variables in 3.0129T. Full details are available on GitHub [1],[4] but we outline the steps in Fig. 3. In this counterexample, UAV 1 starts very close to the left perimeter heading right, and UAVs 2 and 3 start in the middle of segment 3 headed left. UAVs 1 and 2 meet near the middle of the perimeter and head left toward what they believe to be their shared segment boundary. This is very close to the left perimeter endpoint because, due to initial conditions, they believe the left perimeter endpoint to be much

---

[4] A spreadsheet with counterexample values for all model variables is located under AADL_sandbox_projects/DPSS-3-AlgB-for-paper/results_20180815_eispi.

farther away than it actually is. Then they split, and UAV 1 learns where the
left perimeter endpoint actually is, but UAV 2 does not. UAV 2 heads right and
meets UAV 3 shortly afterward, and they move to what they believe to be their
shared segment boundary, which is likewise very close to the right perimeter
endpoint. Then they split, and UAV 3 learns where the right perimeter endpoint
is, but UAV 2 does not. UAV 2 heads left, meets UAV 1 shortly after, and
learns correct "left" coordination variables. However, UAV 2 still believes the
right perimeter endpoint to be farther away than it actually is, so UAV 1 and 2
estimate their shared segment boundary to be near the middle of the perimeter.
They then head toward this point and split apart, with UAV 1 headed left and
still not having correct "right" coordination variables. UAV 2 and 3 then meet,
exchange information, and now both have correct coordination variables. They
go to their actual shared boundary, split apart, and UAV 2 heads left toward
UAV 1. UAV 1 and 2 then meet on segment 1, exchange information, and now
all UAVs have correct coordination variables.

The counterexample reveals a key intuition that was missing in Lemma 1.
The original argument did not fully consider the effects of initial conditions and
so only considered a case in which UAVs came close to *one* end of the perimeter
without actually reaching it. The counterexample shows it can happen at *both*
ends if initial conditions cause the UAVs to believe the perimeter endpoints to
be farther away than they actually are. This could happen if the perimeter were
to quickly shrink, causing the system to essentially "reinitialize" with incorrect
coordination variables.

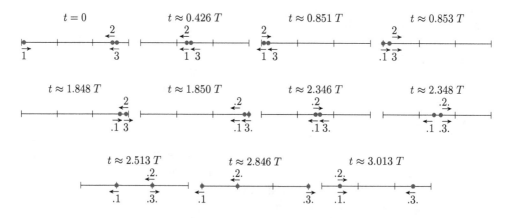

Fig. 3. Counterexample to Lemma 1. Dots to the left of a UAV number indicate it has
correct "left" variables, and likewise for the right.

Analysis for three UAVs for Algorithm B completed in 18 days on a machine
with 256 GB RAM and 80 cores.

5   Discussion and Conclusions

Formal modeling and analysis through AGREE had many benefits. First, it allowed us to analyze DPSS, a decentralized protocol for distributing a surveillance task across multiple UAVs. Though the original publication on DPSS provided a convincing human-generated proof and simulation results to support claims about its convergence bounds, analysis revealed that one of the key lemmas was incorrect. Furthermore, the counterexample returned by AGREE provided insight into why it was incorrect. Second, formal modeling in and of itself allowed us to find what were essentially technical typos in the original paper. For example, the formula for dividing the perimeter across UAVs only accounted for changes in estimates of the right perimeter endpoint and not the left, so we corrected the formula for our model. We also discovered that certain key aspects of the protocol were underspecified. In particular, it is unclear what should happen if more than two UAVs meet at the same time. Analysis showed this occurring for as little as three UAVs in Algorithm B, and simulations in the original paper showed this happening frequently, but this behavior was not explicitly described. Here, we decided that if all three UAVs meet to the left of UAV 3's estimated segment, UAV 3 immediately heads right and the other two follow the normal protocol to escort each other to their shared border. Otherwise, the UAVs all travel left together to the boundary between segments 2 and 3, then UAV 3 breaks off and heads right while the other two follow the normal protocol.

This brings us to a discussion of challenges and limitations. First, in terms of more than two UAVs meeting at a time, simulations in the original paper implement a more complex behavior in which UAVs head to the closest shared boundary and then split apart into smaller and smaller groups until reaching the standard case of two co-located UAVs. This behavior requires a more complex AGREE model that can track "cliques" of more than two UAVs, and it is difficult to validate the model due to long analysis run times. Second, we noted in Sect. 4 that in our model, UAV coordination variables N_{R_i} and N_{L_i} have an upper bound of 20. In fact, with an earlier upper bound of 3, we found the bound for Lemma 1 to be $(3 + \frac{1}{3})T$ and did not consider that it would depend on upper bounds for N_{R_i} and N_{L_i}. We therefore cannot conclude that even $(3 + \frac{2}{3})T$ is the convergence time for Lemma 1. Third and related to the last point, model checking with AGREE can only handle up to three UAVs for Algorithm B. Due to these limitations, we cannot say for sure what the upper bound for DPSS actually is, even if we believe it to be $5T$. If it is higher, then it takes DPSS longer to converge, meaning it can handle less frequent changes than originally believed. We are therefore attempting to transition to theorem provers such as ACL2 [9] and PVS [12] to develop a proof of convergence bounds for an arbitrary number of UAVs, upper bound on N_{R_i} and N_{L_i}, and perimeter length (which was set to a fixed size to make the model small enough to analyze).

In terms of recommendations and lessons learned, it was immensely useful to work with the author of DPSS to formalize our model. Multi-agent protocols like DPSS are inherently complex, and it is not surprising that the original paper contained some typos, underspecifications, and errors. In fact, the original paper explains DPSS quite well and is mostly correct, but it is still challenging for formal methods experts to understand complex systems from other disciplines, so access to subject matter experts can greatly speed up formalization.

Acknowledgment. We thank John Backes for his guidance on efficiently modeling DPSS in AGREE and Aaron Fifarek for running some of the longer AGREE analyses.

References

1. OpenUxAS GitHub repository, dpssModel branch. https://github.com/afrl-rq/OpenUxAS/tree/dpssModel
2. Alur, R., Moarref, S., Topcu, U.: Compositional synthesis of reactive controllers for multi-agent systems. In: Chaudhuri, S., Farzan, A. (eds.) CAV 2016. LNCS, vol. 9780, pp. 251–269. Springer, Cham (2016). https://doi.org/10.1007/978-3-319-41540-6_14
3. Cofer, D., Gacek, A., Miller, S., Whalen, M.W., LaValley, B., Sha, L.: Compositional verification of architectural models. In: Goodloe, A.E., Person, S. (eds.) NFM 2012. LNCS, vol. 7226, pp. 126–140. Springer, Heidelberg (2012). https://doi.org/10.1007/978-3-642-28891-3_13
4. de Moura, L., Bjørner, N.: Z3: an efficient SMT solver. In: Ramakrishnan, C.R., Rehof, J. (eds.) TACAS 2008. LNCS, vol. 4963, pp. 337–340. Springer, Heidelberg (2008). https://doi.org/10.1007/978-3-540-78800-3_24
5. Feiler, P.H., Lewis, B.A., Vestal, S.: The SAE architecture analysis & design language (AADL): a standard for engineering performance critical systems. In: IEEE International Conference Computer Aided Control System Design, pp. 1206–1211. IEEE (2006)
6. Fisher, M., Dennis, L., Webster, M.: Verifying autonomous systems. Commun. ACM **56**(9), 84–93 (2013)
7. Gacek, A., Backes, J., Whalen, M., Wagner, L., Ghassabani, E.: The JKIND model checker. In: Chockler, H., Weissenbacher, G. (eds.) CAV 2018. LNCS, vol. 10982, pp. 20–27. Springer, Cham (2018). https://doi.org/10.1007/978-3-319-96142-2_3
8. Guo, M., Tumova, J., Dimarogonas, D.V.: Cooperative decentralized multi-agent control under local LTL tasks and connectivity constraints. In: 2014 IEEE 53rd Annual Conference on Decision and Control (CDC), pp. 75–80. IEEE (2014)
9. Kaufmann, M., Moore, J.S.: An industrial strength theorem prover for a logic based on common lisp. IEEE Trans. Softw. Eng. **23**(4), 203–213 (1997)
10. Kingston, D., Beard, R.W., Holt, R.S.: Decentralized perimeter surveillance using a team of UAVs. IEEE Trans. Robot. **24**(6), 1394–1404 (2008)
11. Kupermann, O., Vardi, M.: Synthesizing distributed systems. In: Proceedings 16th Annual IEEE Symposium Logic in Computer Science, pp. 389–398. IEEE (2001)
12. Owre, S., Rushby, J.M., Shankar, N.: PVS: a prototype verification system. In: Kapur, D. (ed.) CADE 1992. LNCS, vol. 607, pp. 748–752. Springer, Heidelberg (1992). https://doi.org/10.1007/3-540-55602-8_217

8

StreamLAB: Stream-Based Monitoring of Cyber-Physical Systems

Peter Faymonville, Bernd Finkbeiner,
Malte Schledjewski, Maximilian Schwenger[✉],
Marvin Stenger, Leander Tentrup,
and Hazem Torfah

Reactive Systems Group, Saarland University,
Saarbrücken, Germany
{faymonville,finkbeiner,schledjewski,schwenger,
stenger,tentrup,torfah}@react.uni-saarland.de

Abstract. With ever increasing autonomy of cyber-physical systems, monitoring becomes an integral part for ensuring the safety of the system at runtime. StreamLAB is a monitoring framework with high degree of expressibility and strong correctness guarantees. Specifications are written in RTLola, a stream-based specification language with formal semantics. StreamLAB provides an extensive analysis of the specification, including the computation of memory consumption and run-time guarantees. We demonstrate the applicability of StreamLAB on typical monitoring tasks for cyber-physical systems, such as sensor validation and system health checks.

1 Introduction

In stream-based monitoring, we translate input streams containing data collected at runtime, such as sensor readings, into output streams containing aggregate statistics, such as an average value, a counter, or the integral of a signal. Trigger specifications define thresholds and other logical conditions on the values on these output streams, and raise an alarm or execute some other predefined action if the condition becomes true. The advantage of this setup is great expressiveness and easy-to-reuse, compositional specifications. Existing stream-based languages like Lola [9,12] are based on the synchronous programming paradigm, where all streams are synchronized via a global clock. In each step, the new values of all output streams are computed in terms of the values of the other streams at a previous time step or. This paradigm provides a simple and natural evaluation model that fits well with typical implementations on synchronous hardware. In real-time applications, however, the assumption that all data arrives synchronously is often simply not true. Consider, for example, an autonomous drone with several sensors, such as a GPS module, an inertia measurement unit, and a laser distance meter. While a synchronous arrival of all measured value would be desirable, some sensors' measurement frequency is higher than others. Moreover, the sensors do not necessarily operate on a common clock, so their readings drift apart over time.

In this paper we present the monitoring framework StreamLAB. We lift the synchronicity assumption to allow for monitoring asynchronous systems. Basis for the framework is RTLola, an extension of the steam-based runtime verification language Lola. RTLola introduces two new key concepts into Lola:

1. Variable-rate input streams: we consider input streams that extend at a-priori unknown rates. The only assumption is that each new event has a real-valued timestamp and that the events arrive in-order.
2. Sliding windows: A sliding window aggregates data over a real-time window given in units of time. For example, we might integrate the readings of an airspeed indicator.

As with any semantic extension, the challenge in the design of RTLola is to maintain the efficiency of the monitoring. Obviously, not all RTLola specifications can be monitored with constant memory since the rates of the input streams are unknown, an arbitrary number of events may occur in the span of a fixed real-time unit. Thus, for aggregations such as the mean requiring to store the whole sequence of value, no amount of constant memory will always suffice. We can, nevertheless, again identify an efficiently monitorable fragment that covers many specifications of practical interest. For the space-efficient aggregation over real-time sliding windows, we partition the real-time axis into equally-sized intervals. The size of the intervals is dictated by the rate of the output streams. For certain common types of aggregations, such as the sum or the number of entries, the values within each interval can be pre-aggregated and then only stored in this summarized form. In a static analysis of the specification, we identify parts of the specification with unbounded memory consumption, and compute bounds for all other parts of the specification. In this way, we can determine early, whether a particular specification can be executed on a system with limited memory.

Related Work. There is a rich body of work on monitoring real-time properties. Many monitoring approaches are based on real-time variants of temporal logics [3, 11, 16–18, 24]. Maler and Nickovic present a monitoring algorithm for properties written in signal temporal logic (STL) by reducing STL formulas via a boolean abstraction to formulas in the real-time logic MITL [21]. Building on these ideas, Donze et al. present an algorithm for the monitoring of STL properties over continuous signals [10]. The algorithm computes the robustness degree in which a piecewise-continuous signal satisfies or violates an STL formula. Towards more practical approaches, Basin et al. extend metric logics with parameterization [8]. A monitoring algorithm for the extension is implemented in the tool MonPoly [5]. MonPoly was introduced as a tool for monitoring usage-control policies. Another extension to metric dynamic logic was implemented in

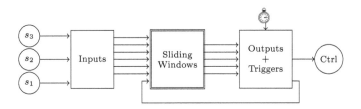

Fig. 1. Illustration of the decoupled input and output using aggregations.

the tool Aerial [7]. However, most monitors generated from temporal logics are limited to Boolean verdicts.

StreamLAB uses the stream-based language RTLola as its core specification language. RTLola builds upon Lola [9,12], which is a stream-based language originally developed for monitoring synchronous hardware circuits, by adding the concepts discussed above. Stream-based monitoring languages are significantly more expressive than temporal logics. Other prominent stream-based monitoring approaches are the *Copilot* framework [23] and the tool BeepBeep 3 [15]. Copilot is a dataflow language based on several declarative stream processing languages [9,14]. From a specification in Copilot, constant space and constant time C programs implementing embedded monitors are generated. The BeepBeep 3 tool uses an SQL-like language that is defined over streams of events. In addition to stream-processing, it contains operators such as slicing, where inputs can be separated into several different traces, and windowing where aggregations over a sliding window can be computed. Unlike RTLola, BeepBeep and Copilot assume a synchronous computation model, where all events arrive at a fixed rate. Two asynchronous real-time monitoring approaches are TeSSLa [19] and Striver [13]. TeSSLa allows for monitoring piece-wise constant signals where streams can emit events at different speeds with arbitrary latencies. Neither language provides the language feature of sliding windows and the definition of fixed-rate output streams. The efficient evaluation of aggregations on sliding windows [20] has previously been studied in the context of temporal logic [4]. Basin et al. present an algorithm for combining the elements of subsequences of a sliding window with an associative operator, which reuses the results of the subsequences in the evaluation of the next window [6].

2   Real-Time Lola

RTLola extends the stream-based specification languages Lola [12] with real-time features. In the stream-based processing paradigm, sensor readings are viewed as input streams to a stream processing engine that computes outputs in form of streams on top of the values of the input streams. For example, the RTLola specification

```
input altitude : Float32
output tooLow := altitude < 200.0
```

checks whether a drone flies with an altitude less than 200 feet. For each reading of the velocity sensor, a new value for the output stream *tooLow* is computed. Streams marked with the "**trigger**"-keyword alert the user when the value of the trigger is true. In the following example, the user is warned when the drone flies below the allowed altitude.

```
trigger tooLow "flying below minimum altitude"
```

Output streams in RTLola are computed from values of the input streams, other output streams and their own past values. If we want to count the number of times the drone dives below 200 feet we can specify the stream

```
output count := (if tooLow then 1 else 0)
   + count.offset(by:-1).defaults(to:0)
```

Here, the stream *count* computes its new values by increasing its latest value by 1 in case the drone currently flies below the permitted altitude. The expression `count.offset(by:-1)` represents the last value of the stream. We call such expressions "lookup expressions". The default operator `e.defaults(to:0)` returns the value 0 in case the value of `e` is not defined. This can happen when a stream is evaluated the first time and looks up its last value.

In RTLola, we do not impose any assumption on the arrival frequency of input streams. Each stream can produce new values individually and at arbitrary points in time. This can lead to problems when a burst of new input values occur in a short amount of time. Subsequently, the monitor needs to evaluate all output streams, exerting a lot of pressure on the system. To prevent that, RTLola distinguishes between two kinds of outputs. *Event-based* outputs are computed whenever new input values arrive and should thus only contain inexpensive operations. All streams discussed above where event-based. In contrast to that, there are *periodic* outputs such as the following:

```
output freqDev @5Hz := altitude.aggregate(over : 200ms,
                                          using: count) < 5
```

Here, *freqDev* will be evaluated every 200 ms as indicated by the "@ 5 Hz" label, independently of arriving input values. The stream *freqDev* does not access the event-based input *altitude* directly, but uses a *sliding window* expression to count the number of times a new value for *altitude* occurred within the last 200 ms. The value of *freqDev* represents the number of measurements the monitor received from the altimeter. Comparing this value against the expected number of readings allows for detecting deviations and thus a potentially damaged sensor.

Sliding windows allow for decoupling event-based and periodic streams, as illustrated in Fig. 1. Since the specifier has no control over the frequency of event-based streams, these streams should be quickly evaluatable. More expensive operations, such as sliding windows, may only be used in periodic streams to increase the monitor's robustness.

2.1 Examples

In the following, we will present several interesting properties showcasing RTLola's expressivity. The specifications are simplified for illustration and thus not immediately applicable to the real-world.

Sensor Validation. When a sensor starts to deteriorate, it can misbehave and drop single measurements. To verify that a GPS sensor produces values at its specified frequency, in this example 10 Hz, we count the number of sensor values in a continuous window and compare it against the expected amount of events in this time frame.

```
input lat: Float32, lon : Float32
output gps_freq@10Hz:=
  lat.aggregate(over: =1s, using: count).defaults(to:9)
trigger gps_freq < 9 "GPS sensor frequency < 9 Hz"
```

Assuming that we have another sensor measuring the true air speed, we can check whether the measured data matches the GPS data using RTLola's computation primitives. For this, we first compute the difference in longitude and latitude between the current and last measurement. The Euclidean distance provides the length of the movement vector, which can be derived discretely by dividing by the amount of time that has passed between two GPS measurements.

```
input velo : Float32
output δlon := lon - lon.offset(by:-1).defaults(to:lon)
output δlat := lat - lat.offset(by:-1).defaults(to:lat)
output gps_dist := sqrt(δlon * δlon + δlat * δlat)
output gps_velo := gps_dist
  / (time - time.offset(by:-1).defaults(to:0.0))
trigger abs(gps_velo - velo) > 0.1 "Deviating velocity"
```

When the pathfinding algorithm of the mission planner takes longer than expected, the system remains in a state without target location and thus hovers in place. Such a hover period can be detected by computing the covered distance in the last seconds. For this, we integrate the assumed velocity. We also exclude a strong headwind as a culprit for the low change in position.

```
input wnd_dir: Float32, wnd_spd : Float32
output dir := arctan(lat/lon)
output headwind := abs(wnd_dir - dir) < 0.2
  ∧ wnd_spd > 10.0
output hovering @ 1Hz := velo.aggregate(over: 5s, using: ∫)
  .defaults(to:0.5) < 0.5 ∧ ¬headwind.hold().defaults(to:⊥)
trigger hovering "Long hover phase"
```

3   Performance Guarantees via Static Analysis

3.1   Type System

RTLola is a strongly-typed specification language. Every expression has two orthogonal types: a value type and a stream type. The *value* type is `Bool`, `String`, `Int`, or `Float`. It indicates the usual semantics of a value or expression and the amount of memory required to store the value. The *stream* type indicates when a value is evaluated. For periodic streams, the stream type defines the frequency in which it is computed. Event-based streams do not have a pre-determined period. The stream type for an event-based stream identifies a set of input streams, indicating that the event-based stream is extended whenever there is, synchronously, an event on all input streams. Event-based streams may also depend on input streams not listed in the type; in such cases, the type system requires an explicit use of the 0-order *sample&hold* operator.

The type system provides runtime guarantees for the monitor: Independently of the arrival of input data, it is guaranteed that all required data is available whenever a stream is extended. Either the data was just received as input event, was computed as output stream value, or the specifier provided a default value. The type system can, thus, eliminate classes of specification problems like unintentionally accessing a slower stream from a faster stream. Whenever possible, the tool provides automatic type inference.

3.2   Sliding Windows

We use two techniques to ensure that we only need a bounded amount of memory to compute sliding windows. Meertens [22] classifies an aggregations $\gamma\colon A^* \to B$ as list homomorphism if it can be split into a mapping function $m\colon A \to T$, an associative reduction function $r\colon T \times T \to T$, a finalization function $f\colon T \to B$, and a neutral element $\varepsilon \in T$ with $\forall t \in T\colon r(t,\varepsilon) = r(\varepsilon,t) = t$. For these functions, rather than aggregating the whole list at once, one can apply m to each element, reduce the intermediate results with an arbitrary precedence, and finalize the result to get the same value. The second technique by Li et al. [20] divides a time interval into panes of equal size. For each pane, we aggregate all inputs and store only the fix amount of intermediate values. The type system ensures that sliding windows only occur in periodic streams so by choosing the pane size as the inverse of the frequency, paning does not change the result. In StreamLAB there are several pre-defined aggregation functions such as count, integration, summation, product, mini-, and maximization available.

3.3   Memory Analysis

StreamLAB computes the worst-case memory consumption of the specification. For this, an annotated dependency graph (ADG) is constructed where each stream s constitutes a node v_s and whenever s accesses s', there is an edge from v_s to $v_{s'}$. Edges are annotated according to the type of access: if s accesses

s' discretely with offset n or with a sliding window aggregation of duration d and aggregation function γ, then the edge $e = (v_s, v_{s'})$ is labeled with $\lambda(e) = n$ or $\lambda(e) = (d, \gamma)$, respectively. Nodes of periodic streams are now annotated with their periodicity, if stream s has period $200\,\text{ms}$ then the node is labeled with $\pi(v_s) = 5\,\text{Hz}$. Memory bounds for discrete-time offsets can be computed as for Lola [9]. We extend this algorithm with new computational rules to determine the memory bounds for real-time expressions. For each edge $e = (v, v')$ in the ADG we can determine how many events of v' must be stored for the computation of v using the rules in Fig. 2. Here, only γ is a list homomorphism. The strict upper bound on required memory is now the sum of the memory requirement of each individual stream. This, however, is only the amount of memory needed for storing values and does not take book-keeping data structures and the internal representation of the specification into account. Assuming reasonably small expressions (depth ≤ 64), this additional memory can be bounded with $1\,\text{kB}$ per stream plus a flat $10\,\text{kB}$ for working memory.

$\pi(v)$	$\pi(v')$	$\lambda(e) = (d, \gamma)$	$\lambda(e) = (d, \gamma^*)$
var	var	$unbounded$	zd
$x\text{Hz}$	var	$unbounded$	$\min(zd, xd)$
var	$y\text{Hz}$	yd	$\min(zd, yd)$
$x\text{Hz}$	$y\text{Hz}$	$\min(xd, yd)$	$\min(xd, yd)$

Fig. 2. Computation of memory bound over the dependency graph.

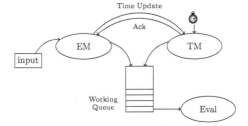

Fig. 3. Illustration of the data flow. The EM manages input events, TM schedules periodic tasks, and Eval manages the evaluation of streams.

4 Processing Engine

The processing engine consists of three components: The *EventManager (EM)* reads events from an input such Standard In or a CSV file and translates string values into the internal representation. The values are mapped to the corresponding input streams in the specification. Using a multiple-sender-single-receiver channel, the EM pushes the event on a working queue. The *TimeManager (TM)* schedules the evaluation of periodic streams. The TM computes the hyper-period of all streams and groups them by equal deadlines. Whenever a deadline is due, the corresponding streams are pushed into the working queue using the same channel as the EM. This ensures that event-based and periodic evaluation cycles occur in the correct order even under high pressure. Lastly, the *Evaluator (Eval)* manages the evaluation of streams and storage of computed values. The Eval repeatedly pops items off the working queue and evaluates the respective streams.

When monitoring a system online, the TM uses the internal system clock for scheduling tasks. When monitoring offline, however, this is no longer possible because the point in time when a stream is due to be evaluated depends on the input event. Thus, before the EM pushes an event on the working queue, it transmits the latest timestamp to the TM. The TM then decides whether some periodic streams need to be evaluated. If so, it effectively goes back in time by pushing the respective task on the working queue before acknowledging the TM. Only upon receiving the acknowledgement, the TM sends the event to the working queue. Figure 3 illustrates the information flow between the components.

5   Experiments

StreamLAB[1] is implemented in Rust. A major benefit of a Rust implementation is the connection to LLVM, which allows a compilation to a large variety of platforms. Moreover, the requirements to the runtime environment are as low as for C programs. This allows StreamLAB to be widely applicable.

The specifications presented in Sect. 2.1 have been tested on traces generated with the state-of-the-art flight simulator ARDUPILOT[2]. Each trace is the result of a drone flying one or more round-trips over Saarland University and provides sensor information for longitude and latitude, true air velocity, wind direction and speed, as well as the number of available GPS satellites. The longest trace consists of slightly less than 433,000 events. StreamLAB successfully detected a variety of errors such as delayed sensor readings, GPS module failures, and phases without significant movement. For an online runtime verification, the monitor reads an event of the simulator's output, processes the input data and pauses until the next event is available. Whenever necessary, periodic streams are evaluated. Online monitoring of a simulation did not allow us to exhaust the capabilities of StreamLAB because the generation of events took significantly longer than processing them. The offline monitoring function of StreamLAB allows the user to specify a delay in which consecutive events are read from a file. By gradually decreasing the delay between events until the pressure was too high, we could determine a maximum input frequency of 647.2 kHz. When disabling the delay and running the monitor at maximum speed, StreamLAB processes a trace of length 432,961 in 0.67 s, so each event takes 1545 ns to process while three threads utilized 146% of CPU. In terms of memory, the maximum resident set size amounted to 16 MB. This includes bookkeeping data structures, the specification, evaluator code, and parts of the C standard library. While the evaluation does not require any heap allocation after the setup phase, the average stack size amounts to less than 1kB. The experiment was conducted on 3.3 GHz Intel Core i7 processor with 16 GB 2133 MHz LPDDR3 RAM.

---

[1] www.stream-lab.org.

[2] ardupilot.org.

6 Outlook

The stream-based monitoring framework StreamLAB demonstrates the applicability of stream monitoring for cyber-physical systems. Previous versions of Lola have successfully been applied to networks and unmanned aircraft systems in cooperation the with German Aerospace Center DLR [1,2,12]. StreamLAB provides a modular, easy-to-understand specification language and design-time feedback for specifiers. This helps to improve the development process for cyber-physical systems. Coupled with the promising experimental results, this lays the foundation for further applications of the framework on real-world systems.

References

1. Adolf, F.-M., Faymonville, P., Finkbeiner, B., Schirmer, S., Torens, C.: Stream runtime monitoring on UAS. In: Lahiri, S., Reger, G. (eds.) RV 2017. LNCS, vol. 10548, pp. 33–49. Springer, Cham (2017). https://doi.org/10.1007/978-3-319-67531-2_3

2. Adolf, F., Faymonville, P., Finkbeiner, B., Schirmer, S., Torens, C.: Stream runtime monitoring on UAS. CoRR arXiv:abs/1804.04487 (2018). http://arxiv.org/abs/1804.04487

3. Alur, R., Henzinger, T.A.: Real-time logics: complexity and expressiveness. In: [1990] Proceedingsof the Fifth Annual IEEE Symposium on Logic in Computer Science, pp. 390–401, June 1990. https://doi.org/10.1109/LICS.1990.113764

4. Basin, D., Bhatt, B.N., Traytel, D.: Almost event-rate independent monitoring of metric temporal logic. In: Legay, A., Margaria, T. (eds.) TACAS 2017. LNCS, vol. 10206, pp. 94–112. Springer, Heidelberg (2017). https://doi.org/10.1007/978-3-662-54580-5_6

5. Basin, D., Harvan, M., Klaedtke, F., Zălinescu, E.: MONPOLY: monitoring usage-control policies. In: Khurshid, S., Sen, K. (eds.) RV 2011. LNCS, vol. 7186, pp. 360–364. Springer, Heidelberg (2012). https://doi.org/10.1007/978-3-642-29860-8_27

6. Basin, D., Klaedtke, F., Zălinescu, E.: Greedily computing associative aggregations on sliding windows. Inf. Process. Lett. **115**(2), 186–192 (2015). https://doi.org/10.1016/j.ipl.2014.09.009

7. Basin, D., Traytel, D., Krstić, S.: Aerial: almost event-rate independent algorithms for monitoring metric regular properties (2017). https://www21.in.tum.de/~traytel/papers/rvcubes17-aerial_tool/index.html

8. Basin, D.A., Klaedtke, F., Müller, S., Zalinescu, E.: Monitoring metric first-order temporal properties. J. ACM **62**(2), 15:1–15:45 (2015). https://doi.org/10.1145/2699444

9. D'Angelo, B., et al.: Lola: Runtime monitoring of synchronous systems. In: TIME 2005, pp. 166–174. IEEE Computer Society Press, June 2005

10. Donzé, A., Ferrère, T., Maler, O.: Efficient robust monitoring for STL. In: Sharygina, N., Veith, H. (eds.) CAV 2013. LNCS, vol. 8044, pp. 264–279. Springer, Heidelberg (2013). https://doi.org/10.1007/978-3-642-39799-8_19

11. Donzé, A., Maler, O.: Robust satisfaction of temporal logic over real-valued signals. In: Chatterjee, K., Henzinger, T.A. (eds.) FORMATS 2010. LNCS, vol. 6246, pp. 92–106. Springer, Heidelberg (2010). https://doi.org/10.1007/978-3-642-15297-9_9. http://dl.acm.org/citation.cfm?id=1885174.1885183

12. Faymonville, P., Finkbeiner, B., Schirmer, S., Torfah, H.: A stream-based speci-
    fication language for network monitoring. In: Falcone, Y., Sánchez, C. (eds.) RV
    2016. LNCS, vol. 10012, pp. 152–168. Springer, Cham (2016). https://doi.org/10.
    1007/978-3-319-46982-9_10
13. Gorostiaga, F., Sánchez, C.: Striver: stream runtime verification for real-time event-
    streams. In: Colombo, C., Leucker, M. (eds.) RV 2018. LNCS, vol. 11237, pp. 282–
    298. Springer, Cham (2018). https://doi.org/10.1007/978-3-030-03769-7_16
14. Halbwachs, N., Caspi, P., Raymond, P., Pilaud, D.: The synchronous dataflow
    programming language lustre. In: Proceedings of the IEEE, pp. 1305–1320 (1991)
15. Hallé, S.: When RV meets CEP. In: Falcone, Y., Sánchez, C. (eds.) RV 2016. LNCS,
    vol. 10012, pp. 68–91. Springer, Cham (2016). https://doi.org/10.1007/978-3-319-
    46982-9_6
16. Harel, E., Lichtenstein, O., Pnueli, A.: Explicit clock temporal logic. In: LICS 1990,
    pp. 402–413. IEEE Computer Society (1990). https://doi.org/10.1109/LICS.1990.
    113765
17. Jahanian, F., Mok, A.K.L.: Safety analysis of timing properties in real-time sys-
    tems. IEEE Trans. Softw. Eng. **SE-12**(9), 890–904 (1986). https://doi.org/10.
    1109/TSE.1986.6313045
18. Koymans, R.: Specifying real-time properties with metric temporal logic. Real-
    Time Syst. **2**(4), 255–299 (1990). https://doi.org/10.1007/BF01995674
19. Leucker, M., Sánchez, C., Scheffel, T., Schmitz, M., Schramm, A.: Tessla: runtime
    verification of non-synchronized real-time streams. In: Haddad, H.M., Wainwright,
    R.L., Chbeir, R. (eds.) PSAC 2018, pp. 1925–1933. ACM (2018). https://doi.org/
    10.1145/3167132.3167338
20. Li, J., Maier, D., Tufte, K., Papadimos, V., Tucker, P.A.: No pane, no gain: efficient
    evaluation of sliding-window aggregates over data streams. SIGMOD Rec. **34**(1),
    39–44 (2005). https://doi.org/10.1145/1058150.1058158
21. Maler, O., Nickovic, D.: Monitoring temporal properties of continuous signals. In:
    Lakhnech, Y., Yovine, S. (eds.) FORMATS/FTRTFT -2004. LNCS, vol. 3253, pp.
    152–166. Springer, Heidelberg (2004). https://doi.org/10.1007/978-3-540-30206-
    3_12
22. Meertens, L.: Algorithmics: towards programming as a mathematical activity
    (1986)
23. Pike, L., Goodloe, A., Morisset, R., Niller, S.: Copilot: a hard real-time runtime
    monitor. In: Barringer, H., et al. (eds.) RV 2010. LNCS, vol. 6418, pp. 345–359.
    Springer, Heidelberg (2010). https://doi.org/10.1007/978-3-642-16612-9_26
24. Raskin, J.-F., Schobbens, P.-Y.: Real-time logics: fictitious clock as an abstraction
    of dense time. In: Brinksma, E. (ed.) TACAS 1997. LNCS, vol. 1217, pp. 165–182.
    Springer, Heidelberg (1997). https://doi.org/10.1007/BFb0035387

9

Symbolic Monitoring Against Specifications Parametric in Time and Data

Masaki Waga[1,2,3](✉)[iD], Étienne André[1,4,5][iD],
and Ichiro Hasuo[1,2][iD]

[1] National Institute of Informatics, Tokyo, Japan
mwaga@nii.ac.jp
[2] SOKENDAI (The Graduate University for Advanced Studies), Tokyo, Japan
[3] JSPS Research Fellow, Tokyo, Japan
[4] Université Paris 13, LIPN, CNRS, UMR 7030, 93430 Villetaneuse, France
[5] JFLI, CNRS, Tokyo, Japan

Abstract. Monitoring consists in deciding whether a log meets a given specification. In this work, we propose an automata-based formalism to monitor logs in the form of actions associated with time stamps and arbitrarily data values over infinite domains. Our formalism uses both timing parameters and data parameters, and is able to output answers symbolic in these parameters and in the log segments where the property is satisfied or violated. We implemented our approach in an ad-hoc prototype SyMon, and experiments show that its high expressive power still allows for efficient online monitoring.

1 Introduction

Monitoring consists in checking whether a sequence of data (a log or a signal) satisfies or violates a specification expressed using some formalism. Offline monitoring consists in performing this analysis after the system execution, as the technique has access to the entire log in order to decide whether the specification is violated. In contrast, online monitoring can make a decision earlier, ideally as soon as a witness of the violation of the specification is encountered.

Using existing formalisms (e.g., the metric first order temporal logic [14]), one can check whether a given bank customer withdraws more than 1,000 € every week. With formalisms extended with data, one may even *identify* such customers. Or, using an extension of the signal temporal logic (STL) [18], one can ask: "is that true that the value of variable x is always copied to y exactly 4 time units later?" However, questions relating time and data using parameters become much harder (or even impossible) to express using existing formalisms: "what are the users and time frames during which a user withdraws more than half of the total bank withdrawals within seven days?" And even, can we *synthesize* the durations (not necessarily 7 days) for which this specification holds? Or "what is the set of variables for which there exists a duration within which their value is always copied to another variable?" In addition, detecting periodic behaviors without knowing the period can be hard to achieve using existing formalisms.

In this work, we address the challenging problem to monitor logs enriched with both timing information and (infinite domain) data. In addition, we significantly push the existing limits of expressiveness so as to allow for a further level of abstraction using *parameters*: our specification can be both parametric in the *time* and in the *data*. The answer to this symbolic monitoring is richer than a pure Boolean answer, as it *synthesizes* the values of both time and data parameters for which the specification holds. This allows us notably to detect periodic behaviors without knowing the period while being symbolic in terms of data. For example, we can *synthesize variable names* (data) and *delays* for which variables will have their value copied to another data within the aforementioned delay. In addition, we show that we can detect the log *segments* (start and end date) for which a specification holds.

Example 1. Consider a system updating three variables a, b and c (i. e., strings) to values (rationals). An example of log is given in Fig. 1a. Although our work is event-based, we can give a graphical representation similar to that of signals in Fig. 1b. Consider the following property: "for any variable px, whenever an update of that variable occurs, then within strictly less than tp time units, the value of variable b must be equal to that update". The *variable parameter* px is compared with string values and the *timing parameter* tp is used in the timing constraints. We are interested in checking for which values of px and tp this property is violated. This can be seen as a synthesis problem in both the variable and timing parameters. For example, px = c and tp = 1.5 is a violation of the specification, as the update of c to 2 at time 4 is not propagated to b within 1.5 time unit. Our algorithm outputs such violation by a constraint e.g., $px = c \wedge tp \leq 2$. In contrast, the value of any signal at any time is always such that either b is equal to that signal, or the value of b will be equal to that value within at most 2 time units. Thus, the specification holds for any valuation of the variable parameter px, provided tp > 2.

We propose an automata-based approach to perform monitoring parametric in both time and data. We implement our work in a prototype SYMON and perform experiments showing that, while our formalism allows for high expressiveness, it is also tractable even for online monitoring.

We believe our framework balances expressiveness and monitoring performance well: *(i)* Regarding expressiveness, comparison with the existing work is summarized in Table 1 (see Sect. 2 for further details). *(ii)* Our monitoring is *complete*, in the sense that it returns a symbolic constraint characterizing *all* the parameter valuations that match a given specification. *(iii)* We also achieve

Table 1. Comparison of monitoring expressiveness

Work	[7]	[18]	[14]	[13]	[30]	[26]	[4]	[9]	This work
Timing parameters	✓	×	?	?	?	×	✓	×	✓
Data	✓	✓	✓	✓	✓	✓	×	✓	✓
Parametric data	✓	×	✓	✓	✓	✓	×	✓	✓
Memory	×	✓	✓	✓	✓	✓	×	×	✓
Aggregation	×	×	×	✓	✓	×	×	×	✓
Complete parameter identification	✓	N/A	✓✓	✓✓	N/A	N/A	✓	✓	✓

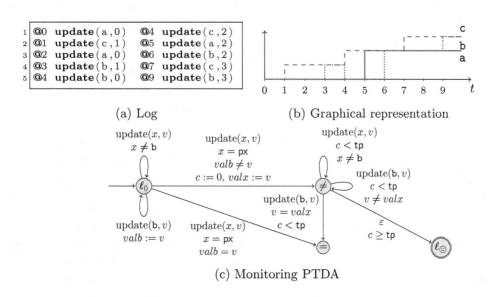

Fig. 1. Monitoring copy to b within tp time units

reasonable monitoring speed, especially given the degree of parametrization in our formalism. Note that it is not easy to formally claim superiority in expressiveness: proofs would require arguments such as the pumping lemma; and such formal comparison does not seem to be a concern of the existing work. Moreover, such formal comparison bears little importance for industrial practitioners: expressivity via an elaborate encoding is hardly of practical use. We also note that, in the existing work, we often observe gaps between the formalism in a theory and the formalism that the resulting tool actually accepts. This is not the case with the current framework.

Outline. After discussing related works in Sect. 2, we introduce the necessary preliminaries in Sect. 3, and our parametric timed data automata in Sect. 4. We present our symbolic monitoring approach in Sect. 5 and conduct experiments in Sect. 6. We conclude in Sect. 7.

2   Related Works

Robustness and Monitoring. Robust (or quantitative) monitoring extends the
binary question whether a log satisfies a specification by asking "by how much"
the specification is satisfied. The quantification of the distance between a signal and a signal temporal logic (STL) specification has been addressed in, e.g.,
[20–23, 25, 27] (or in a slightly different setting in [5]). The distance can be understood in terms of space ("signals") or time. In [6], the distance also copes for
reordering of events. In [10], the *robust pattern matching problem* is considered
over signal regular expressions, by quantifying the distance between the signal
regular expression specification and the *segments* of the signal. For piecewise-
constant and piecewise-linear signals, the problem can be effectively solved using
a finite union of convex polyhedra. While our framework does not fit in robust
monitoring, we can simulate both the robustness w.r.t. time (using timing parameters) and w.r.t. data, e.g., signal values (using data parameters).

Monitoring with Data. The tool MARQ [30] performs monitoring using Quantified Event Automata (QEA) [12]. This approach and ours share the automata-
based framework, the ability to express some first-order properties using "events
containing data" (which we encode using local variables associated with actions),
and data may be quantified. However, [30] does not seem to natively support
specification parametric in time; in addition, [30] does not perform complete
("symbolic") parameters synthesis, but outputs the violating entries of the log.

The metric first order temporal logic (MFOTL) allows for a high expressiveness by allowing universal and existential quantification over data—which can
be seen as a way to express parameters. A monitoring algorithm is presented for
a safety fragment of MFOTL in [14]. Aggregation operators are added in [13],
allowing to compute *sums* or *maximums* over data. A fragment of this logics is
implemented in MONPOLY [15]. While these works are highly expressive, they
do not natively consider timing parameters; in addition, MONPOLY does not
output symbolic answers, i.e., symbolic conditions on the parameters to ensure
validity of the formula.

In [26], binary decision diagrams (BDDs) are used to symbolically represent the observed data in QTL. This can be seen as monitoring data against
a parametric specification, with a symbolic internal encoding. However, their
implementation DEJAVU only outputs *concrete* answers. In contrast, we are
able to provide symbolic answers (both in timing and data parameters), e.g., in
the form of union of polyhedra for rationals, and unions of string constraints
using equalities ($=$) and inequalities ($\neq$).

Freeze Operator. In [18], STL is extended with a freeze operator that can
"remember" the value of a signal, to compare it to a later value of the same
signal. This logic STL* can express properties such as "In the initial 10 s, x
copies the values of y within a delay of 4 s": $\mathbf{G}_{[0,10]} * (\mathbf{G}_{[0,4]} y^* = x)$. While the
setting is somehow different (STL* operates over signals while we operate over
timed data words), the requirements such as the one above can easily be encoded

in our framework. In addition, we are able to *synthesize* the delay within which the values are always copied, as in Example 1. In contrast, it is not possible to determine using STL* which variables and which delays violate the specification.

Monitoring with Parameters. In [7], a log in the form of a dense-time real-valued signal is tested against a parameterized extension of STL, where parameters can be used to model uncertainty both in signal values and in timing values. The output comes in the form of a subset of the parameters space for which the formula holds on the log. In [9], the focus is only on signal parameters, with an improved efficiency by reusing techniques from the *robust* monitoring. Whereas [7,9] fit in the framework of signals and temporal logics while we fit in words and automata, our work shares similarities with [7,9] in the sense that we can express data parameters; in addition, [9] is able as in our work to exhibit the segment of the log associated with the parameters valuations for which the specification holds. A main difference however is that we can use memory and aggregation, thanks to arithmetic on variables.

In [24], the problem of *inferring* temporal logic formulae with constraints that hold in a given numerical data time series is addressed.

Timed Pattern Matching. A recent line of work is that of timed pattern matching, that takes as input a log and a specification, and decides *where* in the log the specification is satisfied or violated. On the one hand, a line of works considers signals, with specifications either in the form of timed regular expressions [11,31–33], or a temporal logic [34]. On the other hand, a line of works considers timed words, with specifications in the form of timed automata [4,36]. We will see that our work can also encode parametric timed pattern matching. Therefore, our work can be seen as a two-dimensional extension of both lines of works: first, we add timing parameters ([4] also considers similar timing parameters) and, second, we add data—themselves extended with parameters. That is, coming back to Example 1, [31–33,36] could only infer the segments of the log for which the property is violated for a given (fixed) variable and a given (fixed) timing parameter; while [4] could infer both the segments of the log and the timing parameter valuations, but not which variable violates the specification.

Summary. We compare related works in Table 1. "Timing parameters" denote the ability to synthesize unknown constants used in timing constraints (e.g., modalities intervals, or clock constraints). "?" denotes works not natively supporting this, although it might be encoded. The term "Data" refers to the ability to manage logs over infinite domains (apart from timestamps). For example, the log in Fig. 1a features, beyond timestamps, both string (variable name) and rationals (value). Also, works based on real-valued signals are naturally able to manage (at least one type of) data. "Parametric data" refer to the ability to express formulas where data (including signal values) are compared to (quantified or unquantified) variables or unknown parameters; for example, in the log in Fig. 1a, an example of property parametric in data is to synthesize the parameters for which the difference of values between two consecutive updates of variable px is always below pv, where px is a string parameter and pv a rational-valued parameter. "Memory" is the ability to remember *past* data; this can be achieved using e.g., the freeze operator of STL*, or variables (e.g., in [14, 26, 30]). "Aggregation" is the ability to aggregate data using operators such as sum or maximum; this allows to express properties such as "A user must not withdraw more than \$10,000 within a 31 day period" [13]. This can be supported using dedicated aggregation operators [13] or using variables ([30], and our work). "Complete parameter identification" denotes the *synthesis* of the set of parameters that satisfy or violate the property. Here, "N/A" denotes the absence of parameter [18], or when parameters are used in a way (existentially or universally quantified) such as the identification is not explicit (instead, the position of the log where the property is violated is returned [26]). In contrast, we return in a *symbolic* manner (as in [4,7]) the exact set of (data and timing) parameters for which a property is satisfied. "$\checkmark$/$\times$" denotes "yes" in the theory paper, but not in the tool.

3   Preliminaries

Clocks, Timing Parameters and Timed Guards. We assume a set $\mathbb{C} = \{c_1, \ldots, c_H\}$ of *clocks*, i.e., real-valued variables that evolve at the same rate. A *clock valuation* is $\nu : \mathbb{C} \to \mathbb{R}_{\geq 0}$. We write $\mathbf{0}$ for the clock valuation assigning 0 to all clocks. Given $d \in \mathbb{R}_{\geq 0}$, $\nu + d$ is s.t. $(\nu + d)(c) = \nu(c) + d$, for all $c \in \mathbb{C}$. Given $R \subseteq \mathbb{C}$, we define the *reset* of a valuation ν, denoted by $[\nu]_R$, as follows: $[\nu]_R(c) = 0$ if $c \in R$, and $[\nu]_R(c) = \nu(c)$ otherwise.

We assume a set $\mathbb{TP} = \{\mathsf{tp}_1, \ldots, \mathsf{tp}_J\}$ of *timing parameters*. A *timing parameter valuation* is $\gamma : \mathbb{TP} \to \mathbb{Q}_+$. We assume $\bowtie \in \{<, \leq, =, \geq, >\}$. A *timed guard tg* is a constraint over $\mathbb{C} \cup \mathbb{TP}$ defined by a conjunction of inequalities of the form $c \bowtie d$, or $c \bowtie \mathsf{tp}$ with $d \in \mathbb{N}$ and $\mathsf{tp} \in \mathbb{TP}$. Given tg, we write $\nu \models \gamma(tg)$ if the expression obtained by replacing each c with $\nu(c)$ and each tp with $\gamma(\mathsf{tp})$ in tg evaluates to true.

Variables, Data Parameters and Data Guards. For sake of simplicity, we assume a *single* infinite domain $\mathbb{D}$ for data. The formalism defined in Sect. 4 can be extended in a straightforward manner to different domains for different variables (and our implementation does allow for different types). The case of *finite* data domain is immediate too. We define this formalism in an *abstract* manner, so as to allow a sort of parameterized domain.

We assume a set $\mathbb{V} = \{v_1, \ldots, v_M\}$ of *variables* valued over $\mathbb{D}$. These variables are internal variables, that allow an high expressive power in our framework, as they can be compared or updated to other variables or parameters. We also assume a set $\mathbb{LV} = \{lv_1, \ldots, lv_O\}$ of *local variables* valued over $\mathbb{D}$. These variables will only be used locally along a transition in the "argument" of the action (e.g., x and v in upate(x, v)), and in the associated guard and (right-hand part of) updates. We assume a set $\mathbb{VP} = \{\mathsf{vp}_1, \ldots, \mathsf{vp}_N\}$ of *data parameters*, i.e., unknown variable constants.

A *data type* $(\mathbb{D}, \mathcal{DE}, \mathcal{DU})$ is made of *(i)* an infinite domain $\mathbb{D}$, *(ii)* a set of admissible Boolean expressions $\mathcal{DE}$ (that may rely on $\mathbb{V}$, $\mathbb{LV}$ and $\mathbb{VP}$), which will define the type of guards over variables in our subsequent automata, and *(iii)* a domain for updates $\mathcal{DU}$ (that may rely on $\mathbb{V}$, $\mathbb{LV}$ and $\mathbb{VP}$), which will define the type of updates of variables in our subsequent automata.

Example 2. As a first example, let us define the data type for rationals. We have $\mathbb{D} = \mathbb{Q}$. Let us define Boolean expressions. A *rational comparison* is a constraint over $\mathbb{V} \cup \mathbb{LV} \cup \mathbb{VP}$ defined by a conjunction of inequalities of the form $v \bowtie d$, $v \bowtie v'$, or $v \bowtie \mathsf{vp}$ with $v, v' \in \mathbb{V} \cup \mathbb{LV}$, $d \in \mathbb{Q}$ and $\mathsf{vp} \in \mathbb{VP}$. $\mathcal{DE}$ is the set of all rational comparisons over $\mathbb{V} \cup \mathbb{LV} \cup \mathbb{VP}$. Let us then define updates. First, a linear arithmetic expression over $\mathbb{V} \cup \mathbb{LV} \cup \mathbb{VP}$ is $\sum_i \alpha_i v_i + \beta$, where $v_i \in \mathbb{V} \cup \mathbb{LV} \cup \mathbb{VP}$ and $\alpha_i, \beta \in \mathbb{Q}$. Let $\mathcal{LA}(\mathbb{V} \cup \mathbb{LV} \cup \mathbb{VP})$ denote the set of arithmetic expressions over $\mathbb{V}$, $\mathbb{LV}$ and $\mathbb{VP}$. We then have $\mathcal{DU} = \mathcal{LA}(\mathbb{V} \cup \mathbb{LV} \cup \mathbb{VP})$.

As a second example, let us define the data type for strings. We have $\mathbb{D} = \mathbb{S}$, where $\mathbb{S}$ denotes the set of all strings. A *string comparison* is a constraint over $\mathbb{V} \cup \mathbb{LV} \cup \mathbb{VP}$ defined by a conjunction of comparisons of the form $v \approx s$, $v \approx v'$, or $v \approx \mathsf{vp}$ with $v, v' \in \mathbb{V} \cup \mathbb{LV}$, $s \in \mathbb{S}$, $\mathsf{vp} \in \mathbb{VP}$ and $\approx \in \{=, \neq\}$. $\mathcal{DE}$ is the set of all string comparisons over $\mathbb{V} \cup \mathbb{LV} \cup \mathbb{VP}$. $\mathcal{DU} = \mathbb{V} \cup \mathbb{LV} \cup \mathbb{S}$, i. e., a string variable can be assigned another string variable, or a concrete string.

A *variable valuation* is $\mu : \mathbb{V} \to \mathbb{D}$. A *local variable valuation* is a partial function $\eta : \mathbb{LV} \nrightarrow \mathbb{D}$. A *data parameter valuation* is $\zeta : \mathbb{VP} \to \mathbb{D}$. Given a data guard $dg \in \mathcal{DE}$, a variable valuation μ, a local variable valuation η defined for the local variables in dg, and a data parameter valuation ζ, we write $(\mu, \eta) \models \zeta(dg)$ if the expression obtained by replacing within dg all occurrences of each data parameter vp_i by $\zeta(\mathsf{vp}_i)$ and all occurrences of each variable v_j (resp. local variable lv_k) with its concrete valuation $\mu(v_j)$ (resp. $\eta(lv_k)$)) evaluates to true.

A parametric data update is a partial function $\mathsf{PDU} : \mathbb{V} \nrightarrow \mathcal{DU}$. That is, we can assign to a variable an expression over data parameters and other variables, according to the data type. Given a parametric data update PDU, a variable valuation μ, a local variable valuation η (defined for all local variables appearing in PDU), and a data parameter valuation ζ, we define $[\mu]_{\eta(\zeta(\mathsf{PDU}))} : \mathbb{V} \to \mathbb{D}$ as:

$$[\mu]_{\eta(\zeta(\mathsf{PDU}))}(v) = \begin{cases} \mu(v) & \text{if } \mathsf{PDU}(v) \text{ is undefined} \\ \eta(\mu(\zeta(\mathsf{PDU}(v)))) & \text{otherwise} \end{cases}$$

where $\eta(\mu(\zeta(\mathsf{PDU}(v))))$ denotes the replacement within the update expression $\mathsf{PDU}(v)$ of all occurrences of each data parameter vp_i by $\zeta(\mathsf{vp}_i)$, and all occur-

Table 2. Variables, parameters and valuations used in guards

	Timed guards		Data guards		
	Clock	Timing parameter	(Data) variable	Local variable	Data parameter
Variable	c	tp	v	lv	vp
Valuation	ν	γ	μ	η	ζ

rences of each variable v_j (resp. local variable lv_k) with its concrete valuation $\mu(v_j)$ (resp. $\eta(lv_k)$). Observe that this replacement gives a value in $\mathbb{D}$, therefore the result of $[\mu]_{\eta(\zeta(\mathsf{PDU}))}$ is indeed a data parameter valuation $\mathbb{V} \to \mathbb{D}$. That is, $[\mu]_{\eta(\zeta(\mathsf{PDU}))}$ computes the new (non-parametric) variable valuation obtained after applying to μ the partial function PDU valuated with ζ.

Example 3. Consider the data type for rationals, the variables set $\{v_1, v_2\}$, the local variables set $\{lv_1, lv_2\}$ and the parameters set $\{\mathsf{vp}_1\}$. Let μ be the variable valuation such that $\mu(v_1) = 1$ and $\mu(v_2) = 2$, and η be the local variable valuation such that $\eta(lv_1) = 2$ and $\eta(lv_2)$ is not defined. Let ζ be the data parameter valuation such that $\zeta(\mathsf{vp}_1) = 1$. Consider the parametric data update function PDU such that $\mathsf{PDU}(v_1) = 2 \times v_1 + v_2 - lv_1 + \mathsf{vp}_1$, and $\mathsf{PDU}(v_2)$ is undefined. Then the result of $[\mu]_{\eta(\zeta(\mathsf{PDU}))}$ is μ' such that $\mu'(v_1) = 2 \times \mu(v_1) + \mu(v_2) - \eta(lv_1) + \zeta(\mathsf{vp}_1) = 3$ and $\mu'(v_2) = 2$.

4　Parametric Timed Data Automata

We introduce here Parametric timed data automata (PTDAs). They can be seen as an extension of parametric timed automata [2] (that extend timed automata [1] with parameters in place of integer constants) with unbounded data variables and parametric variables. PTDAs can also be seen as an extension of some extensions of timed automata with data (see e.g., [16,19,29]), that we again extend with both data parameters and timing parameters. Or as an extension of quantified event automata [12] with explicit time representation using clocks, and further augmented with timing parameters. PTDAs feature both timed guards and data guards; we summarize the various variables and parameters types together with their notations in Table 2.

　　We will associate local variables with actions (which can be see as *predicates*). Let $Dom : \Sigma \to 2^{\mathbb{LV}}$ denote the set of local variables associated with each action. Let $Var(dg)$ (resp. $Var(\mathsf{PDU})$) denote the set of variables occurring in dg (resp. PDU).

Definition 1 (PTDA). *Given a data type* $(\mathbb{D}, \mathcal{DE}, \mathcal{DU})$, *a parametric timed data automaton (PTDA)* $\mathcal{A}$ *over this data type is a tuple* $\mathcal{A} = (\Sigma, L, \ell_0, F, \mathbb{C},$ $\mathbb{TP}, \mathbb{V}, \mathbb{LV}, \mu_0, \mathbb{VP}, E)$, *where:*

1. Σ *is a finite set of actions,*
2. L *is a finite set of locations,* $\ell_0 \in L$ *is the initial location,*
3. $F \subseteq L$ *is the set of accepting locations,*
4. $\mathbb{C}$ *is a finite set of clocks,*
5. $\mathbb{TP}$ *is a finite set of timing parameters,*
6. $\mathbb{V}$ *(resp.* $\mathbb{LV}$*) is a finite set of variables (resp. local variables) over* $\mathbb{D}$,
7. μ_0 *is the initial variable valuation,*
8. $\mathbb{VP}$ *is a finite set of data parameters,*

9. *E is a finite set of edges* $e = (\ell, tg, dg, a, R, \mathsf{PDU}, \ell')$ *where (i)* $\ell, \ell' \in L$ *are the source and target locations, (ii)* tg *is a timed guard, (iii)* $dg \in \mathcal{DE}$ *is a data guard such as* $Var(dg) \cap \mathbb{LV} \subseteq Dom(a)$, *(iv)* $a \in \Sigma$, *(v)* $R \subseteq \mathbb{C}$ *is a set of clocks to be reset, and (vi)* $\mathsf{PDU} : \mathbb{V} \nrightarrow \mathcal{DU}$ *is the parametric data update function such that* $Var(\mathsf{PDU}) \cap \mathbb{LV} \subseteq Dom(a)$.

The domain conditions on dg and PDU ensure that the local variables used in the guard (resp. update) are only those in the action signature $Dom(a)$.

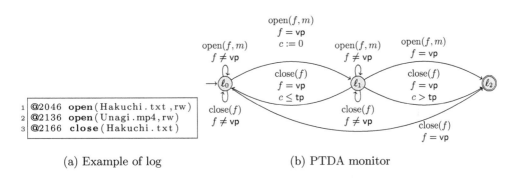

(a) Example of log   (b) PTDA monitor

Fig. 2. Monitoring proper file opening and closing

Example 4. Consider the PTDA in Fig. 2b over the data type for strings. We have $\mathbb{C} = \{c\}$, $\mathbb{TP} = \{\mathsf{tp}\}$, $\mathbb{V} = \emptyset$ and $\mathbb{LV} = \{f, m\}$. $Dom(\text{open}) = \{f, m\}$ while $Dom(\text{close}) = \{f\}$. ℓ_2 is the only accepting location, modeling the violation of the specification.

This PTDA (freely inspired by a formula from [26] further extended with timing parameters) monitors the improper file opening and closing, i.e., a file already open should not be open again, and a file that is open should not be closed too late. The data parameter vp is used to *symbolically* monitor a given file name, i.e., we are interested in opening and closings of this file only, while other files are disregarded (specified using the self-loops in ℓ_0 and ℓ_1 with data guard $f \neq \mathsf{vp}$). Whenever f is opened (transition from ℓ_0 to ℓ_1), a clock c is reset. Then, in ℓ_1, if f is closed within tp time units (timed guard "$c \leq \mathsf{tp}$"), then the system goes back to ℓ_0. However, if instead f is opened again, this is an incorrect behavior and the system enters ℓ_2 via the upper transition. The same occurs if f is closed more than tp time units after opening.

Given a data parameter valuation ζ and a timing parameter valuation γ, we denote by $\gamma|\zeta(\mathcal{A})$ the resulting *timed data automaton (TDA)*, i.e., the non-parametric structure where all occurrences of a parameter vp_i (resp. tp_j) have been replaced by $\zeta(\mathsf{vp}_i)$ (resp. $\gamma(\mathsf{tp}_j)$). Note that, if $\mathbb{V} = \mathbb{LV} = \emptyset$, then $\mathcal{A}$ is a *parametric timed automaton* [2] and $\gamma|\zeta(\mathcal{A})$ is a *timed automaton* [1].

We now equip our TDAs with a concrete semantics.

Definition 2 (Semantics of a TDA). *Given a PTDA $\mathcal{A} = (\Sigma, L, \ell_0, F,$
$\mathbb{C}, \mathbb{TP}, \mathbb{V}, \mathbb{LV}, \mu_0, \mathbb{VP}, E)$ over a data type $(\mathbb{D}, \mathcal{DE}, \mathcal{DU})$, a data parameter valu-
ation ζ and a timing parameter valuation γ, the semantics of $\gamma|\zeta(\mathcal{A})$ is given by
the timed transition system (TTS) $(S, s_0, \rightarrow)$, with*

- $S = L \times \mathbb{D}^M \times \mathbb{R}_{\geq 0}^H$, $s_0 = (\ell_0, \mu_0, \mathbf{0})$,
- $\rightarrow$ *consists of the discrete and (continuous) delay transition relations:*

1. *discrete transitions:* $(\ell, \mu, \nu) \overset{e,\eta}{\mapsto} (\ell', \mu', \nu')$, *there exist* $e = (\ell, tg, dg, a,$
   $R, \mathsf{PDU}, \ell') \in E$ *and a local variable valuation* η *defined exactly for* $Dom(a)$,
   such that $\nu \models \gamma(tg)$, $(\mu, \eta) \models \zeta(dg)$, $\nu' = [\nu]_R$, *and* $\mu' = [\mu]_{\eta(\zeta(\mathsf{PDU}))}$.
2. *delay transitions:* $(\ell, \mu, \nu) \overset{d}{\mapsto} (\ell, \mu, \nu + d)$, *with* $d \in \mathbb{R}_{\geq 0}$.

Moreover we write $((\ell, \mu, \nu), (e, \eta, d), (\ell', \mu', \nu')) \in \rightarrow$ for a combination of a
delay and discrete transition if $\exists \nu'' : (\ell, \mu, \nu) \overset{d}{\mapsto} (\ell, \mu, \nu'') \overset{e,\eta}{\mapsto} (\ell', \mu', \nu')$.

Given a TDA $\gamma|\zeta(\mathcal{A})$ with concrete semantics $(S, s_0, \rightarrow)$, we refer to
the states of S as the *concrete states* of $\gamma|\zeta(\mathcal{A})$. A *run* of $\gamma|\zeta(\mathcal{A})$ is
an alternating sequence of concrete states of $\gamma|\zeta(\mathcal{A})$ and triples of edges,
local variable valuations and delays, starting from the initial state s_0 of
the form $(\ell_0, \mu_0, \nu_0), (e_0, \eta, d_0), (\ell_1, \mu_1, \nu_1), \cdots$ with $i = 0, 1, \ldots$, $e_i \in E$,
$d_i \in \mathbb{R}_{\geq 0}$ and $((\ell_i, \mu_i, \nu_i), (e_i, \eta_i, d_i), (\ell_{i+1}, \mu_{i+1}, \nu_{i+1})) \in \rightarrow$. Given such
a run, the associated *timed data word* is $(a_1, \tau_1, \eta_1), (a_2, \tau_2, \eta_2), \cdots$, where
a_i is the action of edge e_{i-1}, η_i is the local variable valuation associated with that transition, and $\tau_i = \sum_{0 \leq j \leq i-1} d_j$, for $i = 1, 2 \cdots$. For
a timed data word w and a concrete state (ℓ, μ, ν) of $\gamma|\zeta(\mathcal{A})$, we write
$(\ell_0, \mu_0, \mathbf{0}) \overset{w}{\rightarrow} (\ell, \mu, \nu)$ in $\gamma|\zeta(\mathcal{A})$ if w is associated with a run of $\gamma|\zeta(\mathcal{A})$ of
the form $(\ell_0, \mu_0, \mathbf{0}), \ldots, (\ell_n, \mu_n, \nu_n)$ with $(\ell_n, \mu_n, \nu_n) = (\ell, \mu, \nu)$. For a timed
data word $w = (a_1, \tau_1, \eta_1), (a_2, \tau_2, \eta_2), \ldots, (a_n, \tau_n, \eta_n)$, we denote $|w| = n$
and for any $i \in \{1, 2, \ldots, n\}$, we denote $w(1, i) = (a_1, \tau_1, \eta_1), (a_2, \tau_2, \eta_2), \ldots,$
(a_i, τ_i, η_i).

A finite run is *accepting* if its last state (ℓ, μ, ν) is such that $\ell \in F$. The
language $\mathcal{L}(\gamma|\zeta(\mathcal{A}))$ is defined to be the set of timed data words associated with
all accepting runs of $\gamma|\zeta(\mathcal{A})$.

Example 5. Consider the PTDA in Fig. 2b over the data type for strings. Let
$\gamma(\mathsf{tp}) = 100$ and $\zeta(\mathsf{vp}) = \mathtt{Hakuchi.txt}$. An accepting run of the TDA $\gamma|\zeta(\mathcal{A})$
is: $(\ell_0, \emptyset, \nu_0), (e_0, \eta_0, 2046), (\ell_1, \emptyset, \nu_1), (e_1, \eta_1, 90), (\ell_1, \emptyset, \nu_2)(e_2, \eta_2, 30), (\ell_2, \emptyset, \nu_3)$,
where $\emptyset$ denotes a variable valuation over an empty domain (recall that $\mathbb{V} = \emptyset$
in Fig. 2b), $\nu_0(c) = 0$, $\nu_1(c) = 0$, $\nu_2(c) = 90$, $\nu_3(c) = 120$, e_0 is the upper edge
from ℓ_0 to ℓ_1, e_1 is the self-loop above ℓ_1, e_2 is the lower edge from ℓ_1 to ℓ_2,
$\eta_0(f) = \eta_2(f) = \mathtt{Hakuchi.txt}$, $\eta_1(f) = \mathtt{Unagi.mp4}$, $\eta_0(m) = \eta_1(m) = \mathtt{rw}$, and
$\eta_2(m)$ is undefined (because $Dom(\mathsf{close}) = \{f\}$).

The associated timed data word is $(\mathsf{open}, 2046, \eta_0), (\mathsf{open}, 2136, \eta_1),$
$(\mathsf{close}, 2166, \eta_2)$.

Since each action is associated with a set of local variables, given an ordering
on this set, it is possible to see a given action and a variable valuation as a predicate: for example, assuming an ordering of $\mathbb{LV}$ such as f precedes m, then open

with η_0 can be represented as open($\texttt{Hakuchi.txt}, \texttt{rw}$). Using this convention, the log in Fig. 2a corresponds exactly to this timed data word.

5   Symbolic Monitoring Against PTDA Specifications

In symbolic monitoring, in addition to the (observable) actions in Σ, we employ *unobservable* actions denoted by ε and satisfying $Dom(\varepsilon) = \emptyset$. We write Σ_ε for $\Sigma \sqcup \{\varepsilon\}$. We let η_ε be the local variable valuation such that $\eta_\varepsilon(lv)$ is undefined for any $lv \in \mathbb{LV}$. For a timed data word $w = (a_1, \tau_1, \eta_1), (a_2, \tau_2, \eta_2), \ldots,$ (a_n, τ_n, η_n) over Σ_ε, the projection $w{\downarrow}_\Sigma$ is the timed data word over Σ obtained from w by removing any triple (a_i, τ_i, η_i) where $a_i = \varepsilon$. An edge $e = (\ell, tg, dg, a, R, \mathsf{PDU}, \ell') \in E$ is *unobservable* if $a = \varepsilon$, and *observable* otherwise. The use of unobservable actions allows us to encode parametric timed pattern matching (see Sect. 5.3).

We make the following assumption on the PTDAs in symbolic monitoring.

Assumption 1. *The PTDA $\mathcal{A}$ does not contain any loop of unobservable edges.*

5.1   Problem Definition

Roughly speaking, given a PTDA $\mathcal{A}$ and a timed data word w, the symbolic monitoring problem asks for the set of pairs $(\gamma, \zeta) \in (\mathbb{Q}_+)^{\mathbb{TP}} \times \mathbb{D}^{\mathbb{VP}}$ satisfying $w(1, i) \in \gamma|\zeta(\mathcal{A})$, where $w(1, i)$ is a prefix of w. Since $\mathcal{A}$ also contains unobservable edges, we consider w' which is w augmented by unobservable actions.

Symbolic monitoring problem:

INPUT: a PTDA $\mathcal{A}$ over a data type $(\mathbb{D}, \mathcal{DE}, \mathcal{DU})$ and actions Σ_ε, and a timed data word w over Σ

PROBLEM: compute all the pairs (γ, ζ) of timing and data parameter valuations such that there is a timed data word w' over Σ_ε and $i \in \{1, 2, \ldots, |w'|\}$ satisfying $w'{\downarrow}_\Sigma = w$ and $w'(1, i) \in \mathcal{L}(\gamma|\zeta(\mathcal{A}))$. That is, it requires the *validity domain* $D(w, \mathcal{A}) = \{(\gamma, \zeta) \mid \exists w' : i \in \{1, 2, \ldots, |w'|\}, w'{\downarrow}_\Sigma = w$ and $w'(1, i) \in \mathcal{L}(\gamma|\zeta(\mathcal{A}))\}$.

Example 6. Consider the PTDA $\mathcal{A}$ and the timed data word w shown in Fig. 1. The validity domain $D(w, \mathcal{A})$ is $D(w, \mathcal{A}) = D_1 \cup D_2$, where

$$D_1 = \{(\gamma, \zeta) \mid 0 \le \gamma(\mathsf{tp}) \le 2, \zeta(\mathsf{xp}) = \mathsf{c}\} \text{ and } D_2 = \{(\gamma, \zeta) \mid 0 \le \gamma(\mathsf{tp}) \le 1, \zeta(\mathsf{xp}) = \mathsf{a}\}.$$

For $w' = w(1, 3) \cdot (\varepsilon, \eta_\varepsilon, 2.9)$, we have $w' \in \mathcal{L}(\gamma|\zeta(\mathcal{A}))$ and $w'{\downarrow}_\Sigma = w(1, 3)$, where γ and ζ are such that $\gamma(\mathsf{tp}) = 1.8$ and $\zeta(\mathsf{xp}) = \mathsf{c}$, and $w(1, 3) \cdot (\varepsilon, \eta_\varepsilon, 2.9)$ denotes the juxtaposition.

For the data types in Example 2, the validity domain $D(w, \mathcal{A})$ can be represented by a constraint of finite size because the length $|w|$ of the timed data word is finite.

5.2   Online Algorithm

Our algorithm is *online* in the sense that it outputs $(\gamma, \zeta) \in D(w, \mathcal{A})$ as soon as its membership is witnessed, even before reading the whole timed data word w.

Let $w = (a_1, \tau_1, \eta_1), (a_2, \tau_2, \eta_2), \dots (a_n, \tau_n, \eta_n)$ and $\mathcal{A}$ be the timed data word and PTDA given in symbolic monitoring, respectively. Intuitively, after reading (a_i, τ_i, η_i), our algorithm symbolically computes for all parameter valuations $(\gamma, \zeta) \in (\mathbb{Q}_+)^{\mathrm{TP}} \times \mathbb{D}^{\mathrm{VP}}$ the concrete states (ℓ, ν, μ) satisfying $(\ell_0, \mu_0, \mathbf{0}) \xrightarrow{w(1,i)} (\ell, \mu, \nu)$ in $\gamma|\zeta(\mathcal{A})$. Since $\mathcal{A}$ has unobservable edges as well as observable edges, we have to add unobservable actions before or after observable actions in w. By $Conf_i^o$, we denote the configurations after reading (a_i, τ_i, η_i) and no unobservable actions are appended after (a_i, τ_i, η_i). By $Conf_i^u$, we denote the configurations after reading (a_i, τ_i, η_i) and at least one unobservable action is appended after (a_i, τ_i, η_i).

Definition 3 *($Conf_i^o, Conf_i^u$). For a PTDA $\mathcal{A}$ over actions Σ_ε, a timed data word w over Σ, and $i \in \{0, 1, \dots, |w|\}$ (resp. $i \in \{-1, 0, \dots, |w|\}$), $Conf_i^o$ (resp. $Conf_i^u$) is the set of 5-tuples $(\ell, \nu, \gamma, \mu, \zeta)$ such that there is a timed data word w' over Σ_ε satisfying the following: (i) $(\ell_0, \mu_0, \mathbf{0}) \xrightarrow{w'} (\ell, \mu, \nu)$ in $\gamma|\zeta(\mathcal{A})$, (ii) $w'\!\downarrow_\Sigma = w(1, i)$, (iii) The last action $a'_{|w'|}$ of w' is observable (resp. unobservable and its timestamp is less than τ_{i+1}).*

Algorithm 1. Outline of our algorithm for symbolic monitoring

---

> **Input:** A PTDA $\mathcal{A} = (\Sigma_\varepsilon, L, \ell_0, F, \mathbb{C}, \mathrm{TP}, \mathbb{V}, \mathrm{LV}, \mu_0, \mathrm{VP}, E)$ over a data
> type $(\mathbb{D}, \mathcal{DE}, \mathcal{DU})$ and actions Σ_ε, and a timed data
> word $w = (a_1, \tau_1, \eta_1), (a_2, \tau_2, \eta_2), \dots, (a_n, \tau_n, \eta_n)$ over Σ
> **Output:** $\bigcup_{i \in \{1,2,\dots,n+1\}} Result_i$ is the validity domain $D(w, \mathcal{A})$
> 1 $Conf_{-1}^u \leftarrow \emptyset$; $Conf_0^o \leftarrow \{(\ell_0, \mathbf{0}, \gamma, \mu_0, \zeta) \mid \gamma \in (\mathbb{Q}_+)^{\mathrm{TP}}, \zeta \in \mathbb{D}^{\mathrm{VP}}\}$
> 2 **for** $i \leftarrow 1$ **to** n **do**
> 3 $\quad$ compute $(Conf_{i-1}^u, Conf_i^o)$ **from** $(Conf_{i-2}^u, Conf_{i-1}^o)$
> 4 $\quad$ $Result_i \leftarrow \{(\gamma, \zeta) \mid \exists(\ell, \nu, \gamma, \mu, \zeta) \in Conf_{i-1}^u \cup Conf_i^o . \ell \in F\}$
> 5 compute $Conf_n^u$ **from** $(Conf_{n-1}^u, Conf_n^o)$
> 6 $Result_{n+1} \leftarrow \{(\gamma, \zeta) \mid \exists(\ell, \nu, \gamma, \mu, \zeta) \in Conf_n^u . \ell \in F\}$

Algorithm 1 shows an outline of our algorithm for symbolic monitoring (see [35] for the full version). Our algorithm incrementally computes $Conf_{i-1}^u$ and $Conf_i^o$ (line 3). After reading (a_i, τ_i, η_i), our algorithm stores the partial results $(\gamma, \zeta) \in D(w, \mathcal{A})$ witnessed from the accepting configurations in $Conf_{i-1}^u$ and $Conf_i^o$ (line 4). (We also need to try to take potential unobservable transitions and store the results from the accepting configurations *after* the last element of the timed data word (lines 5 and 6).)

Since $(\mathbb{Q}_+)^{\mathrm{TP}} \times \mathbb{D}^{\mathrm{VP}}$ is an infinite set, we cannot try each $(\gamma, \zeta) \in (\mathbb{Q}_+)^{\mathrm{TP}} \times \mathbb{D}^{\mathrm{VP}}$ and we use a symbolic representation for parameter valuations. Similarly to the reachability synthesis of parametric timed automata [28], a set of clock and timing parameter valuations can be represented by a convex polyhedron. For variable valuations and data parameter valuations, we need an appropriate representation depending on the data type $(\mathbb{D}, \mathcal{DE}, \mathcal{DU})$. Moreover, for the termination of Algorithm 1, some operations on the symbolic representation are required.

Theorem 1 (termination). *For any PTDA $\mathcal{A}$ over a data type $(\mathbb{D}, \mathcal{DE}, \mathcal{DU})$ and actions Σ_ε, and for any timed data word w over Σ, Algorithm 1 terminates if the following operations on the symbolic representation V_d of a set of variable and data parameter valuations terminate.*

1. *restriction and update $\{([\mu]_{\eta(\zeta(\mathsf{PDU}))}, \zeta) \mid \exists(\mu, \zeta) \in V_d. (\mu, \eta) \models \zeta(dg)\}$, where η is a local variable valuation, PDU is a parametric data update function, and dg is a data guard;*
2. *emptiness checking of V_d;*
3. *projection $V_d{\downarrow}_{\mathbb{VP}}$ of V_d to the data parameters $\mathbb{VP}$.* □

Example 7. For the data type for rationals in Example 2, variable and data parameter valuations V_d can be represented by convex polyhedra and the above operations terminate. For the data type for strings $\mathbb{S}$ in Example 2, variable and data parameter valuations V_d can be represented by $\mathbb{S}^{|\mathbb{V}|} \times (\mathbb{S} \cup \mathcal{P}_{\mathrm{fin}}(\mathbb{S}))^{|\mathbb{VP}|}$ and the above operations terminate, where $\mathcal{P}_{\mathrm{fin}}(\mathbb{S})$ is the set of finite sets of $\mathbb{S}$.

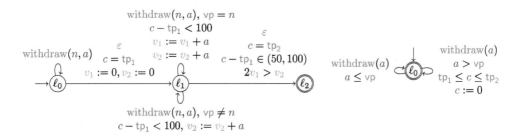

Fig. 3. PTDAs in DOMINANT (left) and PERIODIC (right)

5.3 Encoding Parametric Timed Pattern Matching

The symbolic monitoring problem is a generalization of the parametric timed pattern matching problem of [4]. Recall that parametric timed pattern matching aims at synthesizing timing parameter valuations and *start and end times in the log* for which a log segment satisfies or violates a specification. In our approach, by adding a clock measuring the absolute time, and two timing parameters encoding respectively the start and end date of the segment, one can easily infer the log segments for which the property is satisfied.

Consider the DOMINANT PTDA (left of Fig. 3). It is inspired by a monitoring of withdrawals from bank accounts of various users [15]. This PTDA monitors situations when a user withdraws more than half of the total withdrawals within a time window of $(50, 100)$. The actions are $\Sigma = \{\text{withdraw}\}$

and $Dom(\text{withdraw}) = \{n, a\}$, where n has a string value and a has an integer value. The string n represents a user name and the integer a represents the amount of the withdrawal by the user n. Observe that clock c is never reset, and therefore measures absolute time. The automaton can non-deterministically remain in ℓ_0, or start to measure a log by taking the ε-transition to ℓ_1 checking $c = \text{tp}_1$, and therefore "remembering" the start time using timing parameter tp_1. Then, whenever a user vp has withdrawn more than half of the accumulated withdrawals (data guard $2v_1 > v_2$) in a $(50, 100)$ time window (timed guard $c - \text{tp}_1 \in (50, 100)$), the automaton takes a ε-transition to the accepting location, checking $c = \text{tp}_2$, and therefore remembering the end time using timing parameter tp_2.

6 Experiments

We implemented our symbolic monitoring algorithm in a tool SYMON in C++, where the domain for data is the strings and the integers. Our tool SYMON is distributed at https://github.com/MasWag/symon. We use PPL [8] for the symbolic representation of the valuations. We note that we employ an optimization to merge adjacent polyhedra in the configurations if possible. We evaluated our monitor algorithm against three original benchmarks: COPY in Fig. 1c; and DOMINANT and PERIODIC in Fig. 3. We conducted experiments on an Amazon EC2 c4.large instance (2.9 GHz Intel Xeon E5-2666 v3, 2 vCPUs, and 3.75 GiB RAM) that runs Ubuntu 18.04 LTS (64 bit).

6.1 Benchmark 1: Copy

Our first benchmark COPY is a monitoring of variable updates much like the scenario in [18]. The actions are $\Sigma = \{\text{update}\}$ and $Dom(\text{update}) = \{n, v\}$, where n has a string value representing the name of the updated variables and v has an integer value representing the updated value. Our set consists of 10 timed data words of length 4,000 to 40,000.

The PTDA in COPY is shown in Fig. 1c, where we give an additional constraint $3 < \text{tp} < 10$ on tp. The property encoded in Fig. 1c is "for any variable px, whenever an update of that variable occurs, then within tp time units, the value of b must be equal to that update".

The experiment result is in Fig. 4. We observe that the execution time is linear to the number of the events and the memory usage is more or less constant with respect to the number of events.

6.2 Benchmark 2: Dominant

Our second benchmark is DOMINANT (Fig. 3 left). Our set consists of 10 timed data words of length 2,000 to 20,000. The experiment result is in Fig. 5. We observe that the execution time is linear to the number of the events and the memory usage is more or less constant with respect to the number of events.

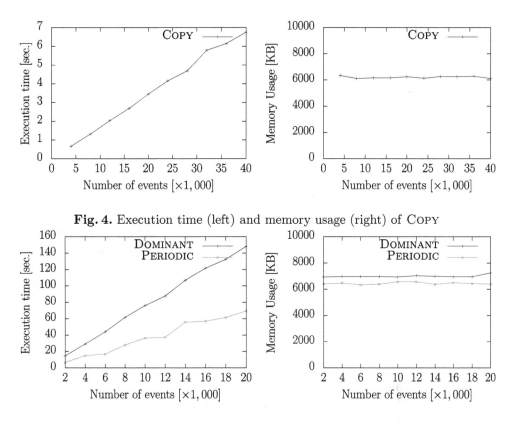

Fig. 4. Execution time (left) and memory usage (right) of COPY

Fig. 5. Execution time (left) and memory usage (right) of DOMINANT and PERIODIC

6.3 Benchmark 3: Periodic

Our third benchmark PERIODIC is inspired by a parameter identification of periodic withdrawals from one bank account. The actions are $\Sigma = \{\text{withdraw}\}$ and $Dom(\text{withdraw}) = \{a\}$, where a has an integer value representing the amount of the withdrawal. We randomly generated a set consisting of 10 timed data words of length 2,000 to 20,000. Each timed data word consists of the following three kinds of periodic withdrawals:

shortperiod One withdrawal occurs every 5 ± 1 time units. The amount of the withdrawal is 50 ± 3.
middleperiod One withdrawal occurs every 50 ± 3 time units. The amount of the withdrawal is 1000 ± 40.
longperiod One withdrawal occurs every 100 ± 5 time units. The amount of the withdrawal is 5000 ± 20.

The PTDA in PERIODIC is shown in the right of Fig. 3. The PTDA matches situations where, for any two successive withdrawals of amount more than vp, the duration between them is within $[\text{tp}_1, \text{tp}_2]$. By the symbolic monitoring, one can identify the period of the

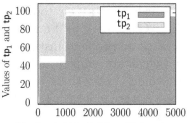

periodic withdrawals of amount greater than
vp is in $[\mathsf{tp}_1, \mathsf{tp}_2]$. An example of the validity
domain is shown in the right figure.

The experiment result is in Fig. 5. We observe that the execution time is linear
to the number of the events and the memory usage is more or less constant with
respect to the number of events.

6.4   Discussion

First, a positive result is that our algorithm effectively performs symbolic monitoring on more than 10,000 actions in one or two minutes even though the
PTDAs feature both timing and data parameters. The execution time in COPY
is 50–100 times smaller than that in DOMINANT and PERIODIC. This is because
the constraint $3 < \mathsf{tp} < 10$ in COPY is strict and the size of the configurations
(i. e., $Conf_i^o$ and $Conf_i^u$ in Algorithm 1) is small. Another positive result is that
in all of the benchmarks, the execution time is linear and the memory usage is
more or less constant in the size of the input word. This is because the size of
configurations (i. e., $Conf_i^o$ and $Conf_i^u$ in Algorithm 1) is bounded due to the
following reason. In DOMINANT, the loop in ℓ_1 of the PTDA is deterministic, and
because of the guard $c - \mathsf{tp}_1 \in (50, 100)$ in the edge from ℓ_1 to ℓ_2, the number of
the loop edges at ℓ_1 in an accepting run is bounded (if the duration between two
continuing actions are bounded as in the current setting). Therefore, $|Conf_i^o|$
and $|Conf_i^u|$ in Algorithm 1 are bounded. The reason is similar in COPY, too.
In PERIODIC, since the PTDA is deterministic and the valuations of the amount
of the withdrawals are in finite number, $|Conf_i^o|$ and $|Conf_i^u|$ in Algorithm 1 are
bounded.

It is clear that we can design ad-hoc automata for which the execution time
of symbolic monitoring can grow much faster (e.g., exponential in the size of
input word). However, experiments showed that our algorithm monitors various
interesting properties in a reasonable time.

COPY and DOMINANT use data and timing parameters as well as memory
and aggregation; from Table 1, no other monitoring tool can compute the valuations satisfying the specification. We however used the parametric timed model
checker IMITATOR [3] to try to perform such a synthesis, by encoding the input
log as a separate automaton; but IMITATOR ran out of memory (on a 3.75 GiB
RAM computer) for DOMINANT with $|w| = 2000$, while SYMON terminates in
14 s with only 6.9 MiB for the same benchmark. Concerning PERIODIC, the only
existing work that can possibly accommodate this specification is [7]. While the
precise performance comparison is interesting future work (their implementation
is not publicly available), we do not expect our implementation be vastly outperformed: in [7], their tool times out (after 10 min) for a simple specification
("$\mathbf{E}_{[0,s_2]}\mathbf{G}_{[0,s_1]}(x < p)$") and a signal discretized by only 128 points.

For those problem instances which MONPOLY and DEJAVU can accommodate (which are simpler and less parametrized than our benchmarks), they tend
to run much faster than ours. For example, in [26], it is reported that they can
process a trace of length 1,100,004 in 30.3 s. The trade-off here is expressivity: for

example, DEJAVU does not seem to accommodate DOMINANT, because DEJAVU does not allow for aggregation. We also note that, while SYMON can be slower than MONPOLY and DEJAVU, it is fast enough for many scenarios of real-world online monitoring.

7   Conclusion and Perspectives

We proposed a symbolic framework for monitoring using parameters both in data and time. Logs can use timestamps and infinite domain data, while our monitor automata can use timing and variable parameters (in addition to clocks and local variables). In addition, our online algorithm can answer symbolically, by outputting all valuations (and possibly log segments) for which the specification is satisfied or violated. We implemented our approach into a prototype SYMON and experiments showed that our tool can effectively monitor logs of dozens of thousands of events in a short time.

Perspectives. Combining the BDDs used in [26] with some of our data types (typically strings) could improve our approach by making it even more symbolic. Also, taking advantage of the polarity of some parameters (typically the timing parameters, in the line of [17]) could improve further the efficiency.

We considered *infinite* domains, but the case of *finite* domains raises interesting questions concerning result representation: if the answer to a property is "neither a nor b", knowing the domain is $\{a, b, c\}$, then the answer should be c.

References

1. Alur, R., Dill, D.L.: A theory of timed automata. Theor. Comput. Sci. **126**(2), 183–235 (1994). https://doi.org/10.1016/0304-3975(94)90010-8
2. Alur, R., Henzinger, T.A., Vardi, M.Y.: Parametric real-time reasoning. In: Kosaraju, S.R., Johnson, D.S., Aggarwal, A. (eds.) STOC, pp. 592–601. ACM, New York (1993). https://doi.org/10.1145/167088.167242
3. André, É., Fribourg, L., Kühne, U., Soulat, R.: IMITATOR 2.5: a tool for analyzing robustness in scheduling problems. In: Giannakopoulou, D., Méry, D. (eds.) FM 2012. LNCS, vol. 7436, pp. 33–36. Springer, Heidelberg (2012). https://doi.org/10.1007/978-3-642-32759-9_6
4. André, É., Hasuo, I., Waga, M.: Offline timed pattern matching under uncertainty. In: Lin, A.W., Sun, J. (eds.) ICECCS, pp. 10–20. IEEE CPS (2018). https://doi.org/10.1109/ICECCS2018.2018.00010
5. Annpureddy, Y., Liu, C., Fainekos, G., Sankaranarayanan, S.: S-TALIRO: a tool for temporal logic falsification for hybrid systems. In: Abdulla, P.A., Leino, K.R.M. (eds.) TACAS 2011. LNCS, vol. 6605, pp. 254–257. Springer, Heidelberg (2011). https://doi.org/10.1007/978-3-642-19835-9_21
6. Asarin, E., Basset, N., Degorre, A.: Distance on timed words and applications. In: Jansen, D.N., Prabhakar, P. (eds.) FORMATS 2018. LNCS, vol. 11022, pp. 199–214. Springer, Cham (2018). https://doi.org/10.1007/978-3-030-00151-3_12

7. Asarin, E., Donzé, A., Maler, O., Nickovic, D.: Parametric identification of temporal properties. In: Khurshid, S., Sen, K. (eds.) RV 2011. LNCS, vol. 7186, pp. 147–160. Springer, Heidelberg (2012). https://doi.org/10.1007/978-3-642-29860-8_12

8. Bagnara, R., Hill, P.M., Zaffanella, E.: The parma polyhedra library: toward a complete set of numerical abstractions for the analysis and verification of hardware and software systems. Sci. Comput. Program. **72**(1–2), 3–21 (2008). https://doi.org/10.1016/j.scico.2007.08.001

9. Bakhirkin, A., Ferrère, T., Maler, O.: Efficient parametric identification for STL. In: HSCC, pp. 177–186. ACM (2018). https://doi.org/10.1145/3178126.3178132

10. Bakhirkin, A., Ferrère, T., Maler, O., Ulus, D.: On the quantitative semantics of regular expressions over real-valued signals. In: Abate, A., Geeraerts, G. (eds.) FORMATS 2017. LNCS, vol. 10419, pp. 189–206. Springer, Cham (2017). https://doi.org/10.1007/978-3-319-65765-3_11

11. Bakhirkin, A., Ferrère, T., Nickovic, D., Maler, O., Asarin, E.: Online timed pattern matching using automata. In: Jansen, D.N., Prabhakar, P. (eds.) FORMATS 2018. LNCS, vol. 11022, pp. 215–232. Springer, Cham (2018). https://doi.org/10.1007/978-3-030-00151-3_13

12. Barringer, H., Falcone, Y., Havelund, K., Reger, G., Rydeheard, D.: Quantified event automata: towards expressive and efficient runtime monitors. In: Giannakopoulou, D., Méry, D. (eds.) FM 2012. LNCS, vol. 7436, pp. 68–84. Springer, Heidelberg (2012). https://doi.org/10.1007/978-3-642-32759-9_9

13. Basin, D.A., Klaedtke, F., Marinovic, S., Zalinescu, E.: Monitoring of temporal first-order properties with aggregations. Form. Methods Syst. Des. **46**(3), 262–285 (2015). https://doi.org/10.1007/s10703-015-0222-7

14. Basin, D.A., Klaedtke, F., Müller, S., Zalinescu, E.: Monitoring metric first-order temporal properties. J. ACM **62**(2), 15:1–15:45 (2015). https://doi.org/10.1145/2699444

15. Basin, D.A., Klaedtke, F., Zalinescu, E.: The MonPoly monitoring tool. In: Reger, G., Havelund, K. (eds.) RV-CuBES. Kalpa Publications in Computing, vol. 3, pp. 19–28. EasyChair (2017)

16. Bouajjani, A., Echahed, R., Robbana, R.: On the automatic verification of systems with continuous variables and unbounded discrete data structures. In: Antsaklis, P., Kohn, W., Nerode, A., Sastry, S. (eds.) HS 1994. LNCS, vol. 999, pp. 64–85. Springer, Heidelberg (1995). https://doi.org/10.1007/3-540-60472-3_4

17. Bozzelli, L., La Torre, S.: Decision problems for lower/upper bound parametric timed automata. Form. Methods Syst. Des. **35**(2), 121–151 (2009). https://doi.org/10.1007/s10703-009-0074-0

18. Brim, L., Dluhos, P., Safránek, D., Vejpustek, T.: STL*: extending signal temporal logic with signal-value freezing operator. Inf. Comput. **236**, 52–67 (2014). https://doi.org/10.1016/j.ic.2014.01.012

19. Dang, Z.: Pushdown timed automata: a binary reachability characterization and safety verification. Theor. Comput. Sci. **302**(1–3), 93–121 (2003). https://doi.org/10.1016/S0304-3975(02)00743-0

20. Deshmukh, J.V., Majumdar, R., Prabhu, V.S.: Quantifying conformance using the Skorokhod metric. Form. Methods Syst. Des. **50**(2–3), 168–206 (2017). https://doi.org/10.1007/s10703-016-0261-8

21. Donzé, A.: Breach, a toolbox for verification and parameter synthesis of hybrid systems. In: Touili, T., Cook, B., Jackson, P. (eds.) CAV 2010. LNCS, vol. 6174, pp. 167–170. Springer, Heidelberg (2010). https://doi.org/10.1007/978-3-642-14295-6_17

22. Donzé, A., Ferrère, T., Maler, O.: Efficient robust monitoring for STL. In: Sharygina, N., Veith, H. (eds.) CAV 2013. LNCS, vol. 8044, pp. 264–279. Springer, Heidelberg (2013). https://doi.org/10.1007/978-3-642-39799-8_19
23. Donzé, A., Maler, O.: Robust satisfaction of temporal logic over real-valued signals. In: Chatterjee, K., Henzinger, T.A. (eds.) FORMATS 2010. LNCS, vol. 6246, pp. 92–106. Springer, Heidelberg (2010). https://doi.org/10.1007/978-3-642-15297-9_9
24. Fages, F., Rizk, A.: On temporal logic constraint solving for analyzing numerical data time series. Theor. Comput. Sci. **408**(1), 55–65 (2008). https://doi.org/10.1016/j.tcs.2008.07.004
25. Fainekos, G.E., Pappas, G.J.: Robustness of temporal logic specifications for continuous-time signals. Theor. Comput. Sci. **410**(42), 4262–4291 (2009). https://doi.org/10.1016/j.tcs.2009.06.021
26. Havelund, K., Peled, D., Ulus, D.: First order temporal logic monitoring with BDDs. In: Stewart, D., Weissenbacher, G. (eds.) FMCAD, pp. 116–123. IEEE (2017). https://doi.org/10.23919/FMCAD.2017.8102249
27. Jakšić, S., Bartocci, E., Grosu, R., Nguyen, T., Ničković, D.: Quantitative monitoring of STL with edit distance. Form. Methods Syst. Des. **53**(1), 83–112 (2018). https://doi.org/10.1007/s10703-018-0319-x
28. Jovanović, A., Lime, D., Roux, O.H.: Integer parameter synthesis for real-time systems. IEEE Trans. Softw. Eng. **41**(5), 445–461 (2015). https://doi.org/10.1109/TSE.2014.2357445
29. Quaas, K.: Verification for timed automata extended with discrete data structure. Log. Methods Comput. Sci. **11**(3) (2015). https://doi.org/10.2168/LMCS-11(3:20)2015
30. Reger, G., Cruz, H.C., Rydeheard, D.: MARQ: monitoring at runtime with QEA. In: Baier, C., Tinelli, C. (eds.) TACAS 2015. LNCS, vol. 9035, pp. 596–610. Springer, Heidelberg (2015). https://doi.org/10.1007/978-3-662-46681-0_55
31. Ulus, D.: MONTRE: a tool for monitoring timed regular expressions. In: Majumdar, R., Kunčak, V. (eds.) CAV 2017, Part I. LNCS, vol. 10426, pp. 329–335. Springer, Cham (2017). https://doi.org/10.1007/978-3-319-63387-9_16
32. Ulus, D., Ferrère, T., Asarin, E., Maler, O.: Timed pattern matching. In: Legay, A., Bozga, M. (eds.) FORMATS 2014. LNCS, vol. 8711, pp. 222–236. Springer, Cham (2014). https://doi.org/10.1007/978-3-319-10512-3_16
33. Ulus, D., Ferrère, T., Asarin, E., Maler, O.: Online timed pattern matching using derivatives. In: Chechik, M., Raskin, J.-F. (eds.) TACAS 2016. LNCS, vol. 9636, pp. 736–751. Springer, Heidelberg (2016). https://doi.org/10.1007/978-3-662-49674-9_47
34. Ulus, D., Maler, O.: Specifying timed patterns using temporal logic. In: HSCC, pp. 167–176. ACM (2018). https://doi.org/10.1145/3178126.3178129
35. Waga, M., André, É., Hasuo, I.: Symbolic monitoring against specifications parametric in time and data. CoRR abs/1905.04486 (2019). arxiv:1905.04486
36. Waga, M., Hasuo, I., Suenaga, K.: Efficient online timed pattern matching by automata-based skipping. In: Abate, A., Geeraerts, G. (eds.) FORMATS 2017. LNCS, vol. 10419, pp. 224–243. Springer, Cham (2017). https://doi.org/10.1007/978-3-319-65765-3_13

Temporal Stream Logic:
Synthesis Beyond the Bools

Bernd Finkbeiner[1], Felix Klein[1(✉)],
Ruzica Piskac[2],
and Mark Santolucito[2]

[1] Saarland University, Saarbrücken, Germany
klein@react.uni-saarland.de
[2] Yale University, New Haven, USA

Abstract. Reactive systems that operate in environments with complex data, such as mobile apps or embedded controllers with many sensors, are difficult to synthesize. Synthesis tools usually fail for such systems because the state space resulting from the discretization of the data is too large. We introduce TSL, a new temporal logic that separates control and data. We provide a CEGAR-based synthesis approach for the construction of implementations that are guaranteed to satisfy a TSL specification for all possible instantiations of the data processing functions. TSL provides an attractive trade-off for synthesis. On the one hand, synthesis from TSL, unlike synthesis from standard temporal logics, is undecidable in general. On the other hand, however, synthesis from TSL is scalable, because it is independent of the complexity of the handled data. Among other benchmarks, we have successfully synthesized a music player Android app and a controller for an autonomous vehicle in the Open Race Car Simulator (TORCS).

1 Introduction

In reactive synthesis, we automatically translate a formal specification, typically given in a temporal logic, into a controller that is guaranteed to satisfy the specification. Over the past two decades there has been much progress on reactive synthesis, both in terms of algorithms, notably with techniques like GR(1)-synthesis [7] and bounded synthesis [20], and in terms of tools, as showcased, for example, in the annual SYNTCOMP competition [25].

In practice however, reactive synthesis has seen limited success. One of the largest published success stories [6] is the synthesis of the AMBA bus protocol. To push synthesis even further, automatically synthesizing a controller for an autonomous system has been recognized to be of critical importance [52]. Despite many years of experience with synthesis tools, our own attempts to synthesize such controllers with existing tools have been unsuccessful. The reason is that the tools are unable to handle the data complexity of the controllers. The controller only needs to switch between a small number of behaviors, like steering during a bend, or shifting gears on high rpm. The number of control states in a typical controller (cf. [18]) is thus not much different from the arbiter in the AMBA case study. However, in order to correctly initiate transitions between control states, the driving controller must continuously process data from more than 20 sensors.

If this data is included (even as a rough discretization) in the state space of the controller, then the synthesis problem is much too large to be handled by any available tools. It seems clear then, that a scalable synthesis approach must separate control and data. If we assume that the data processing is handled by some other approach (such as deductive synthesis [38] or manual programming), is it then possible to solve the remaining reactive synthesis problem?

In this paper, we show scalable reactive synthesis is indeed possible. Separating data and control has allowed us to synthesize reactive systems, including an autonomous driving controller and a music player app, that had been impossible to synthesize with previously available tools. However, the separation of data and control implies some fundamental changes to reactive synthesis, which we describe in the rest of the paper. The changes also imply that the reactive synthesis problem is no longer, in general, decidable. We thus trade theoretical decidability for practical scalability, which is, at least with regard to the goal of synthesizing realistic systems, an attractive trade-off.

We introduce Temporal Stream Logic (TSL), a new temporal logic that includes *updates*, such as $[\![y \leftarrowtail f\ x]\!]$, and predicates over arbitrary function terms. The update $[\![y \leftarrowtail f\ x]\!]$ indicates that the result of applying function f to variable x is assigned to y. The implementation of predicates and functions is not part of the synthesis problem. Instead, we look for a system that satisfies the TSL specification *for all possible interpretations of the functions and predicates.*

This implicit quantification over all possible interpretations provides a useful abstraction: it allows us to *independently* implement the data processing part. On the other hand, this quantification is also the reason for the undecidability of the synthesis problem. If a predicate is applied to the same term *twice*, it must (independently of the interpretation) return the *same* truth value. The synthesis must then implicitly maintain a (potentially infinite) set of terms to which the predicate has previously been applied. As we show later, this set of terms can be used to encode PCP [45] for a proof of undecidability.

We present a practical synthesis approach for TSL specifications, which is based on bounded synthesis [20] and counterexample-guided abstraction refinement (CEGAR) [9]. We use bounded synthesis to search for an implementation up to a (iteratively growing) bound on the number of states. This approach underapproximates the actual TSL synthesis problem by leaving the interpretation of the predicates to the environment. The underapproximation allows

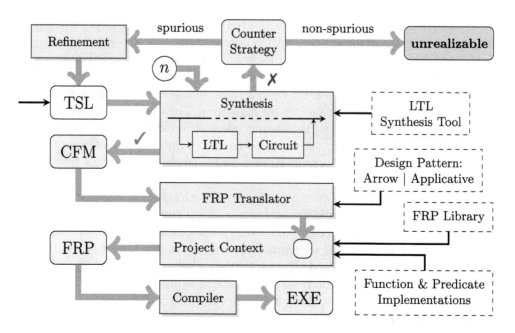

Fig. 1. The TSL synthesis procedure uses a modular design. Each step takes input from the previous step as well as interchangeable modules (dashed boxes).

for inconsistent behaviors: the environment might assign different truth values to the same predicate when evaluated at different points in time, even if the predicate is applied to the same term. However, if we find an implementation in this underapproximation, then the CEGAR loop terminates and we have a correct implementation for the original TSL specification. If we do not find an implementation in the underapproximation, we compute a counter strategy for the environment. Because bounded synthesis reduces the synthesis problem to a safety game, the counter strategy is a reachability strategy that can be represented as a finite tree. We check whether the counter strategy is spurious by searching for a pair of positions in the strategy where some predicate results in different truth values when applied to the same term. If the counter strategy is not spurious, then no implementation exists for the considered bound, and we increase the bound. If the counter strategy is spurious, then we introduce a constraint into the specification that eliminates the incorrect interpretation of the predicate, and continue with the refined specification.

A general overview of this procedure is shown in Fig. 1. The top half of the figure depicts the bounded search for an implementation that realizes a TSL specification using the CEGAR loop to refine the specification. If the specification is realizable, we proceed in the bottom half of the process, where a synthesized implementation is converted to a control flow model (CFM) determining the control of the system. We then specialize the CFM to Functional Reactive Programming (FRP), which is a popular and expressive programming paradigm for building reactive programs using functional programming languages [14].

```
Sys.leaveApp() :
  if (MP.musicPlaying())
    Ctrl.pause()
Sys.resumeApp() :
  pos = MP.trackPos()
  Ctrl.play(Tr,pos)
```

$$\text{ALWAYS} \left(\begin{array}{l} \text{leaveApp Sys} \wedge \text{musicPlaying MP} \\ \quad \rightarrow [\![\text{Ctrl} \leftharpoondown \text{pause}()]\!] \end{array}\right)$$

$$\text{ALWAYS} \left(\begin{array}{l} \text{resumeApp Sys} \\ \quad \rightarrow [\![\text{Ctrl} \leftharpoondown \text{play Tr (trackPos MP)}]\!] \end{array}\right)$$

Fig. 2. Sample code and specification for the music player app.

Our framework supports any FRP library using the *Arrow* or *Applicative* design patterns, which covers most of the existing FRP libraries (e.g. [2,3,10,41]). Finally, the synthesized control flow is embedded into a project context, where it is equipped with function and predicate implementations and then compiled to an executable program.

Our experience with synthesizing systems based on TSL specifications has been extremely positive. The synthesis works for a broad range of benchmarks, ranging from classic reactive synthesis problems (like escalator control), through programming exercises from functional reactive programming, to novel case studies like our music player app and the autonomous driving controller for a vehicle in the Open Race Car Simulator (TORCS).

2 Motivating Example

To demonstrate the utility of our method, we synthesized a music player Android app[1] from a TSL specification. A major challenge in developing Android apps is the temporal behavior of an app through the *Android lifecycle* [46]. The Android lifecycle describes how an app should handle being paused, when moved to the background, coming back into focus, or being terminated. In particular, *resume and restart errors* are commonplace and difficult to detect and correct [46]. Our music player app demonstrates a situation in which a resume and restart error could be unwittingly introduced when programming by hand, but is avoided by providing a specification. We only highlight the key parts of the example here to give an intuition of TSL. The complete specification is presented in [19].

Our music player app utilizes the Android music player library (MP), as well as its control interface (Ctrl). It pauses any playing music when moved to the background (for instance if a call is received), and continues playing the currently selected track (Tr) at the last track position when the app is resumed. In the Android system (Sys), the leaveApp method is called whenever the app moves to the background, while the resumeApp method is called when the app is brought back to the foreground. To avoid confusion between pausing music and pausing the app, we use leaveApp and resumeApp in place of the Android methods

---

[1] https://play.google.com/store/apps/details?id=com.mark.myapplication.

```
bool wasPlaying = false

Sys.leaveApp() :
  if (MP.musicPlaying()) :
    wasPlaying = true
    Ctrl.pause()
  else
    wasPlaying = false

Sys.resumeApp() :
  if (wasPlaying)
    pos = MP.trackPos()
    Ctrl.play(Tr,pos)
```

$$\text{ALWAYS} \Big((\text{leaveApp Sys} \wedge \text{musicPlaying MP}$$
$$\rightarrow [\![\text{Ctrl} \leftarrowtail \text{pause}()]\!])$$
$$\wedge ([\![\text{Ctrl} \leftarrowtail \text{play Tr (trackPos MP)}]\!]$$
$$\text{AS\_SOON\_AS resumeApp Sys}) \Big)$$

Fig. 3. The effect of a minor change in functionality on code versus a specification.

onPause and onResume. A programmer might manually write code for this as shown on the left in Fig. 2.

The behavior of this can be directly described in TSL as shown on the right in Fig. 2. Even eliding a formal introduction of the notation for now, the specification closely matches the textual specification. First, when the user leaves the app and the music is playing, the music pauses. Likewise for the second part, when the user resumes the app, the music starts playing again.

However, assume we want to change the behavior so that the music only plays on resume when the music had been playing before leaving the app in the first place. In the manually written program, this new functionality requires an additional variable `wasPlaying` to keep track of the music state. Managing the state requires multiple changes in the code as shown on the left in Fig. 3. The required code changes include: a conditional in the `resumeApp` method, setting `wasPlaying` appropriately in two places in `leaveApp`, and providing an initial value. Although a small example, it demonstrates how a minor change in functionality may require wide-reaching code changes. In addition, this change introduces a globally scoped variable, which then might accidentally be set or read elsewhere. In contrast, it is a simple matter to change the TSL specification to reflect this new functionality. Here, we only update one part of the specification to say that if the user leaves the app and the music is playing, the music has to play again as soon as the app resumes.

Synthesis allows us to specify a temporal behavior without worrying about the implementation details. In this example, writing the specification in TSL has eliminated the need of an additional state variable, similarly to a higher order `map` eliminating the need for an iteration variable. However, in more complex examples the benefits compound, as TSL provides a modular interface to specify behaviors, offloading the management of multiple interconnected temporal behaviors from the user to the synthesis engine.

3 Preliminaries

We assume time to be discrete and denote it by the set $\mathbb{N}$ of positive integers. A value is an arbitrary object of arbitrary type. $\mathcal{V}$ denotes the set of all values. The Boolean values are denoted by $\mathcal{B} \subseteq \mathcal{V}$. A stream $s\colon \mathbb{N} \to \mathcal{V}$ is a function fixing values at each point in time. An n-ary function $f\colon \mathcal{V}^n \to \mathcal{V}$ determines new values from n given values, where the set of all functions (of arbitrary arity) is given by $\mathcal{F}$. Constants are functions of arity 0. Every constant is a value, i.e., is an element of $\mathcal{F} \cap \mathcal{V}$. An n-ary predicate $p\colon \mathcal{V}^n \to \mathcal{B}$ checks a property over n values. The set of all predicates (of arbitrary arity) is given by $\mathcal{P}$, where $\mathcal{P} \subseteq \mathcal{F}$. We use $B^{[A]}$ to denote the set of all total functions with domain A and image B.

In the classical synthesis setting, inputs and outputs are vectors of Booleans, where the standard abstraction treats inputs and outputs as atomic propositions $\mathcal{I} \cup \mathcal{O}$, while their Boolean combinations form an alphabet $\Sigma = 2^{\mathcal{I} \cup \mathcal{O}}$. Behavior then is described through infinite sequences $\alpha = \alpha(0)\alpha(1)\alpha(2)\ldots \in \Sigma^\omega$. A *specification* describes a relation between input sequences $\alpha \in (2^{\mathcal{I}})^\omega$ and output sequences $\beta \in (2^{\mathcal{O}})^\omega$. Usually, this relation is not given by explicit sequences, but by a fomula in a temporal logic. The most popular such logic is Linear Temporal Logic (LTL) [43], which uses Boolean connectives to specify behavior at specific points in time, and temporal connectives, to relate sub-specifications over time. The realizability and synthesis problems for LTL are 2EXPTIME-complete [44].

An implementation describes a realizing strategy, formalized via infinite trees. A Φ-labeled and Υ-branching tree is a function $\sigma\colon \Upsilon^* \to \Phi$, where Υ denotes the set of branching directions along a tree. Every node of the tree is given by a finite prefix $v \in \Upsilon^*$, which fixes the path to reach a node from the root. Every node is labeled by an element of Φ. For infinite paths $\nu \in \Upsilon^\omega$, the branch $\sigma \wr \nu$ denotes the sequence of labels that appear on ν, i.e., $\forall t \in \mathbb{N}. \ (\sigma \wr \nu)(t) = \sigma(\nu(0) \ldots \nu(t-1))$.

4 Temporal Stream Logic

We present a new logic: Temporal Stream Logic (TSL), which is especially designed for synthesis and allows for the manipulation of infinite streams of arbitrary (even non-enumerative, or higher order) type. It provides a straight-forward notation to specify how outputs are computed from inputs, while using an intuitive interface to access time. The main focus of TSL is to describe temporal control flow, while abstracting away concrete implementation details. This not only keeps the logic intuitive and simple, but also allows a user to identify problems in the control flow even without a concrete implementation at hand. In this way, the use of TSL scales up to any required abstraction, such as API calls or complex algorithmic transformations.

Architecture. A TSL formula φ specifies a reactive system that in every time step processes a finite number of inputs $\mathbb{I}$ and produces a finite number of outputs $\mathbb{O}$. Furthermore, it uses cells $\mathbb{C}$ to store a value computed at time t, which can then be reused in the next time step $t + 1$. An overview of the architecture of such a system is given in Fig. 4a. In terms of behavior, the environment produces infinite

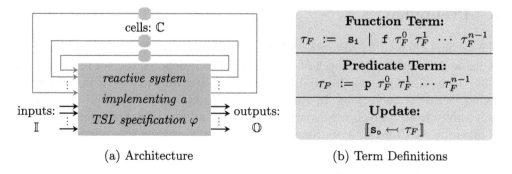

(a) Architecture   (b) Term Definitions

Fig. 4. General architecture of reactive systems that are specified in TSL on the left, and the structure of function, predicate and updates on the right.

streams of input data, while the system uses pure (side-effect free) functions to transform the values of these input streams in every time step. After their transformation, the data values are either passed to an output stream or are passed to a cell, which pipes the output value from one time step back to the corresponding input value of the next. The behaviour of the system is captured by its infinite execution over time.

Function Terms, Predicate Terms, and Updates. In TSL we differentiate between two elements: we use purely functional transformations, reflected by functions $f \in \mathcal{F}$ and their compositions, and predicates $p \in \mathcal{P}$, used to control how data flows inside the system. To argue about both elements we use a term based notation, where we distinguish between function terms τ_F and predicate terms τ_P, respectively. Function terms are either constructed from inputs or cells ($s_i \in \mathbb{I} \cup \mathbb{C}$), or from functions, recursively applied to a set of function terms. Predicate terms are constructed similarly, by applying a predicate to a set of function terms. Finally, an update takes the result of a function computation and passes it either to an output or a cell ($s_o \in \mathbb{O} \cup \mathbb{C}$). An overview of the syntax of the different term notations is given in Fig. 4b. Note that we use curried argument notation similar to functional programming languages.

We denote sets of function and predicate terms, and updates by $\mathcal{T}_F$, $\mathcal{T}_P$ and $\mathcal{T}_U$, respectively, where $\mathcal{T}_P \subseteq \mathcal{T}_F$. We use $\mathbb{F}$ to denote the set of function literals and $\mathbb{P} \subseteq \mathbb{F}$ to denote the set of predicate literals, where the literals s_i, s_o, f and p are symbolic representations of inputs and cells, outputs and cells, functions, and predicates, respectively. Literals are used to construct terms as shown in Fig. 4b. Since we use a symbolic representation, functions and predicates are not tied to a specific implementation. However, we still classify them according to their arity, i.e., the number of function terms they are applied to, as well as by their type: input, output, cell, function or predicate. Furthermore, terms can be compared syntactically using the equivalence relation $\equiv$. To assign a semantic interpretation to functions, we use an assignment function $\langle \cdot \rangle \colon \mathbb{F} \to \mathcal{F}$.

Inputs, Outputs, and Computations. We consider momentary inputs $i \in \mathcal{V}^{[\mathbb{I}]}$, which are assignments of inputs $\mathsf{i} \in \mathbb{I}$ to values $v \in \mathcal{V}$. For the sake of readability let $\mathcal{I} = \mathcal{V}^{[\mathbb{I}]}$. Input streams are infinite sequences $\iota \in \mathcal{I}^\omega$ consisting of infinitely many momentary inputs.

Similarly, a momentary output $o \in \mathcal{V}^{[\mathbb{O}]}$ is an assignment of outputs $\mathsf{o} \in \mathbb{O}$ to values $v \in \mathcal{V}$, where we also use $\mathcal{O} = \mathcal{V}^{[\mathbb{O}]}$. Output streams are infinite sequences $\varrho \in \mathcal{O}^\omega$. To capture the behavior of a cell, we introduce the notion of a computation ς. A computation fixes the function terms that are used to compute outputs and cell updates, without fixing semantics of function literals. Intuitively, a computation only determines which function terms are used to compute an output, but abstracts from actually computing it.

The basic element of a computation is a computation step $c \in \mathcal{T}_F^{[\mathbb{O} \cup \mathbb{C}]}$, which is an assignment of outputs and cells $\mathsf{s_o} \in \mathbb{O} \cup \mathbb{C}$ to function terms $\tau_F \in \mathcal{T}_F$. For the sake of readability let $\mathcal{C} = \mathcal{T}_F^{[\mathbb{O} \cup \mathbb{C}]}$. A computation step fixes the control flow behaviour at a single point in time. A computation $\varsigma \in \mathcal{C}^\omega$ is an infinite sequence of computation steps.

As soon as input streams, and function and predicate implementations are known, computations can be turned into output streams. To this end, let $\langle \cdot \rangle : \mathbb{F} \to \mathcal{F}$ be some function assignment. Furthermore, assume that there are predefined constants $init_\mathsf{c} \in \mathcal{F} \cap \mathcal{V}$ for every cell $\mathsf{c} \in \mathbb{C}$, which provide an initial value for each stream at the initial point in time. To receive an output stream from a computation $\varsigma \in \mathcal{C}^\omega$ under the input stream ι, we use an evaluation function $\eta_{\langle \cdot \rangle} : \mathcal{C}^\omega \times \mathcal{I}^\omega \times \mathbb{N} \times \mathcal{T}_F \to \mathcal{V}$:

$$\eta_{\langle \cdot \rangle}(\varsigma, \iota, t, \mathsf{s_i}) = \begin{cases} \iota(t)(\mathsf{s_i}) & \text{if } \mathsf{s_i} \in \mathbb{I} \\ init_{\mathsf{s_i}} & \text{if } \mathsf{s_i} \in \mathbb{C} \wedge t = 0 \\ \eta_{\langle \cdot \rangle}(\varsigma, \iota, t-1, \varsigma(t-1)(\mathsf{s_i})) & \text{if } \mathsf{s_i} \in \mathbb{C} \wedge t > 0 \end{cases}$$

$$\eta_{\langle \cdot \rangle}(\varsigma, \iota, t, \mathsf{f}\ \tau_0\ \cdots\ \tau_{m-1}) = \langle \mathsf{f} \rangle\ \eta_{\langle \cdot \rangle}(\varsigma, \iota, t, \tau_0)\ \cdots\ \eta_{\langle \cdot \rangle}(\varsigma, \iota, t, \tau_{m-1})$$

Then $\varrho_{\langle \cdot \rangle, \varsigma, \iota} \in \mathcal{O}^\omega$ is defined via $\varrho_{\langle \cdot \rangle, \varsigma, \iota}(t)(\mathsf{o}) = \eta_{\langle \cdot \rangle}(\varsigma, \iota, t, \mathsf{o})$ for all $t \in \mathbb{N}$, $\mathsf{o} \in \mathbb{O}$.

Syntax. Every TSL formula φ is built according to the following grammar:

$$\varphi \ := \ \tau \in \mathcal{T}_P \cup \mathcal{T}_U \ \mid \ \neg \varphi \ \mid \ \varphi \wedge \varphi \ \mid \ \bigcirc \varphi \ \mid \ \varphi \, \mathcal{U} \, \varphi$$

An atomic proposition τ consists either of a predicate term, serving as a Boolean interface to the inputs, or of an update, enforcing a respective flow at the current point in time. Next, we have the Boolean operations via negation and conjunction, that allow us to express arbitrary Boolean combinations of predicate evaluations and updates. Finally, we have the temporal operator next: $\bigcirc \psi$, to specify the behavior at the next point in time and the temporal operator until: $\vartheta \, \mathcal{U} \, \psi$, which enforces a property ϑ to hold until the property ψ holds, where ψ must hold at some point in the future eventually.

Semantics. Formally, this leads to the following semantics. Let $\langle \cdot \rangle \colon \mathbb{F} \to \mathcal{F}$, $\iota \in \mathcal{I}^\omega$, and $\varsigma \in \mathcal{C}^\omega$ be given, then the validity of a TSL formula φ with respect to ς and ι is defined inductively over $t \in \mathbb{N}$ via:

$$\varsigma, \iota, t \vDash_{\langle \cdot \rangle} \mathrm{p}\, \tau_0 \cdots \tau_{m-1} \quad :\Leftrightarrow \quad \eta_{\langle \cdot \rangle}(\varsigma, \iota, t, \mathrm{p}\, \tau_0 \cdots \tau_{m-1})$$
$$\varsigma, \iota, t \vDash_{\langle \cdot \rangle} \llbracket \mathrm{s} \hookleftarrow \tau \rrbracket \quad :\Leftrightarrow \quad \varsigma(t)(\mathrm{s}) \equiv \tau$$
$$\varsigma, \iota, t \vDash_{\langle \cdot \rangle} \neg \psi \quad :\Leftrightarrow \quad \varsigma, \iota, t \nvDash_{\langle \cdot \rangle} \psi$$
$$\varsigma, \iota, t \vDash_{\langle \cdot \rangle} \vartheta \wedge \psi \quad :\Leftrightarrow \quad \varsigma, \iota, t \vDash_{\langle \cdot \rangle} \vartheta \, \wedge \, \varsigma, \iota, t \vDash_{\langle \cdot \rangle} \psi$$
$$\varsigma, \iota, t \vDash_{\langle \cdot \rangle} \bigcirc \psi \quad :\Leftrightarrow \quad \varsigma, \iota, t+1 \vDash_{\langle \cdot \rangle} \psi$$
$$\varsigma, \iota, t \vDash_{\langle \cdot \rangle} \vartheta \, \mathcal{U} \, \psi \quad :\Leftrightarrow \quad \exists t'' \geq t. \, \forall t \leq t' < t''. \, \varsigma, \iota, t' \vDash_{\langle \cdot \rangle} \vartheta \, \wedge \, \varsigma, \iota, t'' \vDash_{\langle \cdot \rangle} \psi$$

Consider that the satisfaction of a predicate depends on the current computation step and the steps of the past, while for updates it only depends on the current computation step. Furthermore, updates are only checked syntactically, while the satisfaction of predicates depends on the given assignment $\langle \cdot \rangle$ and the input stream ι. We say that ς and ι satisfy φ, denoted by $\varsigma, \iota \vDash_{\langle \cdot \rangle} \varphi$, if $\varsigma, \iota, 0 \vDash_{\langle \cdot \rangle} \varphi$.

Beside the basic operators, we have the standard derived Boolean operators, as well as the derived temporal operators: *release* $\varphi \, \mathcal{R} \, \psi \equiv \neg((\neg \psi) \, \mathcal{U} (\neg \varphi))$, *finally* $\Diamond \varphi \equiv true \, \mathcal{U} \, \varphi$, *always* $\Box \varphi \equiv false \, \mathcal{R} \, \varphi$, the *weak* version of *until* $\varphi \, \mathcal{W} \, \psi \equiv (\varphi \, \mathcal{U} \, \psi) \vee (\Box \varphi)$, and *as soon as* $\varphi \, \mathcal{A} \, \psi \equiv \neg \psi \, \mathcal{W} (\psi \wedge \varphi)$.

Realizability. We are interested in the following realizability problem: given a TSL formula φ, is there a strategy $\sigma \in \mathcal{C}^{[\mathcal{I}^+]}$ such that for every input $\iota \in \mathcal{I}^\omega$ and function implementation $\langle \cdot \rangle \colon \mathbb{F} \to \mathcal{F}$, the branch $\sigma \wr \iota$ satisfies φ, i.e.,

$$\exists \sigma \in \mathcal{C}^{[\mathcal{I}^+]}. \, \forall \iota \in \mathcal{I}^\omega. \, \forall \langle \cdot \rangle \colon \mathbb{F} \to \mathcal{F}. \, \sigma \wr \iota, \iota \vDash_{\langle \cdot \rangle} \varphi$$

If such a strategy σ exists, we say σ realizes φ. If we additionally ask for a concrete instantiation of σ, we consider the synthesis problem of TSL.

5   TSL Properties

In order to synthesize programs from TSL specifications, we give an overview of the first part of our synthesis process, as shown in Fig. 1. First we show how to approximate the semantics of TSL through a reduction to LTL. However, due to the approximation, finding a realizable strategy immediately may fail. Our solution is a CEGAR loop that improves the approximation. This CEGAR loop is necessary, because the realizability problem of TSL is undecidable in general.

Approximating TSL with LTL. We approximate TSL formulas with weaker LTL formulas. The approximation reinterprets the syntactic elements, $\mathcal{T}_P$ and $\mathcal{T}_U$, as atomic propositions for LTL. This strips away the semantic meaning of the function application and assignment in TSL, which we reconstruct by later adding assumptions lazily to the LTL formula.

Formally, let $\mathcal{T}_P$ and $\mathcal{T}_U$ be the finite sets of predicate terms and updates, which appear in φ_{TSL}, respectively. For every assigned signal, we partition $\mathcal{T}_U$ into $\biguplus_{\mathrm{s}_\circ \in \mathbb{O} \cup \mathbb{C}} \mathcal{T}_U^{\mathrm{s}_\circ}$. For every $\mathrm{c} \in \mathbb{C}$ let $\mathcal{T}_{U/\mathrm{id}}^{\mathrm{c}} = \mathcal{T}_U^{\mathrm{c}} \cup \{\llbracket \mathrm{c} \hookleftarrow \mathrm{c} \rrbracket\}$, for $\mathrm{o} \in \mathbb{O}$ let

$$\square (\llbracket y \leftarrowtail y \rrbracket \vee \llbracket y \leftarrowtail x \rrbracket) \\ \wedge \Diamond p \, x \to \Diamond p \, y$$

$$\square \neg(y\_to\_y \wedge x\_to\_y) \\ \wedge \square (y\_to\_y \vee x\_to\_y) \\ \wedge \Diamond p\_x \to \Diamond p\_y$$

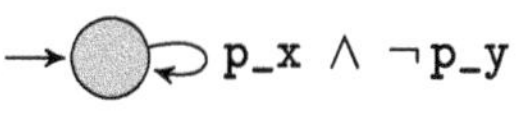

$p\_x \wedge \neg p\_y$

(a) TSL specification   (b) initial approximation   (c) spurious counter-strategy

Fig. 5. A TSL specification (a) with input x and cell y that is realizable. A winning strategy is to save x to y as soon as p(x) is satisfied. However, the initial approximation (b), that is passed to an LTL synthesis solver, is unrealizable, as proven through the counter-strategy (c) returned by the LTL solver.

$\mathcal{T}^{\circ}_{U/\mathrm{id}} = \mathcal{T}^{\circ}_{U}$, and let $\mathcal{T}_{U/\mathrm{id}} = \bigcup_{s_{\circ} \in \mathbb{O} \cup \mathbb{C}} \mathcal{T}^{s_{\circ}}_{U/\mathrm{id}}$. We construct the LTL formula φ_{LTL} over the input propositions $\mathcal{T}_{P}$ and output propositions $\mathcal{T}_{U/\mathrm{id}}$ as follows:

$$\varphi_{LTL} = \square \Big(\bigwedge_{s_{\circ} \in \mathbb{O} \cup \mathbb{C}} \bigvee_{\tau \in \mathcal{T}^{s_{\circ}}_{U/\mathrm{id}}} \big(\tau \wedge \bigwedge_{\tau' \in \mathcal{T}^{s_{\circ}}_{U/\mathrm{id}} \setminus \{\tau\}} \neg\tau'\big) \Big) \wedge \text{SyntacticConversion}(\varphi_{TSL})$$

Intuitively, the first part of the equation partially reconstructs the semantic meaning of updates by ensuring that a signal is not updated with multiple values at a time. The second part extracts the reactive constraints of the TSL formula without the semantic meaning of functions and updates.

Theorem 1 ([19]). *If φ_{LTL} is realizable, then φ_{TSL} is realizable.*

Note that unrealizability of φ_{LTL} does not imply that φ_{TSL} is unrealizable. It may be that we have not added sufficiently many environment assumptions to the approximation in order for the system to produce a realizing strategy.

Example. As an example, we present a simple TSL specification in Fig. 5a. The specification asserts that the environment provides an input x for which the predicate p x will be satisfied eventually. The system must guarantee that eventually p y holds. According to the semantics of TSL the formula is realizable. The system can take the value of x when p x is true and save it to y, thus guaranteeing that p y is satisfied eventually. This is in contrast to LTL, which has no semantics for pure functions - taking the evaluation of p y as an environmentally controlled value that does not need to obey the consistency of a pure function.

Refining the LTL Approximation. It is possible that the LTL solver returns a counter-strategy for the environment although the original TSL specification is realizable. We call such a counter-strategy *spurious* as it exploits the additional freedom of LTL to violate the purity of predicates as made possible by the underapproximation. Formally, a counter-strategy is an infinite tree $\pi \colon \mathcal{C}^{*} \to 2^{\mathcal{T}_{P}}$, which provides predicate evaluations in response to possible update assignments of function terms $\tau_{F} \in \mathcal{T}_{F}$ to outputs $o \in \mathbb{O}$. W.l.o.g. we can assume that $\mathbb{O}$, $\mathcal{T}_{F}$ and $\mathcal{T}_{P}$ are finite, as they can always be restricted to the outputs and terms that appear in the formula. A counter-strategy is spurious, iff there is a branch $\pi \wr \varsigma$ for some computation $\varsigma \in \mathcal{C}^{\omega}$, for which the strategy chooses an inconsistent evaluation of two equal predicate terms at different points in time, i.e.,

---

Algorithm 1. Check-Spuriousness

Input: bound b, counter-strategy $\pi\colon \mathcal{C}^* \to 2^{\mathcal{T}_P}$ (finitely represented using m states)

1: **for all** $v \in \mathcal{C}^{m \cdot b}$, $\tau_P \in \mathcal{T}_P$, $t, t' \in \{0, 1, \ldots, m \cdot b - 1\}$ **do**

2:     **if** $\eta_{\langle\rangle_{\text{id}}}(v, \iota_{\text{id}}, t, \tau_P) \equiv \eta_{\langle\rangle_{\text{id}}}(v, \iota_{\text{id}}, t', \tau_P) \wedge$

        $\tau_P \in \pi(v_0 \ldots v_{t-1}) \wedge \tau_P \notin \pi(v_0 \ldots v_{t'-1})$ **then**

3:         $w \leftarrow \textbf{reduce}\,(v, \tau_P, t, t')$

4:         **return** $\square\left(\bigwedge_{i=0}^{t-1} \bigcirc^i w_i \wedge \bigwedge_{i=0}^{t'-1} \bigcirc^i w_i \to (\bigcirc^t \tau_P \leftrightarrow \bigcirc^{t'} \tau_P)\right)$

5: **return** ``non-spurious''

$$\exists \varsigma \in \mathcal{C}^\omega.\ \exists t, t' \in \mathbb{N}.\ \exists \tau_P \in \mathcal{T}_P.$$
$$\tau_P \in \pi(\varsigma(0)\varsigma(1) \ldots \varsigma(t-1)) \wedge \tau_P \notin \pi(\varsigma(0)\varsigma(1) \ldots \varsigma(t'-1)) \wedge$$
$$\forall \langle \cdot \rangle \colon \mathbb{F} \to \mathcal{F}.\ \eta_{\langle \cdot \rangle}(\varsigma, \pi\wr\varsigma, t, \tau_P) = \eta_{\langle \cdot \rangle}(\varsigma, \pi\wr\varsigma, t', \tau_P).$$

Note that a non-spurious strategy can be inconsistent along multiple branches. Due to the definition of realizability the environment can choose function and predicate assignments differently against every system strategy accordingly.

By purity of predicates in TSL the environment is forced to always return the same value for predicate evaluations on equal values. However, this semantic property cannot be enforced implicitly in LTL. To resolve this issue we use the returned counter-strategy to identify spurious behavior in order to strengthen the LTL underapproximation with additional environment assumptions. After adding the derived assumptions, we re-execute the LTL synthesizer to check whether the added assumptions are sufficient in order to obtain a winning strategy for the system. If the solver still returns a spurious strategy, we continue the loop in a CEGAR fashion until the set of added assumptions is sufficiently complete. However, if a non-spurious strategy is returned, we have found a proof that the given TSL specification is indeed unrealizable and terminate.

Algorithm 1 shows how a returned counter-strategy π is checked for being spurious. To this end, it is sufficient to check π against system strategies bounded by the given bound b, as we use bounded synthesis [20]. Furthermore, we can assume w.l.o.g. that π is given by a finite state representation, which is always possible due to the finite model guarantees of LTL. Also note that π, as it is returned by the LTL synthesizer, responds to sequences of sets of updates $(2^{\mathcal{T}_U/\text{id}})^*$. However, in our case $(2^{\mathcal{T}_U/\text{id}})^*$ is an alternative representation of $\mathcal{C}^*$, due to the additional "single update" constraints added during the construction of φ_{LTL}.

The algorithm iterates over all possible responses $v \in \mathcal{C}^{m \cdot b}$ of the system up to depth $m \cdot b$. This is sufficient, since any deeper exploration would result in a state repetition of the cross-product of the finite state representation of π and any system strategy bounded by b. Hence, the same behaviour could also be generated by a sequence smaller than $m \cdot b$. At the same time, the algorithm iterates over predicates $\tau_P \in \mathcal{T}_P$ appearing in φ_{TSL} and times t and t' smaller than $m \cdot b$. For each of these elements, spuriousness is checked by comparing the output of π for the evaluation of τ_P at times t and t', which should only differ if the inputs to the predicates are different as well. This can only happen, if the passed input terms have been constructed differently over the past. We check it by using the evaluation function η equipped with the identity assignment $\langle \cdot \rangle_{\mathtt{id}} \colon \mathbb{F} \to \mathbb{F}$, with $\langle \mathtt{f} \rangle_{\mathtt{id}} = \mathtt{f}$ for all $\mathtt{f} \in \mathbb{F}$, and the input sequence $\iota_{\mathtt{id}}$, with $\iota_{\mathtt{id}}(t)(\mathtt{i}) = (t, \mathtt{i})$ for all $t \in \mathbb{N}$ and $\mathtt{i} \in \mathbb{I}$, that always generates a fresh input. Syntactic inequality of $\eta_{\langle \cdot \rangle_{\mathtt{id}}}(v, \iota_{\mathtt{id}}, t, \tau_P)$ and $\eta_{\langle \cdot \rangle_{\mathtt{id}}}(v, \iota_{\mathtt{id}}, t', \tau_P)$ then is a sufficient condition for the existence of an assignment $\langle \cdot \rangle \colon \mathbb{F} \to \mathcal{F}$, for which τ_P evaluates differently at times t and t'.

If spurious behaviour of π could be found, then the revealing response $v \in \mathcal{C}^*$ is first simplified using reduce, which reduces v again to a sequence of sets of updates $w \in (2^{\mathcal{T}_{U/\mathtt{id}}})^*$ and removes updates that do not affect the behavior of τ_P at the times t and t' to accelerate the termination of the CEGAR loop. Afterwards, the sequence w is turned into a new assumption that prohibits the spurious behavior, generalized to prevent it even at arbitrary points in time.

As an example of this process, reconsider the spurious counter-strategy of Fig. 5c. Already after the first system response $[\![\mathtt{y} \leftarrowtail \mathtt{x}]\!]$, the environment produces an inconsistency by evaluating p x and p y differently. This is inconsistent, as the cell y holds the same value at time $t = 1$ as the input x at time $t = 0$. Using Algorithm 1 we generate the new assumption $\square([\![\mathtt{y} \leftarrowtail \mathtt{x}]\!] \to (\mathtt{p~x} \leftrightarrow \bigcirc \mathtt{p~y}))$. After adding this strengthening the LTL synthesizer returns a realizability result.

Undecidability. Although we can approximate the semantics of TSL with LTL, there are TSL formulas that cannot be expressed as LTL formulas of finite size.

Theorem 2 ([19])**.** *The realizability problem of TSL is undecidable.*

6   TSL Synthesis

Our synthesis framework provides a modular refinement process to synthesize executables from TSL specifications, as depicted in Fig. 1. The user initially provides a TSL specification over predicate and function terms. At the end of the procedure, the user receives an executable to control a reactive system.

The first step of our method answers the synthesis question of TSL: if the specification is realizable, then a control flow model is returned. To this end, an intermediate translation to LTL is used, utilizing an LTL synthesis solver that produces circuits in the AIGER format. If the specification is realizable, the resulting control flow model is turned into Haskell code, which is implemented as an independent Haskell module. The user has the choice between two different targets: a module built on Arrows, which is compatible with any Arrowized FRP library, or a module built on Applicative, which supports Applicative FRP libraries. Our procedure generates a single Haskell module per TSL specification. This makes naturally decomposing a project according to individual tasks possible. Each module provides a single component, which is parameterized by their initial state and the pure function and predicate transformations. As soon as these are provided as part of the surrounding project context, a final executable can be generated by compiling the Haskell code.

An important feature of our synthesis approach is that implementations for the terms used in the specification are only required after synthesis. This allows

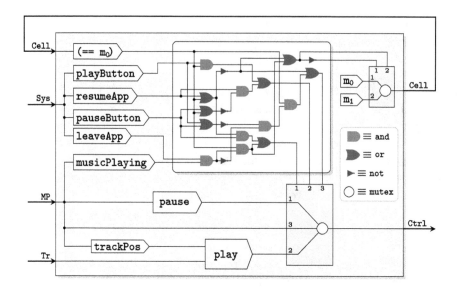

Fig. 6. Example CFM of the music player generated from a TSL specification.

the user to explore several possible specifications before deciding on any term implementations.

Control Flow Model. The first step of our approach is the synthesis of a *Control Flow Model* $\mathcal{M}$ (CFM) from the given TSL specification φ, which provides us with a uniform representation of the control flow structure of our final program.

Formally, a CFM $\mathcal{M}$ is a tuple $\mathcal{M} = (\mathbb{I}, \mathbb{O}, \mathbb{C}, V, \ell, \delta)$, where $\mathbb{I}$ is a finite set of inputs, $\mathbb{O}$ is a finite set of outputs, $\mathbb{C}$ is a finite set of cells, V is a finite set of vertices, $\ell \colon V \to \mathbb{F}$ assigns a vertex a function $\mathsf{f} \in \mathbb{F}$ or a predicate $\mathsf{p} \in \mathbb{P}$, and

$$\delta \colon (\mathbb{O} \cup \mathbb{C} \cup V) \times \mathbb{N} \to (\mathbb{I} \cup \mathbb{C} \cup V \cup \{\bot\})$$

is a dependency relation that relates every output, cell, and vertex of the CFM with $n \in \mathbb{N}$ arguments, which are either inputs, cells, or vertices. Outputs and cells $\mathsf{s} \in \mathbb{O} \cup \mathbb{C}$ always have only a single argument, i.e., $\delta(\mathsf{s}, 0) \not\equiv \bot$ and $\forall m > 0$. $\delta(\mathsf{s}, m) \equiv \bot$, while for vertices $x \in V$ the number of arguments $n \in \mathbb{N}$ align with the arity of the assigned function or predicate $\ell(x)$, i.e., $\forall m \in \mathbb{N}. \ \delta(x, m) \equiv \bot \leftrightarrow m > n$. A CFM is valid if it does not contain circular dependencies, i.e., on every cycle induced by δ there must lie at least a single cell. We only consider valid CFMs.

An example CFM for our music player of Sect. 2 is depicted in Fig. 6. Inputs $\mathbb{I}$ come from the left and outputs $\mathbb{O}$ leave on the right. The example contains a single cell $\mathsf{c} \in \mathbb{C}$, which holds the stateful memory Cell, introduced during synthesis for the module. The green, arrow shaped boxes depict vertices V, which are labeled with functions and predicates names, according to ℓ. For the Boolean decisions that define δ, we use circuit symbols for conjunction, disjunction, and negation. Boolean decisions are piped to a multiplexer gate that selects the respective update streams. This allows each update stream to be passed to an output stream if and only if the respective Boolean trigger evaluates positively, while our construction ensures mutual exclusion on the Boolean triggers. For code generation, the logic gates are implemented using the corresponding dedicated Boolean functions. After building a control structure, we assign semantics to functions and predicates by providing implementations. To this end, we use Functional Reactive Programming (FRP). Prior work has established Causal Commutative Arrows (CCA) as an FRP language pattern equivalent to a CFM [33,34,53]. CCAs are an abstraction subsumed by other functional reactive programming abstractions, such as Monads, Applicative and Arrows [32,33]. There are many FRP libraries using Monads [11,14,42], Applicative [2,3,23,48], or Arrows [10,39,41,51], and since every Monad is also an Applicative and Applicative/Arrows both are universal design patterns, we can give uniform translations to all of these libraries using translations to just Applicative and Arrows. Both translations are possible due to the flexible notion of a CFM.

In the last step, the synthesized FRP program is compiled into an executable, using the provided function and predicate implementations. This step is not fixed to a single compiler implementation, but in fact can use any FRP compiler (or library) that supports a language abstraction at least as expressive as CCA. For example, instead of creating an Android music player app, we could target an FRP web interface [48] to create an online music player, or an embedded FRP library [23] to instantiate the player on a computationally more restricted device. By using the strong core of CCA, we even can directly implement the player in hardware, which is for example possible with the CλaSH compiler [3]. Note that we still need separate implementations for functions and predicates for each target. However, the specification and synthesized CFM always stay the same.

7 Experimental Results

To evaluate our synthesis procedure we implemented a tool that follows the structure of Fig. 1. It first encodes the given TSL specification in LTL and then refines it until an LTL solver either produces a realizability result or returns a non-spurious counter-strategy. For LTL synthesis we use the bounded synthesis tool BoSy [15]. As soon as we get a realizing strategy it is translated to a corresponding CFM. Then, we generate the FRP program structure. Finally, after providing function implementations the result is compiled into an executable.

To demonstrate the effectiveness of synthesizing TSL, we applied our tool to a collection of benchmarks from different application domains, listed in Table 1. Every benchmark class consists of multiple specifications, addressing different features of TSL. We created all specifications from scratch, where we took care that they either relate to existing textual specifications, or real world scenarios. A short description of each benchmark class is given in [19].

For every benchmark, we report the synthesis time and the size of the synthesized CFM, split into the number of cells ($|\mathbb{C}_{\mathcal{M}}|$) and vertices ($|V_{\mathcal{M}}|$) used. The synthesized CFM may use more cells than the original TSL specification if synthesis requires more memory in order to realize a correct control flow.

Table 1. Number of cells $|\mathbb{C}_\mathcal{M}|$ and vertices $|V_\mathcal{M}|$ of the resulting CFM $\mathcal{M}$ and synthesis times for a collection of TSL specifications φ. A * indicates that the benchmark additionally has an initial condition as part of the specification.

Benchmark (φ)	$|\varphi|$	$|\mathbb{I}|$	$|\mathbb{O}|$	$|\mathbb{P}|$	$|\mathbb{F}|$	$|\mathbb{C}_\mathcal{M}|$	$|V_\mathcal{M}|$	Synthesis Time (s)
Button								
default	7	1	2	1	3	3	8	0.364
Music App								
simple	91	3	1	4	7	2	25	0.77
system feedback	103	3	1	5	8	2	31	0.572
motivating example	87	3	1	5	8	2	70	1.783
FRPZoo								
scenario$_0$	54	1	3	2	8	4	36	1.876
scenario$_5$	50	1	3	2	7	4	32	1.196
scenario$_{10}$	48	1	3	2	7	4	32	1.161
Escalator								
non-reactive	8	0	1	0	1	2	4	0.370
non-counting	15	2	1	2	4	2	19	0.304
counting	34	2	2	3	7	3	23	0.527
counting*	43	2	2	3	8	4	43	0.621
bidirectional	111	2	2	5	10	3	214	4.555
bidirectional*	124	2	2	5	11	4	287	16.213
smart	45	2	1	2	4	4	159	24.016
Slider								
default	50	1	1	2	4	2	15	0.664
scored	67	1	3	4	8	4	62	3.965
delayed	71	1	3	4	8	5	159	7.194
Haskell-TORCS								
simple	40	5	3	2	16	4	37	0.680
advanced								
gearing	23	4	1	1	3	2	7	0.403
accelerating	15	2	2	2	6	3	11	0.391
steering								
simple	45	2	1	4	6	2	31	0.459
improved	100	2	2	4	10	3	26	1.347
smart	76	3	2	4	8	5	227	3.375

Table 2. Set of programs that use purity to keep one or two counters in range. Synthesis needs multiple refinements of the specification to proof realizability.

Benchmark (φ)	$|\varphi|$	$|\mathbb{I}|$	$|\mathbb{O}|$	$|\mathbb{P}|$	$|\mathbb{F}|$	$|\mathbb{C}_\mathcal{M}|$	$|V_\mathcal{M}|$	Refinements	Synthesis Time (s)
inrange-single	23	2	1	2	4	2	21	3	0.690
inrange-two	51	3	3	4	7	4	440	6	173.132
graphical-single	55	2	3	2	6	4	343	9	1767.948
graphical-two	113	3	5	4	9	-	-	-	¿10000

The synthesis was executed on a quad-core Intel Xeon processor (E3-1271 v3, 3.6GHz, 32 GB RAM, PC1600, ECC), running Ubuntu 64bit LTS 16.04.

The experiments of Table 1 show that TSL successfully lifts the applicability of synthesis from the Boolean domain to arbitrary data domains, allowing for new applications that utilize every level of required abstraction. For all benchmarks we always found a realizable system within a reasonable amount of time, where the results often required synthesized cells to realize the control flow behavior.

We also considered a preliminary set of benchmarks that require multiple refinement steps to be synthesizable. An overview of the results is given in Table 2. The benchmarks are inspired by examples of the Reactive Banana FRP library [2]. Here, purity of function and predicate applications must be utilized by the system to ensure that the value of one or two counters never goes out of range. Thereby, the system not only needs purity to verify this condition, but also to take the correct decisions in the resulting implementation to be synthesized.

8 Related Work

Our approach builds on the rich body of work on reactive synthesis, see [17] for a survey. The classic reactive synthesis problem is the construction of a finite-state machine that satisfies a specification in a temporal logic like LTL. Our approach differs from the classic problem in its connection to an actual programming paradigm, namely FRP, and its separation of control and data.

The synthesis of *reactive programs*, rather than finite-state machines, has previously been studied for standard temporal logic [21,35]. Because there is no separation of control and data, these approaches do not directly scale to realistic applications. With regard to FRP, a *Curry-Howard correspondence* between LTL and FRP in a dependently typed language was discovered [28,29] and used to prove properties of FRP programs [8,30]. However, our paper is the first, to the best of our knowledge, to study the synthesis of FRP programs from temporal specifications.

The idea to separate control and data has appeared, on a smaller scale, in the synthesis with *identifiers*, where identifiers, such as the number of a client in a mutual exclusion protocol, are treated symbolically [13]. *Uninterpreted functions* have been used to abstract data-related computational details in the synthesis of synchronization primitives for complex programs [5]. Another connection to other synthesis approaches is our CEGAR loop. Similar *refinement loops* also appear in other synthesis appraches, however with a different purpose, such as the refinement of environment assumptions [1].

So far, there is no immediate connection between our approach and the substantial work on *deductive* and *inductive synthesis*, which is specifically concerned with the data-transformation aspects of programs [16,31,40,47,49,50]. Typically, these approaches are focussed on non-reactive sequential programs. An integration of deductive and inductive techniques into our approach for reactive systems is a very promising direction for future work. Abstraction-based synthesis [4,12,24,37] may potentially provide a link between the approaches.

9   Conclusions

We have introduced Temporal Stream Logic, which allows the user to specify the control flow of a reactive program. The logic cleanly separates control from complex data, forming the foundation for our procedure to synthesize FRP programs. By utilizing the purity of function transformations our logic scales independently of the complexity of the data to be handled. While we have shown that scalability comes at the cost of undecidability, we addressed this issue by using a CEGAR loop, which lazily refines the underapproximation until either a realizing system implementation or an unrealizability proof is found.

Our experiments indicate that TSL synthesis works well in practice and on a wide range of programming applications. TSL also provides the foundations for further extensions. For example, a user may want to fix the semantics for a subset of the functions and predicates. Such refinements can be implemented as part of a much richer *TSL Modulo Theory* framework.

References

1. Alur, R., Moarref, S., Topcu, U.: Counter-strategy guided refinement of GR(1) temporal logic specifications. In: Formal Methods in Computer-Aided Design, FMCAD 2013, Portland, OR, USA, 20–23 October 2013, pp. 26–33. IEEE (2013). http://ieeexplore.ieee.org/document/6679387/
2. Apfelmus, H.: Reactive-banana. Haskell library (2012). http://www.haskell.org/haskellwiki/Reactive-banana
3. Baaij, C.: Digital circuit in CλaSH: functional specifications and type-directed synthesis. Ph.D. thesis, University of Twente, January 2015. https://doi.org/10.3990/1.9789036538039, eemcs-eprint-23939
4. Beyene, T.A., Chaudhuri, S., Popeea, C., Rybalchenko, A.: A constraint-based approach to solving games on infinite graphs. In: Jagannathan and Sewell [26], pp. 221–234. https://doi.org/10.1145/2535838.2535860, http://doi.acm.org/10.1145/2535838.2535860
5. Bloem, R., Hofferek, G., Könighofer, B., Könighofer, R., Ausserlechner, S., Spork, R.: Synthesis of synchronization using uninterpreted functions. In: Formal Methods in Computer-Aided Design, FMCAD 2014, Lausanne, Switzerland, 21–24 October 2014, pp. 35–42. IEEE (2014). https://doi.org/10.1109/FMCAD.2014.6987593
6. Bloem, R., Jacobs, S., Khalimov, A.: Parameterized synthesis case study: AMBA AHB. In: Chatterjee, K., Ehlers, R., Jha, S. (eds.) Proceedings 3rd Workshop on Synthesis, SYNT 2014. EPTCS, Vienna, Austria, 23–24 July 2014, vol. 157, pp. 68–83 (2014). https://doi.org/10.4204/EPTCS.157.9
7. Bloem, R., Jobstmann, B., Piterman, N., Pnueli, A., Sa'ar, Y.: Synthesis of reactive(1) designs. J. Comput. Syst. Sci. **78**(3), 911–938 (2012). https://doi.org/10.1016/j.jcss.2011.08.007
8. Cave, A., Ferreira, F., Panangaden, P., Pientka, B.: Fair reactive programming. In: Jagannathan and Sewell [26], pp. 361–372. https://doi.org/10.1145/2535838.2535881, http://doi.acm.org/10.1145/2535838.2535881
9. Clarke, E.M., Grumberg, O., Jha, S., Lu, Y., Veith, H.: Counterexample-guided abstraction refinement for symbolic model checking. J. ACM **50**(5), 752–794 (2003). https://doi.org/10.1145/876638.876643

10. Courtney, A., Nilsson, H., Peterson, J.: The yampa arcade. In: Proceedings of the ACM SIGPLAN Workshop on Haskell, Haskell 2003, Uppsala, Sweden, 28 August 2003, pp. 7–18. ACM, (2003). https://doi.org/10.1145/871895.871897, http://doi.acm.org/10.1145/871895.871897

11. Czaplicki, E., Chong, S.: Asynchronous functional reactive programming for Guis. In: Boehm, H., Flanagan, C. (eds.) ACM SIGPLAN Conference on Programming Language Design and Implementation, PLDI 2013, Seattle, WA, USA, 16–19 June 2013, pp. 411–422. ACM (2013). https://dl.acm.org/citation.cfm?doid=2462156.2462161, http://doi.acm.org/10.1145/2462156.2462161

12. Dimitrova, R., Finkbeiner, B.: Counterexample-guided synthesis of observation predicates. In: Jurdziński, M., Ničković, D. (eds.) FORMATS 2012. LNCS, vol. 7595, pp. 107–122. Springer, Heidelberg (2012). https://doi.org/10.1007/978-3-642-33365-1_9

13. Ehlers, R., Seshia, S.A., Kress-Gazit, H.: Synthesis with identifiers. In: McMillan, K.L., Rival, X. (eds.) VMCAI 2014. LNCS, vol. 8318, pp. 415–433. Springer, Heidelberg (2014). https://doi.org/10.1007/978-3-642-54013-4_23

14. Elliott, C., Hudak, P.: Functional reactive animation. In: Jones, S.L.P., Tofte, M., Berman, A.M. (eds.) Proceedings of the 1997 ACM SIGPLAN International Conference on Functional Programming (ICFP 1997), Amsterdam, The Netherlands, 9–11 June 1997, pp. 263–273. ACM (1997). https://doi.org/10.1145/258948.258973, http://doi.acm.org/10.1145/258948.258973

15. Faymonville, P., Finkbeiner, B., Tentrup, L.: BoSy: an experimentation framework for bounded synthesis. In: Majumdar, R., Kunčak, V. (eds.) CAV 2017. LNCS, vol. 10427, pp. 325–332. Springer, Cham (2017). https://doi.org/10.1007/978-3-319-63390-9_17

16. Feser, J.K., Chaudhuri, S., Dillig, I.: Synthesizing data structure transformations from input-output examples. In: Grove and Blackburn [22], pp. 229–239. https://doi.org/10.1145/2737924.2737977, http://doi.acm.org/10.1145/2737924.2737977

17. Finkbeiner, B.: Synthesis of reactive systems. In: Esparza, J., Grumberg, O., Sickert, S. (eds.) Dependable Software Systems Engineering. NATO Science for Peace and Security Series, D: Information and Communication Security, vol. 45, pp. 72–98. IOS Press (2016)

18. Finkbeiner, B., Klein, F., Piskac, R., Santolucito, M.: Vehicle platooning simulations with functional reactive programming. In: Proceedings of the 1st International Workshop on Safe Control of Connected and Autonomous Vehicles, SCAV@CPSWeek 2017, Pittsburgh, PA, USA, 21 April 2017, pp. 43–47. ACM, (2017). https://doi.org/10.1145/3055378.3055385, http://doi.acm.org/10.1145/3055378.3055385

19. Finkbeiner, B., Klein, F., Piskac, R., Santolucito, M.: Temporal stream logic: Synthesis beyond the bools. CoRR abs/1712.00246 (2019). http://arxiv.org/abs/1712.00246

20. Finkbeiner, B., Schewe, S.: Bounded synthesis. STTT **15**(5–6), 519–539 (2013). https://doi.org/10.1007/s10009-012-0228-z

21. Gerstacker, C., Klein, F., Finkbeiner, B.: Bounded synthesis of reactive programs. In: Automated Technology for Verification and Analysis - 16th International Symposium, ATVA 2018, Los Angeles, CA, USA, 7–10 October 2018, Proceedings, pp. 441–457 (2018). https://doi.org/10.1007/978-3-030-01090-4_26

22. Grove, D., Blackburn, S. (eds.): Proceedings of the 36th ACM SIGPLAN Conference on Programming Language Design and Implementation, Portland, OR, USA, 15–17 June 2015. ACM (2015). http://dl.acm.org/citation.cfm?id=2737924

23. Helbling, C., Guyer, S.Z.: Juniper: a functional reactive programming language for the arduino. In: Janin and Sperber [27], pp. 8–16. https://doi.org/10.1145/2975980.2975982, http://doi.acm.org/10.1145/2975980.2975982

24. Hsu, K., Majumdar, R., Mallik, K., Schmuck, A.K.: Multi-layered abstraction-based controller synthesis for continuous-time systems. In: Proceedings of the 21st International Conference on Hybrid Systems: Computation and Control (part of CPS Week), pp. 120–129. ACM (2018)

25. Jacobs, S., et al.: The 4th reactive synthesis competition (SYNTCOMP 2017): Benchmarks, participants and results. In: SYNT 2017. EPTCS, vol. 260, pp. 116–143 (2017). https://doi.org/10.4204/EPTCS.260.10

26. Jagannathan, S., Sewell, P. (eds.): The 41st Annual ACM SIGPLAN-SIGACT Symposium on Principles of Programming Languages, POPL 2014, San Diego, CA, USA, 20–21 January 2014. ACM (2014). http://dl.acm.org/citation.cfm?id=2535838

27. Janin, D., Sperber, M. (eds.): Proceedings of the 4th International Workshop on Functional Art, Music, Modelling, and Design, FARM@ICFP 2016, Nara, Japan, 24 September 2016. ACM (2016). https://doi.org/10.1145/2975980, http://doi.acm.org/10.1145/2975980

28. Jeffrey, A.: LTL types FRP: linear-time temporal logic propositions as types, proofs as functional reactive programs. In: Claessen, K., Swamy, N. (eds.) Proceedings of the sixth workshop on Programming Languages meets Program Verification, PLPV 2012, Philadelphia, PA, USA, 24 January 2012, pp. 49–60. ACM (2012). https://doi.org/10.1145/2103776.2103783, http://doi.acm.org/10.1145/2103776.2103783

29. Jeltsch, W.: Towards a common categorical semantics for linear-time temporal logic and functional reactive programming. Electr. Notes Theor. Comput. Sci. **286**, 229–242 (2012). https://doi.org/10.1016/j.entcs.2012.08.015

30. Krishnaswami, N.R.: Higher-order functional reactive programming without space-time leaks. In: Morrisett, G., Uustalu, T. (eds.) ACM SIGPLAN International Conference on Functional Programming, ICFP 2013, Boston, MA, USA, 25–27 September 2013, pp. 221–232. ACM (2013). https://doi.org/10.1145/2500365.2500588, http://doi.acm.org/10.1145/2500365.2500588

31. Kuncak, V., Mayer, M., Piskac, R., Suter, P.: Comfusy: a tool for complete functional synthesis. In: Touili, T., Cook, B., Jackson, P. (eds.) CAV 2010. LNCS, vol. 6174, pp. 430–433. Springer, Heidelberg (2010). https://doi.org/10.1007/978-3-642-14295-6_38

32. Lindley, S., Wadler, P., Yallop, J.: Idioms are oblivious, arrows are meticulous, monads are promiscuous. Electr. Notes Theor. Comput. Sci. **229**(5), 97–117 (2011). https://doi.org/10.1016/j.entcs.2011.02.018

33. Liu, H., Cheng, E., Hudak, P.: Causal commutative arrows. J. Funct. Program. **21**(4–5), 467–496 (2011). https://doi.org/10.1017/S0956796811000153

34. Liu, H., Hudak, P.: Plugging a space leak with an arrow. Electr. Notes Theor. Comput. Sci. **193**, 29–45 (2007). https://doi.org/10.1016/j.entcs.2007.10.006

35. Madhusudan, P.: Synthesizing reactive programs. In: Bezem, M. (ed.) Computer Science Logic, 25th International Workshop/20th Annual Conference of the EACSL, CSL 2011, Bergen, Norway, 12–15 September 2011, Proceedings. LIPIcs, vol. 12, pp. 428–442. Schloss Dagstuhl - Leibniz-Zentrum fuer Informatik (2011). https://doi.org/10.4230/LIPIcs.CSL.2011.428

36. Mainland, G. (ed.): Proceedings of the 9th International Symposium on Haskell, Haskell 2016, Nara, Japan, 22–23 September 2016. ACM (2016). https://doi.org/10.1145/2976002, http://doi.acm.org/10.1145/2976002

37. Mallik, K., Schmuck, A.K., Soudjani, S., Majumdar, R.: Compositional abstraction-based controller synthesis for continuous-time systems. arXiv preprint arXiv:1612.08515 (2016)
38. Manna, Z., Waldinger, R.: A deductive approach to program synthesis. ACM Trans. Program. Lang. Syst. **2**(1), 90–121 (1980). https://doi.org/10.1145/357084.357090
39. Murphy, T.E.: A livecoding semantics for functional reactive programming. In: Janin and Sperber [27], pp. 48–53. https://doi.org/10.1145/2975980.2975986http://doi.acm.org/10.1145/2975980.2975986
40. Osera, P., Zdancewic, S.: Type-and-example-directed program synthesis. In: Grove and Blackburn [22], pp. 619–630. https://doi.org/10.1145/2737924.2738007, http://doi.acm.org/10.1145/2737924.2738007
41. Perez, I., Bärenz, M., Nilsson, H.: Functional reactive programming, refactored. In: Mainland [36], pp. 33–44. https://doi.org/10.1145/2976002.2976010, http://doi.acm.org/10.1145/2976002.2976010
42. van der Ploeg, A., Claessen, K.: Practical principled FRP: forget the past, change the future, FRPNow! In: Fisher, K., Reppy, J.H. (eds.) Proceedings of the 20th ACM SIGPLAN International Conference on Functional Programming, ICFP 2015, Vancouver, BC, Canada, 1–3 September 2015, pp. 302–314. ACM (2015). https://doi.org/10.1145/2784731.2784752, http://doi.acm.org/10.1145/2784731.2784752
43. Pnueli, A.: The temporal logic of programs. In: 18th Annual Symposium on Foundations of Computer Science, Providence, Rhode Island, USA, 31 October–1 November 1977, pp. 46–57. IEEE Computer Society (1977). https://doi.org/10.1109/SFCS.1977.32
44. Pnueli, A., Rosner, R.: On the synthesis of an asynchronous reactive module. In: Ausiello, G., Dezani-Ciancaglini, M., Della Rocca, S.R. (eds.) ICALP 1989. LNCS, vol. 372, pp. 652–671. Springer, Heidelberg (1989). https://doi.org/10.1007/BFb0035790
45. Post, E.L.: A variant of a recursively unsolvable problem. Bull. Am. Math. Soc. **52**(4), 264–268 (1946). http://projecteuclid.org/euclid.bams/1183507843
46. Shan, Z., Azim, T., Neamtiu, I.: Finding resume and restart errors in android applications. In: Visser, E., Smaragdakis, Y. (eds.) Proceedings of the 2016 ACM SIGPLAN International Conference on Object-Oriented Programming, Systems, Languages, and Applications, OOPSLA 2016, part of SPLASH 2016, Amsterdam, The Netherlands, 30 October–4 November 2016, pp. 864–880. ACM (2016). https://doi.org/10.1145/2983990.2984011, http://doi.acm.org/10.1145/2983990.2984011
47. Solar-Lezama, A.: Program sketching. STTT **15**(5–6), 475–495 (2013). https://doi.org/10.1007/s10009-012-0249-7
48. Trinkle, R.: Reflex-frp (2017). https://github.com/reflex-frp/reflex
49. Vechev, M.T., Yahav, E., Yorsh, G.: Abstraction-guided synthesis of synchronization. STTT **15**(5–6), 413–431 (2013). https://doi.org/10.1007/s10009-012-0232-3
50. Wang, X., Dillig, I., Singh, R.: Synthesis of data completion scripts using finite tree automata. PACMPL 1(OOPSLA), 62:1–62:26 (2017). https://doi.org/10.1145/3133886, http://doi.acm.org/10.1145/3133886
51. Winograd-Cort, D.: Effects, Asynchrony, and Choice in Arrowized Functional Reactive Programming. Ph.D. thesis, Yale University, December 2015. http://www.danwc.com/s/dwc-yale-formatted-dissertation.pdf
52. Wongpiromsarn, T., Topcu, U., Murray, R.M.: Synthesis of control protocols for autonomous systems. Unmanned Syst. **1**(01), 21–39 (2013)

53. Yallop, J., Liu, H.: Causal commutative arrows revisited. In: Mainland [36], pp. 21–32. https://doi.org/10.1145/2976002.2976019, http://doi.acm.org/10.1145/2976002.2976019

Semi-Quantitative Abstraction and Analysis of Chemical Reaction Networks

Milan Češka[1]([⊠]) and Jan Křetínský[2]

[1] Brno University of Technology, FIT,
IT4I Centre of Excellence, Brno, Czech Republic

ceskam@fit.vutbr.cz

[2] Technical University of Munich, Munich, Germany

Abstract. Analysis of large continuous-time stochastic systems is a computationally intensive task. In this work we focus on population models arising from chemical reaction networks (CRNs), which play a fundamental role in analysis and design of biochemical systems. Many relevant CRNs are particularly challenging for existing techniques due to complex dynamics including stochasticity, stiffness or multimodal population distributions. We propose a novel approach allowing not only to predict, but also to explain both the transient and steady-state behaviour. It focuses on qualitative description of the behaviour and aims at quantitative precision only in orders of magnitude. First we build a compact understandable model, which we then crudely analyse. As demonstrated on complex CRNs from literature, our approach reproduces the known results, but in contrast to the state-of-the-art methods, it runs with virtually no computational cost and thus offers unprecedented scalability.

1 Introduction

Chemical Reaction Networks (CRNs) are a versatile language widely used for *modelling and analysis* of biochemical systems [12] as well as for high-level *programming* of molecular devices [8,40]. They provide a compact formalism equivalent to Petri nets [37], Vector Addition Systems (VAS) [29] and distributed population protocols [3]. Motivated by numerous potential applications ranging from system biology to synthetic biology, various techniques allowing simulation and formal analysis of CRNs have been proposed [2,9,21,24,39], and embodied in the design process of biochemical systems [20,25,32]. The time-evolution of CRNs is governed by the Chemical Master Equation (CME), which describes the probability of the molecular counts of each chemical species. Many important biochemical systems lead to complex dynamics that includes *state space explosion, stochasticity, stiffness, and multimodality* of the population distributions

[23, 44], and that fundamentally limits the class of systems the existing techniques can effectively handle. More importantly, biologist and engineers often seek for plausible explanations why the system under study has or has not the required behaviour. In many cases, a set of system simulations/trajectories or population distributions is not sufficient and the ability to provide an accurate explanation for the temporal or steady-state behaviour is another major challenge for the existing techniques.

In order to cope with the computational complexity of the analysis and in order to obtain explanations of the behaviour, we shift the focus from quantitatively precise results to a more qualitative analysis, closer to how a human would behold the system. Yet we insist on providing at least rough timing information on the behaviour as well as rough classification of probability of different behaviours at the extent of "very likely", "few percent", "barely possible", so that we can conclude on issues such as time to extinction or bimodality of behaviour. This gives rise to our *semi-quantitative* approach. We stipulate that analyses in this framework reflect quantities in orders of magnitude, both for time duration and probabilities, but not more than that. This paradigm shift is reflected on two levels: (1) We abstract systems into semi-quantitative models. (2) We analyse systems in a semi-quantitative way. While each of the two can be combined with a traditional abstraction/analysis, when combined together they provide powerful means to understand systems' behaviour with virtually no computational cost.

Semi-quantitative Models. The states of the models contain information on the current amount of objects of each species as an interval spanning often several orders of magnitude, unless instructed otherwise. For instance, if an amount of a certain species is to be closely monitored (as a part of the input specification/property of the system) then this abstraction can be finer. Similarly, whenever the analysis of a previous version of the abstraction points to the lack of precision in certain states, preventing us to conclude which of the possible behaviours is prevalent, the corresponding refinement can take place. Further, the rates of the transitions are also captured only with such imprecision. The crucial point allowing for existence of such models that are small, yet faithful, is our concept of *acceleration*. It captures certain *sequences* of transitions. It eliminates most of the non-determinism that paralyses other types of abstractions, which are too over-approximative, unable to conclude anything, but safety properties.

Semi-quantitative Analysis. Instead of performing exact transient or steady-state analysis, we can consider most probable transitions and then carefully lift this to most probable temporal behaviours. Technically, this is done by *alternating between transient and steady-state analysis* where only some rates and transitions are taken into account at different stages. In order to further facilitate the resulting insight of the human on the result of the analysis, we provide an algorithm to perform this analysis with virtually no computation effort and thus possibly manually. The trivial computations immediately pinpoint why certain behaviours occur. Moreover, less likely behaviours can also be identified easily, to any desired degree of improbability (dozens of percent, promilles etc.).

To summarise, the first step yields tiny models, allowing for a synoptic observation of the model; due to their size these models can be either analysed easily using standard means, or can be subject to the second step. The second step provides an efficient approximative analysis, which is also very illustrative due to the limited use of quantities. It can be applied to any system; however, it is particularly interesting in connection with the models coming from the first step since (i) no extra effort (size, computation) is wasted on overly precise treatment that is ignored by the other step, and (ii) together they yield an understandable explanation of the behaviour. An entertaining feature of this paradigm is that the stiffer (with rates at hugely different time scales) the system is the easier it is to analyse.

To demonstrate the capabilities of our approach, we consider three challenging and biologically relevant case studies that have been used in literature to evaluate state-of-the-art methods for the CRN analysis. It has been shown that many approaches fail, either due to time-outs or incapability to capture differences in behaviours, and some tailored ones require considerable computational effort, e.g. an hour of computation. Our experiments clearly show that the proposed approach can deliver results that yield qualitatively same information, more understanding and can be computed in minutes by hand (or within a fraction of a second by computer).

Our contribution can be summarized as follows:

- We propose a novel *semi-quantitative* framework for analysis of CRN and similar population models, focusing on explainability of the results and low complexity, with quantitative precision limited to orders of magnitude.
- An algorithm for abstracting CRNs into semi-quantitative models based on interval abstraction of the species population and on transition acceleration.
- An algorithm for semi-quantitative analysis that replaces exact numerical computation by exploring the most probable transitions and alternating transient and steady-state analysis.
- We consider three challenging CRNs thoroughly studied in literature and demonstrate that the semi-quantitative abstraction and analysis gives us a unique tool that is able to accurately predict and explain both transient and steady-state behaviour of complex CRNs in a fraction of a second.

Related Work

To the best of our knowledge, there does not exist any abstraction of CRNs similar to the proposed approach. Indeed, there exist various abstraction and approximation schemes for CRNs that improve the performance and scalability of both the simulation-based and the numerical-based techniques. In the following paragraphs, we discuss the most relevant directions and the links to our approach.

Approximate Semantics for CRNs. For CRNs including large populations of species, fluid (mean-field) approximation techniques can be applied [5] and extended to approximate higher-order moments [15]: these deterministic approximations lead to a set of ordinary differential equations (ODEs). An alternative is to approximate the CME as a continuous-state stochastic process. The Linear Noise Approximation (LNA) is a Gaussian process which has been derived as an approximation of the CME [16,44] and describes the time evolution of expectation and variance of the species in terms of ODEs. Recently, an aggregation scheme over ODEs that aims at understanding the dynamics of large CRNs has been proposed in [10]. In contrast to our approach, the deterministic approximations cannot adequately capture the stochasticity of CRNs caused by low population species.

To mitigate this drawback, various *hybrid models* have been proposed. The common idea of these models is as follows: the dynamics of low population species is described by the discrete stochastic process and the dynamics of large population species is approximated by a continuous process. The particular hybrid models differ in the approximation of the large population species. In [27], a pure deterministic semantics for large population species is used. The moment-based description for medium/high-copy number species was used in [24]. The LNA approximation and an adaptive partitioning of the species according to leap conditions (that is more general than partitioning based on population thresholds) was proposed in [9]. All hybrid models have to deal with interactions between low and large population species. In particular, the dynamics of the stochastic process describing the low-population species is conditioned by the continuous-state describing the concentration of the large-population species. The numerical analysis of such conditioned stochastic process is typically a computationally demanding task that limits the scalability.

In contrast, our approach does not explicitly partition the species, but rather abstracts the concrete species population using an interval abstraction and tries to effectively capture both the stochastic and the deterministic behaviour with the help of the accelerated transitions. As we already emphasised, the proposed abstraction and analysis avoids any numerical computation of precise quantities.

Reduction Techniques for Stochastic Models. A widely studied reduction method for Markov models is state aggregation based on lumping [6] or (bi-)simulation equivalence [4], with the latter notion in its exact [33] or approximate [13] form. Approximate notions of equivalence have led to new abstraction/refinement techniques for the numerical verification of Markov models over finite [14] as well as uncountably-infinite state spaces [1,41,42]. Several approximate aggregation schemes leveraging the structural properties of CRNs were proposed [17,34,45]. Abate et al. proposed an adaptive aggregation that gives formal guarantees on the approximation error, but typically provide lower state space reductions [2]. Our approach shares the idea of abstracting the state space by aggregating some states together. Similarly to [17,34,45], we partition the state space based on the species population, i.e. we also introduce the population levels. In contrast to the aforementioned aggregation schemes, we propose a novel abstraction of the transition relation based on the acceleration. It allows us to avoid the numerical solution of the approximate CME and thus achieve a better reduction while providing an accurate predication of the system behaviour.

Alternative methods to deal with large/infinite state spaces are based on a state truncation trying to eliminate insignificant states, i.e., states reached only with a negligible probability. These methods, including finite state projections [36], sliding window abstractions [26], or fast adaptive uniformisation [35], are able to quantify the total probability mass that is lost due to the truncation, but typically cannot effectively handle systems involving a stiff behaviour and multimodality [9].

Simulation-Based Analysis. Transient analysis of CRNs can be performed using the Stochastic Simulation Algorithm (SSA) [21]. Note that the SSA produces a single realisation of the stochastic process, whereas the stochastic solution of CME gives the probability distribution of each species over time. Although simulation-based analysis is generally faster than direct solution of the stochastic process underlying the given CRN, obtaining good accuracy necessitates potentially large numbers of simulations and can be very time consuming.

Various partitioning schemes for species and reactions have been proposed for the purpose of speeding up the SSA in multi-scale systems [23,38,39]. For instance, Yao et al. introduced the slow-scale SSA [7], where they distinguish between fast and slow species. Fast species are then treated assuming they reach equilibrium much faster than the slow ones. Adaptive partitioning of the species has been considered in [19,28]. In contrast to the simulation-based analysis, our approach (i) provides a compact explanation of the system behaviour in the form of tiny models allowing for a synoptic observation and (ii) can easily reveal less probable behaviours.

2   Chemical Reaction Networks

In this paper, we assume familiarity with standard verification of (continuous-time) probabilistic systems, e.g. [4]. For more detail, see [11, Appendix].

CRN Syntax. A *chemical reaction network (CRN)* $\mathcal{N} = (\Lambda, \mathcal{R})$ is a pair of finite sets, where Λ is a set of *species*, $|\Lambda|$ denotes its size, and $\mathcal{R}$ is a set of reactions. Species in Λ interact according to the reactions in $\mathcal{R}$. A *reaction* $\tau \in \mathcal{R}$ is a triple $\tau = (r_\tau, p_\tau, k_\tau)$, where $r_\tau \in \mathbb{N}^{|\Lambda|}$ is the *reactant complex*, $p_\tau \in \mathbb{N}^{|\Lambda|}$ is the *product complex* and $k_\tau \in \mathbb{R}_{>0}$ is the coefficient associated with the rate of the reaction. r_τ and p_τ represent the stoichiometry of reactants and products. Given a reaction $\tau_1 = ([1, 1, 0], [0, 0, 2], k_1)$, we often refer to it as $\tau_1 : \lambda_1 + \lambda_2 \xrightarrow{k_1} 2\lambda_3$.

CRN Semantics. Under the usual assumption of mass action kinetics, the *stochastic* semantics of a CRN $\mathcal{N}$ is generally given in terms of a discrete-state, continuous-time stochastic process $\mathbf{X}(\mathbf{t}) = (X_1(t), X_2(t), \ldots, X_{|\Lambda|}(t), t \geq 0)$ [16]. The *state change* associated to the reaction τ is defined by $v_\tau = p_\tau - r_\tau$, i.e. the state $\mathbf{X}$ is changed to $\mathbf{X}' = \mathbf{X} + v_\tau$, which we denote as $\mathbf{X} \xrightarrow{\tau} \mathbf{X}'$. For example, for τ_1 as above, we have $v_{\tau_1} = [-1, -1, 2]$. For a reaction to happen in a state $\mathbf{X}$, all reactants have to be in sufficient numbers. The *reachable state space* of $\mathbf{X(t)}$, denoted as $\mathbf{S}$, is the set of all states reachable by a sequence of reactions from a given *initial state* $\mathbf{X}_0$. The set of reactions changing the state $\mathbf{X}_i$ to the state $\mathbf{X}_j$ is denoted as $\mathsf{reac}(\mathbf{X}_i, \mathbf{X}_j) = \{\tau \mid \mathbf{X}_i \xrightarrow{\tau} \mathbf{X}_j\}$.

The behaviour of the stochastic system $\mathbf{X(t)}$ can be described by the (possibly infinite) continuous-time Markov chain (CTMC) $\gamma(\mathcal{N}) = (\mathbf{S}, \mathbf{X}_0, \mathbf{R})$ where the transition matrix $\mathbf{R}(i, j)$ gives the probability of a transition from $\mathbf{X}_i$ to $\mathbf{X}_j$. Formally,

$$\mathbf{R}(i,j) = \sum_{\tau \in \mathsf{reac}(\mathbf{X}_i, \mathbf{X}_j)} k_\tau \cdot C_{\tau,i} \quad \text{where} \quad C_{\tau,i} = \prod_{\ell=1}^{N} \binom{\mathbf{X}_{i,\ell}}{r_\ell} \tag{R}$$

corresponds to the population dependent term of the *propensity function* where $\mathbf{X}_{i,\ell}$ is ℓth component of the state $\mathbf{X}_i$ and r_ℓ is the stoichiometric coefficient of the ℓ-th reactant in the reaction τ. The CTMC $\gamma(\mathcal{N})$ is the accurate representation of CRN $\mathcal{N}$, but—even when finite—not scalable in practice because of the state space explosion problem [25, 31].

3   Semi-quantitative Abstraction

In this section, we describe our abstraction. We derive the desired CTMC conceptually in several steps, which we describe explicitly, although we implement the construction of the final system directly from the initial CRN.

3.1   Over-Approximation by Interval Abstraction and Acceleration

Given a CRN $\mathcal{N} = (\Lambda, \mathcal{R})$, we first consider an interval continuous-time Markov decision process (interval CTMDP[1]), which is a finite abstraction of the infinite $\gamma(\mathcal{N})$. Intuitively, abstract states are given by intervals on sizes of populations with an additional specific that the abstraction captures enabledness of reactions. The transition structure follows the ideas of the standard may abstraction and of the three-valued abstraction of continuous-time systems [30]. A technical difference in the latter point is that we abstract rates into intervals instead of uniformising the chain and then only abstracting transition probabilities into intervals; this is necessary in later stages of the process. The main difference is that we also treat certain sequences of actions, which we call acceleration.

Abstract Domains. The first step is to define the abstract domain for the population sizes. For every species $\lambda \in \Lambda$, we define a finite partitioning A_λ of $\mathbb{N}$ into intervals, reflecting the rough size of the population. Moreover, we want the abstraction to reflect whether a reaction is enabled. Hence we require that

---

[1] Interval CTMDP is a CTMDP with lower/upper bounds on rates. Since it serves only as an intermediate formalism to ease the presentation, we refrain from formalising it here.

$\{0\} \in A_\lambda$ for the case when the coefficients of this species as a reactant is always 0 or 1; in general, for every $i < \max_{\tau \in \mathcal{R}} r_\tau(\lambda)$ we require $\{i\} \in A_\lambda$.

The abstraction $\alpha_\lambda(n)$ of a number n of a species λ is then the $I \in A_\lambda$ for which $n \in I$. The state space of $\alpha(\mathcal{N})$ is the product $\prod_{\lambda \in \Lambda} A_\lambda$ of the abstract domains with the point-wise defined abstraction $\alpha(\boldsymbol{n})_\lambda = \alpha_\lambda(\boldsymbol{n}_\lambda)$.

The abstract domain for the rates according to (R) is the set of all real intervals.

Transitions from an abstract state are defined as the may abstraction as follows. Since our abstraction reflect enabledness, the same set of action is enabled in all concrete states of a given abstract state. The targets of the action in the abstract setting are abstractions of all possible concrete successors, i.e. $succ(s, a) := \{\alpha(\boldsymbol{n}) \mid \boldsymbol{m} \in s, \boldsymbol{m} \xrightarrow{a} \boldsymbol{n}\}$, in other words, the transitions enabled in at least one of the respective concrete states. The abstract rate is the smallest interval including all the concrete rates of the respective concrete transitions. This can be easily computed by the corner-points abstraction (evaluating only the extremum values for each species) since the stoichiometry of the rates is monotone in the population sizes.

High-Level of Non-determinism. The (more or less) standard style of the abstraction above has several drawbacks—mostly related to the high degree of non-determinism for rates—which we will subsequently discuss.

Firstly, in connection with the abstract population sizes, transitions to different sizes only happen non-deterministically, leaving us unable to determine which behaviour is probable. For example, consider the simple system given by $\lambda \xrightarrow{d} \emptyset$ with $k_d = 10^{-4}$ so the degradation happens on average each 10^4 seconds. Assume population discretisation into $[0], [1..5], [6..20], [21..\infty)$ with abstraction depicted in Fig. 1. While the original system obviously moves from $[6..20]$ to $[1..5]$ very probably in less than $15 \cdot 10^4$ seconds, the abstraction cannot even say that it happens, not to speak of estimating the time.

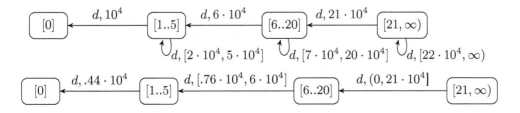

Fig. 1. Above: Interval CTMDP abstraction with intervals on rates and non-determinism. Below: Interval CTMC abstraction arising from acceleration.

Acceleration. To address this issue, we drop the non-deterministic self-loops and transitions to higher/lower populations in the abstract system.[2] Instead,

---

[2] One can also preserve the non-determinism for the special case when one of the transitions leads to a state where some action ceases to be enabled. While this adds more precision, the non-determinism in the abstraction makes it less convenient to handle.

we *"accelerate"* their effect: We consider sequences of these actions that in the concrete system have the effect of changing the population level. In our example above, we need to take the transition 1 to 13 times from [6..20] with various rates depending on the current concrete population, in order to get to [1..5]. This makes the precise timing more complicated to compute. Nevertheless, the expected time can be approximated easily: here it ranges from $\frac{1}{6} \cdot 10^4 = 0.17 \cdot 10^4$ (for population 6) to roughly $(\frac{1}{20} + \frac{1}{19} + \cdots + \frac{1}{6}) \cdot 10^4 = 1.3 \cdot 10^4$ (for population 20). This results in an interval CTMC.[3]

Concurrency in Acceleration. The accelerated transitions can due to higher number of occurrences be considered continuous or deterministic, as opposed to discrete stochastic changes as distinguished in the hybrid approach. The usual differential equation approach would also take into account other reactions that are modelled deterministically and would combine their effect into one equation. In order to simplify the exposition and computation and—as we see later— without much loss of precision, we can consider only the fastest change (or non-deterministically more of them if their rates are similar).[4]

3.2   Operational Semantics: Concretisation to a Representative

The next disadvantage of classical abstraction philosophy, manifested in the interval CTMC above is that the precise-valued intervals on rates imply high computational effort during the analysis. Although the system is smaller, standard transient analysis is still quite expensive.

Concretisation. In order to deal with this issue, the interval can be approximated roughly by the expected time it would take for an average population in the considered range, in our example the "average" representative is 13. Then the first transition occurs with rate $13 \cdot 10^{-4} = 10^{-3}$ and needs to happen 7 times, yielding expected time $7/13 \cdot 10^4 = 0.5 \cdot 10^4$ (ignoring even the precise slow downs in the rates as the population decreases). Already this very rough computation yields relative precision with factor 3 for all the populations in this interval, thus yielding the correct order of magnitude with virtually no effort. We lift the concretisation naturally to states and denote the concretisation of abstract state s by $\gamma(s)$. The complete procedure is depicted in Algorithm 1.

The concretisation is one of the main points where we deliberately drop a lot of quantitative information, while still preserving some to conclude on big quantitative differences. Of course, the precision improves with more precise abstract domains and also with higher differences on the original rates.

---

[3] The waiting times are not distributed according to the rates in the intervals. It is only the expected waiting time (reciprocal of the rate) that is preserved. Nevertheless, for ease of exposition, instead of labelling the transitions with expected waiting times we stick to the CTMC style with the reciprocals and formally treat it as if the label was a real rate.

[4] Typically the classical concurrency diamond appears and the effect of the other accelerated reactions happen just after the first one.

Algorithm 1. Semi-quantitative abstraction CTMC $\alpha(\mathcal{N})$

1:   $A \leftarrow \prod_{\lambda \in \Lambda} A_\lambda$ ▷ States
2: **for** $a \in A$ **do**   ▷ Transitions
3:     $c \leftarrow \gamma(a)$ ▷ Concrete representative
4:     **for** each τ enabled in c **do**
5:         $r \leftarrow$ rate of τ in c ▷ According to (R)
6:         $a' \leftarrow \alpha(c + v_\tau)$ ▷ Successor
7:         set $a \xrightarrow{\tau} a'$ with rate r
8:     **for** self-loop $a \xrightarrow{\tau} a$ **do**   ▷ Accelerate self-loops
9:         $n_\tau \leftarrow \min\{n \mid \alpha(c + n \cdot v_\tau) \neq a\}$ ▷ the number of τ to change the abstract state
10:        $a' \leftarrow \alpha(c + n_\tau \cdot v_\tau)$ ▷ Acceleration successor
11:        instead of the self-loop with rate r, set $a \xrightarrow{\tau} a'$ with rate $n_\tau \cdot r$

It remains to determine the representative for the unbounded interval. In order to avoid infinity, we require an additional input for the analysis, which are deemed upper bounds on possible population of each species. In cases when any upper bound is hard to assume, we can analyse the system with a random one and see if the last interval is reachable with significant probability. If yes, then we need to use this upper bound as a new point in the interval partitioning and try a higher upper bound next time. In general, such conditions can be checked in the abstraction and their violation implies a recommendation to refine the abstract domains accordingly.

Orders-of-Magnitude Abstraction. Such an approximation is thus sufficient to determine most of the time whether the acceleration (sequence of actions) happens sooner or later than e.g. another reaction with rate 10^{-6} or 10^{-2}. Note that this *decision* gets more precise not only as we refine the population levels, but also as the system gets stiffer (the concrete values of the rates differ more), which are normally harder to analyse. For the ease of presentation in our case studies, we shall depict only the magnitude of the rates, i.e. the decadic logarithm rounded to an integer.

Non-determinism and Refinement. If two rates are close to each other, say of the same magnitude (or difference 1), such a rough computation (and rough population discretisation) is not precise enough to determine which of the reactions happens with high probability sooner. Both may be happening roughly at the same pace, or with more information we could conclude one of them is considerably faster. This introduces an uncertainty, showing different behaviours are possible depending on the exact quantities. This indicates points where refinement might be needed if more precise results are required. For instance, with rates of magnitudes 2 and 3, the latter should be happing most of the time, the former only with a few percent chance. If we want to know whether it is rather tens of percent or tenths of percent, we should refine the abstraction.

4   Semi-quantitative Analysis

In this section, we present an approximative analysis technique that describes the most probable transient and steady-state behaviour of the system (also with rough timing) and on demand also the (one or more orders of magnitude) less probable behaviours. As such it is robust in the sense that it is well suited to work with imprecise rates and populations. It is computationally easy (can be done in hand in time required for a computer by other methods), while still yielding significant quantitative results ("in orders of magnitude"). It does not provide exact error guarantees since computing them would be almost as expensive as the classical analysis. It only features trivial limit-style bounds: if the population abstraction gets more and more refined, the probabilities converge to those of the original system; further, the higher the separation between the rate magnitudes, the more precise the approximation is since the other factors (and thus the incurred imprecisions) play less significant role.

Intuitively, the main idea—similar to some multi-rate simulation techniques for stiff systems—is to "simulate" "fast" reactions until the steady state and then examine which slower reactions take place. However, "fast" does not mean faster than some constant, but faster than other transitions in a given state. In other words, we are not distinguishing fast and slow reactions, but tailor this to each state separately. Further, "simulation" is not really a stochastic simulation, but a deterministic choice of the fastest available transition. If a transition is significantly faster than others then this yields what a simulation would yield. When there are transitions with similar rates, e.g. with at most one order of magnitude difference, then both are taken into account as described in the following definition.

Pruned System. Consider the underlying graph of the given CTMC. If we keep only the outgoing transitions with the maximum rate in each state, we call the result *pruned*. If there is always (at most) one transition then the graph consists of several paths leading to cycles. In general when more transitions are kept, it has bottom strongly connected components (bottom SCCs, BSCCs) and some transient parts.

We generalise this concept to *n-pruning* that preserves all transitions with a rate that is not more than n orders of magnitude smaller than the maximum rate in the state. Then the pruning above is 0-pruning, 1-pruning preserves also transitions happening up to 10 times slower, which can thus still happen with dozens of percent, 2-pruning is relevant for analysis where behaviour occurring with units of percent is also tracked etc.

Algorithm Idea. Here we explain the idea of Algorithm 2. The transient parts of the pruned system describe the most probable behaviour from each state until the point where visited states start to repeat a lot (steady state of the pruned system). In the original system, the usual behaviour is then to stay in this SCC C until one of the pruned (slower) reactions occurs, say from state s to state t. This may bring us to a different component of the pruned graph and the analysis process repeats. However, t may also bring us back into C, in which case we stay in the steady-state, which is basically the same as without the transition from s to t. Further, t might be in the transient part leading to C, in which case these states are added to C and the steady state changes a bit, spreading the distribution slightly also to the previously transient states. Finally, t might be leading us into a component D where this run was previous to visiting C. In that case, the steady-state distribution spreads over all the components visited between D and C, putting a probability mass to each with a different order of magnitude depending on all the (magnitudes of) sojourn times in the transient and steady-state phases on the way.

Using the macros defined in the algorithm, the correctness of the computations can be shown as follows. For the time spent in the transient phase (line 16), we consider the slowest sojourn time on the way times the number of such transitions; this is accurate since the other times are by order(s) of magnitude shorter, hence negligible. The steady-state distribution on a BSCC of the

---

Algorithm 2. Semi-quantitative analysis

1: $W \leftarrow \emptyset$ ▷ worklist of SCCs to process
2: add {initial state} to W and assign iteration 0 to it   ▷ artificial SCC to start the process
3: **while** $W \neq \emptyset$ **do**
4:      $C \leftarrow$ pop W
                                                          ▷ Compute and output steady state or its approximation
5:      steady-state of C is approximately $minStayingRate/(m \cdot stayingRate(\cdot))$
6:      **if** C has no exits **then** continue   ▷ definitely bottom SCC, final steady state
                                   ▷ Compute and output exiting transitions and the time spent in C
7:      $exitStates \leftarrow \arg\min_C(stayingRate(\cdot)/exitingRate(\cdot))$ ▷ Probable exit points
8:      $minStayingRate \leftarrow$ minimum rate in C, $m \leftarrow$ #occurrences there
9:      $timeToExit \leftarrow stayingRate(s) \cdot m/(|exitStates| \cdot minStayingRate \cdot exitingRate(s))$
                                                                        for (arbitrary) $s \in exitStates$
10:      **for all** $s \in exitsStates$ **do**   ▷ Transient analysis
11:          $t \leftarrow$ target of the exiting transition
12:          $T \leftarrow$ SCCs reachable in the pruned graph from t
13:          thereby newly reached transitions get assigned iteration of $C + 1$
14:          **for** $D \in T$ **do**
                                                          ▷ Compute and output time to get from t to D
15:              $minRate \leftarrow$ minimum rate on the way from t to D, $m \leftarrow$ #occurrences there
16:              $transTime \leftarrow m/minRate$
                                                                        ▷ Determine the new SCC
17:              **if** $D = C$ **then**   ▷ back to the current SCC
18:                  add to W the union of C and the new transient path τ from t to C
19:                  in later steady-state computation, the states of τ will have probability
                               smaller by a factor of $stayingRate(s)/exitingRate(s)$
20:              **else if** D was previously visited **then**   ▷ alternating between different SCCs
21:                  add to W the merge of all SCCs visited between D and C (inclusively)
22:                  in later steady-state computation, reflect all $timeToExit$ and $transTime$
                                                                        between D and C
23:              **else**   ▷ new SCC
24:                  add D to W

MACROS:

$stayingRate(s)$ is the rate of transitions from s in the pruned graph

$exitingRate(s)$ is the maximum rate of transitions from s not in the pruned graph

pruned graph can be approximated by the $minStayingRate/(m \cdot stayingRate(\cdot))$ on line 5. Indeed, it corresponds to the steady-state distribution if the BSCC is a cycle and the $minStayingRate$ significantly larger than other rates in the BSCC since then the return time for the states is approximately $m/minStayingRate$ and the sojourn time $1/stayingRate(\cdot)$. The component is exited from s with the proportion given by its steady-state distribution times the probability to take the exit during that time. The former is approximated above; the latter can be approximated by the density in 0, i.e. by $exitingRate(s)$, since the staying rate is significantly faster. Hence the candidates for exiting are maximising $exitingRate(\cdot)/stayingRate(\cdot)$ as on line 7. There are $|exitStates|$ candidates for exit and the time to exit the component by a particular candidate s is the expected number of visits before exit, i.e. $stayingRate(s) \cdot exitingRate(s)$ times the return time $m \cdot minStayingRate$, hence the expression on line 9.

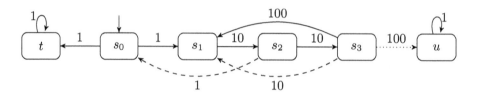

Fig. 2. Alternating transient and steady-state analysis.

For example, consider the system in Fig. 2. Iteration 1 reveals the part with solid lines with two (temporary) BSCCs $\{t\}$ and $\{s_1, s_2, s_3\}$. The former turns out definitely bottom. The latter has a steady state proportional to $(10^{-1}, 10^{-1}, 100^{-1})$. Its most probable exits are the dashed ones, identified in the subsequent iteration 2, probable proportionally to $(1/10, 10/100)$; the expected time to take them is $10 \cdot 2/(2 \cdot 10 \cdot 1) = 1 = 100 \cdot 2/(2 \cdot 10 \cdot 10)$. The latter leads back to the current SCC and does not change the set of BSCCs (hence in our examples below we often either skip or merge such iterations for the sake of readability). In contrast, the former leads to a previous SCC; thereafter $\{s_1, s_2, s_3\}$ is no more a bottom SCC and consequently the third exit to u is not even analysed. Nevertheless, it could still happen with minor probability, which can be seen if we consider 1-pruning instead.

5   Experimental Evaluation and Discussion

In order to demonstrate the applicability and accuracy of our approach, we selected the following three biologically relevant case studies. (1) stochastic model of gene expression [22,24], (2) Goutsias's model [23] describing transcription regulation of a repressor protein in bacteriophage λ and (3) viral infection model [43].

Although the underlying CRNs are quite small (up to 5 species and 10 reaction), their analysis is very challenging: (i) the stochasticity has a strong impact on the dynamics of these systems and thus purely deterministic approximations via ODEs are not accurate, (ii) the systems include species with low, medium, and high populations and thus the resulting state space of the stochastic process is prohibitively large to perform precise numerical analysis and existing reduction/approximation techniques are not sufficient (they are either too imprecise or do not provide sufficient reduction factors), and (iii) the system dynamics leads to bi-modal distributions and/or is affected by stiff reactions.

These models thus represent perfect candidates for evaluating advanced approximation methods including various hybrid approaches [9,24,27]. Although these approaches can handle the models, they typically require tens of minutes or hours of computation time. Similarly simulation-based methods are very time consuming especially in case of very stiff CRN, represented by the viral infection model. We demonstrate that our approach provides accurate predications of the system behaviour and is feasible even when performed manually by a human.

Recall that the algorithm that builds the abstract model of the given CRN takes as input two vectors representing the population discretisation and population bounds. We generally assume that these inputs are provided by users who have a priori knowledge about the system (e.g. in which orders the species population occurs) and that the inputs also reflect the level of details the users are interested in. In the following case studies, we, however, set the inputs only based on the rate orders of the reactions affecting the particular species (unless mentioned otherwise).

5.1   Gene Expression Model

The CRN underlying the gene expression model is described in Table 1. As discussed in [24] and experimentally observed in [18], the system oscillates between two phases characterised by the D_{on} state and the D_{off} state, respectively. Biologists are interested in how the distribution of the D_{on} and D_{off} states is aligned with the distribution of RNA and proteins P, and how the correlation among the distributions depends on the DNA switching rates.

The state vector of the underlying CTMC is given as [P, RNA, D_{off}, D_{on}]. We use very relaxed bounds on the maximal populations, namely the bound 1000 for P and 100 for RNA. Note the DNA invariant $D_{on} + D_{off} = 1$. As in [24], the initial state is given as [10,4,1,0].

We first consider the slow switching rates that lead to a more complicated dynamics including bimodal distributions. In order to demonstrate the refinement step and its effect on the accuracy of the model, we start with a very coarse abstraction. It distinguishes only the zero population and the non-zero populations and thus it is not able to adequately capture the relationship between the DNA state and RNA/P population. The pruned abstract model obtained using Algorithm 1 and 2 is depicted in Fig. 3 (left). The full one before pruning is shown in Fig. 6 [11, Appendix].

The proposed analysis of the model identifies the key trends in the system dynamic. The red transitions, representing iterations 1–3, capture the most probable paths in the system. The green component includes states with DNA on

Table 1. Gene expression. For slow DNA switching, $r_1 = r_2 = 0.05$. For fast DNA switching, $r_1 = r_2 = 1$. The rates are in h^{-1}.

$$D_{off} \xrightarrow{r_1} D_{on} \qquad\qquad D_{on} \xrightarrow{r_2} D_{off} \qquad D_{on} \xrightarrow{10} D_{on} + RNA \qquad\qquad RNA \xrightarrow{1} \emptyset$$

$$RNA \xrightarrow{4} RNA + P \qquad P \xrightarrow{1} \emptyset \qquad\qquad P + D_{off} \xrightarrow{0.0015} P + D_{on}$$

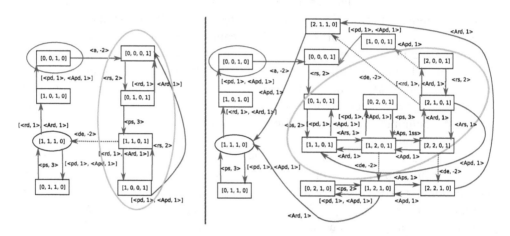

Fig. 3. Pruned abstraction for the gene expression model using the coarse population discretisation (left) and after the refinement (right). The state vector is [P, RNA, D_{off}, D_{on}].

(i.e. $D_{on} = 1$) where the system oscillates. The component is reached via the blue state with D_{off} and no RNAs/P. The blue state is promptly reached from the initial state and then the system waits (roughly 100 h according our rate abstraction) for the next DNA activation. The oscillation is left via a deactivation in the iteration 4 (the blue dotted transition)[5]. The estimation of the exit time computed using Algorithm 2 is also 100 h. The deactivation is then followed by fast red transitions leading to the blue state, where the system waits for the next activation. Therefore, we obtain an oscillation between the blue state and the green component, representing the expected oscillation between the D_{on} and D_{off} states.

As expected, this abstraction does not clearly predict the bimodal distribution on the RNA/P populations as the trivial population levels do not bear any information beside reaction enabledness. In order to obtain a more accurate analysis of the system, we refine the population discretisation using a single level threshold for P and DNA, that is equal to 100 and 10, respectively (the rates in the CRN indicate that the population of P reaches higher values).

Figure 3 (right) depicts the pruned abstract model with the new discretisation (the full model is depicted in Fig. 7 [11, Appendix]. We again obtain the oscillation between the green component representing DNA$_{on}$ states and the blue DNA$_{off}$ state. The states in the green component more accurately predicts

---

[5] In Fig. 3, the dotted transitions denote exit transitions representing the deactivations.

that in the DNA_{on} states the populations of RNA and P are high and drop to zero only for short time periods. The figure also shows orange transitions within the iteration 2 that extend the green component by two states. Note that the system promptly returns from these states back to the green component. After the deactivation in the iteration 4, the system takes (within the same iteration) the fast transitions (solid blue) leading to the blue component where system waits for another activation and where the mRNA/protein populations decrease. The expected time spent in states on blue solid transitions is small and thus we can reliably predict the bimodal distribution of the mRNA/P populations and its correlation with the DNA state. The refined abstraction also reveals that the switching time from the DNA_{on} mode to the DNA_{off} mode is lower. These predications are in accordance with the results obtained in [24]. See Fig. 8 [11, Appendix] that is adopted from [24] and illustrates these results.

To further test the accuracy of our approach, we consider the fast switching between the DNA states. We follow the study in [24] and increase the rates by two orders of magnitude. We use the refined population discretisation and obtain a very similar abstraction as in Fig. 3 (right). We again obtain the oscillation between the green component (DNA_{on} states and nonzero RNA/protein populations) and the blue state (DNA_{off} and zero RNA/protein populations). The only difference is in fact the transition rates corresponding to the activation and deactivation causing that the switching rate between the components is much faster. As a consequence, the system spends a longer period in the blue transient states with D_{off} and nonzero RNA/protein populations. The time spent in these states decreases the correlation between the DNA state and the RNA/protein populations as well as the bimodality in the population distribution. This is again in the accordance with [24].

To conclude this case study, we observe a very aligned agreement between the results obtained using our approach and results in [24] obtained via advanced and time consuming numerical methods. We would like to emphasise that our abstraction and its solution is obtained within a fraction of a second while the numerical methods have to approximate solutions of equations describing high-order conditional moments of the population distributions. As [24] does not report the runtime of the analysis and the implementation of their methods is not publicly available, we cannot directly compare the time complexity.

5.2 Goutsias's Model

Goutsias's model illustrated in Table 2 is widely used for evaluation of various numerical and simulation based techniques. As showed e.g. in [23], the system has with a high probability the following transient behaviour. In the first phase, the system switches with a high rate between the non-active DNA (denoted DNA) and the active DNA (DNA.D). During this phase the population of RNA, monomers (M) and dimers (D) gradually increase (with only negligible oscillations). After around 15 min, the DNA is blocked (DNA.2D) and the population of RNA decreases while the population of M and D is relatively stable. After all RNA degrades (around another 15 min) the system switches to the third

Table 2. Goutsias' Model. The rates are in s^{-1}

$$\text{RNA} \xrightarrow{0.043} \text{RNA} + \text{M} \qquad \text{M} \xrightarrow{7\times10^{-4}} \emptyset \qquad\qquad \text{RNA} \xrightarrow{4\times10^{-3}} \emptyset$$

$$\text{DNA} + \text{D} \xrightarrow{0.002} \text{DNA.D} \qquad \text{DNA.D} \xrightarrow{0.48} \text{DNA} + \text{D}$$

$$\text{DNA.D} + \text{D} \xrightarrow{2\times10^{-4}} \text{DNA.2D} \qquad \text{M+M} \xrightarrow{0.083} \text{D} \qquad\qquad \text{D} \xrightarrow{0.5} \text{M} + \text{M}$$

$$\text{DNA.2D} \xrightarrow{9\times10^{-12}} \text{DNA.D} + \text{D} \qquad \text{DNA.D} \xrightarrow{0.072} \text{RNA} + \text{DNA.D}$$

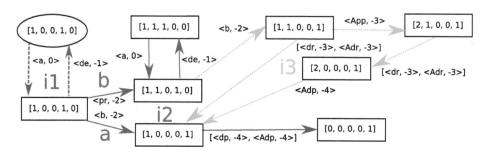

Fig. 4. Pruned abstraction for the Goutsias' model. The state vector is [M + D, RNA, DNA, DNA.D, DNA.2D]

phase where the population of M and D slowly decreases. Further, there is a non-negligible probability that the DNA is blocked at the beginning while the population of RNA is still small and the system promptly dies out.

Although the system is quite suitable for the hybrid approaches (there is no strong bimodality and only a limited stiffness), the analysis still takes 10 to 50 min depending on the required precision [27]. We demonstrate that our approach is able to accurately predict the main transient behaviour as well as the non-negligible probability that the system promptly dies out.

The state vector is given as [M, D, RNA, DNA, DNA.D, DNA.2D] and the initial state is set to [2, 6, 0, 1, 0, 0] as in [27]. We start our analysis with a coarse population discretisation with a single threshold 100 for M and D and a single threshold 10 for RNA. We relax the bounds, in particular, 1000 for M and D, and 100 for RNA. Note that these numbers were selected solely based on the rate orders of the relevant reactions. Note the DNA invariant DNA + DNA.D + DNA.2D = 1.

Figure 4 illustrates the pruned abstract model we obtained (the full model is depicted in Fig. 9 [11, Appendix]. For a better visualisation, we merged the state components corresponding to M and D into one component with M + D. As there is the fast reversible dimerisation, the actual distributions between the population of M and D does not affect the transient behaviour we are interested in.

The analysis of the model shows the following transient behaviour. The purple dotted loop in the iteration i1 represents (de-)activation of the DNA. The expected exit time of this loop is 100 s. According to our abstraction, there are two options (with the same probability) to exit the loop: (1) the path a represents the DNA blocking followed by the quick extinction and (2) the path b corresponds to the production of RNA and its followed by the red loop in the i2 that again represents (de-)activation of the DNA. Note that according our abstraction, this loop contains states with the populations of M/D as well as RNA up to 100 and 10, respectively.

The expected exit time of this loop is again 100 s and there are two options how to leave the loop: (1) the path within the iteration $i3$ (taken with roughly 90%) represents again the DNA blocking and it is followed by the extension of RNA and consequently by the extension of M/D in about 1000 s and (2) the path within the iteration 5 (shown in the full graph in Fig. 9 [11, Appendix]) taken with roughly 10% represents the series of protein productions and leads to the states with a high number of proteins (above 100 in our population discretisation). Afterwards, there is again a series of DNA (de-)activations followed by the DNA blocking and the extinction of RNA. As before, this leads to the extinction of M/D in about 1000 s.

Although this abstraction already shows the transient behaviour leading to the extinction in about 30 min, it introduces the following inaccuracy with respect to the known behaviour: (1) the probability of the fast extinction is higher and (2) we do not observe the clear bell-shape pattern on the RNA (i.e. the level 2 for the RNA is not reached in the abstraction). As in the previous case study, the problem is that the population discretisation is too coarse. It causes that the total rate of the DNA blocking (affected by the M/D population via the mass action kinetics) is too high in the states with the M/D population level 1. This can be directly seen in the interval CTMC representation where the rate spans many orders of magnitude, incurring too much imprecision. The refinement of the M/D population discretisation eliminates the first inaccuracy. To obtain the clear bell-shape patter on RNA, one has to refine also the RNA population discretisation.

5.3   Viral Infection

The viral infection model described in Table 3 represents the most challenging system we consider. It is highly stochastic, extremely stiff, with all species presenting high variance and some also very high molecular populations. Moreover, there is a bimodal distribution on the RNA population. As a consequence, the solution of the full CME, even using advanced reduction and aggregation techniques, is prohibitive due to state-space explosion and stochastic simulation are very time consuming. State-of-the-art hybrid approaches integrating the LNA and an adaptive population partitioning [9] can handle this system but also need a very long execution time. For example, a transient analysis up to time $t = 50$ requires around 20 min and up to $t = 200$ more than an hour.

To evaluate the accuracy of our approach on this challenging model, we also focus on the same transient analysis, namely, we are interested in the distribution of RNA at time $t = 200$. The analysis in [9] predicts a bimodal distribution where, the probability that RNA is zero in around 20% and the remaining probability has Gaussian distribution with mean around 17 and the probability that there

Table 3. Viral Infection. The rates are day^{-1}

$$\text{DNA} + \text{P} \xrightarrow{7\times10^{-6}} \text{V} \qquad \text{DNA} \xrightarrow{0.025} \text{DNA} + \text{R} \qquad \text{RNA} \xrightarrow{0.25} \emptyset$$

$$\text{RNA} \xrightarrow{1} \text{RNA} + \text{DNA} \qquad \text{RNA} \xrightarrow{1000} \text{RNA.} + \text{P} \qquad \text{P} \xrightarrow{1.99} \emptyset$$

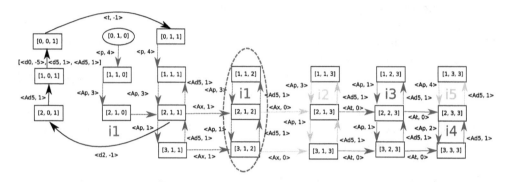

Fig. 5. Pruned abstraction for the viral infection model. The state vector is [P, RNA, DNA].

is more than 30 RNAs is close to zero. This is confirmed by simulation-based analysis in [23] showing also the gradual growth of the RNA population. The simulation-based analysis in [43], however, estimates a lower probability (around 3%) that RNA is 0 and higher mean of the remaining Gaussian distribution (around 23). Recall that obtaining accurate results using simulations is extremely time consuming due to very stiff reactions (a single simulation for $t = 200$ takes around 20 s).

In the final experiments, we analyse the distribution of RNA at time $t = 200$ using our approach. The state vector is given as [P, RNA, DNA] and we start with the concrete state [0, 1, 0]. To sufficiently reason about the RNA population and to handle the very high population of the proteins, we use the following population discretisation: thresholds {10, 1000} for P, {10, 30} for RNA, and {10, 100} for DNA. As before, we use very relaxed bounds 10000, 100, and 1000 for P, RNA, and D, respectively. Note that we ignore the population of the virus V as it does not affect the dynamics of the other species. This simplification makes the visualisation of our approach more readable and has no effect on the complexity of the analysis.

Figure 5 illustrates the obtained abstract model enabling the following transient analysis (the full model is depicted in Fig. 10 [11, Appendix]. In a few days the system reaches from the initial state the loop (depicted by the purple dashed ellipse) within the iteration *i1*. The loop includes states where RNA has level 1, DNA has level 2 and P oscillates between the levels 2 and 3. Before entering the loop, there is a non-negligible probability (orders of percent) that the RNA drops to 0 via the full black branch that returns to transient part of the loop in *i1*. In this branch the system can also die out (not shown in this figure, see the full model) with probability in the order of tenths of percent.

The average exit time of the loop in *i1* is in the order of 10 days and the system goes to the yellow loop within the iteration *i2*, where the DNA level is increased to 3 (RNA level is unchanged and P again oscillates between the levels 2 and 3). The average exit time of the loop in *i2* is again in the order of 10 days and systems goes to the dotted red loop within iteration *i3*. The transition represents the sequence of RNA synthesis that leads to RNA level 2. P oscillates as before. Finally, the system leaves the loop in *i3* (this takes another dozen days) and reaches RNA level 3 in iterations *i4* and *i5* where the DNA level remains at the level 3 and P oscillates. The iteration *i4* and *i5* thus roughly correspond to the examined transient time $t = 200$.

The analysis clearly demonstrates that our approach leads to the behaviour that is well aligned with the previous experiments. We observed growth of the RNA population with a non-negligible probability of its extinction. The concrete quantities (i.e. the probability of the extinction and the mean RNA population) are closer to the analysis in [43]. The quantities are indeed affected by the population discretisation and can be further refined. We would like to emphasise that in contrast to the methods presented in [9, 23, 43] requiring hours of intensive numerical computation, our approach can be done even manually on the paper.

References

1. Abate, A., Katoen, J.P., Lygeros, J., Prandini, M.: Approximate model checking of stochastic hybrid systems. Eur. J. Control **16**, 624–641 (2010)
2. Abate, A., Brim, L., Češka, M., Kwiatkowska, M.: Adaptive aggregation of Markov chains: quantitative analysis of chemical reaction networks. In: Kroening, D., Păsăreanu, C.S. (eds.) CAV 2015. LNCS, vol. 9206, pp. 195–213. Springer, Cham (2015). https://doi.org/10.1007/978-3-319-21690-4_12
3. Angluin, D., Aspnes, J., Eisenstat, D., Ruppert, E.: The computational power of population protocols. Distrib. Comput. **20**(4), 279–304 (2007)
4. Baier, C., Katoen, J.P.: Principles of Model Checking. The MIT Press, Cambridge (2008)
5. Bortolussi, L., Hillston, J.: Fluid model checking. In: Koutny, M., Ulidowski, I. (eds.) CONCUR 2012. LNCS, vol. 7454, pp. 333–347. Springer, Heidelberg (2012). https://doi.org/10.1007/978-3-642-32940-1_24
6. Buchholz, P.: Exact performance equivalence: an equivalence relation for stochastic automata. Theor. Comput. Sci. **215**(1–2), 263–287 (1999)
7. Cao, Y., Gillespie, D.T., Petzold, L.R.: The slow-scale stochastic simulation algorithm. J. Chem. Phys. **122**(1), 014116 (2005)
8. Cardelli, L.: Two-domain DNA strand displacement. Math. Struct. Comput. Sci. **23**(02), 247–271 (2013)
9. Cardelli, L., Kwiatkowska, M., Laurenti, L.: A stochastic hybrid approximation for chemical kinetics based on the linear noise approximation. In: Bartocci, E., Lio, P., Paoletti, N. (eds.) CMSB 2016. LNCS, vol. 9859, pp. 147–167. Springer, Cham (2016). https://doi.org/10.1007/978-3-319-45177-0_10
10. Cardelli, L., Tribastone, M., Tschaikowski, M., Vandin, A.: Maximal aggregation of polynomial dynamical systems. Proc. Natl. Acad. Sci. **114**(38), 10029–10034 (2017)

11. Češka, M., Křetínský, J.: Semi-quantitative abstraction and analysis of chemical reaction networks. Technical report abs/1905.09914, arXiv.org (2019)
12. Chellaboina, V., Bhat, S.P., Haddad, W.M., Bernstein, D.S.: Modeling and analysis of mass-action kinetics. IEEE Control Syst. Mag. **29**(4), 60–78 (2009)
13. Desharnais, J., Laviolette, F., Tracol, M.: Approximate analysis of probabilistic processes: logic, simulation and games. In: Quantitative Evaluation of SysTems (QEST), pp. 264–273. IEEE (2008)
14. D'Innocenzo, A., Abate, A., Katoen, J.P.: Robust PCTL model checking. In: Hybrid Systems: Computation and Control (HSCC), pp. 275–285. ACM (2012)
15. Engblom, S.: Computing the moments of high dimensional solutions of the master equation. Appl. Math. Comput. **180**(2), 498–515 (2006)
16. Ethier, S.N., Kurtz, T.G.: Markov Processes: Characterization and Convergence, vol. 282. Wiley, New York (2009)
17. Ferm, L., Lötstedt, P.: Adaptive solution of the master equation in low dimensions. Appl. Numer. Math. **59**(1), 187–204 (2009)
18. Gandhi, S.J., Zenklusen, D., Lionnet, T., Singer, R.H.: Transcription of functionally related constitutive genes is not coordinated. Nat. Struct. Mol. Biol. **18**(1), 27 (2011)
19. Ganguly, A., Altintan, D., Koeppl, H.: Jump-diffusion approximation of stochastic reaction dynamics: error bounds and algorithms. Multiscale Model. Simul. **13**(4), 1390–1419 (2015)
20. Giacobbe, M., Guet, C.C., Gupta, A., Henzinger, T.A., Paixão, T., Petrov, T.: Model checking gene regulatory networks. In: Baier, C., Tinelli, C. (eds.) TACAS 2015. LNCS, vol. 9035, pp. 469–483. Springer, Heidelberg (2015). https://doi.org/10.1007/978-3-662-46681-0_47
21. Gillespie, D.T.: Exact stochastic simulation of coupled chemical reactions. J. Phys. Chem. **81**(25), 2340–2361 (1977)
22. Golding, I., Paulsson, J., Zawilski, S.M., Cox, E.C.: Real-time kinetics of gene activity in individual bacteria. Cell **123**(6), 1025–1036 (2005)
23. Goutsias, J.: Quasiequilibrium approximation of fast reaction kinetics in stochastic biochemical systems. J. Chem. Phys. **122**(18), 184102 (2005)
24. Hasenauer, J., Wolf, V., Kazeroonian, A., Theis, F.: Method of conditional moments (MCM) for the chemical master equation. J. Math. Biol. 1–49 (2013). https://doi.org/10.1007/s00285-013-0711-5
25. Heath, J., Kwiatkowska, M., Norman, G., Parker, D., Tymchyshyn, O.: Probabilistic model checking of complex biological pathways. Theor. Comput. Sci. **391**(3), 239–257 (2008)
26. Henzinger, T.A., Mateescu, M., Wolf, V.: Sliding window abstraction for infinite Markov chains. In: Bouajjani, A., Maler, O. (eds.) CAV 2009. LNCS, vol. 5643, pp. 337–352. Springer, Heidelberg (2009). https://doi.org/10.1007/978-3-642-02658-4_27
27. Henzinger, T.A., Mikeev, L., Mateescu, M., Wolf, V.: Hybrid numerical solution of the chemical master equation. In: Computational Methods in Systems Biology (CMSB), pp. 55–65. ACM (2010)
28. Hepp, B., Gupta, A., Khammash, M.: Adaptive hybrid simulations for multiscale stochastic reaction networks. J. Chem. Phys. **142**(3), 034118 (2015)
29. Karp, R.M., Miller, R.E.: Parallel program schemata. J. Comput. Syst. Sci. **3**(2), 147–195 (1969)
30. Katoen, J.-P., Klink, D., Leucker, M., Wolf, V.: Three-valued abstraction for continuous-time Markov chains. In: Damm, W., Hermanns, H. (eds.) CAV 2007. LNCS, vol. 4590, pp. 311–324. Springer, Heidelberg (2007). https://doi.org/10.1007/978-3-540-73368-3_37

31. Kwiatkowska, M., Thachuk, C.: Probabilistic model checking for biology. Softw. Syst. Saf. **36**, 165 (2014)
32. Lakin, M.R., Parker, D., Cardelli, L., Kwiatkowska, M., Phillips, A.: Design and analysis of DNA strand displacement devices using probabilistic model checking. J. R. Soc. Interface **9**(72), 1470–1485 (2012)
33. Larsen, K.G., Skou, A.: Bisimulation through probabilistic testing. Inf. Comput. **94**(1), 1–28 (1991)
34. Madsen, C., Myers, C., Roehner, N., Winstead, C., Zhang, Z.: Utilizing stochastic model checking to analyze genetic circuits. In: Computational Intelligence in Bioinformatics and Computational Biology (CIBCB), pp. 379–386. IEEE (2012)
35. Mateescu, M., Wolf, V., Didier, F., Henzinger, T.A.: Fast adaptive uniformization of the chemical master equation. IET Syst. Biol. **4**(6), 441–452 (2010)
36. Munsky, B., Khammash, M.: The finite state projection algorithm for the solution of the chemical master equation. J. Chem. Phys. **124**, 044104 (2006)
37. Murata, T.: Petri nets: properties, analysis and applications. Proc. IEEE **77**(4), 541–580 (1989)
38. Rao, C.V., Arkin, A.P.: Stochastic chemical kinetics and the quasi-steady-state assumption: application to the Gillespie algorithm. J. Chem. Phys. **118**(11), 4999–5010 (2003)
39. Salis, H., Kaznessis, Y.: Accurate hybrid stochastic simulation of a system of coupled chemical or biochemical reactions. J. Chem. Phys. **122**(5), 054103 (2005)
40. Soloveichik, D., Seelig, G., Winfree, E.: DNA as a universal substrate for chemical kinetics. Proc. Natl. Acad. Sci. U. S. A. **107**(12), 5393–5398 (2010)
41. Soudjani, S.E.Z., Abate, A.: Adaptive and sequential gridding procedures for the abstraction and verification of stochastic processes. SIAM J. Appl. Dyn. Syst. **12**(2), 921–956 (2013)
42. Esmaeil Zadeh Soudjani, S., Abate, A.: Precise approximations of the probability distribution of a Markov process in time: an application to probabilistic invariance. In: Ábrahám, E., Havelund, K. (eds.) TACAS 2014. LNCS, vol. 8413, pp. 547–561. Springer, Heidelberg (2014). https://doi.org/10.1007/978-3-642-54862-8_45
43. Srivastava, R., You, L., Summers, J., Yin, J.: Stochastic vs. deterministic modeling of intracellular viral kinetics. J. Theor. Biol. **218**(3), 309–321 (2002)
44. Van Kampen, N.G.: Stochastic Processes in Physics and Chemistry, vol. 1. Elsevier, New York (1992)
45. Zhang, J., Watson, L.T., Cao, Y.: Adaptive aggregation method for the chemical master equation. Int. J. Comput. Biol. Drug Des. **2**(2), 134–148 (2009)

12

Robust Controller Synthesis in Timed Büchi Automata: A Symbolic Approach

Damien Busatto-Gaston[1]([✉]),
Benjamin Monmege[1], Pierre-Alain Reynier[1],
and Ocan Sankur[2]

[1] Aix Marseille Univ, Université de Toulon,
CNRS, LIS, Marseille, France
{damien.busatto,pierre-alain.reynier}@lis-lab.fr,
benjamin.monmege@univ-amu.fr
[2] Univ Rennes, Inria, CNRS, IRISA, Rennes, France
ocan.sankur@irisa.fr

Abstract. We solve in a purely symbolic way the robust controller synthesis problem in timed automata with Büchi acceptance conditions. The goal of the controller is to play according to an accepting lasso of the automaton, while resisting to timing perturbations chosen by a competing environment. The problem was previously shown to be **PSPACE**-complete using regions-based techniques, but we provide a first tool solving the problem using zones only, thus more resilient to state-space explosion problem. The key ingredient is the introduction of branching constraint graphs allowing to decide in polynomial time whether a given lasso is robust, and even compute the largest admissible perturbation if it is. We also make an original use of constraint graphs in this context in order to test the inclusion of timed reachability relations, crucial for the termination criterion of our algorithm. Our techniques are illustrated using a case study on the regulation of a train network.

1 Introduction

Timed automata [1] extend finite-state automata with timing constraints, providing an automata-theoretic framework to design, model, verify and synthesise real-time systems. However, the semantics of timed automata is a mathematical idealisation: it assumes that clocks have infinite precision and instantaneous actions. Proving that a timed automaton satisfies a property does not ensure that a real implementation of it also does. This *robustness* issue is a challenging problem for embedded systems [12], and alternative semantics have been proposed, so as to ensure that the verified (or synthesised) behaviour remains correct in presence of small timing perturbations.

We are interested in a fundamental controller synthesis problem in timed automata equipped with a Büchi acceptance condition: it consists in determining whether there exists an accepting infinite execution.

Thus, the role of the controller is to choose transitions and delays. This problem has been studied numerously in the exact setting [13–15,17,19,27,28]. In the context of robustness, this strategy should be tolerant to small perturbations of the delays. This discards strategies suffering from weaknesses such as Zeno behaviours, or even non-Zeno behaviours requiring infinite precision, as exhibited in [6].

More formally, the semantics we consider is defined as a game that depends on some parameter δ representing an upper bound on the amplitude of the perturbation [7]. In this game, the controller plays against an antagonistic environment that can perturb each delay using a value chosen in the interval $[-\delta, \delta]$. The case of a fixed value of δ has been shown to be decidable in [7], and also for a related model in [18]. However, these algorithms are based on regions, and as the value of δ may be very different from the constants appearing in the guards of the automaton, do not yield practical algorithms. Moreover, the maximal perturbation is not necessarily known in advance, and could be considered as part of the design process.

The problem we are interested in is *qualitative*: we want to determine whether *there exists* a positive value of δ such that the controller wins the game. It has been proven in [25] that this problem is in PSPACE (and even PSPACE-complete), thus no harder than in the exact setting with no perturbation allowed [1]. However, the algorithm heavily relies on regions, and more precisely on an abstraction that refines the one of regions, namely folded orbit graphs. Hence, it is not at all amenable to implementation.

Our objective is to provide an efficient symbolic algorithm for solving this problem. To this end, we target the use of *zones* instead of regions, as they allow an on-demand partitioning of the state space. Moreover, the algorithm we develop explores the reachable state-space in a *forward* manner. This is known to lead to better performances, as witnessed by the successful tool UPPAAL TIGA based on forward algorithms for solving controller synthesis problems [5].

Our algorithm can be understood as an adaptation to the robustness setting of the standard algorithm for Büchi acceptance in timed automata [17]. This algorithm looks for an accepting lasso using a double depth-first search. A major difficulty consists in checking whether a lasso can be robustly iterated, i.e. whether there exists $\delta > 0$ such that the controller can follow the cycle for an infinite amount of steps while being tolerant to perturbations of amplitude at most δ. The key argument of [25] was the notion of aperiodic folded orbit graph of a path in the region automaton, thus tightly connected to regions. Lifting this notion to zones seems impossible as it makes an important use of the fact that valuations in regions are time-abstract bisimilar, which is not the case for zones.

Our contributions are threefold. First, we provide a polynomial time procedure to decide, given a lasso, whether it can be robustly iterated. This symbolic algorithm relies on a computation of the greatest fixpoint of the operator describing the set of controllable predecessors of a path. In order to provide an argument of termination for this computation, we resort to a new notion of branching constraint graphs, extending the approach used in [16,26] and based

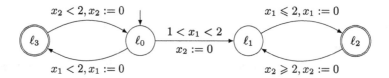

Fig. 1. A timed automaton

on constraint graphs (introduced in [8]) to check iterability of a cycle, without robustness requirements. Second, we show that when considering a lasso, not only can we decide robust iterability, but we can even compute the largest perturbation under which it is controllable. This problem was not known to be decidable before. Finally, we provide a termination criterion for the analysis of lassos. Focusing on zones is not complete: it can be the case that two cycles lead to the same zones, but one is robustly iterable while the other one is not. Robust iterability crucially depends on the real-time dynamics of the cycle and we prove that it actually only depends on the reachability relation of the path. We provide a polynomial-time algorithm for checking inclusion between reachability relations of paths in timed automata based on constraint graphs. It is worth noticing that all our procedures can be implemented using difference bound matrices, a very efficient data structure used for timed systems. These developments have been integrated in a tool, and we present a case study of a train regulation network illustrating its performances.

Integrating the robustness question in the verification of real-time systems has attracted attention in the community, and the recent works include, for instance, robust model checking for timed automata under clock drifts [23], Lipschitz robustness notions for timed systems [11], quantitative robust synthesis for timed automata [2]. Stability analysis and synthesis of stabilizing controllers in hybrid systems are a closely related topic, see e.g. [20,21].

2   Timed Automata: Reachability and Robustness

Let $\mathcal{X} = \{x_1, \ldots, x_n\}$ be a finite set of clock variables. It is extended with a virtual clock x_0, constantly equal to 0, and we denote by $\mathcal{X}_0$ the set $\mathcal{X} \cup \{x_0\}$. An atomic clock constraint on $\mathcal{X}$ is a formula $x - y \leqslant k$, or $x - y < k$ with $x \neq y \in \mathcal{X}_0$ and $k \in \mathbb{Q}$. A constraint is non-diagonal if one of the two clocks is x_0. We denote by $\mathsf{Guards}(X)$ (respectively, $\mathsf{Guards}_{\mathrm{nd}}(X)$) the set of (clock) constraints (respectively, non-diagonal clock constraints) built as conjunctions of atomic clock constraints (respectively, non-diagonal atomic clock constraints).

A clock valuation ν is an element of $\mathbb{R}_{\geqslant 0}^{\mathcal{X}}$. It is extended to $\mathbb{R}_{\geqslant 0}^{\mathcal{X}_0}$ by letting $\nu(x_0) = 0$. For all $d \in \mathbb{R}_{>0}$, we let $\nu + d$ be the valuation defined by $(\nu + d)(x) = \nu(x) + d$ for all clocks $x \in \mathcal{X}$. If $\mathcal{Y} \subseteq \mathcal{X}$, we also let $\nu[\mathcal{Y} \leftarrow 0]$ be the valuation resetting clocks in $\mathcal{Y}$ to 0, without modifying values of other clocks. A valuation ν satisfies an atomic clock constraint $x - y \bowtie k$ (with $\bowtie \in \{\leqslant, <\}$) if $\nu(x) - \nu(y) \bowtie k$. The satisfaction relation is then extended to clock constraints naturally: the satisfaction of constraint g by a valuation ν is denoted by $\nu \models g$. The set of valuations satisfying a constraint g is denoted by $[\![g]\!]$.

A *timed automaton* is a tuple $\mathcal{A} = (L, \ell_0, E, L_t)$ with L a finite set of locations, $\ell_0 \in L$ an initial location, $E \subseteq L \times \mathsf{Guards}_{\mathrm{nd}}(\mathcal{X}) \times 2^{\mathcal{X}} \times L$ is a finite set of edges, and L_t is a set of accepting locations.

An example of timed automaton is depicted in Fig. 1, where the reset of a clock x is denoted by $x := 0$. The semantics of the timed automaton $\mathcal{A}$ is defined as an infinite transition system $[\![\mathcal{A}]\!] = (S, s_0, \rightarrow)$. The set S of states of $[\![\mathcal{A}]\!]$ is $L \times \mathbb{R}_{\geq 0}^{\mathcal{X}}$, $s_0 = (\ell_0, \mathbf{0})$. A transition of $[\![\mathcal{A}]\!]$ is of the form $(\ell, \nu) \xrightarrow{e, d} (\ell', \nu')$ with $e = (\ell, g, \mathcal{Y}, \ell') \in E$ and $d \in \mathbb{R}_{>0}$ such that $\nu + d \models g$ and $\nu' = (\nu + d)[\mathcal{Y} \leftarrow 0]$. We call *path* a possible finite sequence of edges in the timed automaton. The *reachability relation* of a path ρ, denoted by $\mathsf{Reach}(\rho)$ is the set of pairs (ν, ν') such that there is a sequence of transitions of $[\![\mathcal{A}]\!]$ starting from (ℓ, ν), ending in (ℓ', ν') and that follows ρ in order as the edges of the timed automaton. A *run* of $\mathcal{A}$ is an infinite sequence of transitions of $[\![\mathcal{A}]\!]$ starting from s_0. We are interested in Büchi objectives. Therefore, a run is accepting if there exists a final location $\ell_t \in L_t$ that the run visits infinitely often.

As done classically, we assume that every clock is bounded in $\mathcal{A}$ by a constant M, that is we only consider the previous infinite transition system over the subset $L \times [0, M]^{\mathcal{X}}$ of states.

We study the robustness problem introduced in [25], that is stated in terms of games where a controller fights against an environment. After a prefix of a run, the controller will have the capability to choose delays and transitions to fire, whereas the environment perturbs the delays chosen by the controller with a small parameter $\delta > 0$. The aim of the controller will be to find a strategy so that, no matter how the environment plays, he is ensured to generate an infinite run satisfying the Büchi condition. Formally, given a timed automaton $\mathcal{A} = (L, \ell_0, E, L_t)$ and $\delta > 0$, the perturbation game is a two-player turn-based game $\mathcal{G}_\delta(\mathcal{A})$ between a controller and an environment. Its state space is partitioned into $S_C \uplus S_E$ where $S_C = L \times \mathbb{R}_{\geq 0}^{\mathcal{X}}$ belongs to the controller, and $S_E = L \times \mathbb{R}_{\geq 0}^{\mathcal{X}} \times \mathbb{R}_{>0} \times E$ to the environment. The initial state is $(\ell_0, \mathbf{0}) \in S_C$. From each state $(\ell, \nu) \in S_C$, there is a transition to $(\ell, \nu, d, e) \in S_E$ with $e = (\ell, g, \mathcal{Y}, \ell') \in E$ whenever $d > \delta$, and $\nu + d + \varepsilon \models g$ for all $\varepsilon \in [-\delta, \delta]$. Then, from each state $(\ell, \nu, d, (\ell, g, \mathcal{Y}, \ell')) \in S_E$, there is a transition to $(\ell', (\nu + d + \varepsilon)[r \leftarrow 0]) \in S_C$ for all $\varepsilon \in [-\delta, \delta]$. A play of $\mathcal{G}_\delta(\mathcal{A})$ is a finite or infinite path $q_0 \xrightarrow{t_1} q_1 \xrightarrow{t_2} q_2 \cdots$ where $q_0 = (\ell_0, 0)$ and t_i is a transition from state q_{i-1} to q_i, for all $i > 0$. It is said to be maximal if it is infinite or can not be extended with any transition.

A strategy for the controller is a function σ_{Con} mapping each non-maximal play ending in some $(\ell, \nu) \in S_C$ to a pair (d, e) where $d > 0$ and $e \in E$ such that there is a transition from (ℓ, ν) to (ℓ, ν, d, e). A strategy for the environment is a function σ_{Env} mapping each finite play ending in (ℓ, ν, d, e) to a state (ℓ', ν') related by a transition. A play gives rise to a unique run of $[\![\mathcal{A}]\!]$ by only keeping states in V_C. For a pair of strategies $(\sigma_{\mathsf{Con}}, \sigma_{\mathsf{Env}})$, we let $\mathsf{play}_{\mathcal{A}}^\delta(\sigma_{\mathsf{Con}}, \sigma_{\mathsf{Env}})$ denote the run associated with the unique maximal play of $\mathcal{G}_\delta(\mathcal{A})$ that follows the strategies. Controller's strategy σ_{Con} is winning (with respect to the Büchi objective L_t) if for all strategies σ_{Env} of the environment, $\mathsf{play}^\delta_{\mathcal{A}}(\sigma_{\mathsf{Con}}, \sigma_{\mathsf{Env}})$ is infinite and visits infinitely often some location of L_t. The *parametrised robust controller synthesis problem* asks, given a timed automaton $\mathcal{A}$, whether there exists $\delta > 0$ such that the controller has a winning strategy in $\mathcal{G}_\delta(\mathcal{A})$.

Example 1. The controller has a winning strategy in $\mathcal{G}_\delta(\mathcal{A})$, with $\mathcal{A}$ the automaton of Fig. 1, for all possible values of $\delta < 1/2$. Indeed, he can follow the cycle $\ell_0 \to \ell_3 \to \ell_0$ by always picking time delay $1/2$ so that, when arriving in ℓ_3 (resp. ℓ_0) after the perturbation of the environment, clock x_2 (resp. x_1) has a valuation in $[1/2 - \delta, 1/2 + \delta]$. Therefore, he can play forever following this memoryless strategy. For $\delta \geq 1/2$, the environment can enforce reaching ℓ_3 with a value for x_2 at least equal to 1. The guard $x_2 < 2$ of the next transition to ℓ_0 cannot be guaranteed, and therefore the controller cannot win $\mathcal{G}_\delta(\mathcal{A})$. In [25], it is shown that the cycle around ℓ_2 does not provide a winning strategy for the controller for any value of $\delta > 0$ since perturbations accumulate so that the controller can only play it a finite number of times in the worst case.

By [25], the parametrised robust controller synthesis problem is known to be PSPACE-complete. Their solution is based on the region automaton of $\mathcal{A}$. We are seeking for a more practical solution using zones. A zone Z over $\mathcal{X}$ is a convex subset of $\mathbb{R}^{\mathcal{X}}_{\geq 0}$ defined as the set of valuations satisfying a clock constraint g, i.e. $Z = [\![g]\!]$. Zones can be encoded into *difference-bound matrices (DBM)*, that are $|\mathcal{X}_0| \times |\mathcal{X}_0|$-matrices over $(\mathbb{R} \times \{<, \leqslant\}) \cup \{(\infty, <)\}$. We adopt the following notation: for a DBM M, we write $M = (\mathsf{M}, \prec^M)$, where M is the matrix made of the first components, with elements in $\mathbb{R} \cup \{\infty\}$, while $\prec^M$ is the matrix of the second components, with elements in $\{<, \leqslant\}$. A DBM M naturally represents a zone (which we abusively write M as well), defined as the set of valuations ν such that, for all $x, y \in \mathcal{X}_0$, $\nu(x) - \nu(y) \prec^M_{x,y} \mathsf{M}_{x,y}$ (where $\nu(x_0) = 0$). Coefficients of a DBM are thus pairs $(\prec, c)$. As usual, these can be compared: $(\prec, c)$ is less than $(\prec', c')$ (denoted by $(\prec, c) < (\prec', c')$) whenever $c < c'$ or $(c = c', \prec = <$ and $\prec' = \leqslant)$. Moreover, these coefficients can be added: $(\prec, c) + (\prec', c')$ is the pair $(\prec'', c + c')$ with $\prec'' = \leqslant$ if $\prec = \prec' = \leqslant$ and $\prec'' = <$ otherwise.

DBMs were introduced in [4,10] for analyzing timed automata; we refer to [3] for details. Standard operations used to explore the state space of timed automata have been defined on DBMs: intersection is written $M \cap N$, $\mathsf{Pretime}_{>t}(M)$ is the set of valuations such that a time delay of more than t time units leads to the zone M, $\mathsf{Unreset}_R(M)$ is the set of valuations that end in M when the clocks in R are reset. From a robustness perspective, we also consider the operator $\mathsf{shrink}_{[-\delta,\delta]}(M)$ defined as the set of valuations ν such that $\nu + [-\delta, \delta] \subseteq M$ introduced in [24]. Given a DBM M and a rational number δ, all these operations can be effectively computed in time cubic in $|\mathcal{X}|$.

3   Reachability Relation of a Path

Before treating the robustness issues, we start by designing a symbolic (i.e. zone-based) approach to describe and compare the reachability relations of paths in timed automata. This will be crucial subsequently to design a termination criterion in the state space exploration of our robustness-checking algorithm. Solving the inclusion of reachability relations in a symbolic manner has independent interest and can have other applications.

The reachability relation $\mathsf{Reach}(\rho)$ of a path ρ, is a subset of $\mathbb{R}_{\geq 0}^{\mathcal{X} \cup \mathcal{X}'}$ where $\mathcal{X}'$ are primed versions of the clocks, such that each $(\nu, \nu') \in \mathsf{Reach}(\rho)$ iff there is a run from valuation ν to valuation ν' following ρ. Unfortunately, reachability relations $\mathsf{Reach}(\rho)$ are not zones in general, that is, they cannot be represented using only difference constraints. In fact, we shall see shortly that constraints of the form $x - y + z - u \leqslant c$ also appear, as already observed in [22]. We thus cannot rely directly on the traditional difference bound matrices (DBMs) used to represent zones. We instead rely on the constraint graphs that were introduced in [8], and explored in [16] for the parametric case (the latter work considers enlarged constraints, and not shrunk ones as we study here). Our contribution is to use these graphs to obtain a syntactic check of inclusion of the according reachability relations.

Constraint Graphs. Rather than considering the values of the clocks in $\mathcal{X}$, this data structure considers the date X_i of the latest reset of the clock x_i, and uses a new variable τ denoting the global timestamp. Note that the clock values can be recovered easily since $X_i = \tau - x_i$. For the extra clock x_0, we introduce variable X_0 equal to the global timestamp τ (since x_0 must remain equal to 0). A constraint graph defining a zone is a weighted graph whose nodes are $X = \{X_0, X_1, \ldots, X_n\}$. Constraints on clocks are represented by weights on edges in the graph: a constraint $X - Y \prec c$ is represented by an edge from X to Y weighted by $(\prec, c)$, with $\prec \in \{\leqslant, <\}$ and $c \in \mathbf{Q}$. Weights in the graph are thus pairs of the form $(\prec, c)$. Therefore, we can compute shortest weights between two vertices of a weighted graph. A cycle is said to be negative if it has weight at most $(<, 0)$, i.e. $(<, 0)$ or $(\prec, c)$ with $c < 0$.

Encoding Paths. Constraint graphs can also encode tuples of valuations seen along a path. To encode a k-step computation, we make $k + 1$ copies of the nodes, that is, $X^i = \{X_0^i, X_1^i, \ldots, X_n^i\}$ for $i \in \{1, \ldots, k + 1\}$. These copies are also called *layers*. Let us first consider an example on the path ρ consisting of the edge from ℓ_1 to ℓ_2, and the edge from ℓ_2 to ℓ_1, in the timed automaton of Fig. 1. The constraint graph G_ρ is depicted in Fig. 3: in our diagrams of constraint graphs, the absence of labels on an edge means $(\leqslant, 0)$, and we depict with an edge with arrows on both ends the presence of an edge in both directions. The graph has five columns, each containing copies of the variables for that step: they represent the valuations before the first edge, after the first time elapse, after the first reset, after the second time elapse and after the second reset. In general now, each elementary operation can be described by a constraint graph with two layers (X_i) (before) and (X_i') (after).

- The operation $\mathsf{Pretime}_{>t}$ is described by the constraint graph $G_{\mathsf{time}}^{>t}$ with edges $X_i \to X_0$, $X_i \leftrightarrow X_i'$ for $i > 0$, and $X_0 \xrightarrow{(<, -t)} X_0'$. Figure 3 contains two occurrences of $G_{\mathsf{time}}^{>0}$: we always represent with dashed arrows edges that are labelled by $(<, c)$, and plain arrows edges that are labelled with $(\leqslant, c)$; the absence of an edge means that it is labelled with $(<, \infty)$.

- The operation $g \cap \mathsf{Unreset}_{\mathcal{Y}}(\cdot)$, to test a guard g and reset the clocks in $\mathcal{Y}$, is described by the constraint graph $G_{\mathsf{edge}}^{g, \mathcal{Y}}$ with edges $X_0 \leftrightarrow X_0'$ (meaning that the time does not elapse), $X_i \leftrightarrow X_i'$ for i such that clock $x_i \notin \mathcal{Y}$, and $X_i' \leftrightarrow X_0'$ for i such that clock $x_i \in \mathcal{Y}$, and for all clock constraint $x_i - x_j \prec c$ appearing in g, an edge from X_j to X_i labelled by $(\prec, c)$ (since it encodes the fact that $(\tau - X_i) - (\tau - X_j) = X_j - X_i \prec c$). In Fig. 3, we have first $G_{\mathsf{edge}}^{x_1 \leqslant 2, \{x_1\}}$, and then $G_{\mathsf{edge}}^{x_2 \geqslant 2, \{x_2\}}$.

Constraint graphs can be stacked one after the other to obtain the constraint graph of an edge e, and then of a path ρ, that we denote by G_ρ. In the resulting graph, there is one leftmost layer of vertices $(X_i^\ell)_i$ and one rightmost one $(X_i^r)_i$ representing the situation before and after the firing of the path ρ. Once this graph is constructed, the intermediary levels can be eliminated after replacing each edge between the nodes of $X^\ell \cup X^r$ by the shortest path in the graph. This phase is hereafter called *normalisation* of the constraint graph. The normalised version of the constraint graph of Fig. 3 is depicted on its right.

From Constraint Graphs to Reachability Relations. From a logical point of view, the elimination of intermediary layers reflects an elimination of quantifiers in a formula of the first-order theory of real numbers. At the end, we obtain a set of constraints of the form $X_i^k - X_j^{k'} \prec c$ with $k, k' \in \{\ell, r\}$. These constraints do not reflect uniquely the reachability relation $\mathsf{Reach}(\rho)$, in the sense that it is possible that $\mathsf{Reach}(\rho_1) = \mathsf{Reach}(\rho_2)$ but the normalised versions of G_{ρ_1} and G_{ρ_2} are different. For example, if we consider the path ρ^2 obtained by repeating the cycle ρ between ℓ_1 and ℓ_2, the reachability relation does not change ($\mathsf{Reach}(\rho^2) = \mathsf{Reach}(\rho)$), but the normalised constraint graph does ($G_{\rho^2} \neq G_{\rho^1}$): all labels $(\leqslant, 2)$ of the red dotted edges from the rightmost layer to the leftmost layer become $(\leqslant, 4)$, and the labels $(\leqslant, -2)$ of the dashed blue edges become $(\leqslant, -4)$.

We solve this issue by jumping back from variables X_i^k to the clock valuations. Indeed, in terms of clock valuations ν^ℓ and ν^r before and after the path, the constraint $X_i^k - X_j^{k'} \prec c$ (for $k, k' \in \{l, r\}$) rewrites as $(\tau^k - \nu^k(x_i)) - (\tau^{k'} - \nu^{k'}(x_j)) \prec c$, where τ^ℓ is the global timestamp before firing ρ and τ^r the one after. When $k = k'$, variables τ^ℓ and τ^r disappear, leaving a constraint of the form $\nu^k(x_j) - \nu^k(x_i) \prec c$. When $k \neq k'$, we can rewrite the constraint as $\tau^k - \tau^{k'} \prec \nu^k(x_i) - \nu^{k'}(x_j) + c$. We therefore obtain upper and lower bounds on the value of $\tau^r - \tau^\ell$, allowing us to eliminate $\tau^r - \tau^\ell$ considered as a single variable. We therefore obtain in fine a formula mixing constraints of the form

- $\nu^k(x_a) - \nu^k(x_b) \prec p$, with $k \in \{\ell, r\}$, $a \neq b$, and we define $\gamma_{a,b}^k = (\prec, p)$;
- $\nu^\ell(x_a) - \nu^\ell(x_b) + \nu^r(x_c) - \nu^r(x_d) \prec p$, with $a \neq b$ and $c \neq d$, and we define $\gamma_{a,b,c,d} = (\prec, p)$. This constraint can appear in two ways: either from $\nu^r(x_c) - \nu^\ell(x_b) + p_1 \prec_1 \tau^r - \tau^l \prec_2 \nu^l(x_a) - \nu^r(x_d) + p_2$ by eliminating $\tau^r - \tau^l$, or by adding the two constraints of the form $\nu^l(x_a) - \nu^l(x_b) \prec_1 p_1$ and

$\nu^r(x_c) - \nu^r(x_d) \prec_2 p_2$. Thus, $\gamma_{a,b,c,d}$ is obtained as the minimum of the two constraints obtained in this manner. In other terms, in the constraint graph, this constraint is the minimal weight between the sum of the weights of the edges (X_d^r, X_a^l) and (X_b^l, X_c^r), and the sum of the weights of the edges (X_b^l, X_a^l) and (X_d^r, X_c^r). For example, in the path in Fig. 3, we have $\gamma_{0,1,0,2} = (\leqslant, 0)$ since the two constraints are $(\leqslant, 0)$ and $(<, \infty)$, whereas $\gamma_{1,2,2,1} = (\leqslant, 0)$ because the two constraints are $(<, 2)$ and $(\leqslant, 0)$.

Let $\varphi(G)$ be the conjunction of such constraints obtained from a constraint graph G once normalised: this is a quantifier-free formula of the additive theory of reals. We obtain the following property whose proof mimics the one for proving the normalisation of DBMs (and can be derived from the developments of [8]).

Lemma 1. *Let ρ be a path in a timed automaton. If G_ρ contains a negative cycle, then $\mathsf{Reach}(\rho) = \emptyset$. Otherwise, $\mathsf{Reach}(\rho)$ is the set of pairs of valuations (ν^ℓ, ν^r) that satisfy the formula $\varphi(G_\rho)$.*

Checking Inclusion. For a path ρ, we regroup the pairs $(\gamma_{a,b}^l)$, $(\gamma_{a,b}^r)$ and $(\gamma_{a,b,c,d})$ above in a single vector Γ^ρ. We extend the comparison relation $<$ to these vectors by applying it componentwise. These vectors can be used to check equality or inclusion of reachability relations in time $O(|X|^4)$:

Theorem 1. *Let ρ and ρ' be paths in a timed automaton such that $\mathsf{Reach}(\rho)$ and $\mathsf{Reach}(\rho')$ are non empty. Then $\mathsf{Reach}(\rho) \subseteq \mathsf{Reach}(\rho')$ if and only if $\Gamma^\rho \leqslant \Gamma^{\rho'}$.*

Notice that we do not need to check equivalence or implication of formulas $\varphi(G_\rho)$ and $\varphi(G_{\rho'})$, but simply check syntactically constants appearing in these formulas. Moreover, these constants can be stored in usual DBMs on $2 \times |\mathcal{X}_0|$ clocks, allowing for reusability of classical DBM libraries. For the constraint graph in Fig. 3, we have seen that $G_{\rho^2} \neq G_{\rho^1}$, even if $\mathsf{Reach}(\rho^2) = \mathsf{Reach}(\rho)$. However, we can check that $\varphi(G_{\rho^2}) = \varphi(G_\rho)$ as expected.

Computation of Pre and Post. By Lemma 1 and the construction of constraint graphs, one can easily compute $\mathsf{Pre}_\rho(Z) = \{\nu \mid \exists \nu' \in Z \; ((\ell, \nu), (\ell', \nu')) \in \mathsf{Reach}(\rho)\}$ for a given path ρ and zone Z (see [8, 16]). In fact, consider the normalised constraint graph G_ρ on nodes $X^\ell \cup X^r$. To compute $\mathsf{Pre}_\rho(Z)$, one just needs to add the constraints of Z on X^r. This is done by replacing each edge $X_i^r \xrightarrow{w} X_j^r$ by $X_i^r \xrightarrow{\min(Z_{j,i}, w)} X_j^r$ where $Z_{j,i} = (\prec, p)$ defines the constraint of Z on $x_j - x_i$. Then, the normalisation of the graph describes the reachability relation along path ρ ending in zone Z. Furthermore, projecting the constraints to X^ℓ yields $\mathsf{Pre}_\rho(Z)$: this can be obtained by gathering all constraints on pairs of nodes of X^ℓ. A reachability relation can thus be seen as a function assigning to each zone Z its image by ρ. One can symmetrically compute the successor $\mathsf{Post}_\rho(Z) = \{\nu' \mid \exists \nu \in Z \; ((\ell, \nu), (\ell', \nu')) \in \mathsf{Reach}(\rho)\}$ by constraining the nodes X^ℓ and projecting to X^r.

4   Robust Iterability of a Lasso

In this section, we study the perturbation game $\mathcal{G}_\delta(\mathcal{A})$ between the two players (controller and environment), as defined in Sect. 2, when the timed automaton $\mathcal{A}$ is restricted to a fixed *lasso* $\rho_1\rho_2$, i.e. ρ_1 is a path from ℓ_0 to some accepting location ℓ_t, and ρ_2 a cyclic path around ℓ_t. This implies that the controller does not have the choice of the transitions, but only of the delays. We will consider different settings, in which δ is fixed or not.

Controllable Predecessors and their Greatest Fixpoints. Consider an edge $e = (\ell, g, R, \ell')$. For any set $Z \subseteq \mathbb{R}_{\geq 0}^{\mathcal{X}}$, we define the *controllable predecessors of Z* as follows: $\mathsf{CPre}_e^\delta(Z) = \mathsf{Pretime}_{>\delta}(\mathsf{shrink}_{[-\delta,\delta]}(g \cap \mathsf{Unreset}_R(Z)))$. Intuitively, $\mathsf{CPre}_e^\delta(Z)$ is the set of valuations from which the controller can ensure reaching Z in one step, following the edge e, no matter of the perturbations of amplitude at most δ of the environment. In fact, it can delay in $\mathsf{shrink}_{[-\delta,\delta]}(g \cap \mathsf{Unreset}_R(Z))$ with a delay of at least δ, where under any perturbation in $[-\delta, \delta]$, the valuation satisfies the guard, and it ends, after reset, in Z. Results of [24] show that this operator can be computed in cubic time with respect to the number of clocks. We extend this operator to a path ρ by composition, denoted it by $\mathsf{CPre}_\rho^\delta$. Note that $\mathsf{CPre}_\rho^0 = \mathsf{Pre}_\rho$ is the usual predecessor operator without perturbation.

This operator is monotone, hence its greatest fixpoint $\nu X\, \mathsf{CPre}_\rho^\delta(X)$ is well-defined, equal to $\bigcap_{i\geq 0} \mathsf{CPre}_{\rho^i}^\delta(\top)$: it corresponds to the valuations from which the controller can guarantee to loop forever along the path ρ. By definition of the game $\mathcal{G}_\delta(\mathcal{A})$ where $\mathcal{A}$ is restricted to the lasso $\rho_1\rho_2$, the controller wins the game if and only if $\mathbf{0} \in \mathsf{CPre}_{\rho_1}^\delta(\nu X\, \mathsf{CPre}_{\rho_2}^\delta(X))$. As a consequence, our problem reduces to the computation of this greatest fixpoint.

Branching Constraint Graphs. We consider first a fixed (rational) value of the parameter δ, and are interested in the computation of the greatest fixpoint $\nu X\, \mathsf{CPre}_{\rho_2}^\delta(X)$. In [16], constraints graphs were used to provide a termination criterion allowing to compute the greatest fixpoint of the classical predecessor operator CPre_ρ^0. We generalize this approach to deal with the operator $\mathsf{CPre}_\rho^\delta$ and to this end, we need to generalize constraint graphs so as to encode it. Unfortunately, the operator $\mathsf{shrink}_{[-\delta,\delta]}$ cannot be encoded in a constraint graph. Intuitively, this comes from the fact that a constraint graph represents a relation between valuations, while there is no such relation associated with the $\mathsf{CPre}_\rho^\delta$ operator. Instead, we introduce *branching constraint graphs*, that will faithfully represent the $\mathsf{CPre}_\rho^\delta$ operator: unlike constraint graphs introduced so far that have a left layer and a right layer of variables, a branching constraint graph has still a single left layer but several right layers.

We first define a branching constraint graph $G_{\mathsf{shrink}}^\delta$ associated with the operator $\mathsf{shrink}_{[-\delta,\delta]}$ as follows. Its set of vertices is composed of three copies of the $\{X_0, X_1, \ldots, X_n\}$, denoted by primed, unprimed and doubly primed versions. Edges are defined so as to encode the following constraints : $X_i' = X_i$ and $X_i'' = X_i$ for every $i \neq 0$, and $X_0' = X_0 + \delta$ and $X_0'' = X_0 - \delta$. An instance of this graph can be found in several occurrences in Fig. 2.

Proposition 1. *Let Z be a zone and $G^\delta_{\text{shrink}}(Z)$ be the graph obtained from G^δ_{shrink} by adding on primed and doubly primed vertices the constraints defining Z (as for $\text{Pre}_\rho(Z)$ in the end of Sect. 3). Then the constraint on unprimed vertices obtained from the shortest paths in $G^\delta_{\text{shrink}}(Z)$ is equivalent to $\text{shrink}_{[-\delta,\delta]}(Z)$.*

Proof. Given a zone Z and a real number d, we define $Z + d = \{\nu + d \mid \nu \in Z\}$. One easily observes that $\text{shrink}_{[-\delta,\delta]}(Z) = (Z + \delta) \cap (Z - \delta)$. The result follows from the observation that taking two distinct copies of vertices, and considering shortest paths allows one to encode the intersection.   □

Then, for all edges $e = (\ell, g, R, \ell')$, we define the branching constraint graph G^δ_e as the graph obtained by stacking (in this order) the branching constraint graph $G^{>\delta}_{\text{time}}$, G^δ_{shrink} and $G^{g,\mathcal{Y}}_{\text{edge}}$. Note that two copies of the graph $G^{g,\mathcal{Y}}_{\text{edge}}$ are needed, to be connected to the two sets of vertices that are on the right of the graph G^δ_{shrink}. This definition is extended in the expected way to a finite path ρ, yielding the graph G^δ_ρ. In this graph, there is a single set of vertices on the left, and $2^{|\rho|}$ sets of vertices on the right. As a direct consequence of the previous results on the constraint graphs for time elapse, shrinking and guard/reset, one obtains:

Proposition 2. *Let Z be a zone and ρ be a path. We let $G^\delta_\rho(Z)$ be the graph obtained from G^δ_ρ by adding on every set of right vertices the constraints defining Z. Then the constraint on the left layer of vertices obtained from the shortest paths in $G^\delta_\rho(Z)$ is equivalent to $\text{CPre}^\delta_\rho(Z)$.*

An example of the graph $G^\delta_\rho(Z)$ for $\rho = e_1 e_2$, edges considered in Fig. 3, is depicted in Fig. 2 (on the left).

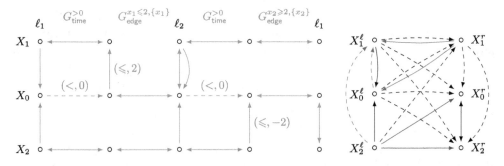

Fig. 2. On the left, the branching constraint graph $G^\delta_{e_1 e_2}$ encoding the operator $\text{CPre}^\delta_{e_1 e_2}$, where e_1 and e_2 refer to edges considered in Fig. 3. Dashed edges have weight $(<, .)$, plain edges have weight $(\leqslant, .)$. Black edges (resp. orange edges, pink edges, red edges, blue edges) are labelled by $(., 0)$ (resp. $(., -\delta)$, $(., \delta)$, $(., 2)$, $(., -2)$). On the right, a decomposition of a path in a branching constraint graph G^δ_ρ. (Color figure online)

We are now ready to prove the following result, generalisation of [16, Lemma 2], that will allow us to compute the greatest fixpoint of the operator CPre^δ_ρ:

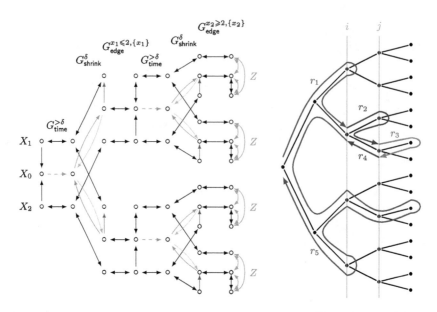

Fig. 3. On the left, the constraint graph of the path $\ell_1 \xrightarrow{x_1 \leqslant 2, x_1 := 0} \ell_2 \xrightarrow{x_2 \geqslant 2, x_2 := 0} \ell_1$. On the right, its normalised version: dashed edges have weight $(<, .)$, plain edges have weight $(\leqslant, .)$, black edges have weight $(., 0)$, red edges have weight $(., 2)$ and blue edges have weight $(., -2)$.

Proposition 3. *Let ρ be a path and δ be a non-negative rational number. We let $N = |\mathcal{X}_0|^2$. If $\mathsf{CPre}_{\rho^{2N+1}}^{\delta}(\top) \subsetneq \mathsf{CPre}_{\rho^{2N}}^{\delta}(\top)$, then $\nu X\, \mathsf{CPre}_{\rho}^{\delta}(X) = \emptyset$.*

Proof. Assume $\mathsf{CPre}_{\rho^{2N+1}}^{\delta}(\top) \subsetneq \mathsf{CPre}_{\rho^{2N}}^{\delta}(\top)$ and consider the zones $\mathsf{CPre}_{\rho^{N+1}}^{\delta}(\top)$ (represented by the DBM M_1) and $\mathsf{CPre}_{\rho^{N}}^{\delta}(\top)$ (represented by the DBM M_2). We have $M_1 \subsetneq M_2$, as otherwise the fixpoint would have already been reached after N steps. By Proposition 2, the zone corresponding to M_1 is associated with shortest paths between vertices on the left in the graph $G_{\rho^{N+1}}^{\delta}$. In the sequel, given a path r in this graph, $w(r)$ denotes its weight. We distinguish two cases:

Case 1: $M_1 \subsetneq M_2$ because of the rational coefficients. Then, there exists an entry $(x, y) \in \mathcal{X}_0^2$ such that $M_1[x, y] < M_2[x, y]$. The value $M_1[x, y]$ is thus associated with a shortest path between vertices X and Y in $G_{\rho^{N+1}}^{\delta}$. We fix a shortest path of minimal length, and denote it by r. As the entry is strictly smaller than in M_2, this shortest path should reach the last copy of the graph G_{ρ}^{δ}. This path can be interpreted as a traversal of the binary tree of depth $|\mathcal{X}_0|^2 + 1$, reaching at least one leaf. We can prove that this entails that there exists a pair of clocks $(u, v) \in \mathcal{X}_0^2$ appearing at two levels $i < j$ of this tree, and a decomposition $r = r_1 r_2 r_3 r_4 r_5$ of the path, such that $w(r_2) + w(r_4) = (\prec, d)$ with $d < 0$ (Property (†)). In addition, in this decomposition, r_3 is included in subgraphs of levels $k \geq j$, and the pair of paths (r_2, r_4) is called a *return path*, following the terminology of [16]. This decomposition is depicted in Fig. 2 (on the right). Intuitively, the property (†) follows from the fact that as r_3 is included in subgraphs of levels $k \geq j$, and because the final zone (on the right) is the zone $\top$ which adds no edges, the concatenation $r' = r_1 r_3 r_5$ is also a valid path from X to Y in $G_{\rho^{N+1}}^{\delta}$, and is shorter than r. We conclude using the fact that r has been chosen as a shortest path of minimal weight.

Property (†) allows us to prove that the greatest fixpoint is empty. Indeed, by considering iterations of ρ, one can repeat the return path associated with (r_2, r_4) and obtain paths from X to Y whose weights diverge towards $-\infty$.

Case 2: $M_1 \subsetneq M_2$ because of the ordering coefficients. We claim that this case cannot occur. Indeed, one can show that the constants will not evolve anymore after the Nth iteration of the fixpoint: the coefficients can only decrease by changing from a non-strict inequality $(\leq, c)$ to a strict one $(<, c)$. This propagation of strict inequalities is performed in at most $|\mathcal{X}_0|^2$ additional steps, thus we have $\mathsf{CPre}_{\rho^{2N+1}}^{\delta}(\top) = \mathsf{CPre}_{\rho^{2N}}^{\delta}(\top)$, yielding a contradiction. □

Compared to the result of [16], the number of iterations needed before convergence grows from $|\mathcal{X}_0|^2$ to $2|\mathcal{X}_0|^2$: this is due to the presence of strict and non-strict inequalities, not considered in [16]. With the help of branching constraint graphs, we have thus shown that the greatest fixpoint can be computed in finite time: this can then be done directly with computations on zones (and not on branching constraint graphs).

Proposition 4. *Given a path ρ and a rational number δ, the greatest fixpoint $\nu X \, \mathsf{CPre}_{\rho}^{\delta}(X)$ can be computed in time polynomial in $|\mathcal{X}|$ and $|\rho|$. As a consequence, one can decide whether the controller has a strategy along a lasso $\rho_1 \rho_2$ in $\mathcal{G}_{\delta}(\mathcal{A})$ in time polynomial in $|\mathcal{X}|$ and $|\rho_1 \rho_2|$.*

Solving the Robust Controller Synthesis Problem for a Lasso. We have shown how to decide whether the controller has a winning strategy for a fixed rational value of δ. We now aim at deciding whether there exists a positive value of δ for which the controller wins the game $\mathcal{G}_{\delta}(\mathcal{A})$ (where $\mathcal{A}$ is restricted to a lasso $\rho_1 \rho_2$). To this end, we will use a parametrised extension of DBMs, namely *shrunk DBMs*, that were introduced in [24] in order to study the parametrised state space of timed automata. Intuitively, our goal is to express *shrinkings* of guards, e.g. sets of states satisfying constraints of the form $g = 1 + \delta < x < 2 - \delta \wedge 2\delta < y$, where δ is a parameter to be chosen. Formally, a shrunk DBM is a pair (M, P), where M is a DBM, and P is a nonnegative integer matrix called a *shrinking matrix*. This pair represents the set of valuations defined by the DBM $M - \delta P$, for any given $\delta > 0$. Considering the example g, M is the guard g obtained by setting $\delta = 0$, and P is made of the integer multipliers of δ. We adopt the following notation: when we write a statement involving a shrunk DBM (M, P), we mean that for some $\delta_0 > 0$, the statement holds for $M - \delta P$ for all $\delta \in (0, \delta_0]$. For instance, $(M, P) = \mathsf{Pretime}_{>\delta}((N, Q))$ means that $M - \delta P = \mathsf{Pretime}_{>\delta}(N - \delta Q)$ for all small enough $\delta > 0$. Shrunk DBMs are closed under standard operations on zones, and as a consequence, the CPre operator can be computed on shrunk DBMs:

Lemma 2. ([25]) *Let $e = (\ell, g, R, \ell')$ be an edge and (M, P) be a shrunk DBM. Then, there exists a shrunk DBM (N, Q), that we can compute in polynomial time, such that $(N, Q) = \mathsf{CPre}_e^\delta((M, P))$.*

Proposition 5. *Given a path ρ, one can compute a shrunk DBM (M, P) equal to the greatest fixpoint of the operator $\mathsf{CPre}_\rho^\delta$. As a consequence, one can solve the parametrised robust controller synthesis problem for a given lasso in time complexity polynomial in the number of clocks and in the length of the lasso.*

Proof. The bound $2|\mathcal{X}_0|^2$ identified previously does not depend on the value of δ. Hence the algorithm for computing a shrunk DBM representing the greatest fixpoint proceeds as follows. It computes symbolically, using shrunk DBMs, the $2|\mathcal{X}_0|^2$-th and $2|\mathcal{X}_0|^2 + 1$-th iterations of the operator $\mathsf{CPre}_\rho^\delta$, from the zone $\top$. By monotonicity, the $2|\mathcal{X}_0|^2 + 1$-th iteration is included in the $2|\mathcal{X}_0|^2$-th. If the two shrunk DBMs are equal, then they are also equal to the greatest fixpoint. Otherwise, the greatest fixpoint is empty. To decide the robust controller synthesis problem for a given lasso, one first computes a shrunk DBM representing the greatest fixpoint associated with ρ_2 and, if not empty, one computes a new shrunk DBM by applying to it the operator $\mathsf{CPre}_{\rho_1}^\delta$. Then, one checks whether the valuation $\mathbf{0}$ belongs to the resulting shrunk DBM. □

Computing the Largest Admissible Perturbation. We say that a perturbation δ is *admissible* if the controller wins the game $\mathcal{G}_\delta(\mathcal{A})$. The parametrised robust controller synthesis problem, solved before just for a lasso, aims at deciding whether *there exists* a positive admissible perturbation. A more ambitious problem consists in determining the *largest admissible* perturbation.

The previous algorithm performs a bounded $(2|\mathcal{X}_0|^2)$ number of computations of the $\mathsf{CPre}_\rho^\delta$ operator. Instead of focusing on arbitrarily small values using shrunk DBMs as we did previously, we must perform a computation for all values of δ. To do so, we consider an extension of the (shrunk) DBMs in which each entry of the matrix (which thus represents a clock constraint) is a piecewise affine function of δ. One can observe that all the operations involved in the computation of the $\mathsf{CPre}_\rho^\delta$ operator can be performed symbolically w.r.t. δ using piecewise affine functions. As a consequence, we obtain the following new result:

Proposition 6. *We can compute the largest admissible perturbation of a lasso.*

Proof. Let $\rho_1 \rho_2$ be a lasso. One first computes a symbolic representation, valid for all values of δ, of the greatest fixpoint of $\mathsf{CPre}_{\rho_2}^\delta$. To do so, one computes the $2|\mathcal{X}_0|^2$-th and $2|\mathcal{X}_0|^2+1$-th iterations of this operator, from the zone $\top$. We denote them by M_1 and M_2 respectively. By monotonicity, the inclusion $M_1(\delta) \subseteq M_2(\delta)$ holds for every $\delta \geq 0$. In addition, both M_1 and M_2 are decreasing w.r.t. δ, thus one can identify the value $\delta_0 = \inf\{\delta \geq 0 \mid M_1(\delta) \subsetneq M_2(\delta)\}$. Then, the greatest fixpoint is equal to M_1 for $\delta < \delta_0$, and to the emptyset for δ at least δ_0. As a second step, one applies the operator CPre_{ρ_1} to the greatest fixpoint. We denote the result by M. To conclude, one can then compute and return the value $\sup\{\delta \in [0, \delta_0[\mid \mathbf{0} \in M(\delta)\}$ of maximal perturbation. □

5 Synthesis of Robust Controllers

We are now ready to solve the parametrised robust controller synthesis problem, that is to find, if it exists, a lasso $\rho_1\rho_2$ and a perturbation δ such that the controller wins the game $\mathcal{G}_\delta(\mathcal{A})$ when following the lasso $\rho_1\rho_2$ as a strategy. As for the symbolic checking of emptiness of a Büchi timed language [17], we will use a double forward analysis to exhaust all possible lassos, each being tested for robustness by the techniques studied in previous section: a first forward analysis will search for ρ_1, a path from the initial location to an accepting location, and a second forward analysis from each accepting location ℓ to find the cycle ρ_2 around ℓ. Forward analysis means that we compute the successor zone $\mathsf{Post}_\rho(Z)$ when following path ρ from zone Z.

Abstractions of Lassos. Before studying in more details the two independent forward analyses, we first study what information we must keep about ρ_1 and ρ_2 in order to still being able to test the robustness of the lasso $\rho_1\rho_2$. A classical problem for robustness is the firing of a *punctual transition*, i.e. a transition where controller has a single choice of time delay: clearly such a firing will be robust for no possible choice of parameter δ. Therefore, we must at least forbid such punctual transitions in our forward analyses. We thus introduce a non-punctual successor operator $\mathsf{Post}_\rho^{\mathrm{np}}$. It consists of the standard successor operator Post_ρ in the timed automaton $\mathcal{A}^{\mathrm{np}}$ obtained from $\mathcal{A}$ by making strict every constraint appearing in the guards ($1 \leq x \leq 2$ becomes $1 < x < 2$). The crucial point is that if a positive delay d can be taken by the controller while satisfying a set of strict constraints, then other delays are also possible, close enough to d. By analogy, a region is said to be *non-punctual* if it contains two valuations separated by a positive time delay. In particular, if such a region satisfies a constraint in $\mathcal{A}$ it also satisfies the corresponding strict constraint in $\mathcal{A}^{\mathrm{np}}$. Therefore, controller wins $\mathcal{G}_\delta(\mathcal{A})$ for some $\delta > 0$ if and only if he wins $\mathcal{G}_\delta(\mathcal{A}^{\mathrm{np}})$ for some $\delta > 0$.

The link between non-punctuality and robustness is as follows:

Theorem 2. *Let $\rho_1\rho_2$ be a lasso of the timed automaton. We have*

$$\exists \delta > 0 \ \ \mathbf{0} \in \mathsf{CPre}_{\rho_1}^\delta(\nu X\, \mathsf{CPre}_{\rho_2}^\delta(X)) \iff \mathsf{Post}_{\rho_1}^{\mathrm{np}}(\mathbf{0}) \cap \left(\bigcup_{\delta>0}\nu X\, \mathsf{CPre}_{\rho_2}^\delta(X)\right) \neq \emptyset$$

Proof. The proof of this theorem relies on three main ingredients:

1. the timed automaton $\mathcal{A}^{\mathrm{np}}$ allows one to compute $\bigcup_{\delta>0} \mathsf{CPre}_e^\delta(Z')$ by classical predecessor operator: $\mathsf{Pre}_e^{\mathrm{np}}(Z') = \bigcup_{\delta>0} \mathsf{CPre}_e^\delta(Z')$;

2. for all edges e, and zones Z and Z', $Z \cap \mathsf{Pre}_e^{\mathrm{np}}(Z') \neq \emptyset$ if and only if $\mathsf{Post}_e^{\mathrm{np}}(Z) \cap Z' \neq \emptyset$: this duality property on predecessor and successor relations always holds, in particular in $\mathcal{A}^{\mathrm{np}}$. These two ingredients already imply that the theorem holds for a path reduced to a single edge e;

3. we then prove the theorem by induction on length of the path using that $\bigcup_{\delta>0} \mathsf{CPre}_{\rho_1\rho_2}^\delta(Z) = \bigcup_{\delta>0} \mathsf{CPre}_{\rho_1}^\delta\left(\bigcup_{\delta'>0} \mathsf{CPre}_{\rho_2}^{\delta'}(Z)\right)$, due to the monotonicity of the $\mathsf{CPre}_{\rho_1}^\delta$ operator. $\qquad\square$

Therefore, in order to test the robustness of the lasso $\rho_1\rho_2$, it is enough to only keep in memory the sets $\mathsf{Post}^{\mathrm{np}}_{\rho_1}(\mathbf{0})$ and $\bigcup_{\delta>0} \nu X\, \mathsf{CPre}^{\delta}_{\rho_2}(X)$.

Non-punctual Forward Analysis. As a consequence of the previous theorem, we can use a classical forward analysis of the timed automaton $\mathcal{A}^{\mathrm{np}}$ to look for the prefix ρ_1 of the lasso $\rho_1\rho_2$. A classical inclusion check on zones allows to stop the exploration, this criterion being complete thanks to Theorem 2. It is worth reminding that we consider only bounded clocks, hence the number of reachable zones is finite, ensuring termination.

Robust Cycle Search. We now perform a second forward analysis, from each possible final location, to find a robust cycle around it. To this end, for each cycle ρ_2, we must compute the zone $\bigcup_{\delta>0} \nu X\, \mathsf{CPre}^{\delta}_{\rho_2}(X)$. This computation is obtained by arguments developed in Sect. 4 (Proposition 4). To enumerate cycles ρ_2, we can again use a classical forward exploration, starting from the universal zone $\top$. Using zone inclusion to stop the exploration is not complete: considering a path ρ_2' reaching a zone Z_2' included in the zone Z_2 reachable using some ρ_2, ρ_2' could be robustly iterable while ρ_2 is not. In order to ensure termination of our analysis, we instead use reachability relations inclusion checks. These tests are performed using the technique developed in Sect. 3, based on constraint graphs (Theorem 1). The correction of this inclusion check is stated in the following lemma, where $\mathsf{Reach}^{\mathrm{np}}_{\rho}$ denotes the reachability relation associated with ρ in the automaton $\mathcal{A}^{\mathrm{np}}$. This result is derived from the analysis based on regions in [25]. Indeed, we can prove that the non-punctual reachability relation we consider captures the existence of non-punctual aperiodic paths in the region automaton, as considered in [25].

Lemma 3. *Let ρ_1 a path from ℓ_0 to some target location ℓ_t. Let ρ_2, ρ_2' be two paths from ℓ_t to some location ℓ, such that $\mathsf{Reach}^{\mathrm{np}}_{\rho_2} \subseteq \mathsf{Reach}^{\mathrm{np}}_{\rho_2'}$. For all paths ρ_3 from ℓ to ℓ_t, $\mathsf{Post}^{\mathrm{np}}_{\rho_1}(\mathbf{0}) \cap (\bigcup_{\delta>0} \nu X\, \mathsf{CPre}^{\delta}_{\rho_2\rho_3}(X)) \neq \emptyset$ implies $\mathsf{Post}^{\mathrm{np}}_{\rho_1}(\mathbf{0}) \cap (\bigcup_{\delta>0} \nu X\, \mathsf{CPre}^{\delta}_{\rho_2'\rho_3}(X)) \neq \emptyset$.*

6   Case Study

We implemented our algorithm in C++. To illustrate our approach, we present a case study on the regulation of train networks. Urban train networks in big cities are often particularly busy during rush hours: trains run in high frequency so even small delays due to incidents or passenger misbehavior can perturb the traffic and end up causing large delays. Train companies thus apply regulation techniques: they slow down or accelerate trains, and modify waiting times in order to make sure that the traffic is fluid along the network. Computing robust schedules with provable guarantees is a difficult problem (see e.g. [9]).

We study here a simplified model of a train network and aim at automatically synthesizing a controller that regulates the network despite perturbations, in order to ensure performance measures on total travel time for each train. Consider a circular train network with m stations $s_0, \ldots, s_{m-1}$ and n trains. We require that all trains are at distinct stations at all times. There is an interval of delays $[\ell_i, u_i]$ attached to each station which bounds the travel time from s_i to $s_{i+1 \bmod m}$. Here the lower bound comes from physical limits (maximal allowed speed, and travel distance) while the upper bound comes from operator specification (e.g. it is not desirable for a train to remain at station for more than 3 min). The objective of each train i is to cycle on the network while completing each tour within a given time interval $[t_1^i, t_2^i]$.

All timing requirements are naturally encoded with clocks. Given a model, we solve the robust controller synthesis problem in order to find a controller choosing travel times for all trains ensuring a Büchi condition (visiting s_1 infinitely often). Given the fact that trains cannot be at the same station at any given time, it suffices to state the Büchi condition only for one train, since its satisfaction of the condition necessarily implies that of all other trains.

Let us present two representative instances and then comment the performance of the algorithm on a set of instances. Consider a network with two trains and m stations, with $[\ell_i, u_i] = [200, 400]$ for each station i, and the objective of both trains is the interval $[250 \cdot m, 350 \cdot m]$, that is, an average travel time between stations that lies in $[250, 350]$. The algorithm finds an accepting lasso: intuitively, by choosing δ small enough so that $m\delta < 50$, perturbations do not accumulate too much and the controller can always choose delays for both trains and satisfy the constraints. This case corresponds to scenario A in Fig. 4. Consider now the same network but with two different objectives: $[0, 300 \cdot m]$ and $[300 \cdot m, \infty)$. Thus, one train needs to complete each

Scenario	m	n	#Clocks	robust?	time
A	6	2	4	yes	4s
B	6	2	4	no	2s
C	6	3	5	no	263s
D	6	3	4	yes	125s
E	6	4	2	yes	53s
F	6	4	2	yes	424s
G	6	4	8		TO
H	6	4	8		TO
I	20	2	2	yes	76s
J	20	2	2	yes	55s
K	30	2	2	yes	579s

Fig. 4. Summary of experiments with different sizes. In each scenario, we assign a different objective to a subset of trains. The answer is *yes* if a robust controller was found, *no* if none exists. TO stands for a time-out of 30 min.

cycle in at most $300 \cdot m$ time units, while the other one in at least $300 \cdot m$ time units. A classical Büchi emptiness check reveals the existence of an accepting lasso: it suffices to move each train in exactly 300 time units between each station. This controller can even recover from perturbations for a bounded number of cycles: for instance, if a train arrives late at a station, the next travel time can be chosen smaller than 300. However, such corrections will cause the distance between the two trains to decrease and if such perturbations happen regularly, the system will eventually enter a deadlock. Our algorithm detects that there is no robust controller for the Büchi objective. This corresponds to the scenario B in Fig. 4.

Figure 4 summarizes the outcome of our prototype implementation on other scenarios. The tool was run on a 3.2 Ghz Intel i7 processor running Linux, with a 30 min time out and 2 GB of memory. The performance is sensitive to the number of clocks: on scenarios with 8 clocks the algorithm ran out of time.

7   Conclusion

Our case study illustrates the application of robust controller synthesis in small or moderate size problems. Our prototype relies on the DBM libraries that we use with twice as many clocks to store the constraints of the normalised constraint graphs. In order to scale to larger models, we plan to study extrapolation operators and their integration in the computation of reachability relations, which seems to be a challenging task. Different strategies can also be adopted for the double forward analysis, switching between the two modes using heuristics, a parallel implementation, etc.

References

1. Alur, R., Dill, D.L.: A theory of timed automata. Theor. Comput. Sci. **126**(2), 183–235 (1994)
2. Bacci, G., Bouyer, P., Fahrenberg, U., Larsen, K.G., Markey, N., Reynier, P.-A.: Optimal and robust controller synthesis. In: Havelund, K., Peleska, J., Roscoe, B., de Vink, E. (eds.) FM 2018. LNCS, vol. 10951, pp. 203–221. Springer, Cham (2018). https://doi.org/10.1007/978-3-319-95582-7_12
3. Bengtsson, J., Yi, W.: Timed automata: semantics, algorithms and tools. In: Desel, J., Reisig, W., Rozenberg, G. (eds.) ACPN 2003. LNCS, vol. 3098, pp. 87–124. Springer, Heidelberg (2004). https://doi.org/10.1007/978-3-540-27755-2_3
4. Berthomieu, B., Menasche, M.: An enumerative approach for analyzing time Petri nets. In: Mason, R.E.A. (ed.) Information Processing 83 - Proceedings of the 9th IFIP World Computer Congress (WCC'83), pp. 41–46. North-Holland/IFIP, September 1983
5. Cassez, F., David, A., Fleury, E., Larsen, K.G., Lime, D.: Efficient on-the-fly algorithms for the analysis of timed games. In: Abadi, M., de Alfaro, L. (eds.) CONCUR 2005. LNCS, vol. 3653, pp. 66–80. Springer, Heidelberg (2005). https://doi.org/10.1007/11539452_9
6. Cassez, F., Henzinger, T.A., Raskin, J.-F.: A comparison of control problems for timed and hybrid systems. In: Tomlin, C.J., Greenstreet, M.R. (eds.) HSCC 2002. LNCS, vol. 2289, pp. 134–148. Springer, Heidelberg (2002). https://doi.org/10.1007/3-540-45873-5_13
7. Chatterjee, K., Henzinger, T.A., Prabhu, V.S.: Timed parity games: complexity and robustness. In: Cassez, F., Jard, C. (eds.) FORMATS 2008. LNCS, vol. 5215, pp. 124–140. Springer, Heidelberg (2008). https://doi.org/10.1007/978-3-540-85778-5_10
8. Comon, H., Jurski, Y.: Timed automata and the theory of real numbers. In: Baeten, J.C.M., Mauw, S. (eds.) CONCUR 1999. LNCS, vol. 1664, pp. 242–257. Springer, Heidelberg (1999). https://doi.org/10.1007/3-540-48320-9_18
9. D'Ariano, A., Pranzo, M., Hansen, I.A.: Conflict resolution and train speed coordination for solving real-time timetable perturbations. IEEE Trans. Intell. Trans. Syst. **8**(2), 208–222 (2007)

10. Dill, D.L.: Timing assumptions and verification of finite-state concurrent systems. In: Sifakis, J. (ed.) CAV 1989. LNCS, vol. 407, pp. 197–212. Springer, Heidelberg (1990). https://doi.org/10.1007/3-540-52148-8_17

11. Henzinger, T.A., Otop, J., Samanta, R.: Lipschitz robustness of timed I/O systems. In: Jobstmann, B., Leino, K.R.M. (eds.) VMCAI 2016. LNCS, vol. 9583, pp. 250–267. Springer, Heidelberg (2016). https://doi.org/10.1007/978-3-662-49122-5_12

12. Henzinger, T.A., Sifakis, J.: The embedded systems design challenge. In: Misra, J., Nipkow, T., Sekerinski, E. (eds.) FM 2006. LNCS, vol. 4085, pp. 1–15. Springer, Heidelberg (2006). https://doi.org/10.1007/11813040_1

13. Herbreteau, F., Srivathsan, B.: Efficient on-the-fly emptiness check for timed büchi automata. In: Bouajjani, A., Chin, W.-N. (eds.) ATVA 2010. LNCS, vol. 6252, pp. 218–232. Springer, Heidelberg (2010). https://doi.org/10.1007/978-3-642-15643-4_17

14. Herbreteau, F., Srivathsan, B., Tran, T.-T., Walukiewicz, I.: Why liveness for timed automata is hard, and what we can do about it. In: FSTTCS 2016, LIPIcs, vol. 65, pp. 48:1–48:14. Schloss Dagstuhl - Leibniz-Zentrum fuer Informatik (2016)

15. Herbreteau, F., Srivathsan, B., Walukiewicz, I.: Efficient emptiness check for timed büchi automata. Formal Methods Syst. Des. **40**(2), 122–146 (2012)

16. Jaubert, R., Reynier, P.-A.: Quantitative robustness analysis of flat timed automata. In: Hofmann, M. (ed.) FoSSaCS 2011. LNCS, vol. 6604, pp. 229–244. Springer, Heidelberg (2011). https://doi.org/10.1007/978-3-642-19805-2_16

17. Laarman, A., Olesen, M.C., Dalsgaard, A.E., Larsen, K.G., van de Pol, J.: Multi-core emptiness checking of timed büchi automata using inclusion abstraction. In: Sharygina, N., Veith, H. (eds.) CAV 2013. LNCS, vol. 8044, pp. 968–983. Springer, Heidelberg (2013). https://doi.org/10.1007/978-3-642-39799-8_69

18. Larsen, K.G., Legay, A., Traonouez, L.-M., Wasowski, A.: Robust synthesis for real-time systems. Theor. Comput. Sci. **515**, 96–122 (2014)

19. Li, G.: Checking timed büchi automata emptiness using LU-abstractions. In: Ouaknine, J., Vaandrager, F.W. (eds.) FORMATS 2009. LNCS, vol. 5813, pp. 228–242. Springer, Heidelberg (2009). https://doi.org/10.1007/978-3-642-04368-0_18

20. Prabhakar, P., Soto, M.G.: Formal synthesis of stabilizing controllers for switched systems. In: Proceedings of the 20th International Conference on Hybrid Systems: Computation and Control, HSCC 2017, New York, NY, USA, pp. 111–120. ACM (2017)

21. Prabhakar, P., Soto, M.G.: Counterexample guided abstraction refinement for stability analysis. In: Chaudhuri, S., Farzan, A. (eds.) CAV 2016. LNCS, vol. 9779, pp. 495–512. Springer, Cham (2016). https://doi.org/10.1007/978-3-319-41528-4_27

22. Quaas, K., Shirmohammadi, M., Worrell, J.: Revisiting reachability in timed automata. In: LICS 2017. IEEE (2017)

23. Roohi, N., Prabhakar, P., Viswanathan, M.: Robust model checking of timed automata under clock drifts. In: Proceedings of the 20th International Conference on Hybrid Systems: Computation and Control, HSCC 2017, New York, NY, USA, pp. 153–162. ACM (2017)

24. Sankur, O., Bouyer, P., Markey, N.: Shrinking timed automata. In: IARCS Annual Conference on Foundations of Software Technology and Theoretical Computer Science (FSTTCS 2011), LIPIcs, vol. 13, pp. 90–102. Schloss Dagstuhl-Leibniz-Zentrum fuer Informatik (2011)

25. Sankur, O., Bouyer, P., Markey, N., Reynier, P.-A.: Robust controller synthesis in timed automata. In: D'Argenio, P.R., Melgratti, H. (eds.) CONCUR 2013. LNCS, vol. 8052, pp. 546–560. Springer, Heidelberg (2013). https://doi.org/10.1007/978-3-642-40184-8_38

26. Tran, T.-T.: Verification of timed automata : reachability, liveness and modelling. (Vérification d'automates temporisés : sûreté, vivacité et modélisation). Ph.D. thesis, University of Bordeaux, France (2016)
27. Tripakis, S.: Checking timed büchi automata emptiness on simulation graphs. ACM Trans. Comput. Log. **10**(3), 15:1–15:19 (2009)
28. Tripakis, S., Yovine, S., Bouajjani, A.: Checking timed büchi automata emptiness efficiently. Formal Methods Syst. Des. **26**(3), 267–292 (2005)

13

BMC for Weak Memory Models: Relation Analysis for Compact SMT Encodings

Natalia Gavrilenko[1,4][(✉)], Hernán Ponce-de-León[2],
Florian Furbach[3], Keijo Heljanko[4],
and Roland Meyer[3]

[1] Aalto University, Helsinki, Finland
[2] fortiss GmbH, Munich, Germany
[3] TU Braunschweig, Brunswick, Germany
[4] University of Helsinki and HIIT, Helsinki, Finland
natalia.gavrilenko@helsinki.fi

Abstract. We present DARTAGNAN, a bounded model checker (BMC) for concurrent programs under weak memory models. Its distinguishing feature is that the memory model is not implemented inside the tool but taken as part of the input. DARTAGNAN reads CAT, the standard language for memory models, which allows to define x86/TSO, ARMv7, ARMv8, POWER, C/C++, and LINUX kernel concurrency primitives. BMC with memory models as inputs is challenging. One has to encode into SMT not only the program but also its semantics as defined by the memory model. What makes DARTAGNAN scale is its relation analysis, a novel static analysis that significantly reduces the size of the encoding. DARTAGNAN matches or even exceeds the performance of the model-specific verification tools NIDHUGG and CBMC, as well as the performance of HERD, a CAT-compatible litmus testing tool. Compared to the unoptimized encoding, the speed-up is often more than two orders of magnitude.

Keywords: Weak memory models · CAT · Concurrency · BMC · SMT

1 Introduction

When developing concurrency libraries or operating system kernels, performance and scalability of the concurrency primitives is of paramount importance. These primitives rely on the synchronization guarantees of the underlying hardware and the programming language runtime environment. The formal semantics of these guarantees are often defined in terms of weak memory models. There is considerable interest in verification tools that take memory models into account [5,9,13,22].

A successful approach to formalizing weak memory models is CAT [11,12,16], a flexible specification language in which all memory models considered so far can be expressed succinctly. CAT, together with its accompanying tool HERD [4], has been used to formalize the semantics not only of assembly for x86/TSO, POWER, ARMv7 and ARMv8, but also high-level programming languages, such as C/C++, transactional memory extensions, and recently the LINUX kernel concurrency primitives [11,15,16,18,20,24,29]. This success indicates the need for universal verification tools that are not limited to a specific memory model.

We present DARTAGNAN [3], a bounded model checker that takes memory models as inputs. DARTAGNAN expects a concurrent program annotated with an assertion and a memory model for which the verification should be conducted. It verifies the assertion on those executions of the program that are valid under the given memory model and returns a counterexample execution if the verification fails. As is typical of BMC, the verification results hold relative to an unrolling bound [21]. The encoding phase, however, is new. Not only the program but also its semantics as defined by the CAT model are translated into an SMT formula.

Having to take into account the semantics quickly leads to large encodings. To overcome this problem, DARTAGNAN implements a novel *relation analysis*, which can be understood as a static analysis of the program semantics as defined by the memory model. More precisely, CAT defines the program semantics in terms of relations between the events that may occur in an execution. Depending on constraints over these relations, an execution is considered valid or invalid. Relation analysis determines the pairs of events that may influence a constraint of the memory model. Any remaining pair can be dropped from the encoding. The analysis is compatible with optimized fixpoint encodings presented in [27,28].

The second novelty is the support for advanced programming constructs. We redesigned DARTAGNAN's heap model, which now has pointers and arrays. Furthermore, we enriched the set of synchronization primitives, including read-modify-write and read-copy-update (RCU) instructions [26]. One motivation for this richer set of programming constructs is the Linux kernel memory model [15] that has recently been added to the kernel documentation [2]. This model has already been used by kernel developers to find bugs in and clarify details of the concurrency primitives. Since the model is expected to be refined with further development of the kernel, verification tools will need to quickly accommodate updates in the specification. So far, only HERD [4] has satisfied this requirement. Unfortunately, it is limited to fairly small programs (litmus tests). The present version of DARTAGNAN offers an alternative with substantially better performance.

We present experiments on a series of benchmarks consisting of 4751 LINUX litmus tests and 7 mutual exclusion algorithms executed on TSO, ARM, and LINUX. Despite the flexibility of taking memory models as inputs, DARTAGNAN's performance is comparable to CBMC [13] and considerably better than that of NIDHUGG [5,9]. Both are model-specific tools. Compared to the previous version of DARTAGNAN [28] and compared to HERD [4], we gain a speed-up of more than two orders of magnitude, thanks to the relation analysis.

Related Work. In terms of the verification task to be solved, the following tools are the closest to ours. CBMC [13] is a scalable bounded model checker supporting TSO, but not ARM. An earlier version also supported POWER.

NIDHUGG [5,9] is a stateless model checker supporting TSO, POWER, and a subset of ARMv7. It is excellent for programs with a small number of executions. RCMC [22] implements a stateless model checking algorithm targeting C11. We cannot directly benchmark against it because the source code of the tool is not yet publicly available, nor do we fully support C11. HERD [4] is the only tool aside from ours that takes a CAT memory model as input. HERD does not scale well to programs with a large number of executions, including some of the LINUX kernel tests. Other verification tasks (e.g., fence insertion to restore sequential consistency) are tackled by MEMORAX [6–8], OFFENCE [14], FENDER [23], DFENCE [25], and TRENCHER [19].

Relation Analysis on an Example. Consider the program (in the .litmus format) given to the left in the figure below. The assertion asks whether there is a reachable state with final values $EBX = 1, ECX = 0$. We analyze the program under the x86-TSO memory model shown below the program. The semantics of the program under TSO is a set of executions. An execution is a graph, similar to the one given below, where the nodes are events and the edges correspond to the relations defined by the memory model. Events are instances of instructions that access the shared memory: R (loads), W (stores, including initial stores), and M (the union of both). The atomic exchange instruction $xchg\,[x], EAX$ gives rise to a pair of read and write events related by a (dashed) rmw edge. Such reads and writes belong to the set A of atomic read-modify-write events.

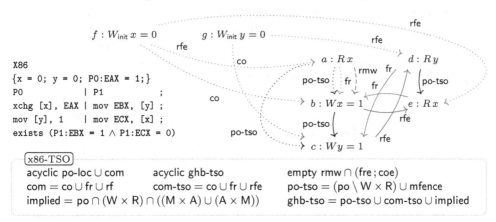

The relations rf, co, and fr model the communication of instructions via the shared memory (reading from a write, coherence, overwriting a read). Their restrictions rfe, coe, and fre denote (external) communication between instructions from different threads. Relation po is the program order within the same thread and po-loc is its restriction to events addressing the same memory location. Edges of mfence relate events separated by a fence. Further relations are derived from these base relations. To belong to the TSO semantics of the program, an execution has to satisfy the constraints of the memory model: empty rmw ∩ (fre ; coe), which enforces atomicity of read-modify-write events, and the two acyclicity constraints.

DARTAGNAN encodes the semantics of the given program under the given memory model into an SMT formula. The problem is that each edge (a, b) that may be present in a relation r gives rise to a variable $r(a, b)$. The goal of our relation analysis is to reduce the number of edges that need to be encoded. We illustrate this on the constraint acyclic ghb-tso. The graph next to the program shows the 14 (dotted and solid) edges which may contribute to the relation ghb-tso. Of those, only the 6 solid edges can occur in a cycle. The dotted edges can be dropped from the SMT encoding. Our relation analysis determines the solid edges—edges that may have an influence on a constraint of the memory model. Additionally, ghb-tso is a composition of various subrelations (e.g., po-tso or co ∪ fr) that also require encoding into SMT. Relation analysis applies to subrelations as well. Applied to all constraints, it reduces the number of encoded edges for all (sub)relations from 221 to 58.

2 Input, Functionality, and Implementation

DARTAGNAN has the ambition of being widely applicable, from assembly over operating system code written in C/C++ to lock-free data structures. The tool accepts programs in PPC, x86, AArch64 assembly, and a subset of C11, all limited to the subsets supported by Herd's .litmus format. It also reads our own .pts format with C11-like syntax [28]. We refer to global variables as memory locations and to local variables as registers. We support pointers, i.e., a register may hold the address of a location. Addresses and values are integers, and we allow the same arithmetic operations for addresses as for regular integer values. Different synchronization mechanisms are available, including variants of read-modify-write, various fences, and RCU instructions [26].

We support the assertion language of HERD. Assertions define inequalities over the values of registers and locations. They come with quantifiers over the reachable states that should satisfy the inequalities.

We use the CAT language [11,12,16] to define memory models. A memory model consists of named relations between events that may occur in an execution. Whether or not an execution is valid is defined by constraints over these relations:

$$\langle MM \rangle ::= \langle const \rangle \mid \langle rel \rangle \mid \langle MM \rangle \wedge \langle MM \rangle \qquad \langle r \rangle ::= \langle b \rangle \mid \langle name \rangle \mid \langle r \rangle \cup \langle r \rangle \mid \langle r \rangle \setminus \langle r \rangle$$

$$\langle const \rangle ::= acyclic(\langle r \rangle) \mid irreflexive(\langle r \rangle) \qquad \mid \langle r \rangle \cap \langle r \rangle \mid \langle r \rangle^{-1} \mid \langle r \rangle^{+} \mid \langle r \rangle^{*} \mid \langle r \rangle; \langle r \rangle$$

$$\mid empty(\langle r \rangle) \qquad \langle b \rangle ::= \text{id} \mid \text{int} \mid \text{ext} \mid \text{po} \mid \text{fencerel}(fence)$$

$$\langle rel \rangle ::= \langle name \rangle := \langle r \rangle \qquad \mid \text{rmw} \mid \text{ctrl} \mid \text{data} \mid \text{addr} \mid \text{loc} \mid \text{rf} \mid \text{co.}$$

CAT has a rich relational language, and we only show an excerpt above. So-called base relations $\langle b \rangle$ model the control flow, data flow, and synchronization constraints. The language provides intuitive operators to derive further relations. One may define relations recursively by referencing named relations. Their semantics is the least fixpoint.

DARTAGNAN is invoked with two inputs: the program, annotated with an assertion over the final states, and the memory model. There are two optional parameters related to the verification. The SMT encoding technique for recursive relations is defined by mode chosen between knastertarski (default) and idl (see below). The parameter alias, chosen between none and andersen (default), defines whether to use an alias analysis for our relation analysis (cf. Sect. 3).

Being a bounded model checker, DARTAGNAN computes an unrolled program with conditionals but no loops. It encodes this acyclic program together with the memory model into an SMT formula and passes it to the Z3 solver. The formula has the form $\psi_{prog} \wedge \psi_{assert} \wedge \psi_{mm}$, where ψ_{prog} encodes the program, ψ_{assert} the assertion, and ψ_{mm} the memory model. We elaborate on the encoding of the program and the memory model. The assertion is already given as a formula.

We model the heap by encoding a new memory location for each variable and a set of locations for each memory allocation of an array. Every location has an address encoded as an integer variable whose value is chosen by the solver. In an array, the locations are required to have consecutive addresses. Instances of instructions are modeled as events, most notably stores (to the shared memory) and loads (from the shared memory).

We encode relations by associating pairs of events with Boolean variables. Whether the pair (e_1, e_2) is contained in relation r is indicated by the variable $r(e_1, e_2)$. Encoding the relations $r_1 \cap r_2$, $r_1 \cup r_2$, $r_1 ; r_2$, $r_1 \setminus r_2$ and r^{-1} is straightforward [27]. For recursively defined and (reflexive and) transitive relations, DARTAGNAN lets the user choose between two methods for computing fixed points by setting the appropriate parameter. The integer-difference logic (IDL) method encodes a Kleene iteration by means of integer variables (one for each pair of events) representing the step in which the pair was added to the relation [27]. The Knaster-Tarski encoding simply looks for a post fixpoint. We have shown in [28] that this is sufficient for reachability analysis.

3 Relation Analysis

To optimize the size of the encoding (and the solving times), we found it essential to reduce the domains of the relations. We determine for each relation a static over-approximation of the pairs of events that may be in this relation. Even more, we restrict the relation to the set of pairs that may influence a constraint of the given memory model. These restricted sets are the *relation analysis* information (of the program relative to the memory model). Technically, we compute, for each relation r, two sets of event pairs, $M(r)$ and $A(r)$. The former contains so-called *may pairs*, pairs of events that may be in relation r. This does not yet take into account whether the may pairs occur in some constraint of the memory model. The *active pairs* $A(r)$ incorporate this information, and hence restrict the set of may pairs. As a consequence of the relation analysis, we only introduce Boolean variables $r(e_1, e_2)$ for the pairs $(e_1, e_2) \in A(r)$ to the SMT encoding.

The algorithm for constructing the may set and the active set is a fixpoint computation. What is unconventional is that the two sets propagate their information in different directions. For $A(r)$, the computation proceeds from the constraints and propagates information down the syntax tree of the CAT memory model. The sets $M(r)$ are computed bottom-up the syntax tree. Interestingly, in our implementation, we do not compute the full fixpoint but let the top-down process trigger the required bottom-up computation.

Both sets are computed as least solutions to a common system of inequalities. As we work over powerset lattices (relations are sets after all), the order of the system will be inclusion. We understand each set $M(r)$ and $A(r)$ as a variable, thereby identifying it with its least solution. To begin with, we give the definition for $A(r)$. In the base case, we have a relation r that occurs in a constraint of the memory model. The inequality is defined based on the shape of the constraint:

$$A(r) \supseteq M(r) \ (empty) \qquad A(r) \supseteq M(r) \cap id \ (irrefl.) \qquad A(r) \supseteq M(r) \cap M(r^+)^{-1} \ (acyclic).$$

For the emptiness constraint, all pairs of events that may be contained in the relation are relevant. If the constraint requires irreflexivity, what matters are the pairs (e, e). If the constraint requires acyclicity, we concentrate on the pairs (e_1, e_2), where (e_1, e_2) may be in relation r and (e_2, e_1) may be in relation r^+. Note how the definition of active pairs triggers the computation of may pairs.

If the relation in the constraint is a composed one, the following inequalities propagate the information about the active pairs down the syntax tree of the CAT memory model:

$$
\begin{aligned}
A(r_1) &\supseteq A(r)^{-1} & & \text{if } r = r_1^{-1} \\
A(r_1) &\supseteq A(r) & & \text{if } r = r_1 \cap r_2 \text{ or } r = r_1 \setminus r_2 \\
A(r_1) &\supseteq A(r) \cap M(r_1) & & \text{if } r = r_1 \cup r_2 \text{ or } r = r_2 \setminus r_1 \\
A(r_1) &\supseteq \{x \in M(r_1) \mid x; M(r_2) \cap A(r) \neq \emptyset\} & & \text{if } r = r_1; r_2 \\
A(r_1) &\supseteq \{x \in M(r_1) \mid M(r_1^*); x; M(r_1^*) \cap A(r) \neq \emptyset\} & & \text{if } r = r_1^+ \text{ or } r = r_1^*.
\end{aligned}
$$

The definition maintains the invariant $A(r) \subseteq M(r)$. If a pair (e_1, e_2) is relevant to relation $r = r_1^{-1}$, then (e_2, e_1) will be relevant to r_1. We do not have to intersect $A(r)^{-1}$ with $M(r)^{-1}$ because $A(r) \subseteq M(r)$ ensures $A(r)^{-1} \subseteq M(r)^{-1}$. We can avoid the intersection with the may pairs for the next case as well. There, $A(r) \subseteq M(r)$ holds by the invariant and $M(r) = M(r_1) \cap M(r_2)$ by definition (see below). For union and the other case of subtraction, the intersection with $M(r_1)$ is necessary. There are symmetric definitions for union and intersection for r_2. For a relation r_1 that occurs in a relational composition $r = r_1; r_2$, the pairs (e_1, e_3) become relevant if they may be composed with a pair (e_3, e_2) in r_2 to obtain a pair (e_1, e_2) relevant to r. Note that for r_2 we again need the may pairs. The definition for r_2 is similar. The definition for the (reflexive and) transitive closure follows the ideas for relational composition.

The definition of the may sets follows the syntax of the CAT memory model bottom-up. With $\oplus \in \{\cup, \cap, \, ;\}$ and $\otimes \in \{+, *, -1\}$, we have:

$$M(r_1 \oplus r_2) \supseteq M(r_1) \oplus M(r_2) \qquad M(r^\otimes) \supseteq M(r)^\otimes \qquad M(r_1 \setminus r_2) \supseteq M(r_1).$$

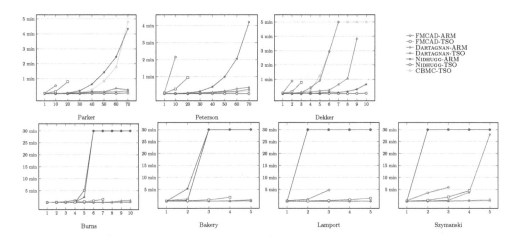

Fig. 1. Impact of the unrolling bound (x-axis) on the verification time (y-axis).

This simply executes the operator of the relation on the corresponding may sets. Subtraction ($r_1 \setminus r_2$) is the exception, it is not sound to over-approximate r_2.

At the bottom level, the may sets are determined by the base relations. They depend on the shape of the relations and the positions of the events in the control flow. The relations loc, co and rf are concerned with memory accesses. What makes it difficult to approximate these relations is our support for pointers and pointer arithmetic. Without further information, we have to conservatively assume that a memory event may access any address. To improve the precision of the may sets for loc, co, and rf, our fixpoint computation incorporates a *may-alias analysis*. We use a control-flow insensitive Andersen-style analysis [17]. It incurs only a small overhead and produces a close over-approximation of the may sets. The analysis returns[1] a set of pairs of memory events $PTS \subseteq (\mathbb{W} \cup \mathbb{R}) \times (\mathbb{W} \cup \mathbb{R})$ such that every pair of events outside PTS definitely accesses different addresses. Here, $\mathbb{W}$ are the store events in the program and $\mathbb{R}$ are the loads. Note that the analysis has to be control-flow insensitive as the given memory model may be very weak [10]. We have $M(\mathsf{loc}) \supseteq PTS$. Similarly, $M(\mathsf{co})$ and $M(\mathsf{rf})$ are defined by PTS restricted to $(\mathbb{W} \times \mathbb{W})$ and $(\mathbb{W} \times \mathbb{R})$, respectively.

We stress the importance of the alias analysis for our relation analysis: loc, co, and rf are frequently used as building blocks of composite relations. Excessive may sets will therefore negatively affect the over-approximations of virtually all relations in a memory model, and keep the overall encoding unnecessarily large.

Illustration. We illustrate the relation analysis on the example from the introduction. Consider constraint **acyclic ghb-tso**. The computation of the active set for the relation **ghb-tso** triggers the calculation of the may set, following the inequality $A(\mathsf{ghb\text{-}tso}) \supseteq M(\mathsf{ghb\text{-}tso}) \cap M(\mathsf{ghb\text{-}tso}^+)^{-1}$. The may set is the union of the may sets for the subrelations, shown by colored (dotted and solid) edges.

---

[1] This is a simplification, Andersen returns points-to sets, and we check by an intersection $PTS(r_1) \cap PTS(r_2)$ whether two registers may alias.

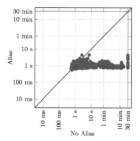
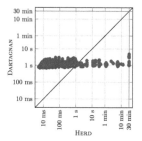

Fig. 2. Execution times (logarithmic scale) on LINUX kernel litmus tests: impact of alias analysis (left) and comparison against HERD (right).

The intersection yields the edges that may lie on cycles of ghb-tso. They are drawn in solid. These solid edges in $A(\text{ghb-tso})$ are propagated down to the sub-relations. For example, $A(\text{po-tso}) \supseteq A(\text{ghb-tso}) \cap M(\text{po-tso})$ yields the solid black edges.

4   Experiments

We compare DARTAGNAN to CBMC [13] and NIDHUGG [5,9], both model-specific tools, and to HERD [4,16] and the DARTAGNAN FMCAD-18 version [3,28] (without relation analysis), both taking CAT models as inputs. We also evaluate the impact of the alias analysis on the execution time.

Benchmarks. For CBMC, NIDHUGG, and the FMCAD-18 DARTAGNAN, we evaluate the performance on 7 mutual exclusion benchmarks executed on TSO (all tools) and a subset of ARMv7 (only NIDHUGG and DARTAGNAN). The results on POWER are similar to those on ARM and thus omitted. We excluded HERD from this experiment since it did not scale even for small unrolling bounds [28]. We set a 5 min timeout for Parker, Dekker, and Peterson as this is sufficient to show the trends in the runtimes, and a 30 min timeout for the remaining benchmarks. To compare against HERD, and to evaluate the impact of the alias analysis, we run 4751 LINUX kernel litmus tests (all tests from [1] without LINUX spinlocks). The tests contain kernel primitives, such as RCU, on the LINUX kernel model. We set a 30 min timeout.

Evaluation. The times for CBMC, NIDHUGG-ARM, and the FMCAD-2018 version of DARTAGNAN grow exponentially for Parker (see Fig. 1). The growth in CBMC and FMCAD-2018 is due to the explosion of the encoding. For the latter, the solver runs out of memory with unrolling bounds 20 (TSO) and 10 (ARM). For NIDHUGG-ARM, the tool explores many unnecessary executions. The verification times for NIDHUGG-TSO and the current version of DARTAGNAN grow linearly. The latter is due to the relation analysis. For Peterson, the results are similar except for CBMC, which matches DARTAGNAN's performance.

For Dekker, NIDHUGG outperforms both CBMC and DARTAGNAN. This is because the number of executions grows slowly compared to the explosion of the number of instructions. The executions in both memory models coincide, making the performance on ARM comparable to that on TSO for NIDHUGG. The difference is due to the optimal exploration in TSO, but not in ARM. Relation analysis has some impact on the performance (see FMCAD-2018 vs. DARTAGNAN), but the encoding size still grows faster than the number of executions.

The benchmarks Burns, Bakery, and Lamport demonstrate the opposite trend: the number of executions grows much faster than the size of the encoding. Here, CBMC and DARTAGNAN outperform NIDHUGG. Notice that for Burns, NIDHUGG performs better on ARM than on TSO with unrolling bound 5. This is counter-intuitive since one expects more executions on ARM. Although the number of executions coincide, the exploration time is higher on TSO due to a different search algorithm. For Szymanski, similar results hold except for DARTAGNAN-ARM where the encoding grows exponentially.

Figure 2 (left) shows the verification times for the current version of DARTAGNAN with and without alias analysis. The alias analysis results in a speed-up of more than two orders of magnitude in benchmarks with several threads accessing up to 18 locations. Figure 2 (right) compares the performance of DARTAGNAN against HERD. We used the Knaster-Tarski encoding and alias analysis since they yield the best performance. HERD outperforms DARTAGNAN on small test instances (less than 1 s execution time). This is due to the JVM startup time and the preprocessing costs of DARTAGNAN. However, on large benchmarks, HERD times out while DARTAGNAN takes less than 10 s.

References

1. Linux kernel litmus test suite. https://github.com/paulmckrcu/litmus
2. Linux Memory Model. https://github.com/torvalds/linux/tree/master/tools/memory-model
3. The Dat3M tool suite. https://github.com/hernanponcedeleon/Dat3M
4. The herdtools7 tool suite. https://github.com/herd/herdtools7
5. Abdulla, P.A., Aronis, S., Atig, M.F., Jonsson, B., Leonardsson, C., Sagonas, K.: Stateless model checking for TSO and PSO. In: Baier, C., Tinelli, C. (eds.) TACAS 2015. LNCS, vol. 9035, pp. 353–367. Springer, Heidelberg (2015). https://doi.org/10.1007/978-3-662-46681-0_28
6. Abdulla, P.A., Atig, M.F., Chen, Y.-F., Leonardsson, C., Rezine, A.: Automatic fence insertion in integer programs via predicate abstraction. In: Miné, A., Schmidt, D. (eds.) SAS 2012. LNCS, vol. 7460, pp. 164–180. Springer, Heidelberg (2012). https://doi.org/10.1007/978-3-642-33125-1_13
7. Abdulla, P.A., Atig, M.F., Chen, Y.-F., Leonardsson, C., Rezine, A.: Counter-example guided fence insertion under TSO. In: Flanagan, C., König, B. (eds.) TACAS 2012. LNCS, vol. 7214, pp. 204–219. Springer, Heidelberg (2012). https://doi.org/10.1007/978-3-642-28756-5_15
8. Abdulla, P.A., Atig, M.F., Chen, Y.-F., Leonardsson, C., Rezine, A.: MEMORAX, a precise and sound tool for automatic fence insertion under TSO. In: Piterman, N., Smolka, S.A. (eds.) TACAS 2013. LNCS, vol. 7795, pp. 530–536. Springer, Heidelberg (2013). https://doi.org/10.1007/978-3-642-36742-7_37

9. Abdulla, P.A., Atig, M.F., Jonsson, B., Leonardsson, C.: Stateless model checking for POWER. In: Chaudhuri, S., Farzan, A. (eds.) CAV 2016. LNCS, vol. 9780, pp. 134–156. Springer, Cham (2016). https://doi.org/10.1007/978-3-319-41540-6_8
10. Alglave, J., Kroening, D., Lugton, J., Nimal, V., Tautschnig, M.: Soundness of data flow analyses for weak memory models. In: Yang, H. (ed.) APLAS 2011. LNCS, vol. 7078, pp. 272–288. Springer, Heidelberg (2011). https://doi.org/10.1007/978-3-642-25318-8_21
11. Alglave, Jade: A Shared Memory Poetics. Thèse de doctorat, L'université Paris Denis Diderot (2010)
12. Alglave, J., Cousot, P., Maranget, L.: Syntax and semantics of the weak consistency model specification language CAT. CoRR, arXiv:1608.07531 (2016)
13. Alglave, J., Kroening, D., Tautschnig, M.: Partial orders for efficient bounded model checking of concurrent software. In: Sharygina, N., Veith, H. (eds.) CAV 2013. LNCS, vol. 8044, pp. 141–157. Springer, Heidelberg (2013). https://doi.org/10.1007/978-3-642-39799-8_9
14. Alglave, J., Maranget, L.: Stability in weak memory models. In: Gopalakrishnan, G., Qadeer, S. (eds.) CAV 2011. LNCS, vol. 6806, pp. 50–66. Springer, Heidelberg (2011). https://doi.org/10.1007/978-3-642-22110-1_6
15. Alglave, J., Maranget, L., McKenney, P.E., Parri, A., Stern, A.S.: Frightening small children and disconcerting grown-ups: Concurrency in the linux kernel. In: ASPLOS, pp. 405–418. ACM (2018)
16. Alglave, J., Maranget, L., Tautschnig, M.: Herding cats: Modelling, simulation, testing, and data mining for weak memory. ACM Trans. Program. Lang. Syst **36**(2), 7:1–7:74 (2014)
17. Andersen, L.O.: Program Analysis and Specialization for the C Programming Language. PhD thesis, University of Copenhagen (1994)
18. Batty, M., Donaldson, A.F., Wickerson, J.: Overhauling SC atomics in C11 and OpenCL. In: POPL, pp. 634–648. ACM (2016)
19. Bouajjani, A., Derevenetc, E., Meyer, R.: Checking and enforcing robustness against TSO. In: Felleisen, M., Gardner, P. (eds.) ESOP 2013. LNCS, vol. 7792, pp. 533–553. Springer, Heidelberg (2013). https://doi.org/10.1007/978-3-642-37036-6_29
20. Chong, N., Sorensen, T., Wickerson, J.: The semantics of transactions and weak memory in x86, Power, ARM, and C++. In: PLDI, pp. 211–225. ACM (2018)
21. Clarke, E.M., Biere, A., Raimi, R., Zhu, Y.: Bounded model checking using satisfiability solving. Form. Methods Syst. Des. **19**(1), 7–34 (2001)
22. Kokologiannakis, M., Lahav, O., Sagonas, K., Vafeiadis, V.: Effective stateless model checking for C/C++ concurrency. PACMPL **2**(POPL), 17:1–7:32 (2018)
23. Kuperstein, M., Vechev, M.T., Yahav, E.: Automatic inference of memory fences. SIGACT News **43**(2), 108–123 (2012)
24. Lahav, O., Vafeiadis, V., Kang, J., Hur, C.-H., Kil, Dreyer, D.: Repairing sequential consistency in C/C++11. In: PLDI, pp. 618–632. ACM (2017)
25. Liu, F., Nedev, N., Prisadnikov, N., Vechev, M.T., Yahav, E.: Dynamic synthesis for relaxed memory models. In: PLDI, pp. 429–440. ACM (2012)
26. McKenney, P.E., Slingwine, J.: Read-copy update: Using execution history to solve concurrency problems. In: Parallel and Distributed Computing and Systems, pp 509–518 (1998)
27. Ponce-de-León, H., Furbach, F., Heljanko, K., Meyer, R.: Portability analysis for weak memory models PORTHOS: **One** *Tool* **for all** *Models*. In: Ranzato, F. (ed.) SAS 2017. LNCS, vol. 10422, pp. 299–320. Springer, Cham (2017). https://doi.org/10.1007/978-3-319-66706-5_15

28. Ponce de León, H., Furbach, F., Heljanko, K., Meyer, R.: BMC with memory models as modules. In: FMCAD, pp. 1–9. IEEE (2018)
29. Pulte, C., Flur, S., Deacon, W., French, J., Sarkar, S., Sewell, P.: Simplifying ARM concurrency: multicopy-atomic axiomatic and operational models for ARMv8. PACMPL **2**(POPL), 19:1–19:29 (2018)

14

Flexible Computational Pipelines for Robust Abstraction-Based Control Synthesis

Eric S. Kim[(✉)] [iD], Murat Arcak [iD], and Sanjit A. Seshia [iD]

UC Berkeley, Berkeley, CA, USA
{eskim,arcak,sseshia}@eecs.berkeley.edu

Abstract. Successfully synthesizing controllers for complex dynamical systems and specifications often requires leveraging domain knowledge as well as making difficult computational or mathematical tradeoffs. This paper presents a flexible and extensible framework for constructing robust control synthesis algorithms and applies this to the traditional abstraction-based control synthesis pipeline. It is grounded in the theory of relational interfaces and provides a principled methodology to seamlessly combine different techniques (such as dynamic precision grids, refining abstractions while synthesizing, or decomposed control predecessors) or create custom procedures to exploit an application's intrinsic structural properties. A Dubins vehicle is used as a motivating example to showcase memory and runtime improvements.

Keywords: Control synthesis · Finite abstraction · Relational interface

1 Introduction

A control synthesizer's high level goal is to automatically construct control software that enables a closed loop system to satisfy a desired specification. A vast and rich literature contains results that mathematically characterize solutions to different classes of problems and specifications, such as the Hamilton-Jacobi-Isaacs PDE for differential games [3], Lyapunov theory for stabilization [8], and fixed-points for temporal logic specifications [11,17]. While many control synthesis problems have elegant mathematical solutions, there is often a gap between a solution's theoretical characterization and the algorithms used to compute it. What data structures are used to represent the dynamics and constraints? What operations should those data structures support? How should the control synthesis algorithm be structured? Implementing solutions to the questions above can require substantial time. This problem is especially critical for computationally challenging problems, where it is often necessary to let the user *rapidly* identify and exploit structure through analysis or experimentation.

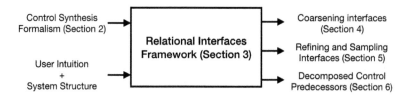

Fig. 1. By expressing many different techniques within a common framework, users are able to rapidly develop methods to exploit system structure in controller synthesis.

1.1 Bottlenecks in Abstraction-Based Control Synthesis

This paper's goal is to enable a framework to develop extensible tools for robust controller synthesis. It was inspired in part by computational bottlenecks encountered in control synthesizers that construct finite abstractions of continuous systems, which we use as a target use case. A traditional abstraction-based control synthesis pipeline consists of three distinct stages:

1. Abstracting the continuous state system into a finite automaton whose underlying transitions faithfully mimic the original dynamics [21,23].
2. Synthesizing a discrete controller by leveraging data structures and symbolic reasoning algorithms to mitigate combinatorial state explosion.
3. Refining the discrete controller into a continuous one. Feasibility of this step is ensured through the abstraction step.

This pipeline appears in tools PESSOA [12] and SCOTS [19], which can exhibit acute computational bottlenecks for high dimensional and nonlinear system dynamics. A common method to mitigate these bottlenecks is to exploit a specific dynamical system's topological and algebraic properties. In MASCOT [7] and CoSyMA [14], multi-scale grids and hierarchical models capture notions of state-space locality. One could incrementally construct an abstraction of the system dynamics while performing the control synthesis step [10,15] as implemented in tools ROCS [9] and ARCS [4]. The abstraction overhead can also be reduced by representing systems as a collection of components composed in parallel [6,13]. These have been developed in isolation and were not previously interoperable.

1.2 Methodology

Figure 1 depicts this paper's methodology and organization. The existing control synthesis formalism does not readily lend itself to algorithmic modifications that reflect and exploit structural properties in the system and specification. We use the theory of relational interfaces [22] as a foundation and augment it to express control synthesis pipelines. Interfaces are used to represent both system models and constraints. A small collection of atomic operators manipulates interfaces and is powerful enough to reconstruct many existing control synthesis pipelines.

One may also add new composite operators to encode desirable heuristics that exploit structural properties in the system and specifications. The last three sections encode the techniques for abstraction-based control synthesis from Sect. 1.1 within the relational interfaces framework. By deliberately deconstructing those techniques, then reconstructing them within a compositional framework it was possible to identify implicit or unnecessary assumptions then generalize or remove them. It also makes the aforementioned techniques interoperable amongst themselves as well as future techniques.

Interfaces come equipped with a refinement partial order that formalizes when one interface abstracts another. This paper focuses on preserving the refinement relation and sufficient conditions to refine discrete controllers back to concrete ones. Additional guarantees regarding completeness, termination, precision, or decomposability can be encoded, but impose additional requirements on the control synthesis algorithm and are beyond the scope of this paper.

1.3 Contributions

To our knowledge, the application of relational interfaces to robust abstraction-based control synthesis is new. The framework's building blocks consist of a collection of small, well understood operators that are nonetheless powerful enough to express many prior techniques. Encoding these techniques as relational interface operations forced us to simplify, formalize, or remove implicit assumptions in existing tools. The framework also exhibits numerous desirable features.

1. It enables compositional tools for control synthesis by leveraging a theoretical foundation with compositionality built into it. This paper showcases a principled methodology to seamlessly combine the methods in Sect. 1.1, as well as construct new techniques.
2. It enables a declarative approach to control synthesis by enforcing a strict separation between the high level algorithm from its low level implementation. We rely on the availability of an underlying data structure to encode and manipulate predicates. Low level predicate operations, while powerful, make it easy to inadvertently violate the refinement property. Conforming to the relational interface operations minimizes this danger.

This paper's first half is domain agnostic and applicable to general robust control synthesis problems. The second half applies those insights to the finite abstraction approach to control synthesis. A smaller Dubins vehicle example is used to showcase and evaluate different techniques and their computational gains, compared to the unoptimized problem. In an extended version of this paper available at [1], a 6D lunar lander example leverages all techniques in this paper and introduces a few new ones.

1.4 Notation

Let $=$ be an *assertion* that two objects are mathematically equivalent; as a special case '$\equiv$' is used when those two objects are sets. In contrast, the operator '$==$' *checks* whether two objects are equivalent, returning true if they are and false otherwise. A special instance of '$==$' is logical equivalence '$\Leftrightarrow$'.

Variables are denoted by lower case letters. Each variable v is associated with a domain of values $\mathcal{D}(v)$ that is analogous to the variable's type. A composite variable is a set of variables and is analogous to a bundle of wrapped wires. From a collection of variables $v_1, \ldots, v_M$ a composite variable v can be constructed by taking the union $v \equiv v_1 \cup \ldots \cup v_M$ and the domain $\mathcal{D}(v) \equiv \prod_{i=1}^{M} \mathcal{D}(v_i)$. Note that the variables $v_1, \ldots, v_M$ above may themselves be composite. As an example if v is associated with a M-dimensional Euclidean space $\mathbb{R}^M$, then it is a composite variable that can be broken apart into a collection of atomic variables $v_1, \ldots, v_M$ where $\mathcal{D}(v_i) \equiv \mathbb{R}$ for all $i \in \{1, \ldots, M\}$. The technical results herein do not distinguish between composite and atomic variables.

Predicates are functions that map variable assignments to a Boolean value. Predicates that stand in for expressions/formulas are denoted with capital letters. Predicates P and Q are logically equivalent (denoted by $P \Leftrightarrow Q$) if and only if $P \Rightarrow Q$ and $Q \Rightarrow P$ are true for all variable assignments. The universal and existential quantifiers $\forall$ and $\exists$ eliminate variables and yield new predicates. Predicates $\exists w P$ and $\forall w P$ do not depend on w. If w is a composite variable $w \equiv w_1 \cup \ldots \cup w_N$ then $\exists w P$ is simply a shorthand for $\exists w_1 \ldots \exists w_N P$.

2 Control Synthesis for a Motivating Example

As a simple, instructive example consider a planar Dubins vehicle that is tasked with reaching a desired location. Let $x = \{p_x, p_y, \theta\}$ be the collection of state variables, $u = \{v, \omega\}$ be a collection input variables to be controlled, $x^+ = \{p_x^+, p_y^+, \theta^+\}$ represent state variables at a subsequent time step, and $L = 1.4$ be a constant representing the vehicle length. The constraints

$$p_x^+ == p_x + v\cos(\theta) \tag{F_x}$$

$$p_y^+ == p_y + v\sin(\theta) \tag{F_y}$$

$$\theta^+ == \theta + \frac{v}{L}\sin(\omega) \tag{F_θ}$$

characterize the discrete time dynamics. The continuous state domain is $\mathcal{D}(x) \equiv [-2,2] \times [-2,2] \times [-\pi,\pi)$, where the last component is periodic so $-\pi$ and π are identical values. The input domains are $\mathcal{D}(v) \equiv \{0.25, 0.5\}$ and $\mathcal{D}(\omega) \equiv \{-1.5, 0, 1.5\}$

Let predicate $F = F_x \wedge F_y \wedge F_\theta$ represent the monolithic system dynamics. Predicate T depends only on x and represents the target set $[-0.4, 0.4] \times [-0.4, 0.4] \times [-\pi, \pi)$, encoding that the vehicle's position must reach a square with any orientation. Let Z be a predicate that depends on variable x^+ that encodes a collection of states at a future time step. Equation (1) characterizes the robust controlled predecessor, which takes Z and computes the set of states from which there exists a non-blocking assignment to u that guarantees x^+ will satisfy Z, despite any non-determinism contained in F. The term $\exists x^+ F$ prevents state-control pairs from blocking, while $\forall x^+ (F \Rightarrow Z)$ encodes the state-control pairs that guarantee satisfaction of Z.

$$\texttt{cpre}(F, Z) = \exists u (\exists x^+ F \wedge \forall x^+ (F \Rightarrow Z)). \tag{1}$$

The controlled predecessor is used to solve safety and reach games. We can solve for a region for which the target T (respectively, safe set S) can be reached (made invariant) via an iteration of an appropriate reach (safe) operator. Both iterations are given by:

Reach Iter: $Z_0 = \bot$ $Z_{i+1} = \text{reach}(F, Z_i, T) = \text{cpre}(F, Z_i) \vee T.$ (2)

Safety Iter: $Z_0 = S$ $Z_{i+1} = \text{safe}(F, Z_i, S) = \text{cpre}(F, Z_i) \wedge S.$ (3)

The above iterations are not guaranteed to reach a fixed point in a finite number of iterations, except under certain technical conditions [21]. Figure 2 depicts an approximate region where the controller can force the Dubins vehicle to enter T. We showcase different improvements relative to a base line script used to generate Fig. 2. A toolbox that adopts this paper's framework is being actively developed and is open sourced at [2]. It is written in python 3.6 and uses the dd package as an interface to CUDD [20], a library in C/C++ for constructing and manipulat-

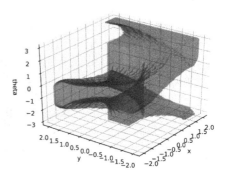

Fig. 2. Approximate solution to the Dubins vehicle reach game visualized as a subset of the state space.

ing binary decision diagrams (BDD). All experiments were run on a single core of a 2013 Macbook Pro with 2.4 GHz Intel Core i7 and 8 GB of RAM.

The following section uses relational interfaces to represent the controlled predecessor $\text{cpre}(\cdot)$ and iterations (2) and (3) as a computational pipeline. Subsequent sections show how modifying this pipeline leads to favorable theoretical properties and computational gains.

3   Relational Interfaces

Relational interfaces are predicates augmented with annotations about each variable's role as an input or output[1]. They abstract away a component's internal implementation and only encode an input-output relation.

Definition 1 (Relational Interface [22]). *An interface $M(i, o)$ consists of a predicate M over a set of input variables i and output variables o.*

For an interface $M(i, o)$, we call (i, o) its input-output *signature*. An interface is a sink if it contains no outputs and has signature like $(i, \varnothing)$, and a source if it contains no inputs like $(\varnothing, o)$. Sinks and source interfaces can be interpreted as sets whereas input-output interfaces are relations. Interfaces encode relations through their predicates and can capture features such as non-deterministic outputs or

---

[1] Relational interfaces closely resemble assume-guarantee contracts [16]; we opt to use relational interfaces because inputs and outputs play a more prominent role.

blocking (i.e., disallowed, error) inputs. A system blocks for an input assignment if there does not exist a corresponding output assignment that satisfies the interface relation. Blocking is a critical property used to declare *requirements*; sink interfaces impose constraints by modeling constrain violations as blocking inputs. Outputs on the other hand exhibit non-determinism, which is treated as an *adversary*. When one interface's outputs are connected to another's inputs, the outputs seek to cause blocking whenever possible.

3.1   Atomic and Composite Operators

Operators are used to manipulate interfaces by taking interfaces and variables as inputs and yielding another interface. We will show how the controlled predecessor $\texttt{cpre}(\cdot)$ in (1) can be constructed by composing operators appearing in [22] and one additional one. The first, output hiding, removes interface outputs.

Definition 2 (Output Hiding [22]). *Output hiding operator* $\texttt{ohide}(w, F)$ *over interface* $F(i, o)$ *and outputs* w *yields an interface with signature* $(i, o \setminus w)$.

$$\texttt{ohide}(w, F) = \exists w F \qquad (4)$$

Existentially quantifying out w ensures that the input-output behavior over the unhidden variables is still consistent with potential assignments to w. The operator $\texttt{nb}(\cdot)$ is a special variant of $\texttt{ohide}(\cdot)$ that hides all outputs, yielding a sink encoding all non-blocking inputs to the original interface.

Definition 3 (Nonblocking Inputs Sink). *Given an interface* $F(i, o)$, *the nonblocking operation* $\texttt{nb}(F)$ *yields a sink interface with signature* $(i, \varnothing)$ *and predicate* $\texttt{nb}(F) = \exists o F$. *If* $F(i, \varnothing)$ *is a sink interface, then* $\texttt{nb}(F) = F$ *yields itself. If* $F(\varnothing, o)$ *is a source interface, then* $\texttt{nb}(F) = \bot$ *if and only if* $F \Leftrightarrow \bot$; *otherwise* $\texttt{nb}(F) = \top$.

The interface composition operator takes multiple interfaces and "collapses" them into a single input-output interface. It can be viewed as a generalization of function composition in the special case where each interface encodes a total function (i.e., deterministic output and inputs never block).

Definition 4 (Interface Composition [22]). *Let* $F_1(i_1, o_1)$ *and* $F_2(i_2, o_2)$ *be interfaces with disjoint output variables* $o_1 \cap o_2 \equiv \varnothing$ *and* $i_1 \cap o_2 \equiv \varnothing$ *which signifies that* F_2's *outputs may not be fed back into* F_1's *inputs. Define new composite variables*

$$io_{12} \equiv o_1 \cap i_2 \qquad (5)$$

$$i_{12} \equiv (i_1 \cup i_2) \setminus io_{12} \qquad (6)$$

$$o_{12} \equiv o_1 \cup o_2. \qquad (7)$$

Composition $\texttt{comp}(F_1, F_2)$ *is an interface with signature* (i_{12}, o_{12}) *and predicate*

$$F_1 \wedge F_2 \wedge \forall o_{12}(F_1 \Rightarrow \texttt{nb}(F_2)). \qquad (8)$$

Interface subscripts may be swapped if instead F_2's *outputs are fed into* F_1.

Interfaces F_1 and F_2 are composed in parallel if $io_{21} \equiv \varnothing$ holds in addition to $io_{12} \equiv \varnothing$. Equation (8) under parallel composition reduces to $F_1 \wedge F_2$ (Lemma 6.4 in [22]) and $\texttt{comp}(\cdot)$ is commutative and associative. If $io_{12} \not\equiv \varnothing$, then they are composed in series and the composition operator is only associative. Any acyclic interconnection can be composed into a single interface by systematically applying Definition 4's binary composition operator. Non-deterministic outputs are interpreted to be *adversarial*. Series composition of interfaces has a built-in notion of robustness to account for F_1's non-deterministic outputs and blocking inputs to F_2 over the shared variables io_{12}. The term $\forall o_{12}(F_1 \Rightarrow \texttt{nb}(F_2))$ in Eq. (8) is a predicate over the composition's input set i_{12}. It ensures that if a potential output of F_1 may cause F_2 to block, then $\texttt{comp}(F_1, F_2)$ must preemptively block.

The final atomic operator is input hiding, which may only be applied to sinks. If the sink is viewed as a constraint, an input variable is "hidden" by an angelic environment that chooses an input assignment to satisfy the constraint. This operator is analogous to projecting a set into a lower dimensional space.

Definition 5 (Hiding Sink Inputs). *Input hiding operator* $\texttt{ihide}(w, F)$ *over sink interface* $F(i, \varnothing)$ *and inputs* w *yields an interface with signature* $(i \setminus w, \varnothing)$.

$$\texttt{ihide}(w, F) = \exists w F \qquad (9)$$

Unlike the composition and output hiding operators, this operator is not included in the standard theory of relational interfaces [22] and was added to encode a controller predecessor introduced subsequently in Eq. (10).

3.2 Constructing Control Synthesis Pipelines

The robust controlled predecessor (1) can be expressed through operator composition.

Proposition 1. *The controlled predecessor operator* (10) *yields a sink interface with signature* $(x, \varnothing)$ *and predicate equivalent to the predicate in* (1).

$$\texttt{cpre}(F, Z) = \texttt{ihide}(u, \texttt{ohide}(x^+, \texttt{comp}(F, Z))). \qquad (10)$$

The simple proof is provided in the extended version at [1]. Proposition 1 signifies that controlled predecessors can be interpreted as an instance of robust composition of interfaces, followed by variable hiding. It can be shown that $\texttt{safe}(F, Z, S) = \texttt{comp}(\texttt{cpre}(F, Z), S)$ because $S(x, \varnothing)$ and $\texttt{cpre}(F, Z)$ would be composed in parallel.[2] Figure. 3 shows a visualization of the safety game's fixed point iteration from the point of view of relational interfaces. Starting from the right-most sink interface S (equivalent to Z_0) the iteration (3) constructs a sequence of sink interfaces $Z_1, Z_2, \ldots$ encoding relevant subsets of the state space. The numerous $S(x, \varnothing)$ interfaces impose constraints and can be interpreted as monitors that raise errors if the safety constraint is violated.

---

[2] Disjunctions over sinks are required to encode $\texttt{reach}(\cdot)$. This will be enabled by the shared refinement operator defined in Definition 10.

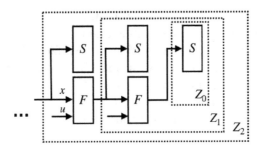

Fig. 3. Safety control synthesis iteration (3) depicted as a sequence of sink interfaces.

3.3 Modifying the Control Synthesis Pipeline

Equation (10)'s definition of cpre($\cdot$) is oblivious to the domains of variables x, u, and x^+. This generality is useful for describing a problem and serving as a blank template. Whenever problem structure exists, pipeline modifications refine the general algorithm into a form that reflects the specific problem instance. They also allow a user to inject implicit preferences into a problem and reduce computational bottlenecks or to refine a solution. The subsequent sections apply this philosophy to the abstraction-based control techniques from Sect. 1.1:

- Sect. 4: Coarsening interfaces reduces the computational complexity of a problem by throwing away fine grain information. The synthesis result is conservative but the degree of conservatism can be modified.
- Sect. 5: Refining interfaces decreases result conservatism. Refinement in combination with coarsening allows one to dynamically modulate the complexity of the problem as a function of multiple criteria such as the result granularity or minimizing computational resources.
- Sect. 6: If the dynamics or specifications are decomposable then the control predecessor operator can be broken apart to refect that decomposition.

These sections do more than simply reconstruct existing techniques in the language of relational interfaces. They uncover some implicit assumptions in existing tools and either remove them or make them explicit. Minimizing the number of assumptions ensures applicability to a diverse collection of systems and specifications and compatibility with future algorithmic modifications.

4   Interface Abstraction via Quantization

A key motivator behind abstraction-based control synthesis is that computing the game iterations from Eqs. (2) and (3) exactly is often intractable for high-dimensional nonlinear dynamics. Termination is also not guaranteed. Quantizing (or "abstracting") continuous interfaces into a finite counterpart ensures that each predicate operation of the game terminates in finite time but at the cost of the solution's precision. Finer quantization incurs a smaller loss of precision but can cause the memory and computational requirements to store and manipulate the symbolic representation to exceed machine resources.

This section first introduces the notion of interface abstraction as a refinement relation. We define the notion of a quantizer and show how it is a simple generalization of many existing quantizers in the abstraction-based control literature. Finally, we show how one can inject these quantizers anywhere in the control synthesis pipeline to reduce computational bottlenecks.

4.1   Theory of Abstract Interfaces

While a controller synthesis algorithm can analyze a simpler model of the dynamics, the results have no meaning unless they can be extrapolated back to the original system dynamics. The following interface refinement condition formalizes a condition when this extrapolation can occur.

Definition 6 (Interface Refinement [22]). *Let $F(i, o)$ and $\hat{F}(\hat{i}, \hat{o})$ be interfaces. $\hat{F}$ is an abstraction of F if and only if $i \equiv \hat{i}$, $o \equiv \hat{o}$, and*

$$nb(\hat{F}) \Rightarrow nb(F) \tag{11}$$

$$\left(nb(\hat{F}) \wedge F\right) \Rightarrow \hat{F} \tag{12}$$

are valid formulas. This relationship is denoted by $\hat{F} \preceq F$.

Definition 6 imposes two main requirements between a concrete and abstract interface. Equation (11) encodes the condition where if $\hat{F}$ accepts an input, then F must also accept it; that is, the abstract component is more aggressive with rejecting invalid inputs. Second, if both systems accept the input then the abstract output set is a superset of the concrete function's output set. The abstract interface is a conservative representation of the concrete interface because the abstraction accepts fewer inputs and exhibits more non-deterministic outputs. If both the interfaces are sink interfaces, then $\hat{F} \preceq F$ reduces down to $\hat{F} \subseteq F$ when $F, \hat{F}$ are interpreted as sets. If both are source interfaces then the set containment direction is flipped and $\hat{F} \preceq F$ reduces down to $F \subseteq \hat{F}$.

The refinement relation satisfies the required reflexivity, transitivity, and antisymmetry properties to be a partial order [22] and is depicted in Fig. 4. This order has a bottom element $\bot$ which is a universal abstraction. Conveniently, the bottom element $\bot$ signifies both boolean false and the bottom of the partial order. This interface blocks for every potential input. In contrast, Boolean $\top$ plays no special role in the partial order. While $\top$ exhibits totally non-deterministic outputs, it also accepts inputs. A blocking input is considered "worse" than non-deterministic outputs in the refinement order. The refinement relation $\preceq$ encodes a direction of conservatism such that any reasoning done over the abstract models is sound and can be generalized to the concrete model.

Theorem 1 (Informal Substitutability Result [22]). *For any input that is allowed for the abstract model, the output behaviors exhibited by an abstract model contains the output behaviors exhibited by the concrete model.*

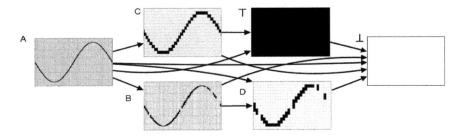

Fig. 4. Example depiction of the refinement partial order. Each small plot on the depicts input-output pairs that satisfy an interface's predicate. Inputs (outputs) vary along the horizontal (vertical) axis. Because B blocks on some inputs but A accepts all inputs $B \preceq A$. Interface C exhibits more output non-determinism than A so $C \preceq A$. Similarly $D \preceq B$, $D \preceq C$, $\top \preceq C$, etc. Note that B and C are incomparable because C exhibits more output non-determinism and B blocks for more inputs. The false interface $\bot$ is a universal abstraction, while $\top$ is incomparable with B and D.

If a property on outputs has been established for an abstract interface, then it still holds if the abstract interface is replaced with the concrete one. Informally, the abstract interface is more conservative so if a property holds with the abstraction then it must also hold for the true system. All aforementioned interface operators preserve the properties of the refinement relation of Definition 6, in the sense that they are monotone with respect to the refinement partial order.

Theorem 2 (Composition Preserves Refinement [22]). *Let* $\hat{A} \preceq A$ *and* $\hat{B} \preceq B$. *If the composition is well defined, then* $\texttt{comp}(\hat{A}, \hat{B}) \preceq \texttt{comp}(A, B)$.

Theorem 3 (Output Hiding Preserves Refinement [22]). *If* $A \preceq B$, *then* $\texttt{ohide}(w, A) \preceq \texttt{ohide}(w, B)$ *for any variable* w.

Theorem 4 (Input Hiding Preserves Refinement). *If* A, B *are both sink interfaces and* $A \preceq B$, *then* $\texttt{ihide}(w, A) \preceq \texttt{ihide}(w, B)$ *for any variable* w.

Proofs for Theorems 2 and 3 are provided in [22]. Theorem 4's proof is simple and is omitted. One can think of using interface composition and variable hiding to horizontally (with respect to the refinement order) navigate the space of all interfaces. The synthesis pipeline encodes one navigated path and monotonicity of these operators yields guarantees about the path's end point. Composite operators such as $\texttt{cpre}(\cdot)$ chain together multiple incremental steps. Furthermore since the composition of monotone operators is itself a monotone operator, any composite constructed from these parts is also monotone. In contrast, the coarsening and refinement operators introduced later in Definitions 8 and 10 respectively are used to move vertically and construct abstractions. The "direction" of new composite operators can easily be established through simple reasoning about the cumulative directions of their constituent operators.

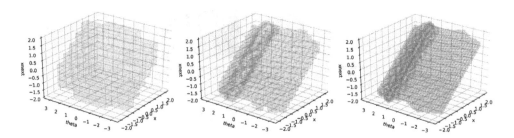

Fig. 5. Coarsening of the F_x interface to $2^3, 2^4$ and 2^5 bins along each dimension for a fixed v assignment. Interfaces are coarsened within milliseconds for BDDs but the runtime depends on the finite abstraction's data structure representation.

4.2 Dynamically Coarsening Interfaces

In practice, the sequence of interfaces Z_i generated during synthesis grows in complexity. This occurs even if the dynamics F and the target/safe sets have compact representations (i.e., fewer nodes if using BDDs). Coarsening F and Z_i combats this growth in complexity by effectively reducing the amount of information sent between iterations of the fixed point procedure.

Spatial discretization or *coarsening* is achieved by use of a quantizer interface that implicitly aggregates points in a space into a partition or cover.

Definition 7. *A quantizer $Q(i,o)$ is any interface that abstracts the identity interface $(i == o)$ associated with the signature (i,o).*

Quantizers decrease the complexity of the system representation and make synthesis more computationally tractable. A coarsening operator abstracts an interface by connecting it in series with a quantizer. Coarsening reduces the number of non-blocking inputs and increases the output non-determinism.

Definition 8 (Input/Output Coarsening). *Given an interface $F(i,o)$ and input quantizer $Q(\hat{i}, i)$, input coarsening yields an interface with signature $(\hat{i}, o)$.*

$$icoarsen(F, Q(\hat{i}, i)) = ohide(i, comp(Q(\hat{i}, i), F)) \tag{13}$$

Similarly, given an output quantizer $Q(o, \hat{o})$, output coarsening yields an interface with signature $(i, \hat{o})$.

$$ocoarsen(F, Q(o, \hat{o})) = ohide(o, comp(F, Q(o, \hat{o}))) \tag{14}$$

Figure 5 depicts how coarsening reduces the information required to encode a finite interface. It leverages a variable precision quantizer, whose implementation is described in the extended version at [1].

The corollary below shows that quantizers can be seamlessly integrated into the synthesis pipeline while preserving the refinement order. It readily follows from Theorems 2, 3, and the quantizer definition.

Corollary 1. *Input and output coarsening operations (13) and (14) are monotone operations with respect to the interface refinement order $\preceq$.*

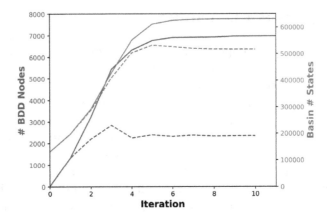

Fig. 6. Number of BDD nodes (red) and number of states in reach basin (blue) with respect to the reach game iteration with a greedy quantization. The solid lines result from the unmodified game with no coarsening heuristic. The dashed lines result from greedy coarsening whenever the winning region exceeds 3000 BDD nodes. (Color figure online)

It is difficult to know a priori where a specific problem instance lies along the spectrum between mathematical precision and computational efficiency. It is then desirable to coarsen dynamically in response to runtime conditions rather than statically beforehand. Coarsening heuristics for reach games include:

- *Downsampling with progress* [7]: Initially use coarser system dynamics to rapidly identify a coarse reach basin. Finer dynamics are used to construct a more granular set whenever the coarse iteration "stalls". In [7] only the Z_i are coarsened during synthesis. We enable the dynamics F to be as well.
- *Greedy quantization*: Selectively coarsening along certain dimensions by checking at runtime which dimension, when coarsened, would cause Z_i to shrink the least. This reward function can be leveraged in practice because coarsening is computationally cheaper than composition. For BDDs, the winning region can be coarsened until the number of nodes reduces below a desired threshold. Figure 6 shows this heuristic being applied to reduce memory usage at the expense of answer fidelity. A fixed point is not guaranteed as long as quantizers can be dynamically inserted into the synthesis pipeline, but is once quantizers are always inserted at a fixed precision.

The most common quantizer in the literature never blocks and only increases non-determinism (such quantizers are called "strict" in [18,19]). If a quantizer is interpreted as a partition or cover, this requirement means that the union must be equal to an entire space. Definition 7 relaxes that requirement so the union can be a subset instead. It also hints at other variants such as interfaces that don't increase output non-determinism but instead block for more inputs.

5 Refining System Dynamics

Shared refinement [22] is an operation that takes two interfaces and merges them into a single interface. In contrast to coarsening, it makes interfaces more precise. Many tools construct system abstractions by starting from the universal abstraction $\bot$, then iteratively refining it with a collection of smaller interfaces that represent input-output samples. This approach is especially useful if the canonical concrete system is a black box function, Simulink model, or source code file. These representations do not readily lend themselves to the predicate operations or be coarsened directly. We will describe later how other tools implement a restrictive form of refinement that introduces unnecessary dependencies.

Interfaces can be successfully merged whenever they do not contain contradictory information. The shared refinability condition below formalizes when such a contradiction does not exist.

Definition 9 (Shared Refinability [22]). *Interfaces $F_1(i, o)$ and $F_2(i, o)$ with identical signatures are shared refinable if*

$$(nb(F_1) \wedge nb(F_2)) \Rightarrow \exists o(F_1 \wedge F_2) \tag{15}$$

For any inputs that do not block for all interfaces, the corresponding output sets must have a non-empty intersection. If multiple shared refinable interfaces, then they can be combined into a single one that encapsulates all of their information.

Definition 10 (Shared Refinement Operation [22]). *The shared refinement operation combines two shared refinable interfaces F_1 and F_2, yielding a new identical signature interface corresponding to the predicate*

$$refine(F_1, F_2) = (nb(F_1) \vee nb(F_2)) \wedge (nb(F_1) \Rightarrow F_1) \wedge (nb(F_2) \Rightarrow F_2). \tag{16}$$

The left term expands the set of accepted inputs. The right term signifies that if an input was accepted by multiple interfaces, the output must be consistent with each of them. The shared refinement operation reduces to disjunction for sink interfaces and to conjunction for source interfaces.

Shared refinement's effect is to move up the refinement order by combining interfaces. Given a collection of shared refinable interfaces, the shared refinement operation yields the least upper bound with respect to the refinement partial order in Definition 6. Violation of (15) can be detected if the interfaces fed into $refine(\cdot)$ are not abstractions of the resulting interface.

5.1 Constructing Finite Interfaces Through Shared Refinement

A common method to construct finite abstractions is through simulation and overapproximation of forward reachable sets. This technique appears in tools such as PESSOA [12], SCOTS [19], MASCOT [7], ROCS [9] and ARCS [4]. By covering a sufficiently large portion of the interface input space, one can construct larger composite interfaces from smaller ones via shared refinement.

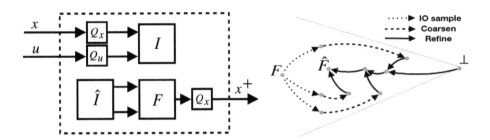

Fig. 7. (Left) Result of sample and coarsen operations for control system interface $F(x \cup u, x^+)$. The I and $\hat{I}$ interfaces encode the same predicate, but play different roles as sink and source. (Right) Visualization of finite abstraction as traversing the refinement partial order. Nodes represent interfaces and edges signify data dependencies for interface manipulation operators. Multiple refine edges point to a single node because refinement combines multiple interfaces. Input-output (IO) sample and coarsening are unary operations so the resulting nodes only have one incoming edge. The concrete interface F refines all others, and the final result is an abstraction $\hat{F}$.

Smaller interfaces are constructed by sampling regions of the input space and constructing an input-output pair. In Fig. 7's left half, a sink interface $I(x \cup u, \varnothing)$ acts as a filter. The source interface $\hat{I}(\varnothing, x \cup u)$ composed with $F(x \cup u, x^+)$ prunes any information that is outside the relevant input region. The original interface refines any sampled interface. To make samples *finite*, interface inputs and outputs are coarsened. An individual sampled abstraction is not useful for synthesis because it is restricted to a local portion of the interface input space. After sampling many finite interfaces are merged through shared refinement. The assumption $\hat{I}_i \Rightarrow \mathrm{nb}(F)$ encodes that the dynamics won't raise an error when simulated and is often made implicitly. Figure 7's right half depicts the sample, coarsen, and refine operations as methods to vertically traverse the interface refinement order.

Critically, refine($\cdot$) can be called within the synthesis pipeline and does not assume that the sampled interfaces are disjoint. Figure 8 shows the results from refining the dynamics with a collection of state-control hyper-rectangles that are randomly generated via uniformly sampling their widths and offsets along each dimension. These hyper-rectangles may overlap. If the same collection of hyper-rectangles were used in MASCOT, SCOTS, ARCS, or ROCS then this would yield a much more conservative abstraction of the dynamics because their implementations are not robust to overlapping or misaligned samples. PESSOA and SCOTS circumvent this issue altogether by enforcing disjointness with an exhaustive traversal of the state-control space, at the cost of unnecessarily coupling the refinement and sampling procedures. The lunar lander in the extended version [1] embraces overlapping and uses two mis-aligned grids to construct a grid partition with p^N elements with only $p^N(\frac{1}{2})^{N-1}$ samples (where p is the number of bins along each dimension and N is the interface input dimension). This technique introduces a small degree of conservatism but its computational savings typically outweigh this cost.

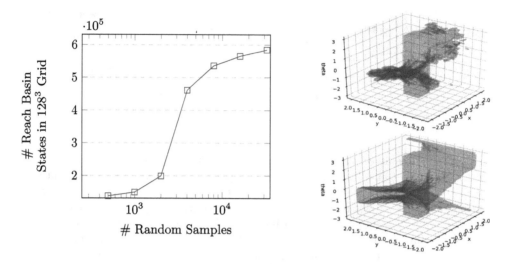

Fig. 8. The number of states in the computed reach basin grows with the number of random samples. The vertical axis is lower bounded by the number of states in the target $131k$ and upper bounded by $631k$, the number of states using an exhaustive traversal. Naive implementations of the exhaustive traversal would require 12 million samples. The right shows basins for 3000 (top) and 6000 samples (bottom).

6 Decomposed Control Predecessor

A decomposed control predecessor is available whenever the system state space consists of a Cartesian product and the dynamics are decomposed component-wise such as F_x, F_y, and F_θ for the Dubins vehicle. This property is common for continuous control systems over Euclidean spaces. While one may construct F directly via the abstraction sampling approach, it is often intractable for larger dimensional systems. A more sophisticated approach abstracts the lower dimensional components F_x, F_y, and F_θ individually, computes $F = \text{comp}(F_x, F_y, F_\theta)$, then feeds it to the monolithic $\text{cpre}(\cdot)$ from Proposition 1. This section's approach is to avoid computing F at all and decompose the monolithic $\text{cpre}(\cdot)$. It operates by breaking apart the term $ohide(x^+, \text{comp}(F, Z))$ in such a way that it respects the decomposition structure. For the Dubins vehicle example $ohide(x^+, \text{comp}(F, Z))$ is replaced with

$$ohide(p_x^+, \text{comp}(F_x, ohide(p_y^+, \text{comp}(F_y, ohide(\theta^+, \text{comp}(F_\theta, Z))))))$$

yielding a sink interface with inputs p_x, p_y, v, θ, and ω. This representation and the original $ohide(x^+, \text{comp}(F, Z))$ are equivalent because $\text{comp}(\cdot)$ is associative and interfaces do not share outputs $x^+ \equiv \{p_x^+, p_y^+, \theta^+\}$. Figure 9 shows multiple variants of $\text{cpre}(\cdot)$ and improved runtimes when one avoids preemptively constructing the monolithic interface. The decomposed $\text{cpre}(\cdot)$ resembles techniques to exploit partitioned transition relations in symbolic model checking [5].

No tools from Sect. 1.1 natively support decomposed control predecessors. We've shown a decomposed abstraction for components composed in parallel

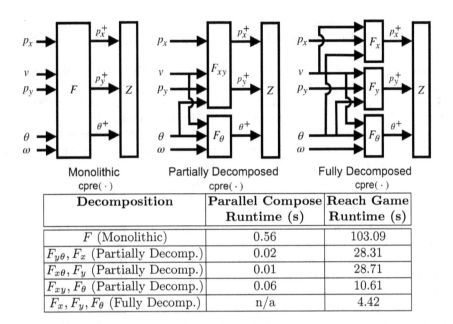

Decomposition	Parallel Compose Runtime (s)	Reach Game Runtime (s)
F (Monolithic)	0.56	103.09
$F_{y\theta}, F_x$ (Partially Decomp.)	0.02	28.31
$F_{x\theta}, F_y$ (Partially Decomp.)	0.01	28.71
F_{xy}, F_θ (Partially Decomp.)	0.06	10.61
F_x, F_y, F_θ (Fully Decomp.)	n/a	4.42

Fig. 9. A monolithic $\mathtt{cpre}(\cdot)$ incurs unnecessary pre-processing and synthesis runtime costs for the Dubins vehicle reach game. Each variant of $\mathtt{cpre}(\cdot)$ above composes the interfaces F_x, F_y and F_θ in different permutations. For example, F_{xy} represents $\mathtt{comp}(F_x, F_y)$ and F represents $\mathtt{comp}(F_x, F_y, F_\theta)$.

but this can also be generalized to series composition to capture, for example, a system where multiple components have different temporal sampling periods.

7 Conclusion

Tackling difficult control synthesis problems will require exploiting *all* available structure in a system with tools that can *flexibly adapt* to an individual problem's idiosyncrasies. This paper lays a foundation for developing an extensible suite of interoperable techniques and demonstrates the potential computational gains in an application to controller synthesis with finite abstractions. Adhering to a simple yet powerful set of well-understood primitives also constitutes a disciplined methodology for algorithm development, which is especially necessary if one wants to develop concurrent or distributed algorithms for synthesis.

References

1. http://arxiv.org/abs/1905.09503
2. https://github.com/ericskim/redax/tree/CAV19
3. Basar, T., Olsder, G.J.: Dynamic Noncooperative Game Theory, vol. 23. Siam, Philadelphia (1999)

4. Bulancea, O.L., Nilsson, P., Ozay, N.: Nonuniform abstractions, refinement and controller synthesis with novel BDD encodings. CoRR, arXiv: abs/1804.04280 (2018)

5. Burch, J., Clarke, E., Long, D.: Symbolic model checking with partitioned transition relations (1991)

6. Gruber, F., Kim, E., Arcak, M.: Sparsity-aware finite abstraction. In: 2017 IEEE 56th Conference on Decision and Control (CDC), December 2017

7. Hsu, K., Majumdar, R., Mallik, K., Schmuck, A.-K.: Multi-layered abstraction-based controller synthesis for continuous-time systems. In: Proceedings of the 21st International Conference on Hybrid Systems: Computation and Control (Part of CPS Week), HSCC 2018, pp. 120–129. ACM, New York (2018)

8. Khalil, H.K., Grizzle, J.W.: Nonlinear Systems, vol. 3. Prentice Hall, Upper Saddle River, New Jersey (2002)

9. Li, Y., Liu, J.: ROCS: a robustly complete control synthesis tool for nonlinear dynamical systems. In: Proceedings of the 21st International Conference on Hybrid Systems: Computation and Control (Part of CPS Week), HSCC 2018, pp. 130–135. ACM, New York (2018)

10. Liu, J.: Robust abstractions for control synthesis: completeness via robustness for linear-time properties. In: Proceedings of the 20th International Conference on Hybrid Systems: Computation and Control, HSCC 2017, pp. 101–110. ACM, New York (2017)

11. Majumdar, R.: Symbolic algorithms for verification and control. Ph.D. thesis, University of California, Berkeley (2003)

12. Mazo Jr., M., Davitian, A., Tabuada, P.: PESSOA: a tool for embedded controller synthesis. In: Touili, T., Cook, B., Jackson, P. (eds.) CAV 2010. LNCS, vol. 6174, pp. 566–569. Springer, Heidelberg (2010). https://doi.org/10.1007/978-3-642-14295-6_49

13. Meyer, P.J., Girard, A., Witrant, E.: Compositional abstraction and safety synthesis using overlapping symbolic models. IEEE Trans. Autom. Control. **63**, 1835–1841 (2017)

14. Mouelhi, S., Girard, A., Gössler, G.: CoSyMA: a tool for controller synthesis using multi-scale abstractions. In: 16th International Conference on Hybrid Systems: Computation and Control, pp. 83–88. ACM (2013)

15. Nilsson, P., Ozay, N., Liu, J.: Augmented finite transition systems as abstractions for control synthesis. Discret. Event Dyn. Syst. **27**(2), 301–340 (2017)

16. Nuzzo, P.: Compositional design of cyber-physical systems using contracts. Ph.D. thesis, EECS Department, University of California, Berkeley, August 2015

17. Piterman, N., Pnueli, A., Sa'ar, Y.: Synthesis of reactive(1) designs. In: Emerson, E.A., Namjoshi, K.S. (eds.) VMCAI 2006. LNCS, vol. 3855, pp. 364–380. Springer, Heidelberg (2005). https://doi.org/10.1007/11609773_24

18. Reißig, G., Weber, A., Rungger, M.: Feedback refinement relations for the synthesis of symbolic controllers. IEEE Trans. Autom. Control. **62**(4), 1781–1796 (2017)

19. Rungger, M., Zamani, M.: SCOTS: a tool for the synthesis of symbolic controllers. In: 19th International Conference on Hybrid Systems: Computation and Control, pp. 99–104. ACM (2016)

20. Somenzi, F.: CUDD: CU Decision Diagram Package. http://vlsi.colorado.edu/~fabio/CUDD/, Version 3.0.0 (2015)

21. Tabuada, P.: Verification and Control of Hybrid Systems. Springer, New York (2009). https://doi.org/10.1007/978-1-4419-0224-5

22. Tripakis, S., Lickly, B., Henzinger, T.A., Lee, E.A.: A theory of synchronous relational interfaces. ACM Trans. Program. Lang. Syst. (TOPLAS) **33**(4), 14 (2011)
23. Zamani, M., Pola, G., Mazo, M., Tabuada, P.: Symbolic models for nonlinear control systems without stability assumptions. IEEE Trans. Autom. Control **57**(7), 1804–1809 (2012)

15

Local and Compositional Reasoning for Optimized Reactive Systems

Mitesh Jain[1]([✉]) and Panagiotis Manolios[2]

[1] Synopsys Inc., Mountain View, USA
mitesh.jain@synopsys.com
[2] Northeastern University, Boston, USA
pete@ccs.neu.edu

Abstract. We develop a compositional, algebraic theory of skipping refinement, as well as local proof methods to effectively analyze the correctness of optimized reactive systems. A verification methodology based on refinement involves showing that any infinite behavior of an optimized low-level implementation is a behavior of the high-level abstract specification. Skipping refinement is a recently introduced notion to reason about the correctness of optimized implementations that run faster than their specifications, *i.e.*, a step in the implementation can skip multiple steps of the specification. For the class of systems that exhibit bounded skipping, existing proof methods have been shown to be amenable to mechanized verification using theorem provers and model-checkers. However, reasoning about the correctness of reactive systems that exhibit unbounded skipping using these proof methods requires reachability analysis, significantly increasing the verification effort. In this paper, we develop two new sound and complete proof methods for skipping refinement. Even in presence of unbounded skipping, these proof methods require only local reasoning and, therefore, are amenable to mechanized verification. We also show that skipping refinement is compositional, so it can be used in a stepwise refinement methodology. Finally, we illustrate the utility of the theory of skipping refinement by proving the correctness of an optimized event processing system.

1 Introduction

Reasoning about the correctness of a reactive system using refinement involves showing that any (infinite) observable behavior of a low-level, optimized implementation is a behavior allowed by the simple, high-level abstract specification. Several notions of refinement like trace containment, (bi)simulation refinement, stuttering (bi)simulation refinement, and skipping refinement [4,10,14,20,22] have been proposed in the literature to directly account for the difference in the abstraction levels between a specification and an implementation. Two attributes of crucial importance that enable us to effectively verify complex reactive systems using refinement are: (1) Compositionality: this allows us to decompose a monolithic proof establishing that a low-level concrete implementation refines a high-level abstract specification into a sequence of simpler refinement proofs, where each of the intermediate refinement proof can be performed independently using verification tools best suited for it; (2) Effective proof methods: analyzing the correctness of a reactive system requires global reasoning about its infinite behaviors, a task that is often difficult for verification tools. Hence it is crucial that the refinement-based methodology also admits effective proof methods that are amenable for mechanized reasoning.

It is known that the (bi)simulation refinement and stuttering (bi)simulation refinement are compositional and support the stepwise refinement methodology [20, 24]. Moreover, the proof methods associated with them are local, *i.e.*, they only require reasoning about states and their successors. Hence, they are amenable to mechanized reasoning. However, to the best of our knowledge, it is not known if skipping refinement is compositional. Skipping refinement is a recently introduced notion of refinement for verifying the correctness of optimized implementations that can "execute faster" than their simple high-level specifications, *i.e.*, a step in the implementation can *skip* multiple steps in the specification. Examples of such systems include superscalar processors, concurrent and parallel systems and optimizing compilers. Two proof methods, *reduced well-founded skipping simulation* and *well-founded skipping simulation* have been introduced to reason about skipping refinement for the class of systems that exhibit bounded skipping [10]. These proof methods were used to verify the correctness of several systems that otherwise were difficult to automatically verify using current model-checkers and automated theorem provers. However, when skipping is unbounded, the proof methods in [10] require reachability analysis, and therefore are not amenable to automated reasoning. To motivate the need for alternative proof methods for effective reasoning, we consider the event processing system (EPS), discussed in [10].

1.1 Motivating Example

An abstract high-level specification, AEPS, of an event processing system is defined as follows. Let E be a set of *events* and V be a set of *state variables*. A *state* of AEPS is a triple $\langle t, Sch, St \rangle$, where t is a natural number denoting the current time; Sch is a set of pairs $\langle e, t_e \rangle$, where $e \in E$ is an event scheduled to be executed at time $t_e \geq t$; St is an assignment to state variables in V. The transition relation for the AEPS system is defined as follows. If at time t there is no $\langle e, t \rangle \in Sch$, *i.e.*, there is no event scheduled to be executed at time t, then t is incremented by 1. Otherwise, we (nondeterministically) choose and execute an event of the form $\langle e, t \rangle \in Sch$. The execution of an event may result in modifying St and also removing and adding a finite number of new pairs $\langle e', t' \rangle$ to Sch. We require that $t' > t$. Finally, execution involves removing the executed event $\langle e, t \rangle$ from Sch. Now consider, tEPS, an optimized implementation of AEPS. As before, a state is a triple $\langle t, Sch, St \rangle$. However, unlike the abstract system which just increments time by 1 when there are no events scheduled at the current time, the optimized system finds the earliest time in future an event is scheduled to execute. The transition relation of tEPS is defined as follows. An event (e, t_e)

with the minimum time is selected, t is updated to t_e and the event e is executed, as in the AEPS. Consider an execution of AEPS and tEPS in Fig. 1. (We only show the prefix of executions). Suppose at $t = 0$, Sch be $\{(e_1, 0)\}$. The execution of event e_1 add a new pair (e_2, k) to Sch, where k is a positive integer. AEPS at $t = 0$, executes the event e_1, adds a new pair (e_2, k) to Sch, and updates t to 1. Since no events are scheduled to execute before $t = k$, the AEPS system repeatedly increments t by 1 until $t = k$. At $t = k$, it executes the event e_2. At time $t = 0$, tEPS executes e_1. The next event is scheduled to execute at time $t = k$; hence it updates in one step t to k. Next, in one step it executes the event e_2. Note that tEPS runs faster than AEPS by *skipping* over abstract states when no event is scheduled for execution at the current time. If $k > 1$, the step from s_2 to s_3 in tEPS neither corresponds to stuttering nor to a single step of the AEPS. Therefore notions of refinement based on stuttering simulation and bisimulation cannot be used to show that tEPS refines AEPS.

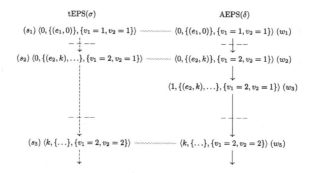

Fig. 1. Event simulation system

It was argued in [10] that skipping refinement is an appropriate notion of correctness that directly accounts for the skipping behavior exhibited by tEPS. Though, tEPS was used to motivate the need for a new notion of refinement, the proof methods proposed in [10] are not effective to prove the correctness of tEPS. This is because, execution of an event in tEPS may add new events that are scheduled to execute at an arbitrary time in future, *i.e.*, in general k in the above example execution is unbounded. Hence, the proof methods in [10] would require unbounded reachability analysis which often is problematic for automated verification tools. Even in the particular case when one can a priori determine an upper bound on k and unroll the transition relation, the proof methods in [10] are viable for mechanical reasoning only if the upper bound k is relatively small.

In this paper, we develop local proof methods to effectively analyze the correctness of optimized reactive systems using skipping refinement. These proof methods reduce global reasoning about infinite computations to local reasoning about states and their successor and are applicable even if the optimized implementation exhibits unbounded skipping. Moreover, we show that the proposed proof methods are complete, *i.e.*, if a system $\mathcal{M}_1$ is a skipping refinement of $\mathcal{M}_2$ under a suitable refinement map, then we can always locally reason about them. We also develop an algebraic theory of skipping refinement. In particular, we show that skipping simulation is closed under relational composition. Thus, skipping refinement aligns with the stepwise refinement methodology. Finally, we illustrate the benefits of the theory of skipping refinement and the associated proof methods by verifying the correctness of optimized event processing systems in ACL2s [3].

2 Preliminaries

A transition system model of a reactive system captures the concept of a state, atomic transitions that modify state during the course of a computation, and what is observable in a state. Any system with a well defined operational semantics can be mapped to a labeled transition system.

Definition 1 Labeled Transition System. *A labeled transition system (TS) is a structure $\langle S, \rightarrow, L \rangle$, where S is a non-empty (possibly infinite) set of states, $\rightarrow \subseteq S \times S$, is a left-total transition relation (every state has a successor), and L is a labeling function whose domain is S.*

Notation: We first describe the notational conventions used in the paper. Function application is sometimes denoted by an infix dot "." and is left-associative. The composition of relation R with itself i times (for $0 < i \leq \omega$) is denoted R^i ($\omega = \mathbb{N}$ and is the first infinite ordinal). Given a relation R and $1 < k \leq \omega$, $R^{<k}$ denotes $\bigcup_{1 \leq i < k} R^i$ and $R^{\geq k}$ denotes $\bigcup_{\omega > i \geq k} R^i$. Instead of $R^{<\omega}$ we often write the more common R^+. $\uplus$ denotes the disjoint union operator. Quantified expressions are written as $\langle Qx : r : t \rangle$, where Q is the quantifier (*e.g.*, $\exists, \forall, min, \bigcup$), x is a bound variable, r is an expression that denotes the range of variable x (*true*, if omitted), and t is a term.

Let $\mathcal{M} = \langle S, \rightarrow, L \rangle$ be a transition system. An $\mathcal{M}$-path is a sequence of states such that for adjacent states, s and u, $s \rightarrow u$. The jth state in an $\mathcal{M}$-path σ is denoted by $\sigma.j$. An $\mathcal{M}$-path σ starting at state s is a *fullpath*, denoted by $fp.\sigma.s$, if it is infinite. An $\mathcal{M}$-segment, $\langle v_1, \ldots, v_k \rangle$, where $k \geq 1$ is a finite $\mathcal{M}$-path and is also denoted by $\vec{v}$. The length of an $\mathcal{M}$-segment $\vec{v}$ is denoted by $|\vec{v}|$. Let INC be the set of strictly increasing sequences of natural numbers starting at 0. The ith partition of a fullpath σ with respect to $\pi \in INC$, denoted by $^{\pi}\sigma^i$, is given by an $\mathcal{M}$-segment $\langle \sigma(\pi.i), \ldots, \sigma(\pi(i+1) - 1) \rangle$.

3 Theory of Skipping Refinement

In this section we first briefly recall the notion of skipping simulation as described in [10]. We then study the algebraic properties of skipping simulation and show that a theory of refinement based on it is compositional and therefore can be used in a stepwise refinement based verification methodology.

The definition of skipping simulation is based on the notion of *matching*. Informally, a fullpath σ matches a fullpath δ under the relation B iff the fullpaths can be partitioned in to non-empty, finite segments such that all elements in a segment of σ are related to the first element in the corresponding segment of δ.

Definition 2 smatch [10]. *Let* $\mathcal{M} = \langle S, \rightarrow, L \rangle$ *be a transition system,* σ, δ *be fullpaths in* $\mathcal{M}$. *For* $\pi, \xi \in INC$ *and binary relation* $B \subseteq S \times S$, *we define*

$$scorr(B, \sigma, \pi, \delta, \xi) \equiv \langle \forall i \in \omega :: \langle \forall s \in {}^\pi \sigma^i :: sB\delta(\xi.i) \rangle \rangle \ and$$
$$smatch(B, \sigma, \delta) \equiv \langle \exists \pi, \xi \in INC :: scorr(B, \sigma, \pi, \delta, \xi) \rangle.$$

Figure 1 illustrates the notion of matching using our running example: σ is the fullpath of the concrete system and δ is a fullpath of the absract system. (The figure only shows the prefix of the fullpaths). The other parameter for matching is the relation B, which is just the identity function. In order to show that $smatch(B, \sigma, \delta)$ holds, we have to find $\pi, \xi \in INC$ satisfying the definition. In Fig. 1, we separate the partitions induced by our choice for π, ξ using $--$ and connect elements related by B with $\sim$. Since all elements of a σ partition are related to the first element of the corresponding δ partition, $scorr(B, \sigma, \pi, \delta, \xi)$ holds, therefore, $smatch(B, \sigma, \delta)$ holds.

Using the notion of matching, skipping simulation is defined as follows. Notice that skipping simulation is defined using a single transition system; it is easy to lift the notion defined on a single transition system to one that relates two transition systems by taking the disjoint union of the transition systems.

Definition 3 Skipping Simulation (SKS). $B \subseteq S \times S$ *is a skipping simulation on a TS* $\mathcal{M} = \langle S, \rightarrow, L \rangle$ *iff for all* s, w *such that* sBw, *both of the following hold.*

(SKS1) $L.s = L.w$
(SKS2) $\langle \forall \sigma: fp.\sigma.s: \langle \exists \delta: fp.\delta.w: smatch(B, \sigma, \delta) \rangle \rangle$

Theorem 1. *Let* $\mathcal{M}$ *be a TS. If* B *is a stuttering simulation (STS) on* $\mathcal{M}$ *then* B *is an SKS on* $\mathcal{M}$.

Proof: Follows directly from the definitions of SKS and STS [18].   □

3.1   Algebraic Properties

We now study the algebraic properties of SKS. We show that it is closed under arbitrary union. We also show that SKS is closed under relational composition. The later property is particularly useful since it enables us to use stepwise refinement and to modularly analyze the correctness of complex systems.

Lemma 1. *Let* $\mathcal{M}$ *be a TS and* $\mathcal{C}$ *be a set of SKS's on* $\mathcal{M}$. *Then* $G = \langle \cup B : B \in \mathcal{C} : B \rangle$ *is an SKS on* $\mathcal{M}$.

Corollary 1. *For any TS* $\mathcal{M}$, *there is a greatest SKS on* $\mathcal{M}$.

Lemma 2. *SKS are not closed under negation and intersection.*

The following lemma shows that skipping simulation is closed under relational composition.

Lemma 3. *Let $\mathcal{M}$ be a TS. If P and Q are SKS's on $\mathcal{M}$, then $R = P; Q$ is an SKS on $\mathcal{M}$.*

Proof: To show that R is an SKS on $\mathcal{M} = \langle S, \rightarrow, L \rangle$, we show that for any $s, w \in S$ such that sRw, SKS1 and SKS2 hold. Let $s, w \in S$ and sRw. From the definition of R, there exists $x \in S$ such that sPx and xQw. Since P and Q are SKS's on $\mathcal{M}$, $L.s = L.x = L.w$, hence, SKS1 holds for R.

To prove that SKS2 holds for R, consider a fullpath σ starting at s. Since P and Q are SKSs on $\mathcal{M}$, there is a fullpath τ in $\mathcal{M}$ starting at x, a fullpath δ in $\mathcal{M}$ starting at w and $\alpha, \beta, \theta, \gamma \in INC$ such that $scorr(P, \sigma, \alpha, \tau, \beta)$ and $scorr(Q, \tau, \theta, \delta, \gamma)$ hold. We use the fullpath δ as a witness and define $\pi, \xi \in INC$ such that $scorr(R, \sigma, \pi, \delta, \xi)$ holds.

We define a function, r, that given i, corresponding to the index of a partition of τ under β, returns the index of the partition of τ under θ in which the first element of τ's i^{th} partition under β resides. $r.i = j$ iff $\theta.j \leq \beta.i < \theta(j+1)$. Note that r is indeed a function, as every element of τ resides in exactly one partition of θ. Also, since there is a correspondence between the partitions of α and β, (by $scorr(P, \sigma, \alpha, \tau, \beta)$), we can apply r to indices of partitions of σ under α to find where the first element of the corresponding β partition resides. Note that r is non-decreasing: $a < b \Rightarrow r.a \leq r.b$.

We define $\pi\alpha \in INC$, a strictly increasing sequence that will allow us to merge adjacent partitions in α as needed to define the strictly increasing sequence π on σ used to prove SKS2. Partitions in π will consist of one or more α partitions. Given i, corresponding to the index of a partition of σ under π, the function $\pi\alpha$ returns the index of the corresponding partition of σ under α.

$$\pi\alpha(0) = 0$$

$$\pi\alpha(i) = \min j \in \omega \text{ s.t. } |\{k : 0 < k \leq j \wedge r.k \neq r(k-1)\}| = i$$

Note that $\pi\alpha$ is an increasing function, *i.e.*, $a < b \Rightarrow \pi\alpha(a) < \pi\alpha(b)$. We now define π as follows.

$$\pi.i = \alpha(\pi\alpha.i)$$

There is an important relationship between r and $\pi\alpha$

$$r(\pi\alpha.i) = \cdots = r(\pi\alpha(i+1) - 1)$$

That is, for all α partitions that are in the same π partition, the initial states of the corresponding β partitions are in the same θ partition.

We define ξ as follows: $\xi.i = \gamma(r(\pi\alpha.i))$.

We are now ready to prove SKS2. Let $s \in {}^{\pi}\sigma^i$. We show that $sR\delta(\xi.i)$. By the definition of π, we have

$$s \in {}^{\alpha}\sigma^{\pi\alpha.i} \vee \cdots \vee s \in {}^{\alpha}\sigma^{\pi\alpha(i+1)-1}$$

Hence,

$$sP\tau(\beta(\pi\alpha.i)) \vee \cdots \vee sP\tau(\beta(\pi\alpha(i+1)-1))$$

Note that by the definition of r (apply r to $\pi\alpha.i$):

$$\theta(r(\pi\alpha.i)) \leq \beta(\pi\alpha.i) < \theta(r(\pi\alpha.i)+1)$$

Hence,

$$\tau(\beta(\pi\alpha.i))Q\delta(\gamma(r(\pi\alpha.i))) \vee \cdots \vee \tau(\beta(\pi\alpha(i+1)-1))Q\delta(\gamma(r(\pi\alpha(i+1)-1)))$$

By the definition of ξ and the relationship between r and $\pi\alpha$ described above, we simplify the above formula as follows.

$$\tau(\beta(\pi\alpha.i))Q\delta(\xi.i) \vee \cdots \vee \tau(\beta(\pi\alpha(i+1)-1))Q\delta(\xi.i)$$

Therefore, by the definition of R, we have that $sR\delta(\xi.i)$ holds. $\square$

Theorem 2. *The reflexive transitive closure of an SKS is an SKS.*

Theorem 3. *Given a TS $\mathcal{M}$, the greatest SKS on $\mathcal{M}$ is a preorder.*

Proof. Let G be the greatest SKS on $\mathcal{M}$. From Theorem 2, G^* is an SKS. Hence $G^* \subseteq G$. Furthermore, since $G \subseteq G^*$, we have that $G = G^*$, *i.e.*, G is reflexive and transitive. $\square$

3.2   Skipping Refinement

We now recall the notion of skipping refinement [10]. We use skipping simulation, a notion defined in terms of a single transition system, to define skipping refinement, a notion that relates *two* transition systems: an *abstract* transition system and a *concrete* transition system. Informally, if a concrete system is a skipping refinement of an abstract system, then its observable behaviors are also behaviors of the abstract system, modulo skipping (which includes stuttering). The notion is parameterized by a *refinement map*, a function that maps concrete states to their corresponding abstract states. A refinement map along with a labeling function determines what is observable at a concrete state.

Definition 4 Skipping Refinement. *Let $\mathcal{M}_A = \langle S_A, \xrightarrow{A}, L_A \rangle$ and $\mathcal{M}_C = \langle S_C, \xrightarrow{C}, L_C \rangle$ be transition systems and let $r : S_C \to S_A$ be a refinement map. We say $\mathcal{M}_C$ is a skipping refinement of $\mathcal{M}_A$ with respect to r, written $\mathcal{M}_C \lesssim_r \mathcal{M}_A$, if there exists a binary relation B such that all of the following hold.*

1. $\langle \forall s \in S_C :: sBr.s \rangle$ and

2. B is an SKS on $\langle S_C \uplus S_A, \xrightarrow{C} \uplus \xrightarrow{A}, \mathcal{L} \rangle$ where $\mathcal{L}.s = L_A(s)$ for $s \in S_A$, and $\mathcal{L}.s = L_A(r.s)$ for $s \in S_C$.

Next, we use the property that skipping simulation is closed under relational composition to show that skipping refinement supports modular reasoning using a stepwise refinement approach. In order to verify that a low-level complex implementation $\mathcal{M}_C$ refines a simple high-level abstract specification $\mathcal{M}_A$ one proceeds as follows: starting with $\mathcal{M}_A$ define a sequence of intermediate systems leading to the final complex implementation $\mathcal{M}_C$. Any two successive systems in the sequence differ only in relatively few aspects of their behavior. We then show that, at each step in the sequence, the system at the current step is a refinement of the previous one. Since at each step, the verification effort is focused only on the few differences in behavior between two systems under consideration, proof obligations are simpler than the monolithic proof. Note that this methodology is orthogonal to (horizontal) modular reasoning that infers the correctness of a system from the correctness of its sub-components.

Theorem 4. Let $\mathcal{M}_1 = \langle S_1, \xrightarrow{1}, L_1 \rangle$, $\mathcal{M}_2 = \langle S_2, \xrightarrow{2}, L_2 \rangle$, and $\mathcal{M}_3 = \langle S_3, \xrightarrow{3}, L_3 \rangle$ be TSs, $p : S_1 \to S_2$ and $r : S_2 \to S_3$. If $\mathcal{M}_1 \lesssim_p \mathcal{M}_2$ and $\mathcal{M}_2 \lesssim_r \mathcal{M}_3$, then $\mathcal{M}_1 \lesssim_{p;r} \mathcal{M}_3$.

Proof: Since $\mathcal{M}_1 \lesssim_p \mathcal{M}_2$, we have an SKS, say A, such that $\langle \forall s \in S_1 :: sA(p.s) \rangle$. Furthermore, without loss of generality we can assume that $A \subseteq S_1 \times S_2$. Similarly, since $\mathcal{M}_2 \lesssim_r \mathcal{M}_3$, we have an SKS, say B, such that $\langle \forall s \in S_2 :: sB(r.s) \rangle$ and $B \subseteq S_2 \times S_3$. Define $C = A; B$. Then we have that $C \subseteq S_1 \times S_3$ and $\langle \forall s \in S_1 :: sCr(p.s) \rangle$. Also, from Theorem 2, C is an SKS on $\langle S_1 \uplus S_3, \xrightarrow{1} \uplus \xrightarrow{3}, \mathcal{L} \rangle$, where $\mathcal{L}.s = L_3(s)$ if $s \in S_3$ else $\mathcal{L}.s = L_3(r(p.s))$.

Formally, to establish that a complex low-level implementation $\mathcal{M}_C$ refines a simple high-level abstract specification $\mathcal{M}_A$, one defines intermediate systems $\mathcal{M}_1, \ldots \mathcal{M}_n$, where $n \geq 1$ and establishes the following: $\mathcal{M}_C = \mathcal{M}_0 \lesssim_{r_0} \mathcal{M}_1 \lesssim_{r_1} \ldots \lesssim_{r_{n-1}} \mathcal{M}_n = \mathcal{M}_A$. Then from Theorem 4, we have that $\mathcal{M}_C \lesssim_r \mathcal{M}_A$, where $r = r_0; r_1; \ldots; r_{n-1}$. We illustrate the utility of this approach in Sect. 5 by proving the correctness of an optimized event processing systems.

Theorem 5. Let $\mathcal{M} = \langle S, \to, L \rangle$ be a TS. Let $\mathcal{M}' = \langle S', \xrightarrow{'}, L' \rangle$ where $S' \subseteq S$, $\xrightarrow{'} \subseteq S' \times S'$, $\xrightarrow{'}$ is a left-total subset of $\to^+$, and $L' = L|_{S'}$. Then $\mathcal{M}' \lesssim_I \mathcal{M}$, where I is the identity function on S'.

Corollary 2. Let $\mathcal{M}_C = \langle S_C, \xrightarrow{C}, L_C \rangle$ and $\mathcal{M}_A = \langle S_A, \xrightarrow{A}, L_A \rangle$ be TSs, $r : S_C \to S_A$ be a refinement map. Let $\mathcal{M}'_C = \langle S'_C, \xrightarrow{C'}, L'_C \rangle$ where $S'_C \subseteq S_C$, $\xrightarrow{C'}$ is a left-total subset of $\xrightarrow{C}{}^+$, and $L'_C = L_C|_{S'_C}$. If $\mathcal{M}_C \lesssim_r \mathcal{M}_A$ then $\mathcal{M}'_C \lesssim_{r'} \mathcal{M}_A$, where r' is $r|_{S'_C}$.

We now illustrate the usefulness of the theory of skipping refinement using our running example of event processing systems. Consider MPEPS, that uses a priority queue to find a non-empty set of events (say E_t) scheduled to execute at the current time and executes them. We allow the priority queue in MPEPS to be deterministic or nondeterministic. For example, the priority queue may deterministically select a single event in E_t to execute, or based on considerations such as resource utilization it may execute some subset of events in E_t in a single step. When reasoning about the correctness of MPEPS, one thing to notice is that there is a difference in the data structures used in the two systems: MPEPS uses a priority queue to effectively find the next set of events to execute in the scheduler, while AEPS uses a simple abstract set representation for the scheduler. Another thing to notice is that MPEPS can "execute faster" than AEPS in two ways: it can increment time by more than 1 and it can execute more than one event in a single step. The theory of skipping refinement developed in this paper enables us to separate out these concerns and apply a stepwise refinement approach to effectively analyse MPEPS.

First, we account for the difference in the data structures between MPEPS and AEPS. Towards this we define an intermediate system MEPS that is identical to MPEPS except that the scheduler in MEPS is now represented as a set of event-time pairs. Under a refinement map, say p, that extracts the set of event-time pairs in the priority queue of MPEPS, a step in MPEPS can be matched by a step in MEPS. Hence, MPEPS $\lesssim_p$ MEPS. Next we account for the difference between MEPS and AEPS in the number of events the two systems may execute in a single step. Towards this, observe that the state space of MEPS and tEPS are equal and the transition relation of MEPS is a left-total subset of the transitive closure of the transition relation of tEPS. Hence, from Theorem 5, we infer that MPEPS is a skipping refinement of tEPS using the identity function, say I_1, as the refinement map, $i.e.$, MEPS $\lesssim_{I_1}$ tEPS. Next observe that the state spaces of tEPS and AEPS are equal and the transition relation of tEPS is a left-total subset of the transitive closure of the transition relation of AEPS. Hence, from Theorem 5, tEPS is a skipping refinement of AEPS using the identity function, say I_2, as the refinement map, $i.e.$, tEPS $\lesssim_{I_2}$ AEPS. Finally, from the transitivity of skipping refinement (Theorem 4), we conclude that MPEPS $\lesssim_{p'}$ AEPS, where $p' = p; I_1; I_2$.

4   Mechanised Reasoning

To prove that a transition system $\mathcal{M}_C$ is a skipping refinement of a transition system $\mathcal{M}_A$ using Definition 3, requires us to show that for any fullpath from $\mathcal{M}_C$ we can find a matching fullpath from $\mathcal{M}_A$. However, reasoning about existence of infinite sequences can be problematic using automated tools. In this section, we develop sound and complete local proof methods that are applicable even if a system exhibits unbounded skipping. We first briefly present the proof methods, reduced well-founded skipping and well-founded skipping simulation, developed in [10].

Definition 5 Reduced Well-founded Skipping [10]. $B \subseteq S \times S$ *is a reduced well-founded skipping relation on TS* $\mathcal{M} = \langle S, \rightarrow, L \rangle$ *iff:*

(RWFSK1) $\langle \forall s, w \in S : sBw : L.s = L.w \rangle$

(RWFSK2) There exists a function, $rankt : S \times S \to W$, such that $\langle W, \prec \rangle$ is well-founded and

$$\langle \forall s, u, w \in S : s \to u \wedge sBw :$$

    (a) $(uBw \wedge rankt(u, w) \prec rankt(s, w)) \vee$

    (b) $\langle \exists v : w \to^{+} v : uBv \rangle \rangle$

Definition 6 Well-founded Skipping [10]. *$B \subseteq S \times S$ is a well-founded skipping relation on TS $\mathcal{M} = \langle S, \to, L \rangle$ iff:*

(WFSK1) $\langle \forall s, w \in S : sBw : L.s = L.w \rangle$

(WFSK2) There exist functions, $rankt : S \times S \to W$, $rankl : S \times S \times S \to \omega$, such that $\langle W, \prec \rangle$ is well-founded and

$$\langle \forall s, u, w \in S : s \to u \wedge sBw :$$

    (a) $\langle \exists v : w \to v : uBv \rangle \vee$

    (b) $(uBw \wedge rankt(u, w) \prec rankt(s, w)) \vee$

    (c) $\langle \exists v : w \to v : sBv \wedge rankl(v, s, u) < rankl(w, s, u) \rangle \vee$

    (d) $\langle \exists v : w \to^{\geq 2} v : uBv \rangle \rangle$

Theorem 6 [10]. *Let $\mathcal{M} = \langle S, \to, L \rangle$ be a TS and $B \subseteq S \times S$. The following statements are equivalent*

(i) B is a SKS on $\mathcal{M}$;
(ii) B is a WFSK on $\mathcal{M}$;
(iii) B is a RWFSK on $\mathcal{M}$.

Recall the event processing systems AEPS and tEPS described in Sect. 1.1. When no events are scheduled to execute at a given time, say t, tEPS increments time t to the earliest time in future, say $k > t$, at which an event is scheduled for execution. Execution of an event can add an event that is scheduled to be executed at an arbitrary time in future. Therefore, we cannot apriori determine an upper-bound on k. Using any of the above two proof-methods to reason about skipping refinement would require unbounded reachability analysis (conditions RWFSK2b and WFSK2d), often difficult for automated verification tools. To redress the situation, we develop two new proof methods of SKS; both require only local reasoning about steps and their successors.

Definition 7 Reduced Local Well-founded Skipping. *$B \subseteq S \times S$ is a local well-founded skipping relation on TS $\mathcal{M} = \langle S, \to, L \rangle$ iff:*

(RLWFSK1) $\langle \forall s, w \in S : sBw : L.s = L.w \rangle$

(RLWFSK2) There exist functions, $rankt : S \times S \longrightarrow W$, $rankls : S \times S \longrightarrow \omega$ such that $\langle W, \prec \rangle$ is well founded, and, a binary relation $\mathcal{O} \subseteq S \times S$

such that

$\langle \forall s, u, w \in S : sBw \wedge s \rightarrow u :$
  (a) $(uBw \wedge rankt(u, w) \prec rankt(s, w)) \vee$
  (b) $\langle \exists v : w \rightarrow v : u\mathcal{O}v\rangle\rangle$
and
$\langle \forall x, y \in S : x\mathcal{O}y :$
  (c) $xBy \vee$
  (d) $\langle \exists z : y \rightarrow z : x\mathcal{O}z \wedge rankls(z, x) < rankls(y, x)\rangle\rangle$

Observe that to prove that a relation is an RLWFSK on a transition system, it is sufficient to reason about single steps of the transition system. Also, note that RLWFSK does not differentiate between skipping and stuttering on the right. This is based on an earlier observation that skipping subsumes stuttering. We used this observation to simplify the definition. However, it can often be useful to differentiate between skipping and stuttering. Next we define local well-founded skipping simulation (LWFSK), a characterization of skipping simulation that separates reasoning about skipping and stuttering on the right (Fig. 2).

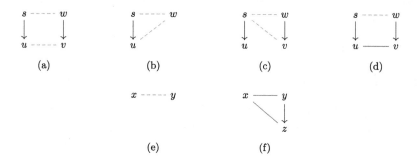

Fig. 2. Local well-founded skipping simulation (orange line indicates the states are related by B and blue line indicate the states are related by $\mathcal{O}$) (Color figure online)

Definition 8 Local Well-founded Skipping. $B \subseteq S \times S$ *is a local well-founded skipping relation on TS* $\mathcal{M} = \langle S, \rightarrow, L\rangle$ *iff:*

(LWFSK1) $\langle \forall s, w \in S : sBw : L.s = L.w\rangle$
(LWFSK2) *There exist functions,* $rankt : S \times S \longrightarrow W$, $rankl : S \times S \times S \longrightarrow \omega$,
        and $rankls : S \times S \longrightarrow \omega$ *such that* $\langle W, \prec\rangle$ *is well founded, and, a*

binary relation $\mathcal{O} \subseteq S \times S$ *such that*

$\langle \forall s, u, w \in S : sBw \wedge s \rightarrow u :$

   (a) $\langle \exists v : w \rightarrow v : uBv \rangle \vee$

   (b) $(uBw \wedge rankt(u, w) \prec rankt(s, w)) \vee$

   (c) $\langle \exists v : w \rightarrow v : sBv \wedge rankl(v, s, u) < rankl(w, s, u) \rangle \vee$

   (d) $\langle \exists v : w \rightarrow v : u\mathcal{O}v \rangle \rangle$

and

$\langle \forall x, y \in S : x\mathcal{O}y :$

   (e) $xBy \vee$

   (f) $\langle \exists z : y \rightarrow z : x\mathcal{O}z \wedge rankls(z, x) < rankls(y, x) \rangle \rangle$

Like RLWFSK, to prove that a relation is a LWFSK, reasoning about single steps of the transition system suffices. However, LWFSK2b accounts for stuttering on the right, and LWFSK2d along with LWFSK2e and LWFSK2f accounts for skipping on the right. Also observe that states related by $\mathcal{O}$ are not required to be labeled identically and may have no observable relationship to the states related by B.

Soundness and Completeness. We next show that RLWFSK and LWFSK in fact completely characterize skipping simulation, *i.e.*, RLWFSK and LWFSK are sound and complete proof rules. Thus if a concrete system $\mathcal{M}_C$ is a skipping refinement of $\mathcal{M}_A$, one can always effectively reason about it using RLWFSK and LWFSK.

Theorem 7. *Let* $\mathcal{M} = \langle S, \rightarrow, L \rangle$ *be a transition system and* $B \subseteq S \times S$. *The following statements are equivalent:*

  (i) B *is an SKS on* $\mathcal{M}$;
  (ii) B *is a WFSK on* $\mathcal{M}$;
  (iii) B *is an RWFSK on* $\mathcal{M}$;
  (iv) B *is an RLWFSK on* $\mathcal{M}$;
  (v) B *is a LWFSK on* $\mathcal{M}$;

Proof: The equivalence of (i), (ii) and (iii) follows from Theorem 6. That (iv) implies (v) follows from the simple observation that RLWFSK2 implies LWFSK2. To complete the proof, we prove the following two implications. We prove below that (v) implies (ii) in Lemma 4 and that (iii) implies (iv) in Lemma 5. □

Lemma 4. *If* B *is a LWFSK on* $\mathcal{M}$, *then* B *is a WFSK on* $\mathcal{M}$.

Proof. Let B be a LWFSK on $\mathcal{M}$. WFSK1 follows directly from LWFSK1. Let *rankt*, *rankl*, and *rankls* be functions, and $\mathcal{O}$ be a binary relation such that LWFSK2 holds. To show that WFSK2 holds, we use the same *rankt* and *rankl* functions and let $s, u, w \in S$ and $s \rightarrow u$ and sBw. LWFSK2a, LWFSK2b and

LWFSK2c are equivalent to WFSK2a, WFSK2b and WFSK2c, respectively, so we show that if only LWFSK2d holds, then WFSK2d holds. Since LWFSK2d holds, there is a successor v of w such that $u\mathcal{O}v$. Since $u\mathcal{O}v$ holds, either LWFSK2e or LWFSK2f must hold between u and v. However, since LWFSK2a does not hold, LWFSK2e cannot hold and LWFSK2f must hold, $i.e.$, there exists a successor v' of v such that $u\mathcal{O}v' \wedge rankls(v', u) < rankls(v, u)$. So, we need a path of at least 2 steps from w to satisfy the universally quantified constraint on $\mathcal{O}$. Let us consider an arbitrary path, δ, such that $\delta.0 = w$, $\delta.1 = v$, $\delta.2 = v'$, $u\mathcal{O}\delta.i$, LWFSK2e does not hold between u and $\delta.i$ for $i \geq 1$, and $rankls(\delta.(i+1), u) < rankls(\delta.i, u)$. Notice that any such path must be finite because $rankls$ is well founded. Hence, δ is a finite path and there exists a $k \geq 2$ such that LWFSK2e holds between u and $\delta.k$. Therefore, WFSK2d holds, $i.e.$, there is a state in δ reachable from w in two or more steps which is related to u by B.   □

Lemma 5. *If B is RWFSK on $\mathcal{M}$, then B is an RLWFSK on $\mathcal{M}$.*

Proof. Let B be an RWFSK on $\mathcal{M}$. RLWFSK1 follows directly from RWFSK1. To show that RLWFSK2 holds, we use any *rankt* function that can be used to show that RWFSK2 holds. We define $\mathcal{O}$ as follows.

$$\mathcal{O} = \{(u, v) : \langle \exists z : v \rightarrow^+ z : uBz \rangle\}$$

We define $rankls(u, v)$ to be the minimal length of a $\mathcal{M}$-segment that starts at v and ends at a state, say z, such that uBz, if such a segment exists and 0 otherwise. Let $s, u, w \in S$, sBw and $s \rightarrow u$. If RWFSK2a holds between s, u, and w, then RLWFSK2a also holds. Next, suppose that RWFSK2a does not hold but RWFSK2b holds, $i.e.$, there is an $\mathcal{M}$-segment $\langle w, a, \ldots, v \rangle$ such that uBv; therefore, $u\mathcal{O}a$ and RLWFSK2b holds.

   To finish the proof, we show that $\mathcal{O}$ and $rankls$ satisfy the constraints imposed by the second conjunct in RLWFSK2. Let $x, y \in S$, $x\mathcal{O}y$ and $x \not{B} y$. From the definition of $\mathcal{O}$, we have that there is an $\mathcal{M}$-segment from y to a state related to x by B; let $\vec{y}$ be such a segment of minimal length. From definition of $rankls$, we have $rankls(y, x) = |\vec{y}|$. Observe that y cannot be the last state of $\vec{y}$ and $|\vec{y}| \geq 2$. This is because the last state in $\vec{y}$ must be related to x by B, but from the assumption we know that $x \not{B} y$. Let y' be a successor of y in $\vec{y}$. Clearly, $x\mathcal{O}y'$; therefore, $rankls(y', x) < |\vec{y}| - 1$, since the length of a minimal $\mathcal{M}$-segment from y' to a state related to x by B, must be less or equal to $|\vec{y}| - 1$.   □

5   Case Study (Event Processing System)

In this section, we analyze the correctness of an optimized event processing system (PEPS) that uses a *priority queue* to find an event scheduled to execute at any given time. We show that PEPS refines AEPS, a simple event processing system described in Sect. 1. Our goal is to illustrate the benefits of the theory of skipping refinement and the associated local proof methods developed in the paper. We use ACL2s [3], an interactive theorem prover, to define the operational semantics of the systems and mechanize a proof of its correctness.

Operational Semantics of PEPS: A state of PEPS system is a triple $\langle \text{tm}, \text{otevs}, \text{mem} \rangle$, where tm is a natural number denoting current time, otevs is a set of timed-event pairs denoting the scheduler that is ordered with respect to a total order te-< on timed-event pairs, and mem is a collection of variable-integer pairs denoting the shared memory. The transition function of PEPS is defined as follows: if there are no events in otevs, then PEPS just increments the current time by 1. Otherwise, it picks the first timed-event pair, say $\langle e, t \rangle$ in otevs, executes it and updates the time to t. The execution of an event may result in adding new timed-events to the scheduler, removing existing timed-events from the scheduler and updating the memory. Finally, the executed timed-event is removed from the scheduler. This is a simple, generic model of an event processing system. Notice that the ability to remove events can be used to specify systems with preemption [23]: an event scheduled to execute at some future time may be canceled (and possibly rescheduled to be executed at a different time in future) as a result of the execution of an event that preempts it. Notice that, for a given total order, PEPS is a deterministic system.

The execution of an event is modeled using three constrained functions that take as input an event, ev, a time, t, and a memory, mem: step-events-add returns the set of new timed-event pairs to add to the scheduler; step-events-rm returns the set of timed-event pairs to remove from the scheduler; and step-memory returns a memory updated as specified by the event. We place minimal constraints on these functions. For example, we only require that step-events-add returns a set of event-time pairs of the form $\langle e, t_e \rangle$ where t_e is greater than the current time t. The constrained functions are defined using the encapsulate construct in ACL2 and can be instantiated with any executable definitions that satisfy these constraints without affecting the proof of correctness of PEPS. Moreover, note that the particular choice of the total order on timed-event pairs is irrelevant to the proof of correctness of PEPS.

Stepwise Refinement: We show that PEPS refines AEPS using a stepwise refinement approach: first we define an intermediate system HPEPS obtained by augmenting PEPS with history information and show that PEPS is a simulation refinement of HPEPS. Second, we show that HPEPS is a skipping refinement of AEPS. Finally, we appeal to Theorems 1 and 4 to infer that PEPS refines AEPS. Note that the compositionality of skipping refinement enables us to decompose the proof into a sequence of refinement proofs, each of which is simpler. Moreover, the history information in HPEPS is helpful in defining the witnessing binary relation and the rank function required to prove skipping refinement.

An HPEPS state is a four-tuple $\langle tm, otevs, mem, h \rangle$, where tm, otevs, mem are respectively the current time, an ordered set of timed events and a collection of variable-integer pairs, and h is the history information. The history information h consists of a Boolean variable valid, time tm, and an ordered set of timed-event pairs otevs and the memory mem. Intuitively, h records the state preceding the current state. The transition function HPEPS is same as the transition function of PEPS except that HPEPS also records the history in h.

PEPS Refines HPEPS: Observe that, modulo the history information, a step of PEPS directly corresponds to a step of HPEPS, *i.e.*, PEPS is a bisimulation refinement of HPEPS under a refinement map that projects a PEPS state $\langle tm, otevs, mem \rangle$ to the HPEPS state $\langle tm, otevs, mem, h \rangle$ where the valid component of h is set to false. But we only prove that it is a simulation refinement, because, from Theorem 1, it suffices to establish that PEPS is a skipping refinement of HPEPS. The proofs primarily require showing that two sets of ordered timed-events that are set equivalent are in fact equal and that adding and removing equivalent sets of timed-event from equal schedulers results in equal schedulers.

HPEPS Refines AEPS: Next we show that HPEPS is a skipping refinement of AEPS under the refinement map R, a function that simply projects an HPEPS state to an AEPS state. To show that HPEPS is a skipping refinement of AEPS under the refinement map R, from Definition 4, we must show as witness a binary relation B that satisfies the two conditions. Let $B = \{(s, R.s) : s \text{ is an HPEPS state}\}$. To establish that B is an SKS on the disjoint union of HPEPS and AEPS, we have a choice of four proof-methods (Sect. 4). Recall that execution of an event can add a new event scheduled to be executed at an arbitrary time in the future. As a result, if we were to use WFSK or RWFSK, the proof obligations from conditions WFSK2d (Definition 5) and RWFSK2b (Definition 6) would require unbounded reachability analysis, something that typically places a big burden on verification tools and their users. In contrast, the proof obligations to establish RLWFSK are local and only require reasoning about states and their successors, which significantly reduces the proof complexity.

RLWFSK1 holds trivially. To prove that RLWFSK2 holds we define a binary relation $\mathcal{O}$ and a rank function *rankls* and show that they satisfy the two universally quantified formulas in RLWFSK2. Moreover, since HPEPS does not stutter we ignore RLWFSK2a, and that is why we do not define *rankt*. Finally, our proof obligation is: for all HPEPS s, u and AEPS state w such that $s \rightarrow u$ and sBw holds, there exists a AEPS state v such that $w \rightarrow v$ and $u\mathcal{O}v$ holds.

Verification Effort: We used the defdata framework in ACL2s, to specify the data definitions for the three systems and the definec construct to introduce function definitions along with their input-contracts (pre-conditions) and output-contracts (post-conditions). In addition to admitting a data definition, defdata proves several theorems about the functions that are extremely helpful in automatically discharging type-like proof obligations. We also developed a library to concisely describe functions using higher-order constructs like map and reduce, which made some of the definitions clearer. ACL2s supports first-order quantifiers via the defun-sk construct, which essentially amounts to the use of Hilbert's choice operator. We use defun-sk to model the transition relation for AEPS (a non-deterministic system) and to specify the proof obligations for proving that HPEPS refines AEPS. However, support for automated reasoning about quantifiers is limited in ACL2. Therefore, we use the domain knowledge, when possible (*e.g.*, a system is deterministic), to eliminate quantifiers in the proof obligations and provide explicit witnesses for existential quantifiers.

The proof makes essential use of several libraries available in ACL2 for reasoning about lists and sets. In addition, we prove a collection of additional lemmas that can be roughly categorized into four categories. First, we have a collection of lemmas to prove the input-output contracts of the functions. Second, we have a collection of lemmas to show that operations on the schedulers in the three systems preserve various invariants, *e.g.*, that any timed-event in the scheduler is scheduled to execute at a time greater or equal to the current time. Third, we have a collection of lemmas to show that inserting and removing two equivalent sets of timed-events from a scheduler results in an equivalent scheduler. And fourth, we have a collection of lemmas to show that two schedulers are equivalent *iff* they are set equal. The above lemmas are used to establish a relationship between priority queues, a data structure used by the implementation system, and sets, the corresponding data structure used in the specification system. The behavioral difference between the two systems is accounted for by the notion of skipping refinement. This separation significantly eases understanding as well as mechanical reasoning about the correctness of reactive systems. We have 8 top-level proof obligations and a few dozen supporting lemmas. The entire proof takes about 120 s on a machine with 2.2 GHz Intel Core i7 with 16 GB main memory.

6   Related Work

Several notions of correctness have been proposed in the literature and their properties been widely studied [2,5,11,16,17]. In this paper, we develop a theory of skipping refinement to effectively prove the correctness of optimized reactive systems using automated verification tools. These results establish skipping refinement on par with notions of refinement based on (bi)simulation [22] and stuttering (bi)simulation [20,24], in the sense that skipping refinement is (1) compositional and (2) admits local proofs methods. Together the two properties have been instrumental in significantly reducing the proof complexity in verification of large and complex systems. We developed the theory of skipping refinement using a generic model of transition systems and place no restrictions on the state space size or the branching factor of the transition system. Any system with a well-defined operational semantics can be mapped to a labeled transition system. Moreover, the local proof methods are sound and complete, *i.e.*, if an implementation is a skipping refinement of the specification, we can always use the local proof methods to effectively reason about it.

Refinement-based methodologies have been successfully used to verify the correctness of several realistic hardware and software systems. In [13], several complex concurrent programs were verified using a stepwise refinement methodology. In addition, Kragl and Qadeer [13] also develop a compact representation to facilitate the description of programs at different levels of abstraction and associated refinement proofs. Several back-end compiler transformations are proved correct in Compcert [15] using simulation refinement. In [25], several compiler transformations were verified using stuttering refinement and associated local proof methods. Recently, refinement-based methodology has also been applied to verify the correctness of practical distributed systems [8] and a general-purpose operating system microkernel [12]. The full verification of CertiKOS [6,7], an OS kernel, is based on the notion of simulation refinement. Refinement based approaches have also been extensively used to verify microprocessor designs [1,9,19,21,26]. Skipping refinement was used to verify the correctness of optimized memory controllers and a JVM-inspired stack machine [10].

7 Conclusion and Future Work

In this paper, we developed the theory of skipping refinement. Skipping refinement is designed to reason about the correctness of optimized reactive systems, a class of systems where a single transition in a concrete low-level implementation may correspond to a sequence of observable steps in the corresponding abstract high-level specification. Examples of such systems include optimizing compilers, concurrent and parallel systems and superscalar processors. We developed sound and complete proof methods that reduce global reasoning about infinite computations of such systems to local reasoning about states and their successors. We also showed that the skipping simulation is closed under composition and therefore is amenable to modular reasoning using a stepwise refinement approach. We experimentally validated our results by analyzing the correctness of an optimized event-processing system in ACL2s. For future work, we plan to precisely classify temporal logic properties that are preserved by skipping refinement. This would enable us to transfer temporal properties from specifications to implementations, after establishing refinement.

References

1. Aagaard, M.D., Cook, B., Day, N.A., Jones, R.B.: A framework for microprocessor correctness statements. In: Margaria, T., Melham, T. (eds.) CHARME 2001. LNCS, vol. 2144, pp. 433–448. Springer, Heidelberg (2001). https://doi.org/10.1007/3-540-44798-9_33
2. Basten, T.: Branching bisimilarity is an equivalence indeed!. Inf. Process. Lett. **58**, 141–147 (1996)
3. Chamarthi, H.R., Dillinger, P., Manolios, P., Vroon, D.: The ACL2 sedan theorem proving system. In: Abdulla, P.A., Leino, K.R.M. (eds.) TACAS 2011. LNCS, vol. 6605, pp. 291–295. Springer, Heidelberg (2011). https://doi.org/10.1007/978-3-642-19835-9_27
4. Clarke, E.M., Grumberg, O., Browne, M.C.: Reasoning about networks with many identical finite-state processes. In: PODC (1986)
5. van Glabbeek, R.J.: The linear time-branching time spectrum (extended abstract). In: Baeten, J.C.M., Klop, J.W. (eds.) CONCUR 1990. LNCS, vol. 458, pp. 278–297. Springer, Heidelberg (1990). https://doi.org/10.1007/BFb0039066

6. Gu, L., Vaynberg, A., Ford, B., Shao, Z., Costanzo, D.: CertiKOS: a certified kernel for secure cloud computing. In: APSys (2011)
7. Gu, R., et al.: Deep specifications and certified abstraction layers. In: POPL (2015)
8. Hawblitzel, C., et al.: IronFleet: Proving practical distributed systems correct. In: SOSP (2015)
9. Hosabettu, R., Gopalakrishnan, G., Srivas, M.: Formal verification of a complex pipelined processor. Form. Methods Syst. Des. **23**, 171–213 (2003)
10. Jain, M., Manolios, P.: Skipping refinement. In: Kroening, D., Păsăreanu, C.S. (eds.) CAV 2015. LNCS, vol. 9206, pp. 103–119. Springer, Cham (2015). https://doi.org/10.1007/978-3-319-21690-4_7
11. Klarlund, N.: Progress measures and finite arguments for infinite computations. Ph.D. thesis (1990)
12. Klein, G., Sewell, T., Winwood, S.: Refinement in the formal verification of the seL4 microkernel. In: Hardin, D. (ed.) Design and Verification of Microprocessor Systems for High-Assurance Applications, pp. 323–339. Springer, Boston (2010). https://doi.org/10.1007/978-1-4419-1539-9_11
13. Kragl, B., Qadeer, S.: Layered concurrent programs. In: Chockler, H., Weissenbacher, G. (eds.) CAV 2018. LNCS, vol. 10981, pp. 79–102. Springer, Cham (2018). https://doi.org/10.1007/978-3-319-96145-3_5
14. Lamport, L.: What good is temporal logic. Information processing (1993)
15. Leroy, X., Blazy, S.: Formal verification of a c-like memory model and its uses for verifying program transformations. J. Autom. Reason. **41**, 1–31 (2008)
16. Liu, X., Yu, T., Zhang, W.: Analyzing divergence in bisimulation semantics. In: POPL (2017)
17. Lynch, N.A., Vaandrager, F.W.: Forward and backward simulations: I. Untimed systems. Inf. Comput. (1995)
18. Manolios, P.: Mechanical verification of reactive systems. Ph.D. thesis, University of Texas (2001)
19. Manolios, P.: Correctness of pipelined machines. In: Hunt, W.A., Johnson, S.D. (eds.) FMCAD 2000. LNCS, vol. 1954, pp. 181–198. Springer, Heidelberg (2000). https://doi.org/10.1007/3-540-40922-X_11
20. Manolios, P.: A compositional theory of refinement for branching time. In: Geist, D., Tronci, E. (eds.) CHARME 2003. LNCS, vol. 2860, pp. 304–318. Springer, Heidelberg (2003). https://doi.org/10.1007/978-3-540-39724-3_28
21. Manolios, P., Srinivasan, S.K.: A complete compositional reasoning framework for the efficient verification of pipelined machines. In: ICCAD (2005)
22. Milner, R.: An algebraic definition of simulation between programs. In: Proceedings of the 2nd International Joint Conference on Artificial Intelligence (1971)
23. Misra, J.: Distributed discrete-event simulation. ACM Comput. Surv. **18**, 39–65 (1986)
24. Namjoshi, K.S.: A simple characterization of stuttering bisimulation. In: Ramesh, S., Sivakumar, G. (eds.) FSTTCS 1997. LNCS, vol. 1346, pp. 284–296. Springer, Heidelberg (1997). https://doi.org/10.1007/BFb0058037
25. Namjoshi, K.S., Zuck, L.D.: Witnessing program transformations. In: Logozzo, F., Fähndrich, M. (eds.) SAS 2013. LNCS, vol. 7935, pp. 304–323. Springer, Heidelberg (2013). https://doi.org/10.1007/978-3-642-38856-9_17
26. Ray, S., Jr Hunt, W.A.: Deductive verification of pipelined machines using first-order quantification. In: Alur, R., Peled, D.A. (eds.) CAV 2004. LNCS, vol. 3114, pp. 31–43. Springer, Heidelberg (2004). https://doi.org/10.1007/978-3-540-27813-9_3

Permissions

The contributors of this book come from diverse backgrounds, making this book a truly international effort. This book will bring forth new frontiers with its revolutionizing research information and detailed analysis of the nascent developments around the world.

We would like to thank all the contributing authors for lending their expertise to make the book truly unique. They have played a crucial role in the development of this book. Without their invaluable contributions this book wouldn't have been possible. They have made vital efforts to compile up to date information on the varied aspects of this subject to make this book a valuable addition to the collection of many professionals and students.

This book was conceptualized with the vision of imparting up-to-date information and advanced data in this field. To ensure the same, a matchless editorial board was set up. Every individual on the board went through rigorous rounds of assessment to prove their worth. After which they invested a large part of their time researching and compiling the most relevant data for our readers.

The editorial board has been involved in producing this book since its inception. They have spent rigorous hours researching and exploring the diverse topics which have resulted in the successful publishing of this book. They have passed on their knowledge of decades through this book. To expedite this challenging task, the publisher supported the team at every step. A small team of assistant editors was also appointed to further simplify the editing procedure and attain best results for the readers.

Apart from the editorial board, the designing team has also invested a significant amount of their time in understanding the subject and creating the most relevant covers. They scrutinized every image to scout for the most suitable representation of the subject and create an appropriate cover for the book.

The publishing team has been an ardent support to the editorial, designing and production team. Their endless efforts to recruit the best for this project, has resulted in the accomplishment of this book. They are a veteran in the field of academics and their pool of knowledge is as vast as their experience in printing. Their expertise and guidance has proved useful at every step. Their uncompromising quality standards have made this book an exceptional effort. Their encouragement from time to time has been an inspiration for everyone.

The publisher and the editorial board hope that this book will prove to be a valuable piece of knowledge for researchers, students, practitioners and scholars across the globe.

List of Contributors

Grigory Fedyukovich and Aarti Gupta
Princeton University, Princeton, USA

Sumanth Prabhu and Kumar Madhukar
TCS Research, Pune, India

Qinheping Hu, Jason Breck, John Cyphert and Loris D'Antoni
University of Wisconsin-Madison, Madison, USA

Thomas Reps
GrammaTech, Inc., Ithaca, USA

Rayna Dimitrova
University of Leicester, Leicester, UK

Bernd Finkbeiner and Hazem Torfah
Saarland University, Saarbrücken, Germany

Jennifer A. Davis
Collins Aerospace, Cedar Rapids, IA 52498, USA

Laura R. Humphrey
Air Force Research Lab, Dayton, OH 45433, USA

Derek B. Kingston
Aurora Flight Sciences, Manassas, VA 20110, USA

Stella Lau
MIT, Cambridge, USA
University of Cambridge, Cambridge, UK

Victor B. F. Gomes, Kayvan Memarian, Jean Pichon-Pharabod and Peter Sewell
University of Cambridge, Cambridge, UK

Natalia Gavrilenko
Aalto University, Helsinki, Finland
University of Helsinki and HIIT, Helsinki, Finland

Hernán Ponce-de-León
fortiss GmbH, Munich, Germany

Florian Furbach and Roland Meyer
TU Braunschweig, Brunswick, Germany

Keijo Heljanko
University of Helsinki and HIIT, Helsinki, Finland

Guy Katz
The Hebrew University of Jerusalem, Jerusalem, Israel

Derek A. Huang, Duligur Ibeling, Kyle Julian, Christopher Lazarus, Rachel Lim, Parth Shah, Shantanu Thakoor, Haoze Wu, Aleksandar Zeljić, David L. Dill, Mykel J. Kochenderfer and Clark Barrett
Stanford University, Stanford, USA

Peter Faymonville, Bernd Finkbeiner, Malte Schledjewski, Maximilian Schwenger, Marvin Stenger, Leander Tentrup and Hazem Torfah
Reactive Systems Group, Saarland University, Saarbrücken, Germany

Pranav Ashok, Jan Křetínský and Maximilian Weininger
Technical University of Munich, Munich, Germany

Milan Češka
Brno University of Technology, FIT, IT4I Centre of Excellence, Brno, Czech Republic

Masaki Waga
National Institute of Informatics, Tokyo, Japan
SOKENDAI (The Graduate University for Advanced Studies), Tokyo, Japan
JSPS Research Fellow, Tokyo, Japan

Ichiro Hasuo
National Institute of Informatics, Tokyo, Japan
SOKENDAI (The Graduate University for Advanced Studies), Tokyo, Japan

Étienne André
National Institute of Informatics, Tokyo, Japan
Université Paris 13, LIPN, CNRS, UMR 7030, 93430 Villetaneuse, France
JFLI, CNRS, Tokyo, Japan

Bernd Finkbeiner and Felix Klein
Saarland University, Saarbrücken, Germany

Ruzica Piskac and Mark Santolucito
Yale University, New Haven, USA

Eric S. Kim, Murat Arcak and Sanjit A. Seshia
UC Berkeley, Berkeley, CA, USA

Damien Busatto-Gaston, Benjamin Monmege and Pierre-Alain Reynier
Aix Marseille Univ, Université de Toulon, CNRS, LIS, Marseille, France

Ocan Sankur
Univ Rennes, Inria, CNRS, IRISA, Rennes, France

Mitesh Jain
Synopsys Inc., Mountain View, USA

Panagiotis Manolios
Northeastern University, Boston, USA

Index